Equity and Education Since *Brown v. Board*

Equity and Education Since *Brown v. Board*

Where Do We Go From Here?

Edited by
Na'ilah Suad Nasir and
Linda Darling-Hammond

TEACHERS COLLEGE PRESS
TEACHERS COLLEGE | COLUMBIA UNIVERSITY
NEW YORK AND LONDON

Published by Teachers College Press,® 1234 Amsterdam Avenue, New York, NY 10027

Copyright © 2025 by Teachers College, Columbia University

Cover painting: Jacob Lawrence, *The Library*. Tempera on fiberboard, 1960, Smithsonian American Art Museum, © 2024 The Jacob and Gwendolyn Knight Lawrence Foundation, Seattle / Artists Rights Society (ARS), New York.

All rights reserved. No part of this publication may be reproduced or transmitted in any form or by any means, electronic or mechanical, including photocopy, or any information storage and retrieval system, without permission from the publisher. For reprint permission and other subsidiary rights requests, please contact Teachers College Press, Rights Dept.: tcpressrights@tc.columbia.edu

Library of Congress Cataloging-in-Publication Data

Names: Nasir, Na'ilah Suad, editor. | Darling-Hammond, Linda, 1951– editor.
Title: Equity and education since Brown v. Board : where do we go from here? / Edited by Na'ilah Suad Nasir and Linda Darling-Hammond.
Other titles: Equity and education since Brown versus Board
Description: New York, NY : Teachers College Press, [2025] | Includes bibliographical references and index.
Identifiers: LCCN 2024039563 (print) | LCCN 2024039564 (ebook) | ISBN 9780807786956 (hardcover) | ISBN 9780807786949 (paperback) | ISBN 9780807783009 (epub)
Subjects: LCSH: Educational equalization—United States—History. | Topeka (Kan.). Board of Education—Trials, litigation, etc. | Brown, Oliver, 1918-1961—Trials, litigation, etc. | African Americans—Education—History. | Segregation in education—United States—History. | African Americans—Civil rights—History.
Classification: LCC LC213.2 .E655 2025 (print) | LCC LC213.2 (ebook) | DDC 379.2/60973—dc23/eng/20241010
LC record available at https://lccn.loc.gov/2024039563
LC ebook record available at https://lccn.loc.gov/2024039564

ISBN 978-0-8077-8694-9 (paper)
ISBN 978-0-8077-8695-6 (hardcover)
ISBN 978-0-8077-8300-9 (ebook)

Printed on acid-free paper
Manufactured in the United States of America

Contents

Introduction: Expanding on the Blueprint: The Significance of *Brown* for Education Now
Na'ilah Suad Nasir and Naomi Mae W. 1

1. *Brown* at 70: Progress, Pushback, and Policies That Matter 13
   Linda Darling-Hammond and Sean Darling-Hammond

2. The Dream of Integration and the Politics of Resegregation: The Continuing Battle Over the Legacy of *Brown v. Board of Education* 56
   Gary Orfield

3. Where Do We Go From Here? Assessing the Limits and Possibilities of Education for Black People in the United States 70 Years After *Brown* 81
   Joaquín M. S. Noguera and Pedro A. Noguera

4. Reclaiming the Promise of *Brown*: The Integration of Desegregation and School Funding Reform 98
   Rucker C. Johnson and Ary Amerikaner

5. But What About the Teachers? The Forgotten Narratives of Black Teachers in the Midst of *Brown* 140
   Gloria Ladson-Billings

6. Facing the Rising Sun: Black Teachers' Positive Impact Post-*Brown* 161
   Travis J. Bristol and Desiree Carver-Thomas

7. The Complex Braid of *Brown*: How Conceptualizations
and Initiatives Within the African American Community
of Research, Practice, and Activism Have Influenced
the Advance of Knowledge and Practice in Education   196
Carol D. Lee

8. *Brown v. Board of Education* and the Democratic
Purposes of Public Education   224
Kent McGuire

Notes   241

Index   244

About the Editors and Contributors   256

Equity and Education Since *Brown v. Board*

INTRODUCTION

Expanding on the Blueprint
The Significance of *Brown* for Education Now

Na'ilah Suad Nasir and Naomi Mae W.

There is no doubt that the set of decisions that constituted *Brown v. Board of Education* in 1954 represented a sea change in how our nation enacted policy with respect to race and inequality. While *Brown* was, obviously, about access to quality schools it was also about so much more than that. Legislation protecting the rights of Black children and families in education led to other changes in policy in housing, voting, transportation, and employment laws (Noguera & Noguera, this volume). And yet, the problems the *Brown* decision was intended to fix—the conditions of segregation and inequality in schools—are, by any measure, still strikingly far from what the architects of *Brown* imagined 70 years ago (Orfield, 2024, this volume). As Darling-Hammond and Darling-Hammond and Noguera and Noguera note in their chapters in this book, differentials in achievement between Black and White students are 50% larger today than they were 35 years ago; schools are still profoundly segregated in the south; and in northern cities, many states have cut spending to education, with lower spending in high-poverty areas where there are more students of color and the needs are greater, and Black students are less likely to attend college and more likely to carry high debt loads when they do attend.

How are we to make sense of both the important legacy of the *Brown* decision, and the failure to make significant progress on equity in educational opportunities and resources? And perhaps more importantly, what are the lessons from *Brown*, and what is the path forward, given the current social, political, and educational context? This book takes up these important questions, with chapters written by leading scholars and thinkers on educational inequality and desegregation, educational policy, and teaching and learning. The volume takes an honest look at the progress since *Brown*, documenting the shifts over time on key aspects of education including school segregation, achievement trends in relation to policies and practices over time, the diversity of the teaching force, access to resources, the role of Black scholars and community activism, and the relationship between democracy and education. The book offers an historical look at the impacts of the *Brown* decision, but importantly, also offers guidance for the road ahead—promising policies, practices, and directions for the schools we need. The eight chapters that comprise the book are at once reflective and forward-leaning, and they consider what we learned from the journey of *Brown*, and what we need to do next to usher in a new era where we truly attend to the educational needs of all students, and provide widespread opportunities to learn and thrive.

SUMMARY OF THE CHAPTERS

Eight chapters comprise the volume, and together they offer wide-ranging historical analysis and commentary on the *Brown* decision, and consider the implications of *Brown* for education today.

In Chapter 1, *Brown* at 70: Progress, Pushback, and Policies That Matter, Linda Darling-Hammond and Sean Darling-Hammond provide a wide-angle look at trends in educational inequality since *Brown*. They focus on four key areas that are critical to educational outcomes: eliminating poverty and the accumulated effects of segregation in communities, ensuring access to equitable school resources, ensuring access to high-quality teachers and curriculum, and ensuring access to safe, inclusive school environments. For each area they document the progress, the pushback, and the policies that have and could matter to improve student outcomes. They offer analyses of trends that showed the reduction of opportunity gaps in the 1960s and early 1970s, then the widening of gaps in subsequent years. They also provide evidence of the kinds of policies that would make a significant difference in these opportunity gaps, and chart a path forward.

In Chapter 2, The Dream of Integration and the Politics of Resegregation: The Continuing Battle Over the Legacy of *Brown v. Board of Education*, Gary Orfield considers how we got here, and traces the 128-year history of school segregation and desegregation from *Plessy* to *Brown* to the present. He details the legal cases that led up to *Brown*, the historic nature of the *Brown* decision, and the slow dismantling of the impact and implementation of *Brown* through subsequent court cases. He argues that the *Brown* decision, and the resulting progress in desegregation in the 1960s and 1970s was the result of "a social movement, serious Presidential leadership, Congressional action, and a Court that finally took decisive moves." In the wake of those decisive moves, an increasingly conservative Supreme Court, and federal administrations that did not take progressive action on educational equity and integration, dismantled the legacy of *Brown* such that there has been only nominal progress of desegregation and educational equity in 70 years.

Expanding on the Blueprint

In Chapter 3, Where Do We Go From Here? Assessing the Limits and Possibilities of Education for Black People in the United States 70 Years After *Brown*, Joaquín Noguera and Pedro Noguera consider first both the failures and the wins of *Brown*—what we gained and what we lost. They examine the sobering history of inequality, and the myriad ways those inequities are instantiated in current systems. They use the Los Angeles Unified School District (LAUSD) as a case study to illustrate how the accumulation of school factors and factors beyond schools creates conditions that perpetuate the cycle of inequality for children of color. Ultimately, they contend moving forward will require an educational equity agenda that includes attention to multiracial communities as well as cooperation between cities, county governments, school districts, and social movements. They also argue for the need to include Black communities themselves in order to understand what they want for their children with respect to education.

In Chapter 4, Reclaiming the Promise of *Brown*: The Integration of Desegregation and School Funding Reform, Rucker Johnson and Ary Amerikaner examine the two core goals underlying *Brown*—school integration and school resource equity—and explore the feasibility of achieving educational equity utilizing either a focus on integration *or* a focus on school resource equity, versus the power of them together. They argue school funding reform alone could equalize resources, but will not provide the same social benefit without attention to diversity and integration; diversity and school reassignment strategies cannot get us to outcomes without attention to resource equity. Johnson and Amerikaner also claim there is an urgent need for a recommitment to advancing integrated and well-resourced public schools, and that such a recommitment is critical if we are to realize the potential of a "multiethnic . . . globally competitive, international, 21st-century knowledge economy."

Chapter 5, But What About the Teachers? The Forgotten Narratives of Black Teachers in the Midst of *Brown,* written by Gloria Ladson-Billings, focuses on the importance of Black teachers in the civil rights struggle in education and the education of Black children. She details the staggering loss of over 35,000 Black teachers in the wake of the *Brown* decision, and the detrimental effects on not only Black children, but on all children. She offers poignant examples of talented and excellent Black educators who were lost during *Brown*, and the multidimensional aspects of their excellence and contributions, including their connection with students, their high standards for learning, innovation in curriculum and instruction, and their role in the Black community. She also ponders what it meant for Black students to desegregate schools post-*Brown* without the care and protection of Black teachers.

Chapter 6, Facing the Rising Sun: Black Teachers' Positive Impact Post-*Brown*, written by Travis Bristol and Desiree Carver-Thomas, continues the discussion of the role and impact of Black teachers. They underscore Ladson-Billings's arguments about the historical and current role that Black teachers have played in supporting the achievement of Black students (and all students), drawing on both quantitative and qualitative evidence on the impact of Black teachers on students and learning. They also take up the critical topic of how we increase the pipeline of teachers of color into the profession. They frame the chapter by identifying this moment as a "second Nadir." They argue, much like in the period preceding *Brown*, we are in a time of retrenchment and regressive policies on race, diversity, and inclusion nationally, and highlight key policy and practice strategies that will support progress even in the face of current challenges.

In Chapter 7, The Complex Braid of *Brown*: How Conceptualizations and Initiatives Within the African American Community of Research, Practice, and Activism Have Influenced the Advance of Knowledge and Practice in Education, Carol D. Lee highlights the important role of the Black community in advancements in education. She argues that *Brown* was both a victory and an ongoing challenge, and that it underscored the desire on the part of Black people to both have access to being full citizens politically, socially, and culturally, and to draw upon the historical beliefs, values, and legacies of their ancestors and traditions. She highlights the multiple ways in which organizing within the Black community has affected change for all communities, and challenges us to consider what the current role of public education is, and how it can prepare young people both intellectually and civically.

And finally in Chapter 8, *Brown v. Board of Education* and the Democratic Purposes of Public Education, Kent McGuire argues that it is time for a renewed purpose of public education focused on building our democracy. He argues this will require a new frame, and is an intentional move away from the kinds of education reforms of the 1990s and 2000s focused on testing and accountability. Instead, he stipulates that we need to center the kinds of competencies, skills, knowledge, and civic reasoning capabilities young people will need to be stewards of our democracy. McGuire further contends that these shifts suggest the need for a new civil rights agenda that leans into the role of educational equity in supporting a robust and thriving society, and considers the kinds of specific purposes and design components that could animate such an education system.

These chapters provide critical and forward-leaning analyses and directions toward what is, to be sure, a critical juncture in our education system. They also raise a myriad of reflections, tensions, and areas we might newly consider in looking at the blueprint left from *Brown*. Together, they continue to bend us toward a new arc in the justice movement with ideas about the kinds of education systems and learning environments we will need to steward an equitable future. Below, we take up a few key challenges and raise some additional provocations.

REFLECTING ON THE SUCCESSES AND FAILURES OF *BROWN*

One throughline across the chapters in this book is whether *Brown* was a success or a failure. Most authors land in a place that acknowledges it was both a success and a failure. By some metrics, *Brown* has clearly failed—Darling-Hammond and Darling-Hammond, Noguera and Noguera, and Orfield all note the failure not only to provide equitable educational opportunity along a number of dimensions, but also to desegregate schools. Ladson-Billings and Bristol and Carver-Thomas also describe the significant failure in relation to Black teachers. The mass layoffs of Black teachers, principals, and administrators had cascading negative effects on the Black community, and on Black students, in that they lost an entire generation of teachers and school leaders who cared for them and taught with excellence. Further, diversity in the teaching and school leadership professions never recovered (Givens, 2023; Siddle-Walker, 2009).

Across chapters, authors also identify important progress during the time that *Brown* was implemented in the 1960s and 1970s, leading to significant reductions in opportunity gaps and resulting achievement gains. Johnson and Amerikaner further underscore the importance of this progress to the long-term academic and social mobility outcomes for students. And *Brown* succeeded in another way as well. The *Brown* decision fueled the civil rights movement, and became a "symbol of America's commitment to racial integration" (p. 98). It also, as Noguera and Noguera point out, gave rise to landmark legislation in sectors like housing, employment, transportation, and voting, thus changing the entire legal landscape of the country. Indeed, *Brown* was one of the most significant legal cases in history related to education policy, born of community struggle, protest, and advocacy to make schools more equitable, and constituted a critical step forward in the United States reflecting the vision for equal schools.

There is also some attention in the chapters to why *Brown* was unable to create the kinds of changes for equity in our education systems that were imagined. Orfield raises the massive collective resistance in White communities and among lawmakers. Darling-Hammond and Darling-Hammond, Orfield, and McGuire highlight the move to regressive social and educational policies in the early 1980s and the ways these policies further entrenched social and education inequality. Noguera and Noguera speak to the continued racialized and inequitable school conditions for Black children and along with Darling-Hammond and Darling-Hammond describe the consistent, systematic underfunding of public schools for low-income communities of color.

However, what's alluded to yet not fully articulated is that what undermined *Brown* was the same thing that caused the need for this legislation in the first place—the pervasiveness of White supremacy in the United States and globally. In their new book, *Radical Brown: Keeping the*

Promise to America's Children, Margaret Beale Spencer and Nancy Dowd (2024) argue that at the core of the policy and social context that preceded *Brown*, and the resistance that followed it, was the set of deep and abiding beliefs about Black inferiority that no policy or legal decision could supersede. They write: "We identify the individual, human, developmental consequences of sustained beliefs concerning inferiority and sustained conditions of privilege for the task of constructing common humanity. These complex consequences cannot be ignored lest we repeat the process of reconstructing inequality" (Spencer & Dowd, 2024, p. 31). They argue that there is a direct link between the condition and purposes of slavery and the purpose of segregation—to "replace, restore, and redeem White supremacy and racial hierarchy. The purpose was dehumanization and psychological harm" (Spencer & Dowd, 2024, p. 63). It is important to acknowledge that the core of the resistance to desegregation was White supremacy, and the goal behind policies that maintain the conditions of profound inequality is to preserve White supremacy. And, in this remembering and acknowledgment, we must hold that policy contexts are always reflective of the social context, and both must be addressed to create lasting change.

CONSIDERING THE HARMS OF *BROWN*

Also mentioned, but not fully articulated across the chapters is the notion that *Brown*, while well-intentioned and providing societal progress on issues of racial inequality, did so at a steep cost to Black teachers, school leaders, communities, and students. Ladson-Billings and Bristol and Carver highlight the cost in terms of the loss of Black teachers and the passion, excellence, and care they bring to Black students and to all students. Ladson-Billings also notes the cost to Black communities, in the mass layoffs of Black teachers, and how a key pathway to the Black middle class was obliterated.

Yet, there is another kind of loss that must be an enduring part of our discussion: the psychological and developmental harm to Black people, and indeed to all people. In *Troubled Waters*, a novel about the climate crisis and Black families and resistance, Heglar writes about a Black character, Cora Mae, who as a 5-year-old girl was the first to integrate a school in Nashville, Tennessee. In one scene in the book, as an elder Cora is recounting to her granddaughter Corrine about her experiences when she integrated her elementary school. For 4 years Cora was at the "White folks school" until her mother insisted that she return to her neighborhood Black school for middle school to be with other Black children. Cora speaks to how her mother noticed the "toll" it was taking on her. Granddaughter Corrine asks, "what kind of toll?" Cora responds,

> My personality changed . . . I used to be real talkative, outgoing. I used to laugh a lot. Made friends easy. But then I just shrank into myself. I started to be nervous all the time. I started to stutter . . . Every little sound, every movement somebody would make near me would just make me jump out of my skin.
>
> Watching Grandma wince, it occurred to Corrine that Black women—celebrated the world over for their extraordinary ability to bend and bend and bend—can, in fact, break. Into a million little shards. (Heglar, 2024, p. 310)

This reflection from Cora underscores the psychological harm incurred by Black children who integrated White schools, without their families, communities, or teachers. Heglar, in this fictional account, articulates a profound and lasting trauma on the part of Black people. This trauma was also experienced at the community level, as adults witnessed this assault on Black children. Often, these children entered their new all-White elementary school escorted alone or by the National Guard through a crowd of angry, jeering White adults calling out racial epithets and threats of violence. Ladson-Billings (this volume) conveys the story of one Black man who had left his segregated Black school to attend an all-White school. He says,

> We went over there by ourselves. All the trophies and medals our Black school had won over the years as football, basketball, baseball, and track champions stayed back at our old school. And our teachers did not go with us. We entered that building all by ourselves. We entered unprotected. (p. 141)

What does it mean for a child to experience school and the world in a way that makes them feel "unprotected" and alone? How might that impact not only learning, but also one's sense of self-esteem, and identity? And, how might this impact one's community across generations? These psychological costs of *Brown* must also be attended to in our recounting and remembering.

STARTING WITH THE NEEDS AND DESIRES OF COMMUNITIES

Several of the chapters wrestled in different ways with the question of whether resource equity is the goal or whether integration is the goal, especially in light of the ways that inequality has been perpetuated, even in desegregated schools. While Johnson and Amerikaner argue strongly that the path forward must include both desegregation and resource equity, Noguera and Noguera are not so sure. What seems to be missing, to some degree, in this debate is the centering of Black families, communities, and young people, and what they want, value, need, and desire in their schools.

In *Ethical Ambition* (2003), renowned critical race theory legal scholar and civil rights lawyer Derrick Bell reflects on his life as an activist, civil rights attorney, and acclaimed Black legal scholar. In one recollection, Bell writes about what he viewed as a key flaw in the strategy of the civil rights lawyers during desegregation in the 1970s. He speaks of how the attorneys, while well-intentioned, did not listen to Black parents' resistance to bussing their children into White schools in Boston. Bell (2003) says of the lawyers who were convinced that desegregation was the only way to equal schooling of Black children, that ". . . their optimism was based less on evidence than wish, and a generation of children paid the price for that error" (p. 157). He reflected,

> When I worked with the NAACP Legal Defense Fund and the federal government, I labored mightily to desegregate public schools across the South. I too was committed to achieving racial balance as the best means to desegregate schools. And I too was insufficiently sensitive to how much would be lost when black schools were closed with most of the black teachers and principals dismissed. Worst of all, I knew that black children and their parents would have to seek the equal educational opportunity we lawyers promised them in often hostile and always alien schools that remained dominated by Whites. (Bell, 2003, p. 157)

He laments how the lawyers of his time did not take enough care to listen to family and community concerns about the psychological toll their children would face by integrating into White schools under the conditions of White resistance. Bell cautioned that those who are most directly affected must be centered, consulted, and ultimately listened to lest we repeat harmful mistakes that we have been wisely forewarned about.

The chapters in this book provide an expanded blueprint to think about the path forward. It is critical to do so with the desires and needs of young people and families at the forefront. Given the high levels of residential segregation, it may be prudent to consider how we provide a high-quality education for each student in their home communities (James-Galloway & Harris, 2021; Wilson, Mae W., & Horne, 2023). Darling-Hammond and Darling-Hammond (this volume) write ". . . the promise of *Brown* rests on a widespread social understanding that the path to our mutual well-being is built on equal educational opportunity" (p. 42). It may well be that this equal opportunity could be imagined within young people's home communities where there would be investment in the children, neighborhoods, resources, facilities, materials, and well-trained teachers in and from the community (Baldridge, 2019; Davis et al., 2023; Ewing, 2018; Todd-Breland, 2018; Vossoughi et al., 2016; Wilson, Nickson, & Ransom, 2023).

BROWN AS AN ORGANIZING EXPERIMENT

As we reflect on the meaning of *Brown*, and the lessons we can learn from it (and what happened in its aftermath), there is an additional set of lessons to be learned. In many ways, the *Brown* decision was a collective victory—it was the product of organizing and activism on the part of communities, families, young people, and many Black professionals including lawyers, teachers, and preachers. *Brown*, which occurred early in the Civil Rights Movement, can be considered an experiment in social change. Veteran Indigenous and Black activists and grassroots organizers Kelly Hayes and Mariame Kaba in *Let this Radicalize You* remind us that activism and organizing is about building anew; creating a world in which all have access and opportunity to a full life that communities desire for themselves rooted in an ethos of care and mutual aid. This world-building through experimentation (Hayes & Kaba, 2023) was at the heart of *Brown*.

Brown came out of advocacy and organizing work with the goal of greater justice and equity, and massive social change. Neither Black nor White communities had any idea how educating their children together would pan out in the experiment of desegregation. It was all speculative because integration was not common, nor had it occurred at scale. Theories of organizing (Hayes & Kaba, 2023; Kaba, 2021) stipulate that an important aspect of movement building is taking stock and reassessing. Now, 70 years later, we can assess *Brown* as the experiment it was. As noted in the section above, not enough care went into how Black children could be harmed in the implementation of *Brown* and the degree of violent White resistance. In the wake of *Brown*, schools were bombed, churches were bombed, homes were bombed, Black children and families received death threats, Black people were lynched and murdered and, within the integrated school halls, Black children were traumatized (Coles & Powell, 2019; Dumas, 2014, 2016; Massey & Denton, 1993). The collective psychological toll from this trauma must inform how we are to move forward in the press for educational equity and opportunity.

Kaba (2021) in her book on abolitionist organizing and justice poignantly notes, "it's only on the other side of folks who are interested in social transformation and change where failure is not supposed to be spoken about or a sign that you're horrible or that your ideas don't have merit" and instead, we must accept failure is inevitable and we need to ". . . be building a million different experiments" (p. 166). Experiments fail, but they also have to be done for strategies to be devised and answers to be found—they are our "life in rehearsal" (Maynard & Simpson, 2022). And in our devising post-*Brown*, we ask, what can we learn from experimentation? What were the talking points, strategies, and tactics of the larger movement and how did *Brown* fit in it? Who was uplifted and who was invisibilized? How were people listened to and how were concerns assuaged or dismissed? What might we learn from Black children and families who were harmed and continue to be harmed by institutions they were led into? How can we better strategize and dream of an experiment of educational opportunity and justice with those who are most marginalized to lead? How can we implement community-initiated ideas with fidelity and then iterate until we get it right? From an organizing perspective, the experiment of *Brown* can be utilized, assessed, and analyzed like a blueprint, and it can support us in collectively considering a path forward.

FUTURE DIRECTIONS

Across the volume, there are a number of policy recommendations to support equitable schools where rich and deep learning can happen. These include a call to better support the preparation and retention of teachers, resource equity, and to consider a renewed commitment to achieving integrated schools. It is also important to note, however, that there is a fundamental assumption and frame for schooling that will be critical to create the kinds of teaching and learning environments that serve all communities. McGuire (this volume) makes the point that we have lost sight of the public mission and value of education. Any direction forward will need to reinvigorate the idea that in many ways was at the center of *Brown*, that schools are key institutions in society that support us in creating and stewarding the next generation. As such, they are a collective public good, which exists to serve the interests of the society as a whole. Toward this end, then, the question that Lee (this volume) poses at the end of her chapter is particularly important. She asks, "What is the role of public education in preparing young people to engage in civic reasoning, problem solving and discourse?" This question takes to heart the role of schools in stewarding a society forward.

EDUCATIONAL EQUITY IN THE CURRENT MOMENT

To expand the blueprint, we have to thoroughly understand what's at stake with educational equity. We are in the midst of not just the aftermath of policies that decimated the social safety net and expanded opportunity and wealth gaps (Darling-Hammond & Darling-Hammond, this volume), we are also facing a set of intersecting national and global challenges that are nothing short of staggering: climate change, global oppression and war, dehumanization in the face of massive technological innovation, massive social inequality, housing shortages and record numbers of houseless individuals and families, a health care and student debt crisis, and a shrinking middle class. And yet, as Ruha Benjamin (2022) reminds us in her important work on transforming society through everyday choices—*Viral Justice*—". . . just because this is a long-term struggle does not mean we throw up our hands in resignation or defeat" (p. 139). Rather, just like the yet uninvented solutions to our current plight, the *Brown* decision was once inconceivable.

Yet, the very fact that we can credit *Brown* for some of our seismic societal shifts 70 years later bears witness to the reality that we have done the inconceivable before. In quoting Butler's *Earthseed: The Book of the Living*, Benjamin (2022) reshares,

> We can,
> Each of us,
> Do the impossible
> As long as we can convince ourselves
> That it has been done before. (p. 209)

Vanessa Siddle-Walker (personal communication, October 10, 2024) has made the argument that Black teachers in the 1930s, 1940s, and 1950s created the civil rights generation. They taught so that young Black people would be well-prepared, critically engaged, and with a strong sense of themselves in connection to their communities. What is the generation of learners and citizens that our society needs for schools to give rise to now? What teaching and learning is required to prepare the next generation for such monumental tasks? And, what policies do we need and what kind of movement do we need to build to get us there? These are the questions we will need to answer, collectively, and with the most marginalized students, families, and communities at the center.

REFERENCES

Baldridge, B. J. (2019). *Reclaiming community: Race and the uncertain future of youth work*. Stanford University Press.

Bell, D. (2003). *Ethical ambition: Living a life of meaning and worth*. Bloomsbury USA.

Benjamin, R. (2022). *Viral justice: How we grow the world we want*. Princeton University Press.

Coles, J. A., & Powell, T. (2019). A BlackCrit analysis on Black urban youth and suspension disproportionality as anti-Black symbolic violence. *Race Ethnicity and Education*, 23(1), 113–133. https://doi.org/10.1080/13613324.2019.1631778

Davis, N. R., Marchand, A. D., Moore, S. S., Greene, D., & Colby, A. (2023). We who believe in freedom: *Freedom Schools* as a critical context for the positive, sociopolitical development of Black youth. *Race Ethnicity and Education*, 26(1), 34–53. https://doi.org/10.1080/13613324.2021.1969901

Dumas, M. J. (2014). 'Losing an arm': Schooling as a site of black suffering. *Race Ethnicity and Education*, 17(1), 1–29. https://doi.org/10.1080/13613324.2013.850412

Dumas, M. J. (2016). Against the dark: Antiblackness in education policy and discourse. *Theory into Practice*, 55(1), 11–19. https://doi.org/10.1080/00405841.2016.1116852

EdBuild (2019). *Fractured*. https://edbuild.org/content/fractured/fractured-full-report.pdf

Ewing, E. L. (2018). *Ghosts in the schoolyard: Racism and school closings on Chicago's South Side*. University of Chicago Press.

Givens, J. (2023). *Fugitive pedagogy: Carter G. Woodson and the art of Black teaching*. Harvard University Press.

Hayes, K., & Kaba, M. (2023). *Let this radicalize you: Organizing and the revolution of reciprocal care*. Haymarket Books.

Heglar, M. A. (2024). *Troubled waters*. Harper Muse.

James-Gallaway, A. D., & Harris, T. (2021). We been relevant: Culturally relevant pedagogy and Black women teachers in segregated schools. *Educational Studies, 57*(2), 124–141. https://doi.org/10.1080/00131946.2021.1878179

Kaba, M. (2021). *We do this 'til we free us: Abolitionist organizing and transforming justice* (Vol. 1). Haymarket Books.

Massey, D. S., & Denton, N. E. (1993). *American apartheid: Segregation and the making of the underclass*. Harvard University Press.

Maynard, R., & Simpson, L. B. (2022). *Rehearsals for living*. Knopf Canada.

Siddle-Walker, V. (2009). *Hello professor: A Black principal and principal leadership in the segregated south*. University of North Carolina Press.

Spencer, M. B., & Dowd, N. E. (2024). *Radical Brown: Keeping the promise to America's children*. Harvard Education Press.

Todd-Breland, E. (2018). *A political education: Black politics and education reform in Chicago since the 1960s*. University of North Carolina Press.

Vossoughi, S., Hooper, P. K., & Escudé, M. (2016). Making through the lens of culture and power: Toward transformative visions for educational equity. *Harvard Educational Review, 86*(2), 206–232. https://doi.org/10.17763/0017-8055.86.2.206

Wilson, C. M., Mae W., N., & Horne, J. D. (2023). Ignited fire: Learning from Black youth activists to cultivate justice-driven educational leadership. *International Journal of Qualitative Studies in Education*, 1–21. https://doi.org/10.1080/09518398.2023.2233919

Wilson, C. M., Nickson, D., & Ransom, K. C. (2023). Spiriting urban educational justice: The leadership of African American mothers organizing for school equity and local control. *Journal of Educational Change, 24*, 265–290. https://doi.org/10.1007/s10833-021-09443-1

CHAPTER 1

Brown at 70
Progress, Pushback, and Policies That Matter

*Linda Darling-Hammond
and Sean Darling-Hammond*[1]

THE CONTEXT OF *BROWN*

Although the United States has prided itself on the notion that equality is central to our national mandate, the Declaration that "all men are created equal" long meant that White men with financial means were created sufficiently "equal" to have access to the franchise and other social benefits enshrined in law. It has taken centuries to begin to imagine equality for all citizens of the United States, and that task is not yet accomplished. While the U.S. Supreme Court ostensibly rejected the doctrine of legal segregation in its 1954 ruling in *Brown v. Board of Education*, both segregation and the unequal access to educational resources that it enables persist to this day.

While progress has occurred, each major advance toward greater equality has been accompanied by strong pushback—a phenomenon we see today as Southern states legislate that the history of systemic racism be left untaught while actions to suppress voting and others to reinforce inequality proceed apace. These efforts reprise those described by Carter G. Woodson in *The Mis-Education of the Negro* (1933), when governments and influential leaders sought to prohibit the inclusion of documents like the Declaration of Independence and the Constitution in Black schools' curriculum, lest they raise questions about the meaning of these rights for Black citizens.

This chapter takes stock of the current status of equity and outlines both the progress and pushback since *Brown* in four major areas that are critical to educational outcomes:

- Eliminating poverty and the accumulated effects of segregation in communities;
- Ensuring access to equitable school resources;

- Ensuring access to high-quality teachers and curriculum; and
- Ensuring access to safe, inclusive school environments.

Continuing challenges in all of these areas build on a long legacy. Legally sanctioned discrimination in access to education is older than the American nation itself. From the time the Southern states made it illegal to teach an enslaved person to read and throughout the 19th century and into the 20th, African Americans have faced *de jure* and *de facto* exclusion from schools throughout the nation enforced through both education policies and housing policies and maintained by redlining and other segregative practices.

Even in the North, when "common schools" were established, they were not integrated, nor were they treated equally. In 1857, for example, a group of African American leaders protested to a New York State investigating committee that the New York Board of Education spent $16 per White child and only one cent per Black child for school buildings. While Black students occupied schools described as "dark and cheerless," White students had access to buildings that were "splendid, almost palatial edifices, with manifold comforts, conveniences, and elegancies" (Tyack, 1974, p. 119).

A century later, when *Brown* consolidated five lawsuits from different states in a complaint to the Supreme Court, there was consistent evidence that, in multiple states where schools were segregated by law, significant disparities in educational access and quality pertained. These began with the allocation of resources. For example, despite the 1896 *Plessy v. Ferguson* decision that articulated the principle of "separate but equal," Alabama spent $37 on each White child and only $7 on each Black child in 1930; South Carolina's ratio was more than 10 to 1, at $53 per pupil for White children and $5 per pupil for Black children. In Clarendon County, South Carolina, Black children comprised 87% of the student population but received only one-third of the county's total funding for their education (Irons, 2002).

White schools had more and better-paid teachers and smaller class sizes, newer and more plentiful desks and textbooks, significantly better and safer facilities, longer school years, and a much richer curriculum aimed at more privileged vocations. The curriculum in Black schools was frequently geared to menial work and lacked courses in advanced mathematics, sciences, history, and world languages. In many communities, education for Black students ended after primary school, with no options for education after the 4th or 5th grade. The *Brown* decision heavily weighed these resource disparities in coming to the unanimous conclusion that "separate but equal has no place in the Constitution."

The judgment was to be implemented with "all deliberate speed," a phrase fraught with internal contradictions that allowed radically different interpretations. It was met with an organized campaign Southern authorities termed "massive resistance," ranging from ignoring the opinion to closing public schools while using public funds to send White students to private schools, and using force and intimidation to prevent Black parents from enrolling their children in White schools. Advocates had to sue hundreds of school districts across the country to enforce desegregation. It took nearly 2 decades to get a judgment from the Supreme Court in *Swann v. Charlotte-Mecklenburg Board of Education* (1971) that segregation was to be dismantled "root and branch," specifying factors to be considered to eliminate the effects of segregation and empowering federal district courts to act to do so. These efforts enabled a period of progress, though, as we describe below, pushback occurred again during the 1980s and at multiple junctures since, including today.

THE CURRENT STATUS OF EQUITY

Extensive civil rights activity during the 1960s activated court cases and legislation that led to desegregation and school finance reform efforts. The passage of the Civil Rights Act of 1964 provided the federal government with a mechanism to enforce school integration for recipients of federal funds, enabling the Department of Justice to address violations of the law through investigation and litigation. And the 1965 Elementary and Secondary Education Act (ESEA) significantly expanded federal funding of education, with implications for recipients of those funds that they needed to comply with federal civil rights law (George & Darling-Hammond, 2019).

The Elementary and Secondary Education Act targeted resources to communities with the most need, recognizing that where a child grows up should not determine where he or she ends up. Congress enacted the Emergency School Aid Act, which supported desegregation, the development of magnet schools, and other strategies to improve urban and poor rural schools. These efforts to level the playing field for children were supported by intensive investments in bringing and keeping talented individuals in teaching, improving teacher education, and investing in research and development, and they were accompanied by increased investments in urban and poor rural schools through the Great Society's War on Poverty.

Childhood poverty was reduced by half during the 1960s, from 27% to 14%. Employment and welfare supports reduced childhood poverty to levels about 60% of what they are today and greatly improved children's access to health care (DeSilver, 2014). These investments paid off in measurable ways. By the mid-1970s, urban schools spent as much as suburban schools and paid their teachers as well, perennial teacher shortages had nearly ended, and gaps in educational attainment had closed substantially. Federally funded curriculum investments transformed teaching in many schools. Innovative schools flourished in many cities and achievement gaps in reading and mathematics shrank considerably. Financial aid for higher education was sharply increased, especially for need-based scholarships and loans. For a brief period in the mid-1970s, Black and Latino high school graduates attended college at the same rate as Whites (National Center for Education Statistics [NCES], n.d.; USA Facts, n.d.).

K–12 Educational Achievement

As we detail below, the effects of these equity-oriented policies were substantial for a generation of students. Overall, the Black–White achievement gap was cut by more than half during the 1970s and early 1980s, as Figure 1.1 also shows. Had this progress been continued, the achievement gap would have been fully closed by the beginning of the 21st century.

However, the gains from the Great Society programs were pushed back during the 1980s, when most targeted federal programs supporting investments in college access and K–12 schools in urban and poor rural areas were reduced or eliminated, and federal aid to schools was cut from 12% to 6% of a shrinking pot of total spending on education. Meanwhile, childhood poverty rates, homelessness, and lack of access to health care grew with cuts in other federal programs supporting housing subsidies, health care, and child welfare. Investments in the education of students of color that

Figure 1.1. *Trends in Student Performance by Race*

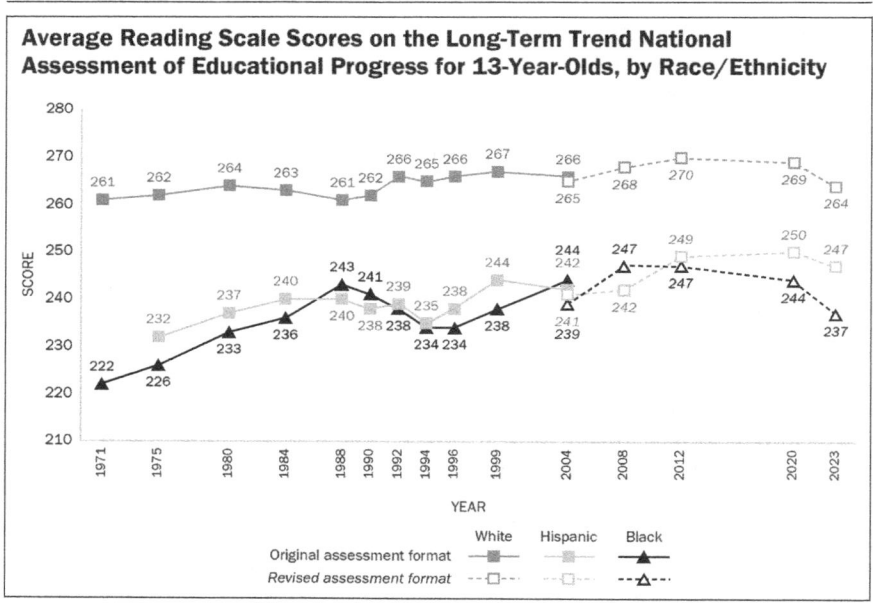

Source: U.S. Department of Education, National Center for Education Statistics, National Assessment of Educational Progress (NAEP), various years, 1971–2023 Long-Term Trend (LTT) Reading and Mathematics Assessments.

characterized the school desegregation and finance reforms of the 1960s and 1970s have never been fully reestablished in the years since.

President Reagan cut funding to the Civil Rights Division of the Department of Justice, and the federal government stopped advocating for enforcement of court desegregation orders (Asante-Muhammad, 2013). Coupled with an end to federal payments to districts to support desegregation efforts in Reagan's first budget, along with state and district antipathy to desegregation, progress was reversed (Frankenberg et al., 2017, pp. 1–18; Pear 1982). Racial desegregation efforts in public education peaked in the late 1980s, with 44% of African American students attending majority-White schools (Millhiser, 2015). Resegregation occurred as the federal government not only stopped encouraging courts to end desegregation, but also began weighing in on the side of districts seeking to end desegregation orders. After the *Parents Involved in Community Schools v. Seattle School District* lawsuit, decided by the Supreme Court in 2007, which challenged the efforts of the Seattle school district to assign students in ways that would create racially integrated schools, the Bush administration issued a "Dear Colleague" letter interpreting the case as prohibiting consideration of race in school assignments. While the Obama administration issued guidance to clarify how districts could constitutionally continue with voluntary desegregation plans, that guidance was rescinded by the Trump administration. One account noted in 2017:

> During George W. Bush's administration, almost 200 districts shed their court orders. With just 176 districts left, Trump's Justice Department could bring an end to the 63-year-old effort to erase the legacy of Jim Crow in the American education system, at a time when nearly 8.4 million black and Latino children are learning in segregated and high-poverty schools. (Felton, 2017, para. 60)

Starting in 1988, the achievement gap began to grow again, and stark differences reemerged between segregated urban schools and their suburban counterparts, which often spent twice as much on education. Achievement gaps between Black and White students in reading and mathematics are 50% larger now than they were 35 years ago.

While some states have made investments that have translated into improvements, over the last 15 years, average achievement for 13-year-old Black students in reading has declined steeply on the National Assessment of Educational Progress (NAEP). (See Figure 1.1.) These drops began during the era introduced by the No Child Left Behind Act (enacted in 2002 and in effect until 2015), which focused the nation on closing test score gaps by applying punitive sanctions to schools with scores not moving fast enough to show "100% proficiency." Although the law was launched with a temporary increase in funds for high-poverty schools, the promised ongoing additional funding did not materialize, and many states focused on testing without investing in the resources needed to achieve higher standards. During the Great Recession (2008–2012) many states slashed education budgets, and most states were spending less on education in 2017 than they had in 2007 (Farrie & Sciarra, 2020).

The law also required severe sanctions—including school closures, replacement by charter schools, or "reconstitution" of staff if test scores did not improve rapidly toward a "100% proficiency" benchmark. Ironically, the most underresourced schools serving students of color in high-need communities—especially Black students—were those that, in the name of equity, were most often closed or reconstituted (Pearman et al., 2023), their teachers and leaders fired or reassigned on the assumption that they alone were the reason for low test scores. Large numbers of Black teachers, now known to be critical to the achievement of Black students, were lost to the profession during this time (Carver-Thomas, 2018; Carver-Thomas & Darling-Hammond, 2017b). Communities that lost their schools suffered, as did students who were uprooted. The closures and mobility often negatively affected academic performance for those students (Gordon et al., 2018), and in many cases created "school deserts" in Black communities, such as those in parts of Chicago and Philadelphia, where there are no longer any public schools at all. As one study of this phenomenon noted: "areas with high-quality schools are significantly wealthier and Whiter than school deserts. . . . (I)f students do not have geographic access to good schools, then school choice policies do not, in fact, offer choice" (Alexander & Massaro, 2020, p. 787).

Many of these communities had just barely begun to recover when the COVID-19 pandemic set in. The effects of the pandemic have only exacerbated the challenges faced by children and families of color, as they experienced the results of greater infection and mortality rates, unemployment, housing and food instability, and the digital divide—which prevented many children from engaging in education and their parents from engaging in telehealth, job searches, access to benefits, or deliveries of groceries and medicine.

The share of families of color living in poverty increased immediately. Despite a gradual decline in rates prior to the pandemic, these numbers shifted for the worse between 2019 and 2020, with a reversal of progress, and a widening of the gap by race/ethnicity and family structure. As Child Trends reported in 2021:

> Poverty rates among Latino children rose by 4.2 percentage points, from 23.0 percent to 27.3 percent, and by 2.8 percentage points among Black children, from 26.4 percent to 29.2 percent. . . . In contrast, the rates of White and Asian children in poverty remained relatively stable. In addition, children in female-headed families also saw a large increase in the poverty rate, by 4.1 percentage points, from 33.4 percent to 37.4 percent. (Chen & Thomson, 2021)

President Biden's American Rescue Plan Act sought to address this growing poverty with income tax credits for low-income families that once again cut child poverty in half for 1 year, plus food and housing security initiatives that prevented evictions and ensured sustenance. However, these initiatives were not continued by the Congress after they expired.

Throughout the country, profound and long-standing inequalities were highlighted the moment schooling became remote: It became apparent that students from low-income families often had little access to computers and connectivity to use for distance learning, and their schools were often the least well-staffed and resourced to provide the tools and supports needed. Since school doors have reopened, educators have struggled to address student trauma and learning lags, as well as the results of personnel shortages that emerged with COVID-19 surges and quarantines and have continued with retirements and resignations, especially from the highest-need schools.

The effects of these challenges were made clear when the 2022 National Assessment of Educational Progress (NAEP) results were released for the first time since 2019. Drops in scores, seen for all students, were most severe for low-income students and students of color. Dr. Peggy Carr, commissioner of the National Center for Education Statistics (NCES), which issued the report, described the results as "almost 2 decades of educational progress washed away" (Brangham & Hastings, 2022).

Indeed, as Figure 1.1 illustrates, by 2023, reading scores for Black 13-year-olds had fallen to their lowest level in the last quarter century, and the achievement gap between White and Black students grew wider than it had been since 1999.

High School Attainment

In 1950, only 14% of Black citizens over the age of 25 had graduated from high school, as compared to 36% of White citizens at that time (NCES, 2019a). Since then, high school attainment has grown more common, and 88% of Black Americans over the age of 25 now hold a high school degree (Day, 2020). However, there is still a noticeable racial/ethnic gap in 4-year graduation rates for current students. In 2019–2020, the "on-time" graduation rate ranged from 93% for Asian students and 90% for White students to 83% for Latinx students, 81% for Black students, and 75% for Native American students (NCES, 2023). (See Figure 1.2.)

Higher Education

Educational limitations—including less access for Black students to advanced college preparatory classes in high school (Leung et al., 2020)—plus lack of family resources and cuts in federal funding for financial aid extend these disparities into higher education. While enrollment in higher education

Figure 1.2. *Graduation Rates by Race/Ethnicity, 2019-2020*

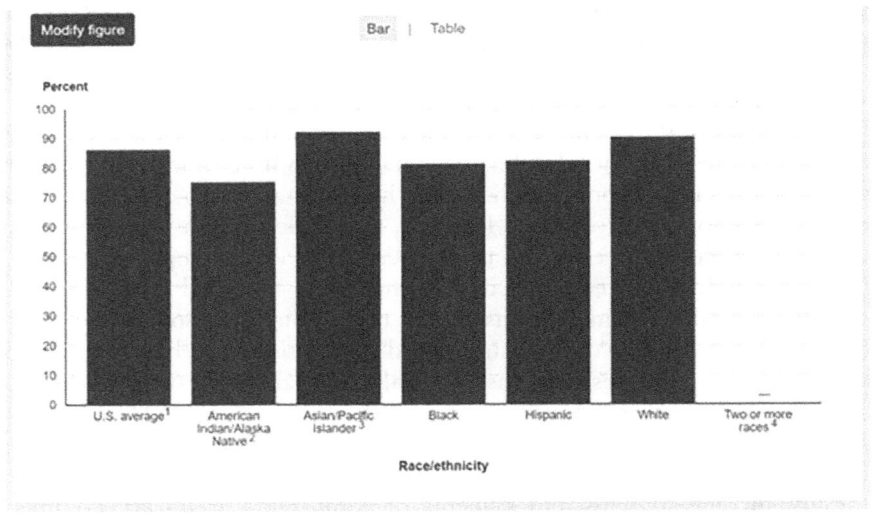

Source: National Center for Education Statistics (2023). Public high school graduation rates. *Condition of Education*. U.S. Department of Education. http://nces.ed.gov/programs/coe/indicator/coi#2

for Black 18- to 24-year-olds increased from 15% in 1970 to 38% in 2010, the rates for White and Asian peers in 2010 were 43% and 64%, respectively (NCES, 2022). Since 2010, total Black enrollment in higher education has dropped significantly, from 3.04 million to 2.38 million in 2020, a 22% decrease; and according to the National Student Clearinghouse, it continued to drop by another 9% over the next 2 years, until it stabilized in 2023 (NCES, 2022; National Student Clearinghouse Research Center, 2024).

These declines, which occurred to enrollments for most other groups to a lesser degree, were a function of economic challenges encountered during the pandemic by many families—especially those who have been historically most economically vulnerable.

And Black students must go into greater debt to attend college. A recent Brookings Institution report found that Black college graduates carry about 50% more debt than their White peers when they receive their bachelor's degrees, and that gap more than triples over the next 4 years, as Black graduates have to borrow more for graduate school and pay more in interest on a growing loan balance. They also go on to earn less than White graduates, which makes these loans more difficult to pay off, and they have higher rates of debt default (Scott-Clayton & Li, 2016; see also Marcus, 2023). Financial challenges also contribute to the lower college graduation rates Black students experience, at 40% after 6 years for those who entered college in 2010, compared to those for Asian students (74%), White students

(64%), Hispanic students (54%), and Pacific Islander students (51%). The rates for Native American students were comparable to those of Black students at 39% (NCES, 2019b).

In the face of these ongoing disparities, the Supreme Court's speculation in *Grutter v. Bollinger* (2003) that affirmative action in higher education would not be needed after 25 years seems laughable. However, as part of contemporary pushback, the Supreme Court effectively ended affirmative action in higher education in 2023 with its decision that the admissions programs at Harvard and the University of North Carolina, which account for race at various stages in the process, violate the Equal Protection Clause of the 14th Amendment to the U.S. Constitution (*Students for Fair Admissions [SFFA] v. Harvard*, 2023; *SFFA v. UNC*, 2023).

POLICIES THAT MATTER

To achieve equality, it is important to understand the anatomy of inequality in the United States, so that it can be dismantled in full. This anatomy begins with a legacy of poverty and segregation, which were increasingly connected through segregated housing policies and redlining that prevented investments in Black neighborhoods for many decades. Though officially ended in 1968 with the Fair Housing Act, the practice continued for decades thereafter, and the effects live on today. Inequality in school funding is layered onto these conditions, producing unequal access to well-qualified educators accompanied by high rates of turnover in many poorly resourced, highly segregated schools. This, in combination with ongoing implicit bias and lack of resources, contributes to unequal access to high-quality curriculum, and, in many instances, to dysfunctional schools characterized by a punitive culture and high rates of exclusionary discipline that further disengage students from school (see Figure 1.3).

Under our current educational system, so-called "achievement gaps" for children of color begin early—even before they enter school—and widen over time (Shapiro, 2017; see also, for example, Rothstein, 2004). This is a function of significant *opportunity* gaps in multiple areas of children's lives (Carter & Welner, 2013). Addressing these conditions requires purposeful policies motivated by a vision that marries equity with educational quality by creating well-resourced schools that are also supportive, inclusive, engaging, culturally responsive, and culturally sustaining.

Eliminating Poverty and the Accumulated Effects of Segregation

Following the theft of labor and wealth accumulation imposed by slavery, centuries of discrimination in employment, housing, and education have contributed to dramatic disparities in financial resources for Black and

Figure 1.3. *The Anatomy of Inequality*

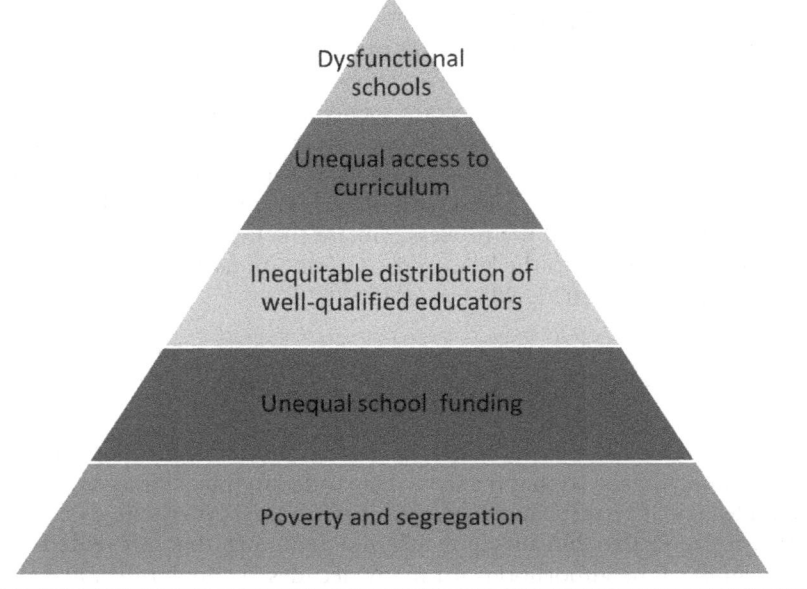

Source: L. Darling-Hammond, Learning Policy Institute.

White families. The Federal Reserve estimates that in 2019, the average Black and Latinx households in the United States earned about half as much as the average White household, and White families had about seven times the average wealth of Black families, at $983,400 vs. $142,500, respectively. These disparities, and overall wealth inequality in the United States, grew dramatically during the 30 years between 1989 and 2019 (Aladangady & Forde, 2021). (See Figure 1.4.) The gap in median wealth was even more stark at $188,200 vs. $24,100, a comfortable six-figure cushion for White families vs. a figure well below the poverty line for Black families.

These disparities began to grow as a function of the Reagan administration policies described earlier that began the process of lowering taxes on the wealthy and reducing governmental expenditures for housing, income, and education that supported lower-income families, a set of policies further expanded in the two Bush administrations and the Trump administration.

Today, more than half of children attending U.S. public schools qualify for free or reduced-price lunch—the highest percentage since the National Center for Education Statistics began tracking this figure decades ago. Furthermore, U.S. children living in poverty have a much weaker safety net than their peers in other industrialized countries, where universal health care, housing subsidies, and high-quality, universally available child care are

Figure 1.4. *Household Net Worth and Income*

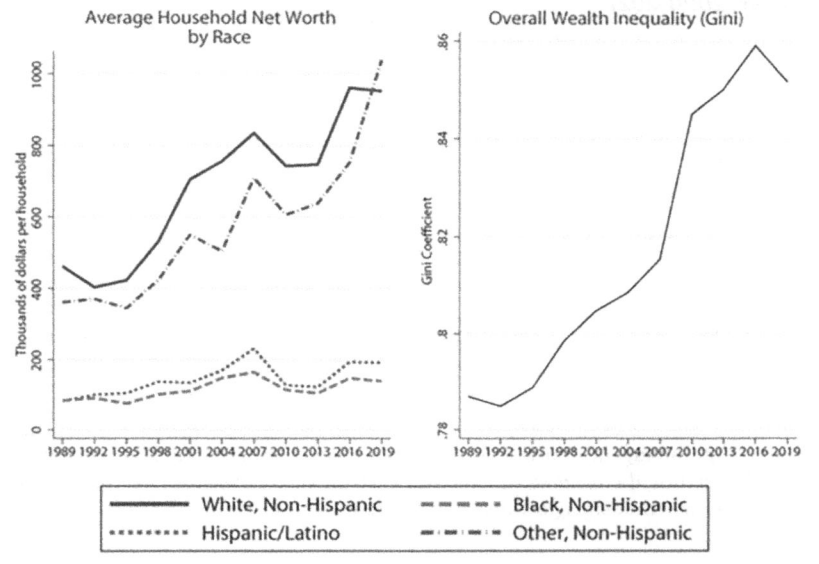

Source: Aladangady, A. & Forde, A. (2021). *Wealth inequality and the racial wealth gap*. FEDS Notes. Board of Governors of the Federal Reserve. https://doi.org/10.17016/2380-7172.2861

the norm. Recent data from the Organisation for Economic Co-operation and Development (OECD, 2017) show that the United States falls in the bottom tier of countries in terms of child poverty, hunger, infant mortality, and access to books in the home.

A 2023 report from the Federal Interagency Forum on Child and Family Statistics shows that, while child poverty rates were declining through 2021, more than one-quarter of Black children (27.3%) were in families below the poverty line ($27,479 for a two-parent, two-child family) (see Figure 1.5). Because of the child tax credit that was part of COVID-19 recovery dollars, this was the lowest rate in more than 3 decades. However, the overall rate of children in poverty more than doubled in the following year when the tax credit was discontinued—the largest year-over-year increase on record (Koutavas, 2023).

Citing the U.S. General Accounting Office, the Centers for Disease Control and Prevention (CDC), and a large body of research, Richard Rothstein's *The Color of Law* (2017) evaluates a long list of factors contributing to low achievement for low-income children and particularly students of color, ranging from lack of access to eyeglasses, disproportionate instances of lead poisoning, iron-deficiency anemia, asthma, and substandard pediatric care, to housing instability, food insufficiency, and neighborhood

Figure 1.5. *Percentage of Children Ages 0-17 Living in Poverty by Race and Hispanic Origin, 2000-2021*

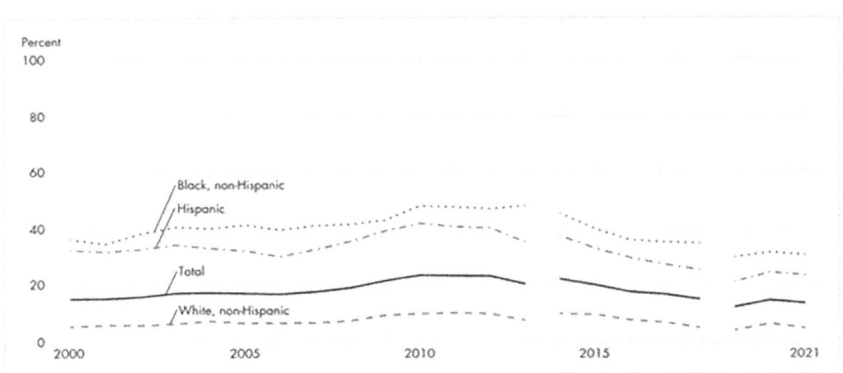

Source: Federal Interagency Forum on Child and Family Statistics. (2023*). America's children: Key national indicators of well-being, 2023.* U.S. Government Printing Office, p. 33. https://www.childstats.gov/americaschildren/eco1.asp

dangers. All of these circumstances have been amplified by the aftereffects of redlining, which created legalized segregated neighborhoods in which banks and governments would not invest to improve housing, parks, or businesses.

These neighborhoods have also accumulated environmental hazards. In 1987, the Commission for Racial Justice published *Toxic Wastes and Race,* which found race to be the most potent factor in predicting the location of waste facility sites. A 2021 study showed that "Black Americans are 75% more likely to live in close proximity to oil and gas facilities," resulting in "higher rates of cancer and asthma, [with] Black children twice as likely to develop asthma as their peers" (Garza, 2021). The catastrophe in Flint, Michigan, which left a predominantly Black community with levels of lead in their water that produced neurological disabilities for more than one-third of children was not an isolated event. There are millions of children exposed to lead in their homes and schools, with as many as 6% of Black children (and 2% of White children) experiencing levels associated with lead poisoning (Fortner, 2021; Nelson, 2016).

Manuel Pastor and colleagues (2004) have further documented environmental inequalities such as the siting of toxic facilities in low-income communities of color, and estimate that the side effects of these hazards account for as much as half of the performance differential between students living in Los Angeles neighborhoods with the lowest and highest risk levels, even after controlling for poverty and other demographic factors.

Clearly, addressing these conditions of children's lives—eliminating the opportunity gaps associated with poverty and environmental challenges—is a fundamental aspect of the march to equity. Another War on Poverty is needed, as is the return of a set of housing, income, employment, and environmental policies that support community health and well-being. The American Rescue Act suggested what is possible, with increased supports in all of these areas associated with sharp, though temporary, reductions in poverty. In addition, the Infrastructure Investment and Jobs Act of 2021 included a $3.5 billion superfund to clean up highly polluted toxic waste sites around the country, about 60% of which are in low-income communities of color, and nearly $3 billion more for lead pipe removal nationwide (Shivaram, 2021).

Meanwhile, investments in community schools that are designed to support children's thriving can wrap around students with the supports they need. A growing number of states, including California, Maryland, New Mexico, and New York, have invested in such schools in high-poverty communities. These schools offer integrated supports for physical and mental health, as well as social services of many kinds; expanded and enriched learning time before and after school and in the summer with community connections both for enrichment and for project-based academic work; family and community engagement; and collaborative leadership and practices that engage staff, families, and community organizations in a common understanding of child development that guides joint efforts. Together, these features have been found to support stronger attendance, achievement, and attainment for students, and better life outcomes (Maier et al., 2017).

Achieving Equitable School Resources

The conditions of family poverty and impoverishment of communities affect children's access to education from a very early age.

Resources for Preschool: Low-income children have less access to preschool in the United States. In 2019, just over half (53%) of 4-year-old children living in poverty were enrolled in preschool compared with 76% of their counterparts in families earning $125,000 a year (Karoly & Cannon, 2021). While affluent families can afford the hefty expense of private preschool, children from low-income families have to compete for limited slots in public preschool programs. The federal Head Start program and most state public preschool programs have never been funded to reach all eligible children.

Preschool has long been known to matter greatly for short- and long-term school and life success, with strong returns on investment well into adulthood. Studies find that quality preschool experiences are associated with stronger school achievement skills; a reduced need for special education or grade retention; increased high school graduation, college attendance, and completion rates; and increased wages and employability in adult life (Heckman & Masterov, 2007; Reynolds et al., 2011). Nobel Prize–winning economist James Heckman has estimated that every dollar invested in a high-quality early childhood education produces returns of 7% to 10% annually (Heckman, 2011).

High-quality programs that get better results employ teachers with specialized training in early childhood (Bueno et al., 2010) who focus on developmentally appropriate learning goals in small classes with low student–teacher ratios that enable personalization (Barnett, 2011). A recent study in California found that preschool quality is associated with larger developmental gains, but that, of all groups, Black students were least likely to have access to high-quality settings (Sussman et al., 2022).

Resources for K–12: Continued inequities deriving from our school funding systems mean that the best-supported students in our highest-spending states and districts experience school spending many times greater than our most poorly supported students. While some experience a rich array of curriculum offerings taught by highly experienced teachers in small classes supported by extensive resources, others attend school where buildings are crumbling, classes are overcrowded, instructional materials are inadequate, and staff are often transient and underprepared.

In 2018, only 12 states spent at least 5% more in the districts serving the greatest proportion of underserved students of color than those serving the fewest (see Figure 1.6). Meanwhile, 20 states spent less on those districts, despite the greater needs of their students. On average, districts serving the largest populations of Black, Latinx, or Indigenous students (those in the top quartile) received about $1,800 (13%) less per student in state and local funding than those serving the fewest (in the bottom quartile).

The disparities in funding have serious consequences for academic outcomes: Research shows that money matters, as it is a precondition for resources that have significant impacts on student achievement, such as class sizes, curriculum, and access to qualified teachers (Baker, 2017). Civil rights data show that the odds of high-minority schools having uncertified and inexperienced teachers are four times those of predominantly White schools, a function of lower salaries and poorer working conditions. These differences translate into differences in access to quality curriculum and teaching, and ultimately in achievement (Cardichon et al., 2020).

A number of studies have found strong relationships between racial segregation and racial achievement gaps; indeed, the racial composition of a school has educational impacts for students beyond those associated with socioeconomic status, particularly due to resource inequities characterizing racially isolated schools (Ayscue et al., 2017). In a case that challenged school desegregation efforts in Jefferson County, Kentucky, and Seattle, Washington, more than 550 scholars signed on to a social science report filed as an amicus brief, which summarized extensive research showing the

Figure 1.6. *School Funding by Race: Per-Pupil Funding Differences Between Districts in the Top and Bottom Quartiles of Students of Color, by State*

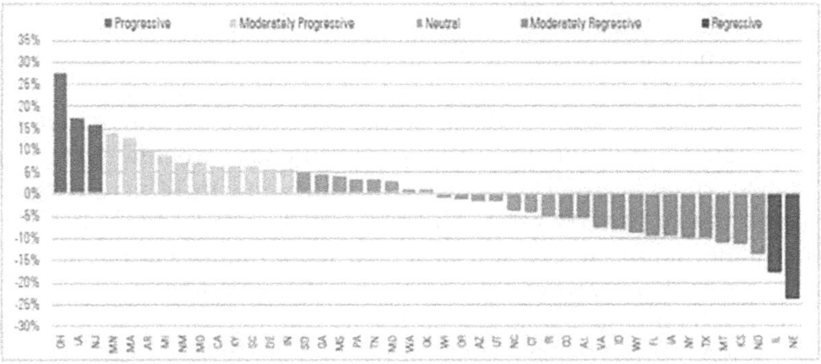

Source: *Funding Gaps 2018*, by I. Morgan and A. Amerikaner, 2018, The Education Trust. https://edtrust.org/resource/funding-gaps-2018

persisting inequalities of segregated minority schools. The scholars concluded that:

> More often than not, segregated minority schools offer profoundly unequal educational opportunities. This inequality is manifested in many ways, including fewer qualified, experienced teachers, greater instability caused by rapid turnover of faculty, fewer educational resources, and limited exposure to peers who can positively influence academic learning. No doubt as a result of these disparities, measures of educational outcomes, such as scores on standardized achievement tests and high school graduation rates, are lower in schools with high percentages of nonwhite students. (American Educational Research Association, 2007)

While school finance reform efforts have met with decades of opposition from state defendants and critics arguing that money doesn't make a difference (Hanushek, 2003, p. 4), the relationship between funding and outcomes has been established over the last decade by multiple studies in a number of states using stronger data sets and statistical methods than were once available (Jackson, 2020). One comprehensive cross-state study of school finance reforms experienced by children born between 1955 and 1985 found that, in places where new formulas enabled 10% more funding for schools serving low-income students, thus improving staffing and programs and reducing class sizes, graduation rates improved by more than 10 percentage points, educational attainment increased, along with employment and adult wages, and the poverty gap for adults was substantially reduced, all of which are associated with large social benefits (Jackson et al., 2016). These improved outcomes were associated with smaller student–teacher ratios, larger salaries for teachers, and longer school years.

It is largely this greater access to resources that has driven improved outcomes from desegregation. A large-scale study on students born between 1945 and 1970 found that graduation rates climbed by 2 percentage points for every year a Black student attended an integrated school (Johnson, 2019). A Black student exposed to court-ordered desegregation for 5 years experienced a 15% increase in wages and an 11 percentage point decline in annual poverty rates. The differences are related to the fact that schools under court supervision benefited from higher per-pupil spending and smaller student–teacher ratios, among other resources.

The results of equalizing school district funding can be seen in Massachusetts and New Jersey. As a result of school finance litigation that resulted in progressive funding reforms during the 1990s, these states catapulted to the two top-ranked states in the nation in terms of student achievement and graduation rates. Achievement gaps also narrowed, as the reforms reallocated money on the basis of student needs, with more going to high-need students in low-income districts, establishing quality preschool for those students, and making investments in stronger teaching from pre-K through grade 12 (Darling-Hammond, L., 2019b, p. 13).

Although the two states maintained these efforts for many years, steadily reducing disparities, litigators in both states are concerned about recent slippages in funding that have caused them to return to court. In both cases, ongoing segregation combined with poverty is at the root of the concerns. In New Jersey, a mediated settlement is expected to result in both interdistrict desegregation plans and new investments in schools (Koruth, 2024).

ACCESS TO QUALITY TEACHERS AND CURRICULUM

Part of the rationale for ongoing school finance litigation has been the challenge of unequal access to well-prepared educators, as low-wealth districts offer poorer salaries and working conditions (Darling-Hammond, L., 2010). School equity cases in more than 20 states have found that by every measure of qualifications—certification, subject matter background, pedagogical training, selectivity of college attended, test scores, or experience—students of color and students from low-income families typically have the least qualified teachers and the least intellectually challenging curriculum. Data from the most recent Civil Rights Data Collection (CRDC) show that schools serving the largest number of students of color employ four times as many uncertified teachers and nearly twice as many inexperienced teachers as those serving the fewest (Cardichon et al., 2020). CRDC data also show that these schools offer many fewer advanced courses and a more impoverished curriculum (Leung et al., 2020).

Frequent shortages in high-minority schools are associated with increased class sizes, canceled course offerings, and the hiring of underqualified teachers. Research finds that individuals who enter teaching without having completed preparation—either through emergency permits or alternative pathways—are typically less effective and have significantly higher turnover rates, which both harm student achievement and create churn that exacerbates shortages (Boyd et al., 2006; Carver-Thomas & Darling-Hammond, 2017a); Clotfelter et al., 2007b; Clotfelter et al., 2010; Darling-Hammond et al., 2005; Ronfeldt et al., 2013). Indeed, the percentage of underprepared teachers in a district is strongly and negatively associated with student achievement, especially for historically underserved students of color (Podolsky et al., 2019).

Many studies have found that the most important in-school predictor of student achievement is teacher qualifications, and that the effects are largest for Black and Latinx students (Goe, 2007; Kyriakides et al., 2013). In one vivid example, a large-scale study in North Carolina found that student achievement gains were significantly larger when students had teachers who were experienced, prepared and licensed before entry, and National Board Certified, an acknowledgment of expertise that is closely related to teachers' abilities to teach diverse students for deeper learning. Together, these variables had more effect on student achievement gains than the effects of race and parent education combined. However, these well-prepared teachers were inequitably distributed, with the most advantaged students disproportionately receiving the most experienced and expert teachers (Clotfelter et al., 2007a; Podolsky et al., 2019).

Meanwhile, a growing body of research shows that Black teachers enable greater achievement and attainment for Black students (Carver-Thomas, 2018). Yet because training to become a teacher is costly and generally unsubsidized, comprehensive preparation programs have been less accessible to potential candidates of color, who carry significantly more college debt than White candidates (Darling-Hammond et al., 2023). This has produced a profession that is currently 80% White even as students of color are now a majority in public schools.

Ironically, as Ladson-Billings (this volume) points out, many extraordinary Black teachers were a casualty of desegregation, and as Bristol and Carver-Thomas (this volume) note, even when Black teachers are recruited, their likelihood of staying in teaching is reduced by the difficulty of affording preparation, as well as less access to mentoring and placement in especially challenging schools that are underresourced.

Investing in strong teacher education and mentoring enables teachers to use strategies that encourage higher-order learning and that respond to students' experiences, cultural contexts, and learning approaches

(Darling-Hammond & Bransford, 2005). Among other things, knowing how to plan and manage a classroom allows teachers to focus on the kind of complex teaching that is needed to develop higher-order skills. Since the novel tasks required for complex problem-solving are more difficult to manage than the routine tasks associated with learning simple skills, lack of classroom management ability can lead teachers to "dumb down" the curriculum to control student work more easily (Carter & Doyle, 1987).

These teaching challenges reinforce the long-standing inequalities in access to a curriculum focused on higher-order thinking skills, which has long been denied to students of color both to justify lower investments in their schools and because of fears that young people would fail to accept their place in the social order if they had greater access to more empowering knowledge. Just as it was forbidden to teach enslaved people to read or to teach the nation's founding documents in Black schools in the South, it has been rare for schools to offer or admit Black students to the advanced curriculum reserved for the most advantaged students (Darling-Hammond et al., 2007).

Curriculum differences have been defended as appropriate to the different, socially sanctioned expectations the education system has held for children. In the 30 years of lawsuits to bring equitable funding to New Jersey, for example, education leaders justified as appropriate for the students the curriculum differences between places like predominantly White Princeton, which offered world languages starting in preschool and a bevy of Advanced Placement courses in high school, and predominantly Black Camden, which offered neither. In 1976, New Jersey State Education Commissioner Fred Burke expressed the view that has often surfaced in state resistance to equalization of funding: "Urban children, even after years of remediation, will not be able to perform in school as well as their suburban counterparts.... We are just being honest" (Burke, 1976).

For these reasons, as Harvard professor Jal Mehta explains,

> Deeper learning has historically been the province of the advantaged—those who could afford to send their children to the best private schools and to live in the most desirable school districts. Research on both inequality across schools and tracking within schools has suggested that students in more affluent schools and top tracks are given the kind of problem-solving education that befits the future managerial class, whereas students in lower tracks and higher-poverty schools are given the kind of rule-following tasks that mirror much of factory and other working-class work. To the degree that race mirrors class, these inequalities in access to deeper learning are shortchanging Black and Latino/a students. (Mehta, 2014)

This was part of the plan for the tracking systems that were developed in the early 1990s to separate students within school buildings according to decisions made about the specific vocations they would be enabled to hold. These tracks were justified by eugenicists' "evidence" about differential intelligence. Psychologist and IQ test developer Lewis Terman, a professor at Stanford University, declared that 80% of the immigrants he tested appeared to be "feeble-minded," and he further concluded in his 1922 book *Intelligence Tests and School Reorganization*: "Indians, Mexicans, and negroes . . . should be segregated in special classes. . . . They cannot master abstractions, but they can often be made efficient workers" (Terman et al., 1922, pp. 27–28).

The conception of schools as a sorting mechanism, selecting only a few students for thinking work, has reinforced both tracking, starting early in elementary school, and cross-school differentials in curriculum opportunities, even as educational expectations in the society and the labor market have changed dramatically. The result of this practice is that challenging curricula are rationed to a very small proportion of students, and few students of color ever encounter the kinds of deeper learning opportunities students in high-achieving countries typically experience (Oakes, 2005).

There are exceptions to these established norms, and they demonstrate what is possible when teams of diverse and talented teachers are recruited to teach a challenging, deeper learning curriculum in schools designed to be student-centered, intellectually challenging, and supportive.

Studies of schools that successfully support deeper learning for students of color and those from low-income communities engage in a number of common practices, including:

- authentic instruction and assessment (e.g., project-based and collaborative learning, performance-based assessment, and connections to relevant topics related to student identities and the world beyond school);
- personalized supports for learning (e.g., advisory systems, differentiated instruction, and social and emotional learning and skill building); and
- supports for educator learning through reflection, collaboration, leadership, and professional development (Noguera et al., 2015, pp. 8–12; see also Friedlaender et al., 2014 and Zeiser, 2014).

In untracked settings in which students are receiving a message that all can succeed, they engage in mastery learning experiences through which they undertake meaningful questions, conduct inquiries together, present and vet their answers to one another, and continue to revise their findings and products until they have more deeply understood the concepts. By revising their work, students learn that they can become competent by applying purposeful effort (often guided by rubrics that identify what they have done well and what is left to do), and they develop cognitive strategies that they can transfer to future work. In many of these schools, students publicly present exhibitions or portfolios of their work at the end of a grade level or for graduation to demonstrate how they are mastering competencies that guide a school's curriculum. As students take agency in the learning process, they come to understand both how they learn and what they care about, which propels their work going forward. They develop a growth mindset and the motivation to continue to define questions and pursue deeper learning about matters they care about, including pathways to college and careers.

Examples include hundreds of public schools serving predominantly students of color and new immigrant students launched as part of the Boston and Los Angeles Pilot Schools, those associated with the Center for Collaborative Education in New York and Boston, the small schools initiative in Chicago, and networks like New Tech High, Big Picture, Internationals, Envision, and others. An example that has scaled significantly is Linked Learning, a network of schools that now number more than 600 in California, with many others across the country. The models are typically new small schools or academies within larger school buildings that integrate rigorous academics with career-based learning and real-world workplace experiences. They include schools with themes and industry relationships ranging from engineering and medical sciences to arts, technology, and law, among many others.

These student-centered environments eliminate the divide between academic and vocational tracks that once divided students substantially by race and class. They emphasize supportive relationships between students and teachers in academic environments that are challenging, culturally and community-connected, relevant, collaborative, and student-directed. Students are assessed on their mastery of knowledge and skills through projects connected to real-life situations, and they have multiple opportunities to demonstrate that mastery. The schools are connected to their communities through industry partners and relationships with other community organizations that provide internships and other learning opportunities; industry and community representatives participate, along with teachers, in evaluating authentic student work. Educators are supported in creating a student-centered learning environment as they design their school or academy and regularly evolve their work with feedback from student surveys and other insights.

Life Academy of Health and Bioscience in Oakland, CA, a nonselective 6th- through 12th-grade public school focused on the health professions and the biological sciences, illustrates what is possible. Serving largely Black and Latinx students, 99% of whom are low-income and 30% of whom are English learners, the school offers all students college and career preparation coursework through an inquiry-based pedagogy that includes cross-disciplinary projects, health and science career internships, a 4-year advisory program that ensures each student has a staff member who knows them well and advocates for their needs, multiple performance-based exhibitions that include a scholarly senior exhibition completing a research paper defended much like a dissertation in graduate school. Like all schools in Oakland, the school is also a community school offering wraparound supports and extended learning time for students. The school had a 97% graduation rate in 2022–2023 and sends 100% of its graduates to 2- or 4-year colleges, with students going to schools like UC–Berkeley and UCLA, as well as Stanford, University of San Francisco, and Smith College (Life Academy School Accountability Report Card, 2023). This is the type of setting that achieves equity and excellence, enabling students to develop the skills to succeed in college, career, and life.

ACCESS TO POSITIVE AND INCLUSIVE SCHOOL CLIMATES

These kinds of schools offer positive and inclusive contexts for learning that are critically important for student success. Advances in the science of learning and development have clarified that psychological safety is a biologically necessary condition for effective learning (Darling-Hammond et al., 2020). Thus, to achieve educational equity, we must ensure that students of all backgrounds have access to positive and inclusive scholastic environments.

However, despite long-standing concerns about the impacts of exclusionary discipline on student well-being (Whiteside, 1975), schools across the country, especially those serving Black students, were encouraged to implement zero-tolerance policies starting in the Reagan years, with rapidly increasing rates of suspensions and expulsions from school from the 1980s through 2010, when the harmful effects of these policies were brought to light by the Obama administration (González, 2021). These policies required educators to use exclusionary discipline approaches as responses for even minor and nonviolent offenses, including tardiness, talking, texting, sleeping in class, or failing to follow instructions—all with little consideration of the context or consequences. The inequitable implementation of these policies generated stark racial disparities in exposure to exclusionary discipline, and today, despite federal policy efforts to reduce reliance on such approaches (U.S. Department of Education & U.S. Department of Justice, 2014), many schools, and particularly schools that serve Black students, continue to suspend and expel students at alarming rates (Government Accountability Office [GAO], 2018).

As we have noted, teachers in schools that serve more Black students are on average less experienced and less well prepared than teachers in schools that serve more White students (Leung-Gagné et al., 2022) and may, therefore, rely more heavily on discipline in part because they lack strategies for managing student behavior in positive ways. This is concerning, as mounting evidence indicates that exclusionary discipline reduces students' sense of connection to school and mental well-being and can lead to dropout and incarceration (Fabelo et al., 2011; Losen & Gillespie, 2012; Morris & Perry, 2016). In short, research indicates that exposure to exclusionary discipline is anathema to the psychological safety necessary for learning, and that Black students are more likely to be exposed to exclusionary discipline. This section describes what is known about the impacts of exclusion and punishment on student achievement and well-being, racial disparities in exclusionary discipline, and the promise of alternatives to exclusionary discipline—such as restorative practices, social and emotional learning, and positive behavioral interventions and supports—to create educational environments that empower students of all backgrounds to learn.

Harms of Exclusion, Punishment, and Racial Disparities

As we describe below, exclusionary punishments harm students' academic performance, their mental and physical health, and their life paths, and, while they affect all students, those harms are more prevalent for Black students and other students of color.

Academic harms: Research has linked exposure to exclusionary discipline with declines in academic performance, including lower GPAs and higher rates of school dropout (Schollenberger, 2015). Econometric research has also estimated that exposure to punitive environments *causes* declines in academic achievement for students, generally, and particularly for Black students (Bacher-Hicks et al., 2019). Researchers have also identified links between racial disparities in exclusionary discipline and racial disparities in academic achievement, suggesting that the persistent discipline gap discussed above may partially explain stubborn achievement gaps (Pearman et al., 2019).

Behavioral, mental health, and school climate harms: Many schools leverage exclusionary discipline practices to try to incentivize positive behavior changes. However, research has found that exposure to exclusionary discipline may lead students to distrust and feel defiant toward adults in their schools (Pesta, 2021; Way, 2011). More recent research has even estimated that after being suspended, students misbehave *more* than similarly situated students who were not suspended (LiCalsi et al., 2021), suggesting that suspension may actually have criminogenic effects whereby suspensions beget more misbehavior and, subsequently, more suspension. Students who experience suspensions also exhibit higher rates of behavioral and mental health challenges, including substance experimentation and addiction, mental health disorders (including depressive symptoms and borderline personality disorder), antisocial behaviors in adolescence, suicide, and involvement in mental health systems (Duarte et al., 2023; Eyllon et al., 2022; Fothergill et al., 2008; Gould et al., 1996; Hemphill et al., 2006; Kramer et al., 2017; Ramey, 2018; Rushton et al., 2002; Slade, 2004; Talluri et al.,

2014). The link between exclusionary discipline and suicide risk is particularly concerning given that the suicide rate among Black youth is currently growing at a rapid and unprecedented rate (Cubbage & Adams, 2023).

Perhaps unsurprisingly, given the way exclusionary discipline may impact the mental health milieux of a school, research suggests that exclusionary discipline may harm the overall school climate both among students who are suspended and even among those who are not (Lacoe & Steinberg, 2019). Many studies estimate that, for Black students specifically, direct exposure to exclusionary discipline harms a variety of academic, behavioral, mental health, and school climate outcomes. However, under the notion that *vicarious* exposure to exclusionary discipline may also harm Black students' sense of well-being, recent research has also explored the impact of exposure to discipline disparities and has found that Black students exposed to larger Black–White discipline gaps exhibit higher rates of adjustment problems (Bottiani et al., 2017) and that even among Black students who have not themselves experienced a suspension, being in a school with a larger Black–White discipline gap is related to lower feelings of belongingness in the school (Darling-Hammond, S., 2023a).

Carceral harms: In a seminal exploration of the correlates of exposure to discipline, researchers followed tens of thousands of students for over a decade after graduation. They found that, compared to students who were not suspended in high school, those who were suspended were 2.6 times more likely to have been arrested, and were about 4.5 times more likely to have been sentenced to serve time in either a juvenile or an adult correctional facility (Schollenberger, 2015). Researchers leveraging econometric techniques have found, similarly, that exposure to exclusionary discipline causes increases in downstream arrest and confinement rates for students of all racial backgrounds, but particularly for Black students (Bacher-Hicks et al., 2019).

Persistence and Pervasiveness of Racial Disparities in Exclusion and Punishment

Data collected by the Department of Education's Office of Civil Rights through the periodic Civil Rights Data Collection (CRDC) have demonstrated that racial disparities in exclusionary discipline and punishment appear across all student populations and scholastic contexts (Darling-Hammond, S., 2023a; Darling-Hammond & Ho, 2023; GAO, 2018). For example, whereas 3% of White students in 2017–2018 received an Out-of-School Suspension (OSS), a full 12% of Black students in the same year received an OSS (see Figure 1.7). The Black OSS rate was approximately 3.6 times higher than the White OSS rate. The same was true when looking at specific student subpopulations (e.g., the OSS rate for Black girls was 5.2 times higher than the OSS rate for White girls) and when looking at students

Figure 1.7. *Percentage of White Versus Black Students Receiving an Out-of-School Suspension (OSS) in the 2017-2018 School Year, Across Student Populations and School Contexts*

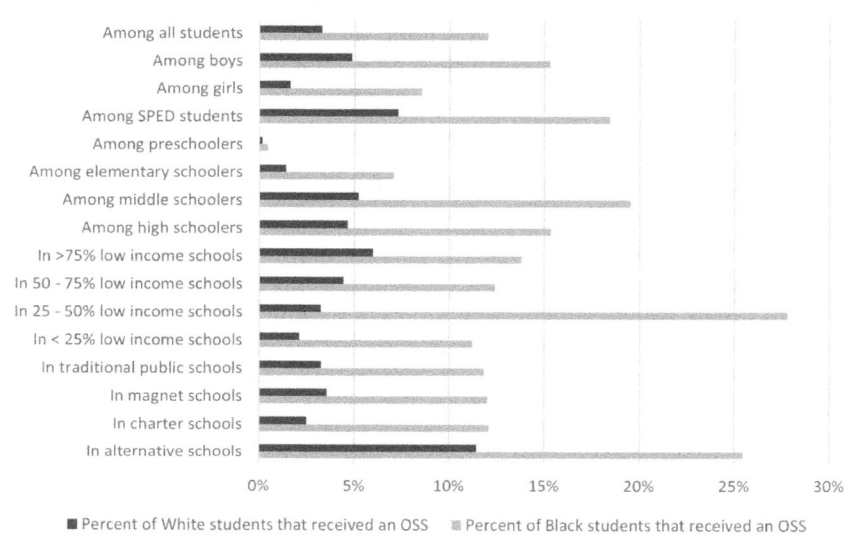

Source: "No Matter How You Slice It: The Persistence and Pervasiveness of Disproportionate Punishment for Black Students," by S. Darling-Hammond and E. Ho, *SocArxiv*. https://doi.org/10.31235/osf.io/khtsa

who attended particular types of schools (e.g., the OSS rate for Black preschoolers was 2.8 times higher than the OSS rate for White preschoolers, and the OSS rate for Black charter school students was 4.8 times higher than the OSS rate for White charter school students). Finally, the same was true when looking across each type of punishment a student might experience, including in-school suspensions, expulsions, corporal punishment, referrals to law enforcement, and school-related arrests. Similar trends emerged in an analysis of the most recent wave of CRDC data (collected in the 2020–2021 school year), evidencing that racial disparities in exclusion and punishment are not only pervasive but also persistent (Darling-Hammond & Ho, 2023).

Sources of Racial Disparities in Exclusionary Discipline

Critically, research from a variety of fields has surfaced evidence that Black–White disparities in exclusionary discipline are not merely a function of racial disparities in misbehavior. Instead, differential treatment by educators seems to be a critical driver. In a randomized controlled vignette experiment, researchers documented that teachers respond to behavior by Black students more punitively than they do to identical behavior by White students (Okonofua & Eberhardt, 2015). Evidence of bias emerges as early as preschool. In an eye-tracking study, researchers found that when they asked preschool teachers to find instances of problem behavior in a video of children playing, these teachers focused a disproportionate amount of their attention on Black boys (Gilliam et al., 2016).

Studies using student administrative data echo these points, finding that Black students are more likely to receive suspensions than White students, even when the students: have misbehaved a similar number of times, are engaged in the same incident of misbehavior (i.e., in a conflict with one another), have similar prior behavioral tendencies, or are in schools with similar racial compositions (Barrett et al., 2021; Gregory et al., 2016; Huang & Cornell, 2017; Shi & Zhu, 2022). When researchers have conducted "decomposition analyses" to compare factors that might contribute to Black–White disparities in exclusionary discipline rates, they have concluded that differential treatment is the largest contributor and explains about five times more variation than differences in behavior (Owens & McLanahan, 2020).

Safety Beyond Teachers: School Psychologists, School Counselors, and School Police

Psychological safety in schools is not merely a function of the practices of teachers. Instead, staff throughout the school play critical roles in creating psychologically appropriate conditions for learning.

School psychologists can play an instrumental role in improving outcomes for students and schools (Müller et al., 2021) by helping students address behavioral goals—such as reducing impulsivity, aggressive behavior, delinquent behavior, and social withdrawal (Lepage et al., 2004; Owens et al., 2008)—and by helping schools improve teacher efficacy (Vu et al., 2013) and reduce disciplinary referrals (Hawken, 2006).

School counselors can help students process challenging life situations and emotions (such as loss and grief; Guidry et al., 2013). Research indicates that school counselors can improve students' sense of connection to school (Lapan et al., 2014), academic achievement (Carrell & Hoekstra, 2014), college application rate (Bryan et al., 2011), and postsecondary enrollment rate (Belasco, 2013), and may help reduce schools' discipline rates (Lapan et al., 2012).

Research on the effects of student exposure to school psychologists, school counselors, and other school-based mental health providers has generally been positive. In contrast, research on the effects of exposure to school *police* has indicated that school police may increase exposure to discipline (Curran et al., 2019; Fisher & Hennessy, 2016) and damage school climate (Allen & Noguera, 2023), and that, for Black students, exposure to racially biased school police may lead to anxiety, depression, and psychological distress (Darling-Hammond, S., 2023b).

Despite the benefits of school counselors, and the comparative harms of school police, research has found that over 1.7 million students attend schools that have school police officers but lack even a single school counselor (Whitaker et al., 2019). Black students are more likely than students of other races to attend a school with a school police officer (Kidane & Rauscher, 2023).

Of course, many schools employ school police, and recruit exclusionary discipline methods, to ensure safety. However, research suggests that these practices not only fail to enhance safety, but may actually increase misbehavior. What, then, *can* schools do to ensure students' physical safety, and create the kinds of psychologically safe environments needed for students to learn?

Relational Alternatives to Exclusion and Punishment

In response to research documenting disparities in, and harms of, exclusionary discipline and punishment, many schools and districts have implemented alternative approaches to ensuring school safety. These include restorative practices, positive behavioral interventions and supports, and social and emotional learning. Research on these practices suggests that they have promise to increase the psychological safety of schools that serve students of all backgrounds.

For example, there has been recent growth in literature exploring the multifaceted benefits of student exposure to *restorative practices* (RP). RP practices can be loosely grouped into two types of practices: (1) community-building practices (e.g., weekly community-building circles where students and teachers share their emotional worlds and deepen social connections) and (2) harm-repair practices (e.g., conflict resolution conversations and convenings to help students and staff heal social bonds when conflicts emerge). Studies of RP have found strong evidence that exposure to these practices is related to reductions in misbehavior (Cook et al., 2018; Darling-Hammond, S., 2023a; Duong et al., 2019; Goldys, 2016; Lewis, 2009; McCold, 2002; McCold, 2008; McMorris et al., 2013) and exclusionary discipline (Armour, 2014; Augustine et al., 2018; Baker 2009; Darling-Hammond, S., 2023a; Goldys, 2016; González, 2015; Gregory et al., 2018; Gregory et al., 2021; Hashim et al., 2018; Jain et al., 2014; Mansfield et al., 2016; Riestenberg, 2003; Sumner et al., 2010), and improvements in school climate (Acosta et al., 2019; Augustine et al., 2018; Cook et al., 2018; Darling-Hammond, S., 2023a; Duong et al., 2019; Goldys, 2016; Grant et al., 2022; Jain et al., 2014; Lansing School District, 2008; McMorris et al., 2013; Terrill 2018). More limited research evidence suggests that the implementation of RP can help improve academic performance (Darling-Hammond, 2023a; Jain et al., 2014; Kerstetter, 2016; McMorris et al., 2013; Norris, 2009; Sadler, 2021;), improve student mental health (Darling-Hammond, S., 2023a), and reduce racial disparities in both academic achievement (Darling-Hammond, S., 2023a) and discipline (Armour, 2014; Darling-Hammond, S., 2023a; González, 2015; Gregory et al., 2016; Gregory et al., 2018; Hashim et al., 2018; Jain et al., 2014).

Other alternatives to exclusionary discipline have found support in research evidence, including Positive Behavioral Interventions and Support (PBIS) and Social and Emotional Learning (SEL) programs. PBIS is a framework for responding to student behavior (whether positive or unwanted) in a consistent and strategic manner that is designed to generate intrinsic motivation for students to follow school rules. Research on PBIS has found that it can reduce misbehavior, victimization, and bullying (Ögülmüs & Vuran, 2016), as well as reduce office referral and discipline rates (Gage et al., 2018; Noltemeyer et al., 2019). PBIS programs that prioritize recognizing and celebrating students' *good* behavior may also be particularly effective at reducing racial disparities in exclusionary discipline (Barclay et al., 2022). SEL programs provide curriculum and support to teachers and other school staff so they teach students core social and emotional skills such as self-awareness, self-regulation, empathy, and conflict resolution. Research on SEL has indicated that SEL programs can improve social and emotional skills, and can also improve students' attitudes about school, behavior, and academic performance (Durlak et al., 2011).

Taken together, research on RP, PBIS, and SEL suggests that these practices can be more effective than exclusionary discipline at reducing student misbehavior. Moreover, they can play a critical role in engendering environments characterized by psychological safety and, not surprisingly, can help improve student academic performance. When implemented equitably and effectively, these practices help reduce racial disparities in both discipline and academic achievement.

THE POLICIES WE NEED

The long list of disparities we have recounted, which have come to appear inevitable in the United States, are not the norm in developed nations around the world, which typically fund their education systems centrally and equally, with additional resources often going to the schools where students' needs are greater. These more equitable investments made by high-achieving nations are also steadier and more focused on critical elements of the system: access to high-quality early learning, a universally high quality of teachers and teaching, the development of curriculum and assessments that encourage ambitious learning by both students and teachers, and the design of schools as learning organizations that support continuous reflection and improvement. With the exception of a few states with enlightened long-term leadership, the United States has failed to maintain focused investments on these essential elements.

As noted in *The Civil Rights Road to Deeper Learning* (Darling-Hammond & Darling-Hammond, 2022), there is still a long road to travel to access quality learning opportunities for all students, and reaching the destination includes civil rights enforcement and equity policies to ensure access to healthy environments, supportive learning conditions and opportunities, well-resourced and inclusive schools, skillful teaching, and high-quality curriculum. To make good on our national obligation to provide equitable access to high-quality education, policymakers at the federal, state, and local levels need to cultivate universally available high-quality curricular opportunities within well-resourced schools, investments that ensure an adequate and equitably distributed supply of well-prepared educators, and supportive wraparound services (e.g., counseling, health care, social services, and academic supports) to counteract the adverse conditions that many students experience.

(1) To create **healthy environments** for children's well-being, we need to mend the tattered safety net for children and families, as the American Rescue Act plan began to do, with investments in nutrition, health care, and child tax credits that reduced child poverty by half in 2021 (Parolin et al., 2021). Those supports should be made permanent in federal law. Ongoing investments are also needed to reduce toxins in the environment, continuing the work of the Infrastructure Investment and Jobs Act of 2021, which reestablished efforts to clean up toxic waste, mostly in communities of color. And, like the economic investments that supported urban renewal in the 1970s, policymakers need to invest in rebuilding communities that have been cordoned off from investment and opportunity through decades of redlining, so that families in these communities can thrive. Rebuilding communities should include reestablishing and improving schools in neighborhoods that have become "school deserts" (Alexander & Massaro , 2020) as a result of punitive school closure policies, and developing community school models that organize whole child supports promoting students' physical and mental health, social welfare, and academic success, along with families' access to health care, social services, and adult education (Maier et al., 2017).

(2) To ensure *adequate and equitable resources* that address the needs of children and families, we need to redouble *school finance reform* efforts to achieve state policies that provide funding based

on pupil needs—such as poverty, homelessness, English learner status, and special education status—rather than as a function of property tax wealth in local communities. Because school funding and segregation continue to be strongly linked, reengagement of federal support for *desegregation* is also needed, through investments in such programs as the Magnet Schools Assistance Program and the Diversity Act to enable districts and states to pursue both intra-district and inter-district solutions to the conflation of poverty and segregation that has produced a growing number of apartheid schools (Brittain et al., 2019). A federal right to education can also be argued—despite the Supreme Court's 5–4 ruling in 1973 that the Constitution does not provide such a right (*San Antonio v. Rodriguez*)[2]—as federal requirements have since created mandates sanctioning schools that do not follow federally specified procedures and achieve federally specified goals, without ensuring equitable access to resources—including dollars, qualified educators, and standards-based curriculum needed to accomplish those goals (Darling-Hammond, L., 2019a). This right could be enforced both through existing, unenforced provisions of the Elementary and Secondary Education Act (ESEA) (such as those requiring comparability in educator qualifications across schools and those requiring resource audits of schools identified as in need of improvement) and through *accountability systems* that focus on students' opportunities to learn, along with multiple measures of meaningful learning and attainment. Such systems should emphasize indicators of students' access to educational resources, including well-qualified educators, a rich curriculum, high-quality instructional materials (including digital access at home and school), and a positive school climate.

(3) A key on-ramp to equity is access to high-quality *preschool education* that offers key learning resources to close opportunity and achievement gaps before school begins, offering a deeper learning curriculum from the start, when children are developing their initial brain architecture as they explore, inquire, communicate, and play. Federal and state investments should ensure that all 3- and 4-year-olds have access to such learning opportunities, as those in many countries and in some American communities do.

(4) Access to *equitable teaching and curriculum* requires both equitable investments in schools and in the development of a *diverse, well-prepared, culturally responsive and stable teaching force* in all schools. To achieve this goal a robust national teacher policy (Darling-Hammond, L., DiNapoli, M., Jr., & Kini, T., 2023) would: fully cover preparation costs for recruits who teach in high-need

fields or locations; support improved programs that prepare teachers to learn in partner schools connected to universities (like teaching hospitals) that instantiate best practices and support culturally responsive learning focused on 21st-century skills for all candidates; provide high-quality mentoring for all beginning teachers, which would reduce churn, enhance teaching quality, and heighten student achievement; and design recruitment incentives to attract and retain expert, experienced teachers who can teach and coach others in high-need schools—teachers like those certified by the National Board for Professional Teaching Standards who are skilled in teaching for deeper learning and have been found to be highly effective as teachers and mentors (National Research Council, 2008; Zhu et al., 2019).

(5) In addition, access to a thinking curriculum for all students will require a recognition that all students deserve and can benefit from cognitively challenging, authentic learning opportunities that develop higher order skills and the ability to apply them. This, in turn, will require redesigning schools from the factory model assembly line designed to select and sort students for predetermined social roles to schools designed to find and develop students' talents in settings organized for engagement, development, and support.

(6) Finally, developing *safe and inclusive schools* will require ongoing civil rights enforcement that has been essential to pave a path toward nonexclusionary school discipline practices for students of color and students with disabilities. The Office of Civil Rights's ability to monitor suspension and expulsion rates using the Civil Rights Data Collection has been critical, as has its guidance supporting school implementation of relational practices (e.g., restorative practices, social and emotional learning, and positive behavioral interventions and supports) that create strong communities, teach conflict resolution, and support positive discipline as an alternative. Though repealed by the Trump administration, the OCR guidance should be reissued to help districts support productive policies (Cardichon & Darling-Hammond, 2019). As in California, states can include suspension rates in their accountability systems and support access to training in positive discipline and restorative practices to substantially reduce exclusionary discipline and create environments in which all students know they belong (Cardichon & Darling-Hammond, 2019, pp. 10–11).

Ultimately, the promise of *Brown* rests on a widespread social understanding that the path to our mutual well-being is built on equal educational opportunity. In our current knowledge-based economy, all members of society benefit when every young person is prepared to find a successful pathway to their future, contributing through their talents and their taxes to the social progress and social safety net that support us all and to a world in which we can collectively solve the massive problems our world faces in the 21st century.

REFERENCES

Acosta, J., Chinman, M., Ebener, P., Malone, P. S., Phillips, A., & Wilks, A. (2019). Evaluation of a whole-school change intervention: Findings from a two-year cluster-randomized trial of the restorative practices intervention. *Journal of Youth and Adolescence, 48*, 876–890. https://doi.org/10.1007/s10964-019-01013-2

Aladangady, A., & Forde, A. (2021). *Wealth inequality and the racial wealth gap.* FEDS Notes. Board of Governors of the Federal Reserve. https://www.federalreserve.gov/econres/notes/feds-notes/wealth-inequality-and-the-racial-wealth-gap-20211022.html

Alexander, M., & Massaro, V. A. (2020). School deserts: Visualizing the death of the neighborhood school. *Policy Futures in Education, 18*(6), 787–805. https://doi.org/10.1177/1478210320951063

Allen, T., & Noguera, P. (2023). A web of punishment: Examining Black student interactions with school police in Los Angeles. *Educational Researcher, 0*(0). https://doi.org/10.3102/0013189X221095547

American Educational Research Association. Brief *amicus curiae* filed in *Parents Involved in Community Schools v. Seattle School District No. 1*, 551 U.S. 701 (2007).

Armour, M. (2014). *Ed White Middle School restorative discipline evaluation: Implementation and impact, 2012/2013 sixth & seventh grade.* The Institute for Restorative Justice and Restorative Dialogue. http://sites.utexas.edu/irjrd/files/2016/01/Year-2-Final-EW-Report.pdf

Asante-Muhammad, D. (2013, March 11). The Reagan era: Turning back racial equality gains. *Huffington Post.* https://www.huffingtonpost.com/dedrick-muhammad/the-reagan-eraturning-bac_b_2838625.html

Augustine, C. H., Engberg, J., Grimm, G. E., Lee, E., Wang, E. L., Christianson, K., & Joseph, A. A. (2018). *Can restorative practices improve school climate and curb suspensions? An evaluation of the impact of restorative practices in a mid-sized urban school district.* RAND. https://www.rand.org/pubs/research_reports/RR2840.html

Ayscue, J., Frankenberg, E., & Siegel-Hawley, G. (2017). *The complementary benefits of racial and socioeconomic diversity in schools.* National Coalition on School Diversity.

Bacher-Hicks, A., Billings, S., & Deming, D. (2019). *The school to prison pipeline: Long-run impacts of school suspensions on adult crime.* National Bureau of Economic Research. https://doi.org/10.3386/w26257

Baker, B. D. (2017). *How money matters for schools*. Learning Policy Institute. https://learningpolicyinstitute.org/sites/default/files/product-files/How_Money_Matters_REPORT.pdf

Baker, M. (2009). *DPS Restorative Justice Project: Year three*. Denver Public Schools.

Barclay, C. M., Castillo, J., & Kincaid, D. (2022). Benchmarks of equality? School-Wide Positive Behavioral Interventions and Supports and the discipline gap. *Journal of Positive Behavior Interventions, 24*(1), 4–16. https://doi.org/10.1177/10983007211040097

Barnett, S. (2011, September 22). *Preschool effectiveness and access*. Presented at the Equity and Excellence Commission.

Barrett, N., McEachin, A., Mills, J. N., & Valant, J. (2021). Disparities and discrimination in student discipline by race and family income. *Journal of Human Resources, 56*(3), 711–748. https://www.muse.jhu.edu/article/798142

Belasco, A. S. (2013). Creating college opportunity: School counselors and their influence on postsecondary enrollment. *Research in Higher Education, 54*(7), 781–804. https://doi.org/10.1007/s11162-013-9297-4

Bottiani, J. H., Bradshaw, C. P., & Mendelson, T. (2017). A multilevel examination of racial disparities in high school discipline: Black and white adolescents' perceived equity, school belonging, and adjustment problems. *Journal of Educational Psychology, 109*(4), 532–545. https://doi.org/10.1037/edu0000155

Boyd, D., Grossman, P., Lankford, H., Loeb, S., & Wyckoff, J. (2006). How changes in entry requirements alter the teacher workforce and affect student achievement. *Education Finance and Policy, 1*(2), 176–216.

Brangham, W., & Hastings, D. (2022, October 24). 'Nation's Report Card' shows test scores at lowest level in decades. *PBS NewsHour*. https://www.pbs.org/newshour/show/nations-report-card-shows-test-scores-at-lowest-level-in-decades

Brittain, J., Willis, L., & Cookson, P. W., Jr. (2019). *Sharing the wealth: How regional finance and desegregation plans can enhance educational equity*. Learning Policy Institute.

Bryan, J., Moore-Thomas, C., Day-Vines, N. L., & Holcomb-McCoy, C. (2011). School counselors as social capital: The effects of high school college counseling on college application rates. *Journal of Counseling & Development, 89*(2), 190–199. https://doi.org/10.1002/j.1556-6678.2011.tb00077.x

Bueno, M., Darling-Hammond, L., & Gonzales, D. (2010). *A matter of degrees: Preparing teachers for the pre-K classroom*. Pew Center on the States.

Burke, F. (1976, April 2). *New Jersey Star Ledger*.

Cardichon, J., & Darling-Hammond, L. (2019). *Protecting students' civil rights: The federal role in school discipline*. Learning Policy Institute. https://learningpolicyinstitute.org/product/student-civil-rights-school-discipline-report

Cardichon, J., Darling-Hammond, L., Yang, M., Scott, C., Shields, P. M., & Burns, D. (2020). *Inequitable opportunity to learn: Student access to certified and experienced teachers*. Learning Policy Institute. https://learningpolicyinstitute.org/sites/default/files/product-files/CRDC_Teacher_Access_REPORT.pdf

Carrell, S. E., & Hoekstra, M. (2014). Are school counselors an effective education input? *Economic Letters, 125*(1), 66–69. https://doi.org/10.1016/j.econlet.2014.07.020

Carter, K., & Doyle, W. (1987). Teachers' knowledge structures and comprehension processes. In J. Calderhead (Ed.), *Exploring teacher thinking* (pp. 147–160). Cassell.

Carter, P. L., & Welner, K. G. (Eds.). (2013). *Closing the opportunity gap: What America must do to give every child an even chance.* Oxford University Press.

Carver-Thomas, D. (2018). *Diversifying the teaching profession: How to recruit and retain teachers of color.* Learning Policy Institute. https://doi.org/10.54300/559.310

Carver-Thomas, D., & Darling-Hammond, L. (2017a). *Teacher turnover: Why it matters and what we can do about it.* Learning Policy Institute. https://doi.org/10.54300/454.278

Carver-Thomas, D. and Darling-Hammond, L. (2017b). Why Black women teachers leave and what can be done about it. *Black Female Teachers.* (*Advances in Race and Ethnicity in Education, Vol. 6*), Emerald Publishing Limited, pp. 159–184. https://doi.org/10.1108/S2051-231720170000006009

Chen, Y., & Thomson, D. (2021, June 3). *Child poverty increased nationally during COVID, especially among Latino and Black children.* Child Trends. https://www.childtrends.org/publications/child-poverty-increased-nationally-during-covid-especially-among-latino-and-black-children

Civil Rights Act of 1964, P.L. 88–352, Stat. 241 (1964).

Clotfelter, C. T., Ladd, H. F., & Vigdor, J. L. (2007a). *How and why do teacher credentials matter for student achievement?* [NBER Working Paper #12828]. National Bureau of Economic Research. https://www.nber.org/papers/w12828

Clotfelter, C. T., Ladd, H. F., & Vigdor, J. L. (2007b). Teacher credentials and student achievement: Longitudinal analysis with student fixed effects. *Economics of Education Review, 26*(6), 673–682.

Clotfelter, C. T., Ladd, H. F., & Vigdor, J. L. (2010). Teacher credentials and student achievement in high school: A cross-subject analysis with student fixed effects. *Journal of Human Resources, 45*(3), 655–681.

Commission for Racial Justice. (1987). *Toxic wastes and race in the United States.* United Church of Christ. https://ia802506.us.archive.org/28/items/toxicwastesrace/toxicwastesrace_text.pdf

Cook, C. R., Coco, S., Zhang, Y., Fiat, A. E., Duong, M., Renshaw, T., Long, A. C., & Frank, S. (2018). Cultivating positive teacher–student relationships: Preliminary evaluation of the establish–maintain–restore (EMR) method. *School Psychology Review, 47*(3), 226–243. https://doi.org/10.17105/SPR-2017-0025.V47-3

Cubbage, J., & Adams, L. (2023). *Still ringing the alarm: An enduring call to action for Black youth suicide prevention.* Johns Hopkins Center for Gun Violence Solutions and Johns Hopkins Bloomberg School of Public Health, Department of Mental Health. https://publichealth.jhu.edu/sites/default/files/2023-08/2023-august-still-ringing-alarm.pdf

Curran, F. C., Fisher, B. W., Viano, S., & Kupchik, A. (2019). Why and when do school resource officers engage in school discipline? The role of context in shaping disciplinary involvement. *American Journal of Education, 126*(1), 33–63. https://www.journals.uchicago.edu/doi/abs/10.1086/705499

Darling-Hammond, K., & Darling-Hammond, L. (2022). *The civil rights road to deeper learning.* Teachers College Press.

Darling-Hammond, L. (2010). *The flat world and education: How America's commitment to equity will determine our future.* Teachers College Press.

Darling-Hammond, L. (2018). Education and the path to one nation, indivisible. In F. Harris & A. Curtis (Eds.), *Healing our divided society: Investing in America fifty years after the Kerner report* (pp. 193–207). Temple University Press.

Darling-Hammond, L. (2019a). Assuring essential educational resources through a federal right to education. In Kimberly Jenkins Robinson (Ed.), *A federal right to education: Fundamental questions for our democracy* (pp. 235–260). New York University Press.

Darling-Hammond, L. (2019b). *Investing for student success: Lessons from state school finance reforms.* Learning Policy Institute. https://learningpolicyinstitute.org/product/investing-student-success-school-finance-reforms-report

Darling-Hammond, L., & Bransford, J. (Eds.). (2005). *Preparing teachers for a changing world: What teachers should learn and be able to do.* Jossey-Bass.

Darling-Hammond, L., DiNapoli, M., Jr., & Kini, T. (2023). *The federal role in ending teacher shortages.* Learning Policy Institute. https://doi.org/10.54300/649.892

Darling-Hammond, L., Flook, L., Cook-Harvey, C., Barron, B., & Osher, D. (2020). Implications for educational practice of the science of learning and development. *Applied Developmental Science, 24*(2), 97–140. https://doi.org/10.1080/10888691.2018.1537791

Darling-Hammond, L., Holtzman, D. J., Gatlin, S. J., & Heilig, J. V. (2005). Does teacher preparation matter? Evidence about teacher certification, Teach for America, and teacher effectiveness. *Education Policy Analysis Archives, 13*(42), 51.

Darling-Hammond, L., Williamson, J., & Hyler, M. (2007). Securing the right to learn: The quest for an empowering curriculum for African American citizens. *Journal of Negro Education, 76*(3), 281–296.

Darling-Hammond, S. (2023a). *Fostering belonging, transforming schools: The impact of restorative practice.* Learning Policy Institute. https://learningpolicyinstitute.org/media/4046/download?inline&file=Restorative_Practices_REPORT.pdf

Darling-Hammond, S. (2023b). *Perceived school resource officer bias and Black student mental health.* EdArXiv Preprints. https://doi.org/10.35542/osf.io/wkhcp

Darling-Hammond, S., & Ho, E. (2023, October 27). No matter how you slice it: The persistence and pervasiveness of disproportionate punishment for Black students. *SocArXiv.* https://doi.org/10.31235/osf.io/khtsa

Day, J. C. (2020, June 10). *Black high school attainment nearly on par with national average.* U.S. Census Bureau. https://www.census.gov/library/stories/2020/06/black-high-school-attainment-nearly-on-par-with-national-average.html

DeSilver, D. (2014). *Who's poor in America? 50 years into the 'War on Poverty.'* The Pew Research Center. https://www.pewresearch.org/short-reads/2014/01/13/whos-poor-in-america-50-years-into-the-war-on-poverty-a-data-portrait

Duong, M. T., Pullmann, M. D., Buntain-Ricklefs, J., Lee, K., Benjamin, K. S., Nguyen, L., & Cook, C. R. (2019). Brief teacher training improves student behavior and student–teacher relationships in middle school. *School Psychology, 34*(2), 212–221. https://doi.org/10.1037/spq0000296

Duarte, C. D., Moses, C., Brown, M., Kajeepeta, S., Prins, S. J., Scott, J., & Mujahid, M. S. (2023). Punitive school discipline as a mechanism of structural marginalization with implications for health inequity: A systematic review of quantitative studies in the health and social sciences literature. *Annals of the New York Academy of Sciences, 1519*(1), 129–152.

Durlak, J. A., Weissberg, R. P., Dymnicki, A. B., Taylor, R. D., & Schellinger, K. B. (2011). The impact of enhancing students' social and emotional learning: A meta-analysis of school-based universal interventions. *Child Development, 82*(1), 405–432. https://doi.org/10.1111/j.1467-8624.2010.01564.x

Eyllon, M., Salhi, C., Griffith, J. L., & Lincoln, A. K. (2022). Exclusionary school discipline policies and mental health in a national sample of adolescents without histories of suspension or expulsion. *Youth & Society, 54*(1), 84–103.

Fabelo, T., Thompson, M., Plotkin, M., Carmichael, D., Marchbanks, M., III, & Booth, E. (2011). *Breaking schools' rules: A statewide study of how school discipline relates to students' success and juvenile justice involvement*. The Council of State Governments Justice Center & Public Policy Research Institute.

Farrie, D., & Sciarra, D. G. (2020). *$600 billion lost: State funding on public education following the Great Recession*. Education Law Center. https://edlawcenter.org/assets/$600%20Billion/$600%20Billion%20Lost.pdf

Federal Interagency Forum on Child and Family Statistics. (2023). *America's children: Key national indicators of well-being, 2023*. U.S. Government Printing Office. https://www.childstats.gov/pdf/ac2023/ac_23.pdf

Felton, E. (2017, September 6). The Department of Justice is overseeing the resegregation of American schools. *The Nation*. https://www.thenation.com/article/archive/the-department-of-justice-is-overseeing-the-resegregation-of-american-schools

Fisher, B. W., & Hennessy, E. A. (2016). School resource officers and exclusionary discipline in U.S. high schools: A systematic review and meta-analysis. *Adolescent Research Review, 1*, 217–233. https://ed.buffalo.edu/content/dam/ed/safety-conference/Fisher%20%26%20Hennessey%20(2016).pdf

Fortner, S. (2021). Erasing the redline: Addressing lead poisoning and environmental racism through research, education, and advocacy. *Liberal Education, 107*(1). https://www.aacu.org/liberaleducation/articles/erasing-the-redline

Fothergill, K. E., Ensminger, M. E., Green, K. M., Crum, R. M., Robertson, J., & Juon, H. S. (2008). The impact of early school behavior and educational achievement on adult drug use disorders: A prospective study. *Drug and Alcohol Dependence, 92*(1–3), 191–199.

Frankenberg, E., Hawley, G., Ee, J., & Orfield, G. (2017). *Southern schools: More than half a century after the Civil Rights revolution*. Civil Rights Project.

Friedlaender, D., Burns, D., Lewis-Charp, H., Cook-Harvey, C. M., Zheng, X., & Darling-Hammond, L. (2014). *Student-centered schools: Closing the opportunity gap*. Stanford Center for Opportunity Policy in Education.

Gage, N. A., Whitford, D. K., & Katsiyannis, A. (2018). A review of schoolwide positive behavior interventions and supports as a framework for reducing disciplinary exclusions. *The Journal of Special Education, 52*(3), 142–151. https://doi.org/10.1177/0022466918767847

Garza, F. (2021, February 11). America's dirty divide: How environmental racism leaves the vulnerable behind. *The Guardian*. https://www.theguardian.com/us-news/2021/feb/11/environmental-racism-americas-dirty-divide

George, J., & Darling-Hammond, L. (2019). *The federal role and school integration: Brown's promise and present challenges*. Learning Policy Institute.

https://learningpolicyinstitute.org/product/federal-role-school-integration-browns-promise-report

Gilliam, W. S., Maupin, A. N., Reyes, C. R., Accavitti, M., & Shic, F. (2016). *Do early educators' implicit biases regarding sex and race relate to behavior expectations and recommendations of preschool expulsions and suspensions?* Yale University Child Study Center. https://medicine.yale.edu/childstudy/zigler/publications/Preschool%20Implicit%20Bias%20Policy%20Brief_final_9_26_276766_5379_v1.pdf

Goe, L. (2007). *The link between teacher quality and student outcomes: A research synthesis.* National Comprehensive Center for Teacher Quality. https://eric.ed.gov/?id=ED521219

Goldys, P. (2016). Restorative practices: From candy and punishment to celebration and problem-solving circles. *Journal of Character Education, 12*(1), 75–80. https://eric.ed.gov/?id=EJ1151544

González, T. (2015). Socializing schools: Addressing racial disparities in discipline through restorative justice. In D. Losen (Ed.), *Closing the school discipline gap: Equitable remedies for excessive exclusion* (pp. 151–165). Teachers College Press.

González, T. (2021). Race, school policing, and public health. *Stanford Law Review, 73*, 180–193. https://review.law.stanford.edu/wp-content/uploads/sites/3/2021/06/73-Stan.-L.-Rev.-Online-180-Gonzalez.pdf

Gordon, M. F., de la Torre, M., Cowhy, J. R., Moore, P. T., Sartain, L. S., & Knight, D. (2018). *School closings in Chicago: Staff and student experiences and academic outcomes.* University of Chicago Consortium on School Research. https://consortium.uchicago.edu/sites/default/files/2019-02/School%20Closings%20in%20Chicago-May2018-Consortium-Exec-Summary.pdf

Gould, M. S., Fisher, P., Parides, M., Flory, M., & Shaffer, D. (1996). Psychosocial risk factors of child and adolescent completed suicide. *Archives of General Psychiatry, 53*(12), 1155–1162.

Government Accountability Office. (2018). *Discipline disparities for Black students, boys, and students with disabilities.* https://www.gao.gov/assets/gao-18-258.pdf

Grant, A. A., Mac Iver, D. J., & Mac Iver, M. A. (2022). The impact of restorative practices with Diplomas Now on school climate and teachers' turnover intentions: Evidence from a cluster multi-site randomized control trial. *Journal of Research on Educational Effectiveness.* https://doi.org/10.1080/19345747.2021.2018745

Gregory, A., Clawson, K., Davis, A., & Gerewitz, J. (2016). The promise of restorative practices to transform teacher-student relationships and achieve equity in school discipline. *Journal of Educational and Psychological Consultation, 26*(4), 325–353. https://doi.org/10.1080/10474412.2014.929950

Gregory, A., Huang, F. L., & Ward-Seidel, A. R. (2021). *Evaluation of the Whole School Restorative Practices Project: One-year implementation and impact on discipline incidents* [Technical report]. Rutgers University.

Gregory, A., Huang, F. L., Anyon, Y., Greer, E., & Downing, B. (2018). An examination of restorative interventions and racial equity in out-of-school suspensions. *School Psychology Review, 47*(2), 167–182. https://doi.org/10.17105/SPR-2017-0073.V47-2

Guidry, K., Simpson, C., Test, T., & Bloomfield, C. (2013). Ambiguous Loss and Its Effects on Children: Implications and Interventions for School Counselors. *Journal of School Counseling, 11*(15), http://files.eric.ed.gov/fulltext/EJ1034744.pdf

Hanushek, E. (2003). The structure of analysis and argument in plaintiff expert reports for *Williams v. State of California* [Narrative statement for expert testimony]. http://www.decentschools.org/expert_reports/hanushek_report.pdf

Hashim, A., Strunk, K., & Dhaliwal, T. (2018). Justice for all? Suspension bans and restorative justice programs in the Los Angeles Unified School District. *Peabody Journal of Education, 93*(2), 174–189. https://doi.org/10.1080/0161956X.2018.1435040

Hawken, L. S. (2006). School psychologists as leaders in the implementation of a targeted intervention: The Behavior Education Program. *School Psychology Quarterly, 21*(1), 91–111. https://doi.org/10.1521/scpq.2006.21.1.91

Heckman, J. J. (2011). The economics of inequality, the value of early childhood education. *The American Educator, 35*(1), 31–35.

Heckman, J. J., & Masterov, D. V. (2007). The productivity argument for investing in young children. *Review of Agricultural Economics, 29*(3), 446–493.

Hemphill, S. A., Toumbourou, J. W., Herrenkohl, T. I., McMorris, B. J., & Catalano, R. F. (2006). The effect of school suspensions and arrests on subsequent adolescent antisocial behavior in Australia and the United States. *Journal of Adolescent Health, 39*, 736–744.

Huang, F. L., & Cornell, D. G. (2017). Student attitudes and behaviors as explanations for the Black–White suspension gap. *Children and Youth Services Review, 73*, 298–308. https://doi.org/10.1016/j.childyouth.2017.01.002

Infrastructure Investment and Jobs Act. HR 3684 (2021). https://www.congress.gov/117/bills/hr3684/BILLS-117hr3684enr.pdf

Irons, P. (2002). *Jim Crow's schools*. Viking Press.

Jackson, C. K. (2020). Does school spending matter? The new literature on an old question. In L. Tach, R. Dunifon, & D. L. Miller (Eds.), *Confronting inequality: How policies and practices shape children's opportunities* (pp. 165–186). American Psychological Association. https://doi.org/10.1037/0000187-008

Jackson, C. K., Johnson, R. C., & Persico, C. (2016). The effect of school spending on educational and economic outcomes: Evidence from school finance reforms. *Quarterly Journal of Economics, 13*(1), 157–218. https://doi.org/10.1093/qje/qjv036

Jain, S., Bassey, H., Brown, M., & Kalra, P. (2014). *Restorative justice in Oakland schools: Implementation and impacts*. Oakland Unified School District. http://www.instituteforrestorativeinitiatives.org/uploads/1/6/3/2/16320200/exec_summary_-_rj_ousd_report_2014.pdf

Johnson, R. C. (2019). *Children of the dream*. Basic Books.

Karoly, L. A., & Cannon, J. S. (2021). *Making preschool investments count through the American families Act*. RAND Corporation. https://www.rand.org/pubs/commentary/2021/06/making-preschool-investments-count-through-the-american.html

Kerstetter, K. (2016). A different kind of discipline: Social reproduction and the transmission of non-cognitive skills at an urban charter school. *Sociological Inquiry, 86*(4), 512–539. https://doi.org/10.1111/soin.12128

Kidane, S., & Rauscher, E. (2023). *Unequal Exposure to School Resource Officers, by Student Race, Ethnicity, and Income*. Urban Institute. https://www.urban.org/research/publication/unequal-exposure-school-resource-officers-student-race-ethnicity-and-income

Koruth, M. A. (2024). NJ school segregation lawsuit parties want more time to negotiate before trial. Here's why. Northjersey.com. https://www.northjersey.com/story/news/education/2024/02/10/nj-school-segregation-lawsuit-parties-make-progress-in-talks/72525281007

Koutavas, A., Yera, C., Collyer, S., Curran, M., Harris, D., & Wimer, C. (2023). *What would 2022 child poverty rates have looked like if an expanded child tax credit had still been in place?* [Brief, Vol. 7, No. 3]. Center on Poverty and Social Policy, Columbia University. https://www.povertycenter.columbia.edu/publication/2023/what-2022-child-poverty-rates-would-have-looked-like

Kramer, U., Temes, C. M., Magni, L. R., Fitzmaurice, G. M., Aguirre, B. A., Goodman, M., & Zanarini, M. C. (2017). Psychosocial functioning in adolescents with and without borderline personality disorder. *Personality and Mental Health, 11*(3), 164–170.

Kyriakides, L., Christoforou, C., & Charalambous, C. Y. (2013). What matters for student learning outcomes: A meta-analysis of studies exploring factors of effective teaching. *Teaching and Teacher Education, 36*, 143–152. https://doi.org/10.1016/j.tate.2013.07.010

Lacoe, J., & Steinberg, M. P. (2019). Do suspensions affect student outcomes? *Educational Evaluation and Policy Analysis, 41*(1), 34–62. https://doi.org/10.3102/0162373718794897

Lansing School District. (2008). *Lansing School District restorative justice annual report, 2007–2008.* http://www.lansingschools.net/downloads/restorative_justice_files/lansing_school_district_restorative_justice_annual_report_07-08.pdf

Lapan, R. T., Wells, R., & McCann, L. A. (2014). Stand tall to protect students: School counselors strengthening school connectedness (J. Petersen, Contributor). *Journal of Counseling & Development, 92*(3), 304–315. https://doi.org/10.1002/j.1556-6676.2014.00158.x

Lapan, R. T., Whitcomb, S. A., & Aleman, N. M. (2012). Connecticut professional school counselors: College and career counseling services and smaller ratios benefit students. *Professional School Counseling, 16*(2). https://doi.org/10.1177/2156759X0001600206

Lepage, K., Kratochwill, T. R., & Elliott, S. N. (2004). Competency-Based behavior consultation training: An evaluation of consultant outcomes, treatment effects, and consumer satisfaction. *School Psychology Quarterly, 19*(1), 1–28. https://doi.org/10.1521/scpq.19.1.1.29406

Leung, M., Cardichon, J., Scott, C., & Darling-Hammond, L. (2020). *Inequitable opportunity to learn: Access to advanced mathematics and science courses.* Learning Policy Institute. https://learningpolicyinstitute.org/media/509/download?inline&file=CRDC_Course_Access_REPORT.pdf

Leung-Gagné, M., McCombs, J., Scott, C., & Losen, D. J. (2022). *Pushed out: Trends and disparities in out-of-school suspension.* Learning Policy Institute. https://learningpolicyinstitute.org/media/3885/download?inline&file=CRDC_School_Suspension_REPORT.pdf

Lewis, S. (2009). *Improving school climate: Findings from schools implementing restorative practices.* International Institute for Restorative Practices. https://www.iirp.edu/pdf/IIRP-Improving-School-Climate-2009.pdf

LiCalsi, C., Osher, D., & Bailey, P. (2021). *The empirical examination of the effects of suspension and suspension severity on behavioral and academic outcomes.*

American Institutes for Research. https://www.air.org/sites/default/files/2021-08/NYC-Suspension-Effects-Behavioral-Academic-Outcomes-August-2021.pdf

Life Academy School Accountability Report Card. (2023). https://sarconline.org/public/print/01612590130575/2022-2023#outcomes

Losen, D. J., & Gillespie, J. (2012). *Opportunities suspended: The disparate impact of disciplinary exclusion from school*. Civil Rights Project.

Maier, A., Daniel, J., Oakes, J., & Lam, L. (2017). *Community schools as an effective school improvement strategy: A review of the evidence*. Learning Policy Institute. https://learningpolicyinstitute.org/product/community-schools-effective-school-improvement-report

Mansfield, K., Rainbolt, S., & Fowler, B. (2016, November 18). *Re-envisioning discipline in complex contexts: An appreciative inquiry of one district's implementation of restorative practices* [Paper presentation]. University Council for Educational Administration Annual Conference, Detroit, MI.

Marcus, J. (2023, May 27). The college-going gap between black and white Americans was always bad. Now it's getting worse. *USA Today*. https://www.usatoday.com/story/news/education/2023/05/15/college-student-gap-between-black-white-americans-worse/70195689007

McCold, P. (2002). *Evaluation of a restorative milieu: CSF Buxmont School/day treatment programs 1999–2001, evaluation outcome technical report*. International Institute of Restorative Practices. http://www.iirp.edu/pdf/erm.pdf

McCold, P. (2008). Evaluation of a restorative milieu: Restorative practices in context. In M. H. Ventura (Ed.), *Restorative justice: From theory to practice* (pp. 99–137). Emerald Group Publishing Limited. https://doi.org/10.1016/S1521-6136(08)00405-3

McMorris, B. J., Beckman, K. J., Shea, G., Baumgartner, J., & Eggert, R. C. (2013). *Applying restorative justice practices to Minneapolis Public Schools students recommended for possible expulsion*. University of Minnesota. https://mch.umn.edu/abstract/applying-restorative-justice-practices-to-minneapolis-public-schools-students-recommended-for-possible-expulsion

Mehta, J. (2014, June 20). Deeper learning has a race problem. *Education Week*. https://www.edweek.org/leadership/opinion-deeper-learning-has-a-race-problem/2014/06

Millhiser, I. (2015, August 13). *American schools are more segregated now than they were in 1968, and the Supreme Court doesn't care*. ThinkProgress. https://thinkprogress.org/american-schools-are-more-segregated-now-than-they-were-in-1968-and-the-supreme-court-doesnt-care-cc7abbf6651c/

Morris, E. W., & Perry, B. L. (2016). The punishment gap: School suspension and racial disparities in achievement. *Social Problems*, *63*(1), 68–86. https://doi.org/10.1093/socpro/spv026

Müller, B., von Hagen, A., Vannini, N., & Büttner, G. (2021). Measurement of the effects of school psychological services: A scoping review. *Frontiers in Psychology*, *12*. https://doi.org/10.3389/fpsyg.2021.606228

National Center for Education Statistics. (n.d.). *College enrollment rates of high school graduates, by race/ethnicity: 1960 to 1997*. https://nces.ed.gov/programs/digest/d98/d98t183.asp

National Center for Education Statistics. (2019a). *Digest of education statistics: Table 104.10: Rates of high school completion and bachelor's degree attainment*. Institute of Education Sciences, U.S. Department of Education. https://nces.ed.gov/programs/digest/d19/tables/dt19_104.10.asp

National Center for Education Statistics. (2019b). *Status and trends in the education of racial and ethnic groups: Indicator 23, Postsecondary graduation rates*. Institute of Education Sciences, U.S. Department of Education. https://nces.ed.gov/programs/raceindicators/indicator_red.asp

National Center for Education Statistics. (2022). *Digest of education statistics: Table 302.60: Percentage of 18 to 24-year-olds enrolled in college*. Institute of Education Sciences, U.S. Department of Education. https://nces.ed.gov/programs/digest/d22/tables/dt22_302.60.asp

National Center for Education Statistics. (2023). Public high school graduation rates. *Condition of Education*. Institute of Education Sciences, U.S. Department of Education. https://nces.ed.gov/programs/coe/indicator/coi

National Research Council. (2008). *Assessing accomplished teaching: Advanced-level certification programs*. The National Academies Press. https://doi.org/10.17226/12224

National Student Clearinghouse Research Center. (2024, January 24). *Current term enrollment estimates: Fall 2023*. https://nscresearchcenter.org/current-term-enrollment-estimates

Nelson, L. (2016, February 15). The Flint water crisis, explained. *Vox*. https://www.vox.com/2016/2/15/10991626/flint-water-crisis

Noguera, P., Darling-Hammond, L., & Friedlaender, D. (2015). *Equal opportunity for deeper learning: Students at the center* [Deeper Learning Research Series]. Jobs for the Future. (pp. 8–12)

Noltemeyer, A., Palmer, K., James, A. G., & Wiechman, S. (2019). School-Wide Positive Behavioral Interventions and Supports (SWPBIS): A synthesis of existing research. *International Journal of School & Educational Psychology, 7*(4), 253–262. https://doi.org/10.1080/21683603.2018.1425169

Norris, A. (2009, March). *Gender and race effects of a restorative justice intervention on school success* [Paper presentation]. American Society of Criminology Annual Conference, Philadelphia, PA.

Oakes, J. (2005). *Keeping track: How schools structure inequality* (2nd ed.). Yale University Press.

Ögülmüş, K., & Vuran, S. (2016). Schoolwide positive behavioral interventions and support practices: Review of studies in the journal of positive behavior interventions. *Educational Sciences: Theory and Practice, 16*(5), 1693–1710. https://eric.ed.gov/?id=EJ1115080

Okonofua, J. A., & Eberhardt, J. L. (2015). Two strikes: Race and the disciplining of young students. *Psychological Science, 26*(5), 617–624. https://doi.org/10.1177/0956797615570365

Organisation for Economic Co-operation and Development. (2017). *How does the United States compare on child well-being?* [Factsheet]. OECD Child Well-Being Data Portal. https://www.oecd.org/en/about/directorates/directorate-for-employment-labour-and-social-affairs.html

Owens, J., & McLanahan, S. S. (2020). Unpacking the drivers of racial disparities in school suspension and expulsion. *Social Forces, 98*(4), 1548–1577. https://doi.org/10.1093/sf/soz095

Owens, J. S., Murphy, C. E., Richerson, L., Girio, E. L., & Himawan, L. K. (2008). Science to practice in underserved communities: the effectiveness of school mental health programming. *Journal of Clinical Child and Adolescent Psychology*, *37*(2), 434–447. https://doi.org/10.1080/15374410801955912

Parolin, Z., Collyer, S., Curran, M. A., & Wimer, C. (2021). The potential poverty reduction effect of the American Rescue Plan (Fact sheet). Center for Poverty and Social Policy, Columbia University. https://static1.squarespace.com/static/610831a16c95260dbd68934a/t/6113eddb3cde100cb68904ee/1628696027691/Poverty-Reduction-Analysis-American-Rescue-Plan-CPSP-2021.pdf

Pastor, M., Jr., Sadd, J. L., & Morello-Frosch, R. (2004). Reading, writing, and toxics: Children's health, academic performance, and environmental justice in Los Angeles. *Environment and Planning C: Politics and Space*, *22*(2), 280–281. https://doi.org/10.1068/c009r

Pear, R. (1982, September 7). Desegregation plans in peril. *The New York Times*. https://www.nytimes.com/1982/09/07/us/desegregation-plans-in-peril.html

Pearman, F. A., II, Curran, F. C., Fisher, B., & Gardella, J. (2019). Are achievement gaps related to discipline gaps? Evidence from national data. *AERA Open*, *5*(4), 1–18. https://doi.org/10.1177/2332858419875440

Pearman, F. A., II, Luong, C., & Greene, D. M. (2023). Examining racial (in)equity in school-closure patterns in California [Working paper]. Policy Analysis for California Education. https://edpolicyinca.org/publications/examining-racial-inequity-school-closure-patterns-california

Pesta, R. (2021). School punishment, deterrence, and race: A partial test of defiance theory. *Crime & Delinquency*, *68*(3), 463–494. https://doi.org/10.1177/00111287211005396

Podolsky, A., Darling-Hammond, L., Doss, C., & Reardon, S. (2019). *California's positive outliers: Districts beating the odds*. Learning Policy Institute. https://learningpolicyinstitute.org/product/positive-outliers-districts-beating-odds-report

Ramey, D. M. (2018). The social construction of child social control via criminalization and medicalization: Why race matters. *Sociological Forum*, *33*(1), 139–64.

Reynolds, A. J., Temple, J. A., Ou, S., Arteaga, I. A., & White, B.A.B. (2011). School-based early childhood education and age-28 well-being: Effects by timing, dosage, and subgroups. *Science*, *333*(6040), 360–364. https://doi.org/10.1126/science.1203618

Riestenberg, N. (2003). *Restorative schools grants final report, January 2002–June 2003: A summary of the grantees' evaluation*. Minnesota Department of Education. http://crisisresponse.promoteprevent.org/webfm_send/1200

Ronfeldt, M., Loeb, S., & Wyckoff, J. (2013). How teacher turnover harms student achievement. *American Educational Research Journal*, *50*(1), 4–36. https://cepa.stanford.edu/content/how-teacher-turnover-harms-student-achievement

Rothstein, R. (2004). *Class and schools: Using social, economic, and educational reform to close the Black–White achievement gap*. Economic Policy Institute.

Rothstein, R. (2017). *The color of law: A forgotten history of how our government segregated America*. Liveright Publishing.

Rushton, J. L., Forcier, M., & Schectman, R. M. (2002). Epidemiology of depressive symptoms in the National Longitudinal Study of Adolescent Health.

Journal of the American Academy of Child and Adolescent Psychiatry, 41(2), 199–205.

Sadler, J. (2021). *No-excuses in restorative justice clothing: The effects of adopting restorative justice in a no-excuse setting* [Doctoral dissertation]. University of North Carolina at Chapel Hill.

San Antonio v. Rodriguez, 411 US 1 (1973).

Schollenberger, T. L. (2015). Racial disparities in school suspension and subsequent outcomes: Evidence from the national longitudinal survey of youth. In D. J. Losen (Ed.), *Closing the school discipline gap: Equitable remedies for excessive exclusion*. Teachers College Press.

Scott-Clayton, J. & Li, J. (2016). *Black-white disparity in student loan debt more than triples after graduation*. Brookings Institution. https://www.brookings.edu/wp-content/uploads/2016/10/es_20161020_scott-clayton_evidence_speaks.pdf

Shapiro, T. M. (2017). *Toxic inequality: How America's wealth gap destroys mobility, deepens the racial divide, and threatens our future*. Basic Books.

Shi, Y., & Zhu, M. (2022). Equal time for equal crime? Racial bias in school discipline. *Economics of Education Review, 88*, 102256. https://doi.org/10.1016/j.econedurev.2022.102256

Shivaram, D. (2021). *EPA rolls out billions to clean up Superfund sites*. NPR. https://www.npr.org/2021/12/18/1065492149/epa-superfund-sites

Slade, E. P. (2004). Racial/ethnic disparities in parent perception of child need for mental health care following school disciplinary events. *Mental Health Services Research, 6*(2), 75–92.

Students for Fair Admissions, Inc. (SFFA) *v. President & Fellows of Harvard College* (Harvard) and *SFFA v. University of North Carolina* (UNC), Nos. 20–1199 & 21–707.

Sumner, D., Silverman, C., & Frampton, M. (2010). *School-based restorative justice as an alternative to zero-tolerance policies: Lessons from West Oakland*. University of California, Berkeley, School of Law. https://www.law.berkeley.edu/files/thcsj/10-2010_School-based_Restorative_Justice_As_an_Alternative_to_Zero-Tolerance_Policies.pdf

Sussman, J., Melnick, H., Newton, E., Kriener-Althen, K., Draney, K., Mangione, P., & Gochyyev, P. (2022). *Preschool quality and child development: How are learning gains related to program ratings?* Learning Policy Institute. https://doi.org/10.54300/422.974

Talluri, R., Wilkinson, A. V., Spitz, M. R., & Shete, S. (2014). A risk prediction model for smoking experimentation in Mexican American youth. *Cancer Epidemiology, Biomarkers & Prevention, 23*(10), 2165–2174.

Terman, L. M., Dickson, V. E., Sutherland, A. H., Franzen, R. H., Tupper, C. R., & Fernald, G. (1922). *Intelligence tests and school reorganization*. World Book Company.

Terrill, S. (2018, March 24). *Discipline that restores: An examination of restorative justice in the school setting* [Paper presentation]. MidAmerica Nazarene University Colloquium, Olathe, KS.

Tyack, D. (1974). *The one best system*. Harvard University Press.

USA Facts. (n.d.). *College enrollment rate by race/ethnicity*. https://usafacts.org/data/topics/people-society/education/higher-education/college-enrollment-rate

U.S. Department of Education & U.S. Department of Justice. (2014). *Joint "dear colleague" letter*. https://www2.ed.gov/about/offices/list/ocr/letters/colleague-201401-title-vi.html

Vu, P., Shanahan, K. B., Rosenfield, S., Gravois, T., Koehler, J., Kaiser, L., Berger, J., Vaganek, M., Gottfredson, G. D., & Nelson, D. (2013). Experimental evaluation of instructional consultation teams on teacher beliefs and practices. *International Journal of School & Educational Psychology, 1*(2), 67–81. https://doi.org/10.1080/21683603.2013.790774

Way, S. M. (2011). School discipline and disruptive student behavior: The moderating effects of student perceptions. *The Sociological Quarterly, 52*(3), 346–375. https://www.jstor.org/stable/23027541

Whitaker A., Torres-Guillen S., Morton M., Jordan H., Coyle S., Mann A., Sun W. (2019). *Cops and no counselors: How the lack of school mental health staff is harming students*. American Civil Liberties Union. https://www.aclu.org/sites/default/files/field_document/030419-acluschooldisciplinereport.pdf

Whiteside, M. (1975). School Discipline: The Ongoing Crisis. *The Clearing House: A Journal of Educational Strategies, Issues and Ideas, 49*(4), 160–162. https://doi.org/10.1080/00098655.1975.11477812

Woodson, C. G. (1933). *The mis-education of the Negro*. Association Press.

Zeiser, K. (2014). *Study of deeper learning outcomes*. American Institutes for Research. https://www.air.org/project/study-deeper-learning-opportunities-and-outcomes

Zhu, B., Gnedko-Berry, N., Borman, T., Manzeske, D. (2019). *Effects of national board certified instructional leaders on classroom practice and student achievement of novice teachers*. American Institutes of Research.

CHAPTER 2

The Dream of Integration and the Politics of Resegregation

The Continuing Battle Over the Legacy of *Brown v. Board of Education*

Gary Orfield

It's been 70 years since *Brown*, and we have not been able to bring our children to school together as we have become a profoundly multiracial society with no racial majority. Since *Brown* we've had 10 presidents, enacted the most important civil rights laws in U.S. history, seen many barriers fall, but we're far from the seemingly simple goal of *Brown*. In fact, we've been going backward for more than 3 decades toward greater degrees of separation—and the separation is double separation, by both race and poverty. Very large educational gaps remain, and there have been no major positive legal or policy developments since the 1970s. Despite all this, there is increasingly powerful evidence that *Brown* was right, that segregation has huge costs for students of color, that diverse schooling can change lives and strengthen the country. Civil rights groups, facing serious legal reverses, continue to seek new paths to achieve *Brown*'s goals.

What happened? Is it true that integration was tried but it failed and was abandoned? Did it fail to help students of color? Was it a zero-sum game, where Whites had to lose so students of color could gain something? Are there deep values or desires in our society that destroy diverse schools and colleges? How did the balance tilt back toward segregation?

The basic story of rising segregation is often described by civil rights opponents as the product of a failed education effort, but the actual driving force was political. The conservative argument is that civil rights law and the courts pushed too hard to force students into schools together and it didn't work. Critics argue that the gains were small, the public was opposed, and that the enterprise failed, resegregating the schools. This study concludes, in contrast, that desegregation produced major lasting gains in the short period of time it was seriously implemented, that many experiences were positive, and that the real cause of the resegregation of the last third of a century was political. Hostile administrations, playing on the politics of racial fear, decimated the federal enforcement process, eliminated aid, and transformed the U.S. Supreme Court. The result was Supreme Court decisions ending desegregation plans even when school districts wanted to continue them and forbidding even major forms of voluntary action through choice systems. Desegregation didn't fail. Its opponents took over the Supreme Court, whose decisions set the basic parameters. Although Martin Luther King, Jr. famously said "The arc of the moral universe is long, but it bends toward justice," the history described here is very different. There wasn't an arc but a major fight to achieve desegregation followed by a long-term strategy to reverse it. School desegregation was seriously undertaken because of a legal struggle, a great social movement, and the strong leadership of a president in the 1960s. It was limited and undone by a political party and presidents identifying with Southern resistance, the strategy of which focused on the Supreme Court and has had increasingly powerful control of the basic rule maker, the Supreme Court, since 1972.

The turn from *Brown* to resegregation is a complex political, legal, and demographic story. It is a story of three presidents, two movements, and eight major Supreme Court decisions. The story began in a court: The Court announced the law but failed to accomplish significant changes in the face of massive resistance. Then a movement and a president created transformative changes, especially in Southern schools where a long history of racial apartheid ended. The most important civil rights law in U.S. history was won after a historic battle. It was seriously enforced for only a few years, but that enforcement made Southern schools the most integrated in the country. Desegregation endured until it was dismantled by the courts. With the conservative movement, two presidents led the attack on desegregation and transformed the Supreme Court, which radically changed desegregation law, blocking even voluntary action. Resegregation was extended to higher education in the 2023 Harvard–UNC decision (*Students for Fair Admissions v. Harvard* and *Students for Fair Admissions v. University of North Carolina*) outlawing affirmative action. In 70 years, except for a brief period in the 1960s, we've never had a sustained effort to make *Brown* the reality in U.S. schools. We have experienced decades of attacks by politicians exploiting fears of racial change. Our high court that opened the door has been turned around and has played a central role in slamming the door again. Yet the vision of *Brown* lives. Schools are our major institution for mobility and opportunity and *Brown* said that their profound racial inequality violated our fundamental law. As those issues become more critical in a polarized nation without a racial majority among its young, it's obvious that the injustice—the segregation in clearly unequal schools that *Brown* addressed—is back.

Seventy years of history since *Brown* encompass many political changes, with 18 presidential terms and historic changes in the nation's population.

A society with more than 80% White students at the time of *Brown* has become a society with a majority of non-White students. A Black–White society has become truly multiracial as massive immigration has increased the Latinx population, making it the nation's largest "minority," and the Asian population, which is now the most educated. There have been huge movements of Black and Latinx families to the suburbs. The share of students poor enough to need free lunches at school has increased substantially. Many parts of the country that had little diversity now have significant non-White population.

The changes that led to *Brown* began after World War II when the United States was suddenly the world's preeminent power. The United States had led the great crusade against the racist Nazi Reich—with a racist segregated army. Social scientists documented the realities of American race relations, including the huge Gunnar Myrdal project and his 1944 book, *An American Dilemma*, and the Court relied on its findings as one of the major bases for the decision. Black and Latinx veterans came back from war experiencing discrimination on many fronts and demanding change. For the first time in its history, the Democratic party adopted a civil rights plank; President Truman issued a report on civil rights. In 1957, the U.S. Commission on Civil Rights was created to study and report on the issues. Both the Truman and Eisenhower administrations recommended to the Supreme Court that there should be action against Southern school segregation. The Supreme Court had begun to open up graduate and professional schools to Black students, but the direct assault on segregated education in four states was the great case, the one that opened up a new era in American life.

CASE 1: *BROWN V. BOARD OF EDUCATION OF TOPEKA*, 1954

The *Brown* decision was one of the most decisive actions of the world's most powerful court. The U.S. Supreme Court's previous leading decisions in the history of race relations had been grim, including the *Dred Scott* decision upholding slavery and helping lead to the Civil War, a series of decisions dismantling the civil rights laws of the Reconstruction and the protections of the 14th Amendment, and, of course, the 1896 *Plessy v. Ferguson* decision establishing "separate but equal" as the law of the land and legitimating hundreds of mandatory segregation laws regulating many aspects of life in many states, including segregation of schools and colleges. The NAACP, founded in 1909 amid extreme segregation, had been struggling for a half century, gradually winning cases that helped build up legal precedents and community support for a major change (Kluger, 1975).

The unanimous *Brown* decision appeared to herald a new era. The Court boldly said that 17 states were violating the Constitution, that segregated schools were "inherently unequal," and that states and communities must radically change their most important public institutions that were preparing their young. But the decision said nothing about *how* this was to be done and there was no definition of what *desegregation* meant. Nine judges and their law clerks weren't about to try to administer the schools of the South. In the *Brown II* decision the next year (1955), the Court held that it was a matter for the local federal judges to figure out and that they should act with "all deliberate speed." The Court did not set goals. The ruling was a decision to punt the responsibility to the federal judges of the South who were told to act "with all deliberate speed," which was a singularly ambiguous command. The job landed on 58 Southern federal judges, who had usually been politically active lawyers, recommended by senior U.S. senators from their states. These were establishment lawyers with no desire to implement a social revolution in communities where all the political leaders were resisting desegregation (Peltason, 1961).

When Arkansas governor Orval Faubus attempted to use the Arkansas National Guard to block desegregation by nine students, and President Eisenhower decided to send in the Army to enforce the court order, there was fierce blowback from across the South, though the Supreme Court stood firm. Usually, when the highest Court rules that something violates a constitutional right, that right becomes effective immediately, and governments and institutions comply without being individually sued. Desegregation did not work that way in the South. With intense resistance, there was no legal authority for the Justice Department to intervene or file cases, and almost no lawyer in the region who would take a case, it's not surprising that there was only token enforcement.

There was soon a very influential U.S. Court of Appeals decision, *Briggs v. Elliott* (1955), which said that *Brown* did not require actual desegregation but only some kind of opportunity for students to choose to transfer to a school of a different race, putting the onus on the Black students who had to come as unwanted intruders to a White school. This was called "freedom of choice" and became the dominant approach. Judges slow-walked the many cases brought by civil rights groups for years and generally ordered extremely little change, such as opening up very limited "freedom of choice" transfers for a decade or more. State legislators created many additional obstacles and there was retaliation against those bringing cases. Southern White leaders discovered that criticizing *Brown* and promising resistance were politically powerful stances in what were still almost all-White electorates. In some of the border states with small Black populations there was some voluntary action, but in the heart of the South, *Brown* was a dead letter for most African American students, and a decade after *Brown*, in spite of many cases brought by civil rights lawyers, 98% of Blacks in the South remained in all-Black schools. There were no Whites in Black schools or being taught by Black teachers. *Brown* was a bold and key historic statement, but it failed to change schools immediately.

Eventually, however, the development of school desegregation law and policy showed a deepening understanding of what was required to actually change schools. It brought policies dealing with the realities of segregation, and of state and local resistance. In 1952, when President Eisenhower was elected, there was no reason to expect major changes. Earl Warren was appointed chief justice by a moderate Republican president in 1953 and served for 16 years. When he took office, *Plessy*'s "separate but equal" had given full legal authority to segregation laws across the South for almost 6 decades, while Congress had taken no significant steps for nearly 80 years. Warren had been a moderate California governor whose record was blemished by his support for the shameful internment of loyal Japanese Americans on racial grounds during World War II. The justices who decided *Brown* had a wide range of views; the president didn't believe in school integration but accepted the Court's ruling. *Brown* was a compromise decision that announced a broad but very general legal goal and called for gradual localized enforcement. By the time Warren left in 1969 all of this had changed. Presidents and Congress had acted, extremely important civil rights laws had been passed, and the Southern schools were deeply changed. Civil rights had been a bipartisan issue but were becoming a seriously partisan one. The Court moved decisively. Step by step, the justices had worked toward unanimous decisions.

Integration activists' goal in the 1950s had been to declare rights and begin changes, but the lack of compliance and the intensity of the resistance defeated the hope for moderate change. In the late 1950s and early 1960s, the Court stood up to open defiance by state authorities (*Cooper v. Aaron*, 358 U.S. 1, 1958), and blocked an effort to simply close public education to avoid desegregation (*Griffin v. County School Board of Prince Edward County*, 377 U.S. 218, 1964) but the Court's actions produced no systemic change. By the end of the Warren Court, the law was requiring rapid systemic change with a focus on outcomes. A series of unanimous decisions reflected an understanding by the Court and the Johnson administration of what it would take to overcome continuing resistance. It had become clear that changing a strongly embedded, fiercely defended, segregated status quo required a systematic plan and serious enforcement. The Court's determination stirred passionate attacks on the Court and calls for the impeachment of the chief justice. The most dramatic changes came after Congress and the president had acted to force action and the Supreme Court affirmed the goals and gave them constitutional force.

The Civil Rights Movement

What actually changed schools: a social movement, serious presidential leadership, Congressional action, and a Court that finally took decisive moves. The social movement, of course, was the Civil Rights Movement that emerged in the late 1950s and early 1960s. The 1956 Montgomery bus boycott showed a powerful new spirit among Southern Blacks, made Martin Luther King, Jr. the leading spokesman of the movement, and led to a Supreme Court decision overturning bus segregation. The next year, King spoke in Washington demanding action on *Brown*, and civil rights groups began to press for enactment of what was called the "Powell amendment" (named for Harlem congressman Adam Clayton Powell, its primary sponsor), which required that schools not complying with *Brown* lose federal aid. This was considered the "nuclear option," violating the tradition of federal–state relationships, and had no chance to be enacted then. The federal government had long passively accepted segregation of the schools and colleges it was aiding and had rarely cut off funds in any grant program.

Over the following years, the movement became a national force, devising bold nonviolent actions, often facing intense resistance, to directly challenge segregation laws. "Freedom riders" risking their lives by defying transportation segregation in the South and Black college students leading lunch counter sit-ins went to jail for trying to force desegregation of public accommodations. Black communities were rising in the face of threatened violence and repression. Protests, spreading across the country, came to a peak in the Birmingham movement in 1963 when a racist sheriff directed a vicious attack on peaceful protesters including children singing hymns, shocking Americans who demanded action. The TV images of segregationist violence galvanized the country, produced demonstrations in many cities, and lit a fire of demands for federal action. Before the dogs and fire hoses attacked peaceful demonstrations by Alabama children, there had not been a major civil rights law passed by Congress in 88 years, and that law had been interpreted away by conservative courts generations ago.

What changed the picture was dramatic action by two Democratic presidents, Kennedy and Johnson, and a huge congressional victory for a bipartisan coalition in enacting the most important civil rights law in American history, the 1964 Civil Rights Act. It was soon followed by a landslide victory for Johnson in the presidential election that gave him power to enforce it. President Kennedy had delayed even modest civil rights actions, but his administration faced intense white Southern political opposition even to small changes. Frustrated and disturbed by racist violence, he announced the historic civil rights bill in a nationally televised address in June 1963, following the Birmingham crisis. The bill was far-reaching, including empowering the Justice Department to include language requiring all recipients of federal dollars to comply with civil rights law or lose federal dollars (Parmet, 1983).

Kennedy was assassinated in Dallas before Congress had taken any action on his bill. His successor, President Johnson, committed his administration to getting the Kennedy proposal enacted. It took an epic congressional struggle and a coalition including many Republicans to defeat fierce Southern resistance to what amounted to a challenge to the region's comprehensive system of racial subordination and exclusions.

Johnson, who had been a powerful Senate leader, put his power directly on the line. The struggle shut down Congress for months before an epic 60-day Southern filibuster could be broken (Whalen & Whalen, 1989), pressing successfully for a truly radical bill that went beyond Kennedy's proposal: the 1964 Civil Rights Act, the most important civil rights law in U.S. history. Johnson successfully negotiated and held together the broad bipartisan coalition needed to enact a law that was even stronger than the initial bill. In a poll taken at the end of the millennium, the law was regarded by the U.S. public as one of the most important events of the 20th century (Caro, 2012; Newport, 2014). The only fundamental national laws expanding the basic rights of non-White Americans passed since 1875 have been the 1964 Civil Rights Act, the 1965 Voting Rights Act, and the Fair Housing Act of 1968, all under Lyndon Johnson. The enactment of the 1964 law, the determination of the Johnson administration to enforce it, and very strong support from the Supreme Court resulted in large steps in desegregating the schools across the South by the early 1970s.

Before the Civil Rights Act, only a very small fraction of Southern school districts had been sued to desegregate. The cases had moved glacially and produced very limited remedies, such as opening up one grade a year for a few voluntary transfers of Black students to White schools. Since almost no lawyer in the South would take one of these cases, most had to be filed by a tiny cadre of civil rights lawyers from outside the South. After the act was passed, however, the U.S. Justice Department was given authority to file or intervene in lawsuits, so school districts were facing a formidable foe that almost never lost a civil rights case. More importantly, the new law contained what its opponents fiercely opposed: a provision, Title VI, that said that resistant Southern school districts could lose all their federal dollars, including the funds from the largest school aid program in U.S. history, enacted in 1965.

Under the Civil Rights Act, the Johnson administration told the more than 2,000 Southern school districts that they must quickly adopt an approved desegregation plan, and defined the requirements for these plans. Within a year, desegregation had begun in virtually all Southern districts. Those that held out lost money and were then sued by the Justice Department. More than 100 had their federal funds cut off. These were the steps that changed the original hope of *Brown* into the reality of the schools. Desegregation began to increase rapidly and, each year, the requirements were raised as obstacles were addressed. By the end of the Johnson administration, the requirements had been expanded to include systematic desegregation of faculty, something that had seemed impossible in the South. The law also provided resources for dealing with community tension, for research, and for helping schools adjust (Orfield, 1969).

The Law

The Civil Rights Act gave the executive branch a full array of tools for actually enforcing the goal of *Brown*. The Justice Department suddenly had power to bring civil rights lawsuits. The small squad of private civil rights lawyers suddenly had the U.S. government on their side and the department virtually never lost a case. The Office of Education (the Department of Education did not yet exist) had the power to develop and enforce regulations requiring actual desegregation and setting deadlines. For the first time the government was collecting and publishing regular national statistics on segregation and desegregation.

The new regulations required that all districts actually submit a plan and meet requirements well beyond those being implemented by many Southern judges. To increase the incentive to comply, President Johnson succeeded in enacting the most sweeping federal school aid law in U.S. history, the Elementary and Secondary Education Act, so schools that complied got a sudden large increase in aid. Until the new laws passed, the vast majority of Southern school districts had not yet been sued and had done nothing. Once the administration made clear that it would actually cut off funds and then the Justice Department would sue the districts anyway, virtually all districts adopted desegregation plans and change sped up quickly. As the federal officials gained experience and tightened the standards, major transformation took place (Orfield, 1969). The federal courts responded by supporting the standards and finally clarifying the legal requirements and ending delay, 14 years after the *Brown* decision. This was the period of most dramatic change, reconstructing basic racial practices in Southern schools, a remarkable and overwhelmingly nonviolent social and educational change. But the powerful implementation of a new vision soon confronted serious opposition.

The Presidents

The three presidents who most strongly affected the trajectory of the *Brown* decision and desegregation are Lyndon Johnson, whose leadership created and implemented the policies that took *Brown* from a theory to a reality in the South; Richard Nixon, who brought the expansion of desegregation policy to a sudden halt by transforming the Supreme Court; and Ronald Reagan, who turned the country firmly back toward *Plessy v. Ferguson* with policies that set in motion the resegregation of U.S. schools. None of the Democratic presidents after Johnson exhibited substantial consequential leadership in this field and all of the Republicans followed the course set by Nixon and Reagan. Donald Trump's appointment of three far-right justices likely consolidated the Reagan reversal for this generation. The period of major coordinated pressure for desegregation by the president, Congress, and the courts was only 5 years out of the last 70. There have been eight conservative GOP presidential terms working actively to roll back civil rights. In the face of strong resistance, desegregation, once accomplished, lasted until it was reversed by the Supreme Court. The turning points toward resegregation came under Richard Nixon and Ronald Reagan.

CASE 2: *GREEN V. NEW KENT COUNTY*, 1968

Civil rights advocates and federal officials feared that school districts angry about the far stronger requirements would try to overturn them by suing the administration in conservative federal district courts. The Supreme Court stepped in with its last major school decision of the Warren Court in 1968, strongly supporting the requirements under the Civil Rights Act, defining a comprehensive set of desegregation principles and holding that they must be implemented immediately.

Dozens of decisions by courts across the South attempted to deal with resistance and barriers created by state and local officials in the 14 years after *Brown*. Judicial decisions outlawed one strategy after another of state resistance. Hostile officials were not allowed to simply shut down public schools and subsidize private vouchers for White-flight schools, as happened in Virginia. The Supreme Court did not allow school districts to split up to avoid desegregation. But the Supreme Court had not answered the fundamental questions left undecided by *Brown*—what were the basic elements required to repair the effects of segregation and when must they be implemented?

In the 1968 *Green* decision, the last major unanimous desegregation decision of the Warren Court, the Court clarified the law. It held that desegregation must be immediate and comprehensive, setting guidelines for all federal courts, cutting off many forms of evasion. For the first time, the Supreme Court gave a clear definition of the essential elements of desegregation and required immediate compliance.

In a decision from what was then a small district, New Kent County, Virginia, near the city of Norfolk, a unanimous Supreme Court said that desegregation must eliminate separate schools and the right to desegregation must be enforced immediately. The Court ruled that desegregation must include not just the composition of student bodies but equality in every facet of school operation—"faculty, staff, transportation, extracurricular activities and facilities." All of these elements must be included. The duty was "prompt and effective disestablishment of a dual system." The decision required a radical and immediate transformation of the schools following 14 years of unwillingness of school districts to act on their own; with extensive evidence that choice plans by themselves would leave the Black schools totally segregated and White schools with only token Black participation, fundamental change was essential. The *Green* decision affirmed the rules developed by the Johnson administration under the Civil Rights Act, told the country what was needed, and demanded every feasible step to end the racial identifiability of schools as White or Black and offering superior or inferior education. It seemed that the fundamental questions had now been answered and an immediate root-and-branch transformation of schools was under way.

Richard Nixon, as a senator and vice president, had been a moderate on civil rights—in what was then the mainstream of his party—and when he ran for vice president alongside Eisenhower for the second time in 1956, the GOP was still receiving a substantial share of the Black vote as the party of Lincoln. In his presidential campaign in 1968, however, he shifted sharply to the right. George Wallace was running a powerful independent candidacy after becoming known for his pledge to defend "segregation forever." Wallace was especially targeting the issue he called "busing," not integration (Frady, 1968). In his nomination fight, Nixon decided to adopt what became known as the "Southern strategy," based largely on pledges to slow down enforcement of voting rights and school desegregation and to appoint conservatives to the Supreme Court. In his campaign in the South, he targeted criticism on urban desegregation proposals. His strategy was a great success in the South and gave him a narrow general election victory over Hubert Humphrey, a strong supporter of integration, whose candidacy was damaged by his party's division over the Vietnam War. It turned out to be a fundamental reorientation of the White South to the GOP and the GOP to the right on school desegregation.

Nixon led an administration that initially included both moderate and conservative Republicans. He had extraordinary opportunities to transform the Supreme Court and to redefine the use of the Civil Rights Act. He doubled down on the Southern strategy. He fired officials who tried to enforce school integration (Panetta & Gall, 1971). He would later push out his HUD Secretary, George Romney (Mitt Romney's father), largely because he wanted subsidized housing to include nonsegregated suburban sites, which Nixon denounced as "forced integration of the suburbs" (Rosenthal, 1971).

In his first term, Nixon had the rare opportunity to appoint four justices, including a new chief justice. Johnson left two vacancies, including the chief justiceship, from a failed effort to name his friend Abe Fortas as chief justice. The Nixon administration, under Attorney General John Mitchell, successfully pressed Justice Fortas to resign and searched systematically for strong conservative justices to turn around the Supreme Court—a practice that would be intensified in future GOP administrations. Two of his Southern nominees were defeated in the Senate partly on the basis of their record on school desegregation and civil rights; these defeats made Nixon only more determined to change the direction of the Court. One of his successful appointees was a conservative lawyer, Lewis Powell, who had helped delay desegregation in Richmond, Virginia, and would have a critical role in future cases. Another, William Rehnquist, was a Justice Department lawyer who, as a clerk on the Supreme Court during the *Brown* case, had argued for continuing the "separate but equal" policy and who had been active in opposing civil rights policy in Phoenix, Arizona. Rehnquist turned out to be the first post-*Brown* justice who became a harsh and consistent critic of desegregation policy (Davis, 1989). Rehnquist would later be appointed chief justice by Ronald Reagan. Both Powell and Rehnquist would play central roles in limiting and reversing desegregation.

All four of Nixon's justices (the others were Warren E. Burger and Harry Blackmun) were part of the 5–4 majorities in 1973 and 1974, discussed below, that shut the door on suburban desegregation and ended the possibility of federal court decisions equalizing funding of public schools, stopping what had been the expansion of court-ordered financial equalization of public education. Nixon saw his Supreme Court choices as "among the most constructive and far-reaching actions of my presidency" (Nixon, 1978, p. 424). They had enduring impacts on the opportunities for Black and Latinx children.

Nixon acted decisively to limit administrative enforcement of the Civil Rights Act. He fired officials in both education and housing who were trying to enforce the laws. He announced that he was opposed to "forced integration of the suburbs"; he threatened to support a constitutional amendment limiting judicial desegregation powers if the Supreme Court ordered desegregation of suburban schools. His administration used the Justice Department's civil rights oversight powers to block and delay desegregation, provoking protests and resignations in the department. Federal courts found his administration guilty of intentional nonenforcement of the Civil Rights Act and, in an extraordinary step, ordered the resumption of enforcement (*Adams v. Richardson*, 1973, the first of numerous decisions in the case).

By the time Congress forced Nixon to resign in disgrace from the presidency, the executive enforcement of desegregation under the Civil Rights Act had been decisively weakened and the Justice Department was representing resisting school districts. The Supreme Court had changed from the source of strong and comprehensive policies on desegregation to the roadblock to the expansion of the rights of minority students, and Lincoln's party was on its way to becoming the party of the White resistance in the South, though the transition was far from complete.

CASE 3: *SWANN V. CHARLOTTE-MECKLENBURG*, 1971

The next great question that came before the Supreme Court was raised by the desegregation of the giant countywide school district serving North

Carolina's largest city and its major suburbs, in the case called *Swann v. Charlotte-Mecklenburg Board of Education* (1971). Much of the law about desegregation had been made with regard to small settings. In the *Brown* case it was about Linda Brown being denied the opportunity to attend her nearest neighborhood school in Topeka, Kansas. In *Green* it was about a small district with no significant residential segregation where Black and White children were being bused past each other in both directions to preserve segregation. The remedy in small districts with limited housing segregation was apparent. But the great challenge was in the districts in the growing metro regions.

The United States had become predominantly urban with massive ghettos and barrios and was going through an enormous spread of suburbs in metropolitan areas after World War II, often with open exclusion of Blacks. The suburbs already had half the metro population by 1960 and were mushrooming. Almost all urban communities had high residential segregation (Taeuber & Taeuber, 1976) and overt discrimination in housing sales was only outlawed nationally in 1968 in a law with very weak enforcement powers. Many city districts had been losing White enrollment as suburbanization grew. With millions of students of color segregated in large metros, that issue came to the courts.

Could a school district comply with *Brown* and *Green* simply by setting up a neighborhood school system in a residentially segregated neighborhood, leaving most students whose rights had been violated over history locked into segregated schools, or did its plan have to create actual integration where possible even if it was necessary to transport students to schools in other neighborhoods? The answer to that question would determine whether millions of students in segregated neighborhoods had any opportunity for integrated education. Two-fifths of U.S. students took buses to school because of distance, including many in the growing suburbs. Could the court order transportation of students to integrated schools? In the *Swann* case, the federal district court had concluded that the *Green* factors could only be realized by massive reassignment of students across a large metropolitan county. President Nixon had attacked the plan in Charlotte during his presidential campaign and his Justice Department opposed the plan. *Swann* was the first major case decided by the Supreme Court headed by Nixon appointee Chief Justice Warren Burger. The decision, which was unanimous, found that busing for the purpose of integration was constitutional. It was the last of the Court's major unanimous decisions on school desegregation. When *Swann* was argued, the Court still had seven members of the Warren Court and only two Nixon appointees (Burger and Blackmun) and there were divisions emerging (Woodward & Armstrong, 1979). The decision was confusing and contained limits and language that would cause major problems later, but it did force rapid desegregation across Southern cities.

Swann supported the use of racial guidelines, setting a range for the desegregation of schools not requiring full racial balance. It held that desegregation orders were not permanent, meaning that local authorities could be able to return to "neighborhood" policies restoring segregation in the future. But the Court did agree that choice plans were not sufficient to fulfil the constitutional requirement established in previous cases. In essence, it supported comprehensive urban desegregation in spite of differences within the Court. *Swann* produced intense political conflict and was opposed by the president and his Justice Department. After the decision was handed down, the Nixon administration refused to enforce it, but was found to be violating the Civil Rights Act and was ordered by the federal court of appeals to apply it broadly. Civil rights attorneys filed cases in many districts winning orders to update existing desegregation plans to meet the new standards, producing a surge of urban desegregation in the major cities of the South and intense political conflict at the beginning of the 1970s.

CASE 4: *KEYES V. SCHOOL DISTRICT NO. 1*, 1973

The next historic decision came just 2 years later, in Denver. Nixon now had four judges on the Supreme Court and *Keyes* produced the first divided decision since *Brown*. Almost 2 decades after *Brown,* the Supreme Court took up two huge issues not yet decided. What rights did students in highly segregated schools have in states where there was no law mandating school segregation but many public and private practices and decisions that produced segregation? This was a crucial question for the large cities of the North and West where non-White students usually lived in segregated neighborhoods and attended schools with virtually no White classmates, suffering the same educational isolation as those in the South but for different reasons. The *Keyes* case began with neighbors in a diverse community objecting to school assignment decisions that were resegregating their neighborhood. The Southwest was already experiencing the immigration surge that would make Latinxes the largest group of minority students. The other big issue in the Denver decision was whether or not Latinxes as well as Blacks had the right to desegregated schools. There had been discriminatory enrollment and curriculum practices for Latinx students in the Southwest for many years, particularly in Texas, isolating children, for example, in "Mexican rooms." Often Latinx children were denied access to regular classes and sent to separate rooms or schools with much more limited instruction. Discrimination was severe. Latinx migration was growing rapidly, and there were serious patterns of segregation as the first national statistics on Latinx segregation were released.

The 7–1 decision (Justice Byron White did not take part) was the last major civil rights victory on desegregation, and it came with limits. The divided court's decision, written by Justice Brennan, supported by four other justices, rejected the idea that segregation was "inherently unequal" regardless of its cause, an idea that existed in some state policies and decisions. Research showed that the educational impact of segregation appeared to be the same whether the children were segregated by law or by other causes. The decision said that you could get a desegregation order for a city only if there was proof of some pattern of substantial official actions causing school segregation. In contrast to the South, where you only had to submit the historic state laws to trigger a remedy, in other regions, including the West, plaintiffs had to study the whole history of school district and other local official decisions that would cause segregation. That created a huge burden of proof, especially in large cities where civil rights groups often could not afford very expensive research and documentation. The Denver case, for example, was only possible because of the work of a local antitrust attorney with expertise in handling vast records and data. In the cases that did go to trial, there was almost always abundant evidence eventually produced showing a complex history of discrimination—issues like intentional selection of school sites or boundaries to reinforce rather than diminish racial segregation, segregated location of subsidized housing and related schools, discriminatory assignment of non-White staff, systematically unequal curriculum, and many other violations. It was not the product of accident or choice of non-White families to be segregated. The *Keyes* decision produced a flurry of new urban cases, but no group had resources to file citywide cases in some of the largest districts, including New York, Los Angeles, and Philadelphia.

The recognition of the rights of Latinx students was a major breakthrough, resting in part on the Civil Rights Commission's documentation of the history of discrimination and inequality. Since the numbers were growing rapidly and segregation was increasing, there was major potential for plans that would produce significant changes.

The *Keyes* case brought the first clear dissent in a school desegregation case since *Brown*. Justice Rehnquist wanted to limit desegregation orders to the states with a history of laws mandating segregation. Justice Powell also dissented in part. Rehnquist described the decision as a "drastic extension of *Brown*." He would consistently fight against it. *Keyes* did not provide lasting remedies and was never seriously enforced by any of the subsequent administrations. In many Southern cities where the Latinx population was beginning to grow, there were already old cases that had not included Latinxes that would be ended before ever recognizing their rights. By the late 1980s, the number of Latinx students was surging and their segregation rapidly increasing.

CASE 5: *SAN ANTONIO INDEPENDENT SCHOOL DISTRICT V. RODRIGUEZ*, 1973

Many opponents of desegregation suggested that equity could be won by what they called "desegregating the dollars"; that is, giving racially divided districts equal funding (separate but equal dollars). There were, of course, large differences in school funding between many low-income, troubled, non-White schools and districts and the affluent suburbs. Redistributing money was often pointed to as the logical way to help solve inequalities, ignoring the *Brown* conclusion about the "inherent" inequality of segregated schools and what happened in the 6 decades under the "separate but equal" formula in *Plessy v. Ferguson*. A decisive case came out of metropolitan San Antonio, Texas, to the Supreme Court. Important cases in states and some in the federal courts had maintained that the "equal protection of the laws" provision must mean, at least, equal resources. Although the federal Constitution says nothing about public education, which did not exist on any scale until long after the Constitution was ratified, public schools were a basic service provided by many states since before the Civil War and there was flagrant inequality. The inequalities were often particularly striking among school districts, often nearby school districts within the same metro area. This was the background of the case filed on behalf of a poor school district in the San Antonio metro, asking for resources. It was, at the time, widely expected that the Court would order a major remedy, possibly even requiring equalization across state lines. The court of appeals had supported the rights claimed by the residents of the poorly funded district, which had a concentration of low-income non-White students.

The case was about inequality. The Court described the basic facts: "The district is situated in the core-city sector of San Antonio in a residential neighborhood that has little commercial or industrial property. The residents are predominantly of Mexican American descent: approximately 90% of the student population is Mexican-American and over 6% is Negro. The average assessed property value per pupil is $5,960—the lowest in the metropolitan area—and the median family income ($4,686) is also the lowest." The majority opinion noted that "Texas virtually concedes that its historically rooted dual system of financing education could not withstand the strict judicial scrutiny that this Court has found appropriate in reviewing legislative judgments that interfere with fundamental constitutional rights" (*San Antonio Independent School District v. Rodriguez*, 1973, pp. 12, 16). But the court's majority, in a decision by Justice Powell, concluded that education was not a federal constitutional right so the court should simply accept Texas's judgment that the status quo of extremely unequal expenditures was good enough. The four dissenters said that *Brown* had seen equal education as a fundamental right and insisted that the equal protection clause of the Constitution did apply. But the decision in this case has blocked any federal right to equal educational resources, the "separate but equal" idea, ever since. (The majority cited research by conservative economist Eric Hanushek for the proposition that money differences didn't really matter much for educational outcomes; with far better data and analytic methods we can now see that money clearly does matter significantly but the *Rodriguez* decision stands [Jackson & Mackevicius, 2024].)

The 5–4 decision was an important turning point with Nixon's and Eisenhower's appointees breaking from the four remaining Democratic appointees, Brennan, White, Douglas, and Marshall. The Court held that there was no right to education in the Constitution, so no basis for ordering equality. It argued that property tax revenues in very unequal districts were legitimate local government activities and cited research suggesting that school funding did not matter anyway. The decision shut the door to financial equalization of schools by federal courts for the last half century. It was a clear sign of a major shift from a central concern with equity to one deferring to local and state governments. In terms of the long history, it rejected half of the *Plessy* equation, "separate but equal," concluding that unequal resources for a fundamental institution do not violate any federal rights.

CASE 6: *MILLIKEN V. BRADLEY*, 1974

Another 5–4 decision the next year decided the fate of metropolitan desegregation and ended the possibility of lasting desegregated education for millions of big city students of color. The case revolved around the desegregation of Detroit's Black students. The Detroit school district was already heavily Black and rapidly losing its White population. The once powerful city was poor and was devastated by a massive 1967 race riot and by a tragically mismanaged federal housing policy that left large sectors of the city abandoned and in ruins. The conservative judge hearing the case at the lower court level found abundant evidence of acts of intentional segregation on the part of both district and state officials. He concluded that the students deserved a desegregation remedy but that, with so few White students now in the city, the only way it would be meaningful was to include the suburban districts. The judge ordered that a plan be drawn up. The decision, supported by the court of appeals, produced a fierce attack from President Nixon and many state governments.

The Supreme Court's 5–4 decision reversing the lower courts held that the traditional autonomy of school districts had greater constitutional weight than desegregation rights. The decision, written by Chief Justice Burger, basically drew a line around the cities, exempting the suburbs from desegregation roles. The decision insisted that the city district should solve the problem, though the lower courts had shown this was impossible. In his dissent, Thurgood Marshall, who had been on the team of civil rights lawyers who won the *Brown* decision, said that the decision meant that there would be no remedy for millions of students stuck in schools intensely segregated by race and poverty in cities with declining resources, since, in the previous year's *Rodriguez* decision, the same 5–4 majority had ruled that there was no constitutional right to equal resources either. So the victims of discrimination in central cities would face a separate and highly unequal future with no rights to change it, a result worse than the *Plessy* formula.

Justice Douglas also dissented: "When we rule against the metropolitan area remedy, we take a step that will likely put the problems of the blacks and our society back to the period that antedated the 'separate but equal' regime of *Plessy v. Ferguson*. The reason is simple. The inner core of Detroit is now rather solidly black; and the blacks, we know, in many instances are likely to be poorer, just as were the Chicanos in *San Antonio School District v. Rodriguez*. By that decision, the poorer school districts must pay their own way. It is therefore a foregone conclusion that we have now given the States a formula whereby the poor must pay their own way." Douglas concluded: "Today's decision, given *Rodriguez,* means that there is no violation of the Equal Protection Clause though the schools are segregated by race and though the black schools are not only 'separate' but 'inferior.'" The Warren Court was now in the rearview mirror.

The case went back to the district court judge in Detroit who had to decide what to do next. Although the decision said that he must desegregate the students, he concluded that it was impossible and that any Detroit-only plan would fail and hurt the city. Instead, he ordered the state to pay for some remedial programs. The Supreme Court, in the 1977 case known as *Milliken II*, upheld the order. Efforts continued for 12 years with little success and the court abandoned the effort (Orfield & Eaton, 1996, p. 155). Federal judge Avern Cohn noted that in spite of the state being required to spend $238 million in 12 years: "These monies were insignificant when considered in light of school district's budget and were insufficient to serve as an incentive for real change." Former Detroit superintendent Arthur Jefferson said: "To even think that it . . . was going to be possible to eradicate those problems caused by segregation in a decade? That's impossible" (Orfield & Eaton, 1996, p. 155). The *Milliken II* orders were used in some other cases, with especially large resources committed in St. Louis and Kansas City. The idea was that the *Rodriguez* limits on equalization didn't hold in a situation where the courts had found unconstitutional discrimination by the state but could not order effective desegregation. In the Supreme Court's 1995 *Missouri v. Jenkins* decision, however, the Court ruled that the state could be required to aid Kansas City only temporarily, whether or not the money was curing the inequalities. It also ruled that money could not be used to even recruit suburbanites to come voluntarily into more integrated city magnet schools. The hope that *Milliken II* would provide some kind of lasting solution for separate-but-equal remedies for proven discrimination only lasted 18 years before that somewhat hopeful pathway was also extinguished. Desegregation had been redefined as a temporary thing; so, now, had extra money for plans to provide funds to try to deal with deep educational inequalities in the schools doomed to segregation by the first *Milliken* decision.

The Movement That Undid Desegregation

The country continually celebrates the Civil Rights Movement. People are proud to claim a role. Schools show films. There are museums and statues. But, so far in this historic struggle, a different, far less celebrated movement is prevailing. It is the movement that Nixon brought into the center of the GOP and that Reagan embraced as a highly ideological, transformative president who changed the national agenda. It didn't start in small Black churches or on protest marches by Black churches, have a national holiday, or create words written on monuments. It started as the segregationist movement of Alabama's George Wallace, South Carolina's Strom Thurmond, the KKK, and many others determined to preserve Southern racial traditions (Ward, 2011). It is supported by very wealthy donors. It includes believers in states' rights, the Tea Party and libertarian movements, "original intent" legal theories, and many others. It became central to political and legal battles when one of America's two national parties adopted its goals and, often, helped elect its leaders. It reached full expression with Donald Trump's campaigns and presidency with overt racial and anti-immigrant bias. It has rallies with enthusiastic crowds. It was relentlessly focused on changing the Supreme Court.

There has not been a Court with a majority of Democratic appointees for more than a half century. This movement, after three Trump appointments, controls the Supreme Court, and it is moving the country backward. Since we have only two national political options, when a movement captures a political party and wins an election, it can change the country. That happened in the 1960s for the civil rights revolution and it happened in the 1970s and 1980s, consolidating in the Reagan–Bush era. By stages, it has virtually eliminated the representation of moderates within the GOP. We are living in the wake of a movement that won, especially on its central goal of reversing the Supreme Court (Keck, 2004; Teles, 2008). It has a large structure of institutions from the Federalist Society to the Heritage Foundation to the anti–civil rights litigation groups, and it has the reach of a huge national political party. Since most scholars don't like it, they often ignore it, to their peril. It has given energy to the rise of the most successful demagogue in the history of American national politics. What has happened to school integration can hardly be understood without understanding this movement and how it has operated. After Nixon's appointments and actions essentially stopped the expansion of desegregation rights and created boundaries that have held, the Supreme Court would turn sharply backwards.

CASE 7: *BOARD OF EDUCATION OF OKLAHOMA CITY V. DOWELL*, 1991

The 1991 decision by Chief Justice Rehnquist was his culminating move in a long history of bitter criticism of school desegregation requirements. He opposed the *Brown* decision, and, according to the White House aide who managed his confirmation, lied about it to the Senate. He was the first open dissenter in the Supreme Court on a major desegregation case in the 1973 *Keyes* decision; he worked hard to try to limit desegregation to the smallest number of schools in a number of cases when he was still in the minority. In the 1991 Oklahoma City case, he dissected desegregation law and left it in tatters.

Rehnquist's decision in *Dowell* defined desegregation as temporary, not permanent, and provided that if a district made what a trial judge thought was a reasonable effort at desegregation, the order should be lifted. The decision took terms from earlier decisions and changed their meanings to justify ending desegregation plans. The 1968 *Green* decision was about the total, multidimensional restructuring of the historically segregated "dual school systems" into an integrated and transformed system eliminating the racial identifiability of schools, making all schools fair and equitable, as the goal of *Brown*. Dual schools were to be replaced by "unitary" schools that were not identifiable by race. The Rehnquist decision took the position that districts were "unitary" when a trial judge said they had made a good effort for a period of time and that *unitary* meant that the judge should dismiss the case and the school district had no further obligations. In fact, it was free to adopt policies that would obviously produce resegregation so long as they said that they did it for some other reason. The court could not look at the effect and the civil rights groups would have to prove intent to get a desegregation plan reinstated, something almost impossible to do unless officials admit their segregative intent. A desegregation order was the one chance for a historically excluded racial group to be fully included in schooling. The great power of federal courts in imposing remedies for unconstitutional action gave leverage to plaintiffs with little or no local political power. There was nothing in the *Green* decision that suggested that school authorities, once they complied for a short time, were authorized to take actions that would quickly resegregate the schools.

What had seemed a clear definition of the goal of *Brown* in *Green* in the late 1960s, equitable and racially integrated education, redefined *Brown* as a temporary punishment for a history of segregation not an ongoing mandate for racial justice. As long as a court order existed, a school district could be prevented from taking any action that would increase racial inequality.

Once it was lifted, however, the same school district could take any of a variety of actions, such as reinstituting segregated neighborhood schools or building schools in a segregated area, so long as the school officials said it was, for example, for efficiency or student convenience. Choice plans could be implemented in ways that favored students from privileged families. The year after the *Dowell* decision the Supreme Court went further, saying in *Freeman v. Pitts* (503 U.S. 467) that even if the district had never implemented all of the *Green* factors, it could be released from continuing parts of the remedy it had implemented. Three years later, the Supreme Court, which had ruled that compensatory educational remedies could be implemented in cases where the courts found desegregation to be impossible in a central city district, ruled in *Missouri v. Jenkins* that *Milliken II* remedies could be dropped after a few years even if there was no evidence that the remedy had actually worked or been carried out well enough or long enough to change things for the victims of segregation.

By 1995 the courts were rapidly dismantling major remaining desegregation orders and abandoning educational remedies across the United States. The law now had reduced desegregation to short-term plans, directed judges to make the orders temporary, removed any national standards for compliance, and eliminated the capacity to order long-term educational remedies for segregated students. The law said that schools that were still separate and unequal had met all their responsibilities and absolved them of continuing responsibility, and created a presumption that almost whatever local political or board officials wanted to do in the future was up to them. *Brown*, which together with the Civil Rights Act had launched a revolution in Southern schools, had been interpreted away into virtual insignificance and the primary responsibility of the courts now was to get out of the way and to end the district's responsibility to continue even a part of the *Green* factors until all had been met even for a short time. Desegregation of Black students had reached its peak in the South shortly before *Dowell*. After *Dowell*, segregation rose in all parts of the United States for the next third of a century and much of the progress of the civil rights revolution was lost, at least for the time.

CASE 8: *PARENTS INVOLVED IN COMMUNITY SCHOOLS V. SEATTLE SCHOOL DIST. NO. 1*, 2007

Beginning in the late 1980s, the Supreme Court began to adopt the theory that it was just as illegal to consider race to produce voluntary desegregation as it was to consider race to produce segregation. In the civil rights era, the consideration of race in order to voluntarily produce desegregation, college access, voting rights, affirmative action in employment, and other fields was considered to be not only legal but admirable. It often was ordered in desegregation remedies so that they would work. The basic idea was that racial discrimination is deeply entrenched in American institutions and you had to take race into consideration positively if you were going to get beyond race. Trying to solve it without considering the race of students was like trying to operate in a body with dangerous cancers without x-rays. If forbidden to consider the race of students, which had been shown to be essential, for example, in successful magnet plans, then not only might the remedies fail but it would make those who, for example, gave special consideration to get some students of color into a college prep program susceptible to being sued for discrimination.

Proving discrimination in individual cases, where those violating could obfuscate and state and local officials could keep inventing new ways to perpetuate the status quo, was often an exercise in futility. Eventually, to get real change it was necessary to suspend normal policies and to produce actual desegregation. When school desegregation had relied on individual action, the *Brown* decision had very limited impact for a decade. After the Civil Rights Act made it possible to require adoption of plans and specify requirements for progress, contrary to the claims of opponents left by the intense media focus on the worst conflicts, most of these changes were tense but peaceful and the schools adapted. Considering race and focusing on outcomes, the Southern schools changed rapidly. A federal survey of nearly a thousand school superintendents at the height of the busing controversy reported, for example, that the vast majority of districts had required no additional police work and that normal education was back in operation within weeks of desegregation (U.S. Commission on Civil Rights, 1976, pp. 145–146).

As the conservatives' theories took hold in a changing Supreme Court, consideration of race with the goal of producing integration was increasingly limited. Finally, in 2007, the Supreme Court agreed to hear cases relating to voluntary desegregation efforts by school boards in Louisville and Seattle to use race-conscious choice plans to foster desegregation in situations where there was no court order. Seattle was the only big city that had desegregated without a court order. Louisville had maintained desegregation voluntarily 2 decades after the court had said its schools were unitary because it had succeeded in increasing integration. Many plans, for instance, had long included "M-to-M" transfer plans where students could transfer from any school where they were a majority to any school where they were a minority, giving preference to moves increasing integration. Magnet schools were set up with specific integration goals and consciously used target recruitment and selection criteria to assure substantial and lasting integration. Both districts were sued by parents whose children had not gotten their favorite choice. In its decision, the Supreme Court's majority asserted that any consideration of a student's race was unconstitutional even if its purpose was to increase diversity and expand the option of integrated schools in segregated cities. This widely criticized decision (which Justice John Paul Stevens, a Republican appointee, said no member of the court he joined 3 decades earlier would have supported), made many voluntary plans unconstitutional and helped lay the groundwork for the 2023 decision ending affirmative action in higher education.

These eight major constitutional decisions and the experience of active enforcement of the Civil Rights Act in the 1960s show that even the most dramatic civil rights success can be lost, that Supreme Court appointments can have vast social impact in a society with an extremely powerful judiciary, that movements and mobilization can make a difference, especially when embraced by a political party, and that celebrations of the *Brown* decision and the role of the great civil rights heroes often neglect to note that the celebrated rights have actually been largely interpreted away and that rights on paper are only real when backed by power and enforcement.

If one were to close the story of leadership and law on desegregation at this point in history, it could seem that the epic story of the nation's struggle over *Brown* and the civil rights revolution was an exercise in futility even though the South is still far from conditions before *Brown* and there are places where integrated schools continue. We have certainly learned that racial segregation and polarization are powerful and durable forces supported by institutions and stereotypes and fears shared by substantial proportions of American society. We have seen that the only president who actually made *Brown* real for millions of students was the first Southerner elected since the Civil War, Lyndon Johnson, and that the two who did most to limit and reverse the progress were Californians who rose, in part, by exploiting White fears in a party that became increasingly focused on activating White fears. Two conservative presidents helped turn the country backward on school integration. A common saying, often attributed to French historian Augustin Thierry, is that the victors write the history. At this point, the opponents of school desegregation seem to be the victors in the 70 years of struggle set off by *Brown* and the Civil Rights Act. Segregation, double segregation by race and class, has been rising for a generation. In another generation I think that there's a good chance that the writers will be producing a different narrative in a society with a declining White minority still dealing with serious racial polarization and, perhaps, generating different, powerful movements and a politics of racial justice. This is not the last act.

There have been two powerful, but very different, movements and many years of struggle over the fate of race in our schools. Right now, it seems normal to accept segregation and make policy about everything else, but this is not the last movement that will change our schools. As the society changes and the understanding of the role of unequal education and the harm of segregation deepens, this issue will come back. There have been crucial big data studies that show the lifelong impacts of desegregation in ways not previously understood. When there are new movements, it will be good to understand the strategies and the legal and political tactics that were effectively used by the current dominant group. The conservatives doubled down on tactics employed by the NAACP Legal Defense Fund in the civil rights era, financed them, and expanded them. Civil rights opponents had a much more focused and sustained drive to control the courts.

Educational aspirations and hope are central realities of the excluded in a highly unequal society where race matters at all stages of life and outcomes are far from equal. The issue will come back because in the 128 years since *Plessy*, we've never succeeded in making separate schools equal on a large scale and in a profoundly multiracial, stratified society, reform movements cannot give up what is probably our most powerful tool for changing it. Race-conscious remedies will be advocated again because it is extremely difficult to change racial outcomes without explicitly focusing on race.

History, of course, continues, and we may have presidents and movements who help turn things back toward the goal of *Brown*. Our experience has shown that it is possible to change deeply rooted institutions, relatively rapidly, with decisive legal and political action. Millions of students were, for the first time, educated in diverse schools in areas that had been absolutely segregated. We now know that there were major lifelong benefits for desegregated students of color and that desegregation did no academic harm to White students while giving them better preparation to live and work in a diverse society. The non-White majority in our schools will become the voting majority; it can profoundly change politics, and, through politics, the courts and the law, if its power is organized. The most resistant forces in the United States, older, poorly educated Whites, are a rapidly shrinking part of our society. There are many reasons to think about a long-term trend toward a very different set of decisions by new leadership. But, given the current Supreme Court, there are powerful obstacles to reform. The conservative movement will surely continue its work to consolidate a status quo preserving advantages for the advantaged. Those who fought against great odds to win the victory in the *Brown* decision and those who led or participated in the social and political movements that led to *Brown* persisted through heartbreaking defeats and overwhelming obstacles. That could happen again. Deeper understanding of why change happened and what have been the consequences for excluded students and segregated communities will be part of any such movement.

REFERENCES

Adams v. Richardson, 356 F. Supp. 92 (D.D.C. 1973). https://law.justia.com/cases/federal/district-courts/FSupp/356/92/1892620/

Board of Education of Oklahoma City v. Dowell, 498 U.S. 237 (1991). https://supreme.justia.com/cases/federal/us/498/237

Briggs v. Elliott, 132 F. Supp. 776, 777 (E.D.S.C. 1955). https://law.justia.com/cases/federal/district-courts/FSupp/132/776/1454854/

Brown v. Board of Education of Topeka, 347 U.S. 483 (1954). https://supreme.justia.com/cases/federal/us/347/483

Brown v. Board of Education of Topeka (Brown II), 349 U.S. 294 (1955). https://supreme.justia.com/cases/federal/us/349/294/

Caro, R. A. (2012). *The years of Lyndon Johnson: The passage of power*. Alfred A. Knopf.

Davis, S. (1989). *Justice Rehnquist and the Constitution*. Princeton University Press.

Frady, M. (1968). *Wallace*. Meridian Books.

Green v. County Sch. Bd. of New Kent County, 391 U.S. 430 (1968). https://supreme.justia.com/cases/federal/us/391/430/

Jackson, C., K., & Mackevicius, C. L. (2024). What impacts can we expect from school spending policy? Evidence from evaluations in the United States. *American Economic Journal: Applied Economics, 16*(1), 412–446.

Keck, T. M. (2004). *The most activist Supreme Court in history: The road to modern judicial conservatism*. University of Chicago Press.

Keyes v. School Dist. No. 1, 413 U.S. 189 (1973). https://supreme.justia.com/cases/federal/us/413/189/

Kluger, R. (1975). *Simple justice: The history of* Brown v. Board of Education *and Black America's struggle for equality*. Vintage Books.

Milliken v. Bradley, 418 U.S. 717 (1974). https://supreme.justia.com/cases/federal/us/418/717/

Milliken v. Bradley, 418 U.S. 717 (1974), Justice Douglas dissent, 759–762. https://supreme.justia.com/cases/federal/us/418/717/

Milliken v. Bradley (Milliken II), 433 U.S. 267, 97 S. Ct. 2749, 53 L. Ed. 2d 745 (1977). https://supreme.justia.com/cases/federal/us/433/267/

Missouri v. Jenkins, 515 U.S. 70 (1995). https://supreme.justia.com/cases/federal/us/515/70/

Myrdal, G. (1944). *An American dilemma: The Negro problem and modern democracy*. Harper & Brothers.

Newport, F. (2014, April 10). Public opinion on civil rights 50 years after the Civil Rights Act of 1964. *Gallup*. https://news.gallup.com/opinion/polling-matters/169361/public-opinion-civil-rights-years-civil-rights-act-1964.aspx

Nixon, R. (1978). *The memoirs of Richard Nixon*. Grosset & Dunlap.

Orfield, G. (1969). *The reconstruction of Southern education: The schools and the 1964 Civil Rights Act*. John Wiley & Sons.

Orfield, G., & Eaton, S. (1996). *Dismantling desegregation: The quiet reversal of* Brown v. Board of Education. New Press.

Panetta, L. E., & Gall, P. (1971). *Bring us together: The Nixon team and the civil rights retreat*. Lippincott.

Parents Involved in Community Schools v. Seattle School Dist. No. 1, 551 U.S. 701 (2007). https://supreme.justia.com/cases/federal/us/551/701

Parmet, H. S. (1983). *JFK: The presidency of John F. Kennedy*. Penguin Books.

Peltason, J. W. (1961). *Fifty-eight lonely men: Southern Federal judges and school desegregation*. Harcourt, Brace & World.

Rosenthal, J. (1971, February 18). President reaffirms opposition to forced suburban integration," *The New York Times*, p. 19.

San Antonio Independent School District v. Rodriguez, 411 U.S. 1 (1973). https://supreme.justia.com/cases/federal/us/411/1

Students for Fair Admissions, Inc. v. President and Fellows of Harvard College, 600 U.S. ___ (2023). https://supreme.justia.com/cases/federal/us/600/20-1199

Swann v. Charlotte-Mecklenburg Board of Education, 402 U.S. 1 (1971). https://supreme.justia.com/cases/federal/us/402/1

Taeuber, K., & Taeuber, A. (1976). *Negroes in cities*. Aldine Publishing Co.

Teles, S. M. (2008). *The rise of the conservative legal movement: The battle for control of the law*. Princeton University Press.

U.S. Commission on Civil Rights. (1976). Fulfilling the letter and spirit of the law: Desegregation of the nation's public schools. Goverment Printing Office.

Ward, J. M. (2011). *Defending White democracy: The making of a segregationist movement & the remaking of racial politics, 1936–1965*. University of North Carolina Press.

Whalen, C., & Whalen, B. (1989). *The longest debate: A legislative history of the 1964 Civil Rights Act*. Seven Locks Press.

Woodward, B., & Armstrong, S. (1979). *The brethren: Inside the Supreme Court*. Simon & Schuster.

CHAPTER 3

Where Do We Go From Here?
Assessing the Limits and Possibilities of Education for Black People in the United States 70 Years After *Brown*

Joaquín M. S. Noguera and Pedro A. Noguera

> A nation that continues year after year to spend more money on military defense than on programs of social uplift is approaching spiritual death. America, the richest and most powerful nation in the world, can well lead the way in this revolution of values. There is nothing to prevent us from paying adequate wages to schoolteachers, social workers and other servants of the public to ensure that we have the best available personnel in these positions which are charged with the responsibility of guiding our future generations. . . . There is nothing, except a tragic death wish, to prevent us from reordering our priorities, so that the pursuit of peace will take precedence over the pursuit of war. There is nothing to keep us from remolding a recalcitrant status quo with bruised hands until we have fashioned it into a brotherhood.
>
> —Martin Luther King Jr., *Where Do We Go from Here: Chaos or Community?*

The profound question posed by Dr. Martin Luther King Jr.—Where do we go from here?—in the last book he published before his assassination aptly captures the critical moment facing Black people in America as they/we ponder possibilities for using education as a resource to advance prospects for better lives. Throughout most of our history in the United States, Black people have viewed education as critical to freedom, prosperity, and justice (Anderson, 1988; King, 2006; Love, 2019; Williams, 2009). Despite this vision, educational opportunities for Black people that would advance our interests and improve our lives collectively have more often than not been out of reach. The question posed by King in 1967, 1 year before his assassination, is as important now as it was then.

As is true with so many other aspects of Black life in America, the history of Black experiences with education has been characterized by great hopes and expectations that have been met with unfulfilled promises. The 2023 U.S. Supreme Court decision requiring institutions of higher education to eliminate all considerations of race in college admissions (*SFFA v. Harvard*, 600 U.S. 181) is just the most recent example of a setback. Affirmative action was created in response to demands from the Civil Rights Movement to end discrimination in all facets of life. While the policy proved to be weak in countering decades of structural barriers and did little to reduce systemic racial inequality in America (in fact, White women benefitted more from the policies aimed at inclusion than any other demographic group) (Crenshaw, 2006; Wise, 1998), it did at least produce a generation of Black professionals—doctors, lawyers, teachers, and others—who disproportionately served Black communities and interests. The Court's 2023 decision effectively ends America's acknowledgment that racial barriers continue to limit access to quality educational opportunities, despite substantial evidence showing that such barriers remain formidable today, though they may no longer be buttressed by legal requirements and rationalizations.

The irony of the Supreme Court decision is that 70 years after *Brown v. Board of Education* we find ourselves with few if any legal remedies to challenge racial injustice in education. Schooling in America continues to be characterized by profound inequities in opportunity that correspond to race, class, and geography, and as numerous studies have shown, disparities in educational opportunity inevitably reinforce disparities in other aspects of life (Apple, 2001; Duncan & Murnane, 2011; Milner, 2021; Stiglitz, 2012).

In this chapter, we consider how race and racial inequality continue to shape the experience of Black students in schools and educational institutions throughout the United States. We begin by exploring the legacy of *Brown* and its significance for schools today. From there we explore the nature of the racial barriers that continue to obstruct educational opportunity for millions of Black children, using the case of Los Angeles to draw attention to the ways in which lack of opportunity within schools corresponds to lack of opportunity and hardship outside of school. Although Black students are the focus of this chapter, we recognize that not only Black children are affected by inequality in educational opportunities. Our goal is to draw lessons from schools that appear to serve Black students well, whether they are integrated or not, so that they can be applied in other schools. Beyond documenting challenges facing Black people in U.S. schools in the third decade of the 21st century, we intend to use this chapter to also explore King's critical question: Where *do* we go from here? As we assess prospects for ensuring equitable educational opportunities for Black people in the United States on the 70th anniversary of the historic *Brown* decision, we believe King's question is as pertinent now as it was in 1967. Throughout this chapter we argue that even in the face of significant constraints created by the exploitative and exclusionary patterns of racial capitalism (Glaude, 2017; Robinson, 2000), education will continue to be important to the future prospects of Black people in America. For this reason, we conclude by describing some of the educational change strategies that are most likely to make it possible for King's dreams of justice to be fulfilled.

REFLECTIONS ON THE STATE OF SCHOOLING FOR BLACK PEOPLE IN THE UNITED STATES 70 YEARS AFTER *BROWN*

Is integrated schooling in the United States a goal still worth pursuing? As we contemplate the significance of the 70th anniversary of the U.S. Supreme Court's *Brown* decision, this basic question carries special pertinence. In theory, integration was pursued to disrupt centuries of legally protected racial hierarchy and provide greater opportunity for people of color. Thurgood Marshall and his allies at the NAACP conceived of integration as a means to expand educational opportunities, with perhaps some residual impact on the healing of an unhealthy society that was engaged in social struggle and transformation. Viewed through the lens of global politics, the issue has been framed as an opportunistic move concerned with global optics (Bell, 1980; Dudziak, 1988), and not simply an act of good will or a reflection of racial reckoning. Rucker Johnson (2011) and others have documented the fierce resistance to integration in most parts of the country (McRae, 2018). In fact, in some states, like California, the State Supreme Court acknowledged the need for desegregation in the state constitution, but little action followed to enforce and protect school integration policies (Orfield & Ee, 2014). Improving educational opportunities in this country has been central to Black peoples' struggle for humanity, dignity, and inclusion in the United States. This connection must be recognized if we are to chart a viable path forward.

Today, all the evidence shows that even as American society is growing more racially and ethnically diverse (Frey, 2020), many of our schools are stunningly homogenous with respect to the race and class composition of the students served. More importantly, the data also shows that in schools where low-income students are concentrated, student achievement tends to be substantially lower than for more affluent students (Reardon, 2016) and prospects for using education as a means to counter inequality appear dim (Chetty et al., 2017).

These are not new developments. After several years of progress in desegregating in the 1960s and 1970s (Johnson, 2011), racially separate schooling has been growing. Moreover, despite rhetoric describing education as the most important civil rights issue of the 21st century espoused by many political leaders (Noguera & Syeed, 2020), no leader or major party has devised a plan to counter the growing racial separation and inequality in schools in American society, nor have they even suggested that this is an issue the nation should be concerned about.

It is important to point out that the nation's lack of progress in creating integrated schools does not mean that the historic *Brown* decision should be regarded as a failure. Most legal scholars still cite *Brown* as groundbreaking and monumental because it established legal precedent for ending legally sanctioned racial discrimination in other aspects of public life, or what might fairly be regarded as "American apartheid" (Hacker, 2010; Wilkerson, 2020). The Supreme Court's unanimous ruling in *Brown* is credited not only with starting the process of eliminating racial barriers in education, but also with setting precedent for the elimination of racial barriers to voting, housing access, employment, transportation, and services in other facets of life (e.g., transportation, health care in America that are essential to full citizenship (Grant-Thomas & Orfield, 2009).

Even as we acknowledge the importance of *Brown* in the struggle for racial justice, we must also acknowledge that its impact on public education has not lived up to the hope that it would produce equality in opportunity. Several studies on the race and class composition of schools in the United States show that they continue to be characterized by a high degree of racial and socioeconomic isolation (Jung et al., 2011). This is the case particularly in the nation's largest metropolitan areas, where the overwhelming majority of students are low income and non-White (Porter, 2022). In large cities like New York, Los Angeles, Houston, and Miami, close to 90% of students are Black, Latinx, or recent immigrants, and the overwhelming majority come from households that qualify for free and reduced-price lunch (Housing Matters, 2023). It is important to note that the concentration of low-income children of color is also common to cities where Whites and Asian Americans make up the majority of residents, such as Denver, Seattle, Milwaukee, and San Diego (Housing Matters, 2023).

In the literature, the persistence of racially separate schooling has typically been explained by two factors: (1) court rulings after *Brown* that weakened the Supreme Court's ruling and undermined its ability to promote desegregation (Orfield & Lee, 2004), especially in the suburbs; and (2) initial rejection of integration through White flight, followed by the creation of new, more segregated school districts, and the continuation of pervasive segregation in residential areas throughout the United States in urban, suburban, and rural communities (Denton, 1996; EdBuild, 2019). While these factors are important to understanding the persistence of racially separate schooling in the United States, it is also essential to acknowledge the role of persistent racism in America, and the way it influences parental choices about school attendance and neighborhood residence (Billingham & Hunt, 2016). Lack of civic and political will and passive acceptance of racially separate schooling (Noguera, 2003; Noguera & Wing, 2008) have all contributed to the lack of progress.

Today, the average Black student attends a school where the student population is 49% Black, even though Blacks comprise 12% of the U.S. population. For Latinx students, the patterns are more extreme. Fifty-seven percent of Latinx students attend schools where the majority of students are Latinx (Orfield & Frankenburg, 2014; U.S. Commission on Civil Rights, 2018). On the whole, Black and Latinx students throughout the United States are likely to attend schools where the majority of children are poor and the resources available to serve them are often inadequate.

While the courts maintained oversight over desegregation efforts, segregation in schools declined significantly. When the courts terminated oversight, segregation in schools increased to new highs. At the height of school desegregation efforts in the 1980s, the achievement gap between Black and White students decreased by more than half in reading and nearly half in math (George & Darling-Hammond, 2019). The *Brown* decision was directed primarily at the 17 states that had laws mandating the segregation of Black people, even though they were not the only states with serious issues of racial discrimination in schooling. Ironically, though the South put up the fiercest resistance to desegregation, today it is the least segregated region in the nation (Orfield & Frankenberg, 2014).

In many parts of the country, children of color experience what might be termed "double segregation"—separation by race and class (Boschma & Brownstein, 2016). Typically, the poorest and most disadvantaged students are concentrated in urban and some rural and suburban schools (Porter, 2022). Many of these schools have low patterns of student achievement and as a result they have been labelled as "failing" by state bureaucracies that theoretically are supposed to help them (Darling-Hammond, 2007). However, the "help" provided to such schools by state departments of education has typically consisted of threats, sanctions, and takeovers, none of which has brought about relief or improvement (Lipman, 2017).

It is widely known that many of the schools serving low-income students of color struggle in part because they are overwhelmed by the wide variety of problems that frequently afflict poor families and communities (including violence, homelessness, hunger, and trauma), and because they have trouble hiring and retaining highly qualified educators (Carver-Thomas & Darling-Hammond, 2019; Simon & Johnson, 2015). Nonetheless, education policymakers typically ignore and fail to address either of these issues and the academic challenges that typically accompany them (Children's Defense Fund, 2017). Instead, under the guise of accountability, policymakers have sought to apply sanctions and a variety of punitive measures in an attempt to pressure schools to improve (Mintrop, 2013). Not only has this strategy failed, but segregation on the basis of race and class is no longer even acknowledged as an obstacle to educational advancement. As we show in the following section, the "accumulation of disadvantage" is a major obstacle to change.

Scholars and commentators, many of whom happen to be Black, have openly questioned the value and importance of racial integration in schools. In 1935, W. E. B. Du Bois questioned whether separate schools were needed for Black folks to receive a proper education. He argued that the outcomes will be healthier and more beneficial when Black children are "in schools where they are wanted, and where they are happy and inspired, than in . . . hells where they are ridiculed and hated." (Du Bois, 1935, p. 331). Scholars like Vanessa Siddle Walker point to the benefits that prior generations experienced from attending schools staffed and led by Black educators who cared for their students, challenged them academically, and never doubted their competence or potential (Siddle Walker, 2000). Other scholars remind us that the Supreme Court's 1898 ruling in *Plessy v. Ferguson*—which called for schools to be "separate but equal"—was never realized. Prior to *Brown*, systemic discrimination and inadequate resource provisions relegated most Black children, and in many cases, Native American, Latinx, and Asian children, to inferior schools and profoundly *unequal* education experiences (Gamoran & An, 2016).

For 20 to 30 years after *Brown*, many communities across the country took *Brown*'s mandate seriously and attempted to integrate schools to undo the legacy of separate and unequal schools. In fact, both authors of this chapter attended such schools in New York and California. However, many communities in the United States resisted attempts to integrate their schools. At this time, the evidence is clear: Not only have we failed to live up to the promise of *Brown*, but we have failed even to deliver on the unfulfilled promise of *Plessy*, that schools would be separate but equal. With few exceptions, poor children of color across the United States not only attend schools that are separated by race and class, but they are also most likely to be enrolled in schools that are profoundly unequal with respect to the educational opportunities they provide (Boschma & Brownstein, 2016).

THE ACCUMULATION OF DISADVANTAGE IN LA COUNTY

Los Angeles County is the metropolitan area with the largest population in the United States. The 2,231 schools and 89 school districts in the county serve close to 1.3 million students (Ed Data, n.d.). Just over 1 million of the students served by schools in the county qualify for free or reduced-price lunch, almost 30,000 children are in foster care (Alliance for Children's Rights, 2020) and a 2023 census of the homeless population found that there were just over 6,200 children who were homeless (Los Angeles Almanac, 2023).

Black students comprise just under 9% of the national student population, a percentage that has been declining for the past 30 years. They are vastly overrepresented among those experiencing hardships, while in contrast they are underrepresented in schools that are regarded as "high performing" based on their academic outcomes. Existing data shows that they are overrepresented in schools with lower indicators on standardized assessments, graduation rates, and the availability and completion of courses needed for college (Noguera et al., 2019). They are also more likely to drop out of school, to be placed in special education, and to be among those who are subject to punitive forms of discipline in school (Swanson, 2022). Additionally, large numbers of Black students live in communities where their health and well-being are more likely to be adversely affected by environmental conditions. As a result, they are more likely than any other group to experience health conditions such as asthma, and less likely to have access to healthy food, parks, and recreational facilities (Noguera et al., 2019).

The report *Beyond the Schoolhouse* (Noguera et al., 2019) sought to draw attention to the ways in which the problems experienced by Black children in school are compounded by the broad array of hardships that many of them face outside of school. When devising strategies to improve school performance and student outcomes, policymakers have typically ignored these connections. For example, Black students are more likely than any other group to experience homelessness, to be placed in foster care, or to be subjected to arrest, in school or outside of it (Noguera et al., 2019). However, even when policymakers have directed additional resources to support schools serving a disproportionate number of children in foster care or experiencing homelessness, they have refused to acknowledge or address the fact that Black children are more likely than any other group to be beset with these hardships.

The report was very clear about the root cause of the problems facing many Black students in LA County. Rather than pointing the finger at educational or political leaders, the authors identified *structural racism* as the underlying cause of the myriad challenges facing Black children and the schools they attend. Structural racism is different from interpersonal racism because it is rooted in the history of racial discrimination and oppression, and not dependent on the conduct or beliefs of racist individuals. We can see that in many cities and urban school districts, people of color hold positions of leadership, yet the legacy of structural racism often remains largely unchanged. Slavery, Jim Crow segregation in housing, redlining, systemic bias, and exclusion by local government and businesses are all features of structural racism (Bonilla-Silva, 2018; Edwards & Noguera, 2022).

What makes structural racism insidious and difficult to counter is that it has become normalized in the popular imagination and in discourse on the problems present in "slums and ghettos." For years, movies and television shows reinforced stereotypes that suggested "bad neighborhoods" were created by "bad" people; people who are lazy, criminally inclined, and substance abusers who make bad choices (Anderson, 1988; Wang, 2019).

Systemic disadvantages caused by redlining and racial discrimination are often overlooked, and structural racism and the continued disinvestment and marginalization of poor Black people remain largely unseen and, therefore, unaddressed.

Similarly, schools where low-income Black and Latinx children are concentrated are assumed to "fail" because they have "bad" students who don't study enough, "bad" teachers who are ineffective, and "bad" parents who don't care (Noguera & Syeed, 2020). Like the neighborhoods where such schools tend to be located, failing the schools is assumed to be a byproduct of failures of the people who study, teach, and send their children there, rather than systemic neglect. When such commonsense notions are unchallenged, policymakers are more likely to respond with threats, pressure, and even school district takeovers, meted out under the guise of accountability, than to pursue policy remedies that would alleviate hardships.

Unlike overt racism, which has increased in recent years with hate crimes on the rise, the problem of structural racism is complex, sometimes subtle, and for many, hard to grasp. However, if we acknowledge the ways in which structural racism shapes the challenges facing schools and communities that serve low-income Black people, we are more likely to devise strategies to counter the ongoing challenges it creates, or at the minimum to strategize how they can be mitigated. Without such an approach, most efforts at school reform will fail.

In many schools that are ostensibly integrated, Black children remain tracked in noncollege prep courses, and overrepresented among those who are subjected to punitive discipline and who are placed in special education (Ahram et al., 2011). Additionally, many of the schools located in racially segregated communities lack the resources and capacity to meet student needs. While hiring more teachers of color, changing the curriculum, adding new technology, or even creating community schools may, when implemented well, be helpful in alleviating some of the challenges facing schools in low-income Black communities and the students they serve, evidence shows they are unlikely to bring about improvement on a larger scale.

However, while doing research on the state of Black children in LA County, the authors decided to look at the data to identify the high schools in the county that were consistently producing the greatest number of Black students who qualified for admission to the California State University (CSU) and the University of California (UC). While the numbers were small, the overwhelming majority of the schools that were so identified were racially integrated schools where Black students comprised less than 10% of the student population (Noguera et al., 2019).

Interestingly, the school that sent the greatest number of Black students to the CSU and UC systems was King-Drew Health Science Magnet. This is a segregated school (*de facto* not *de jure*) located in Watts, a low-income Black and Latinx community. The authors were surprised by the finding.

After all, the school is located in a poor, racially isolated neighborhood, and serves low-income students of color. However, closer examination of the school revealed several factors that helped to explain its relative success: (1) It had a selective admissions process, which meant that students with greater academic needs were typically excluded; (2) it was well-resourced and able to offer a variety of electives, internships, and advanced placement courses, like most suburban schools in affluent communities; (3) it had a positive culture; (4) it had strong and stable leadership and a highly skilled teaching staff; and (5) it had substantial parental involvement. Aside from the selectivity of the admissions process, this list substantially matches the "essentials" that the Chicago Consortium on School Improvement identified as being associated with high-performing schools (Bryk et al., 2010). While the researchers were pleased to have identified King-Drew after being overwhelmed by the dismal array of data on hardships they had collected, they were left wondering: Why does LA and the state of California have only one such school in a low-income Black community?

SO, WHERE *DO* WE GO FROM HERE?

Our attempt at answering Dr. King's profound question is layered. First, we answer it as Black educators who recognize that the educational aspirations of Black people continue to be obstructed by numerous political, social, and economic attacks and challenges. Contending with and finding a way to overcome these challenges is critical to the future of Black people in America. Since the days of slavery when it was illegal to educate Black people (Givens, 2021), large numbers of Black people have embraced education as a means to advance freedom and justice in American society. Those broad goals and aspirations remain relevant today. Much of our thinking about where we go with respect to direction of education policy and strategy, and what we should do to address the significant obstacles that obstruct our collective aspirations, is framed around recognition of both the limitations and the possibilities for change. In this final section, we offer recommendations specifically to Black educators, parents, and students, because at this moment in our history, figuring out how to advance the rights and interests of Black people in the United States is a challenge we cannot ignore or leave to others.

Second, it is important to acknowledge that Black people are not the only ones who have interests at stake in the struggle for educational justice. Race/class segregation and inequality affect the opportunities available to Latinx, Indigenous people, and many low-income White and Asian Americans. Acknowledging that we are not alone is important, because it means we potentially have comrades in this struggle whom we must work with to counter obstacles and advance opportunity. Moreover, as Rucker

Johnson reminds us in his important book *Children of the Dream* (2019), desegregation efforts were most successful when Black parents were supported actively by White allies and others. It is still the case today that building broad coalitions of support for educational justice will be important for avoiding marginalization and foiling attempts by powerful interests to dismiss our efforts as the concerns of fringe activists. There is power in numbers.

Third, to truly respond to the question "Where do we go from here?" we must remember that the struggles for human/civil rights and for educational opportunity have always been deeply intertwined and inextricably connected. Part of the reason we have seen so little progress in advancing racial equity in schools is because reform efforts have been led by academics, policymakers, and to a lesser degree, the courts. Educators, too, have often led this work. But on too many occasions social justice organizations, parents, and unions have been left out.

Policymakers from both parties have done little to advance racial equity in education. They pay lip service to the goal with catchy phrases like "Education is the civil rights issue of the 21st century," but such rhetoric or similar slogans that frequently accompany them have done little to produce change. Sixty years ago, President Lyndon B. Johnson, who was a teacher on the U.S.–Mexico border before he entered politics, connected school integration and civil rights directly. He made the case explicitly through various presidential orders that mandated civil rights and protections, and with the enactment of the Elementary and Secondary Education Act (now called Title I) in 1965. However, since that time both Democrat and Republican politicians have pretended that we could simply talk about King's dream of creating a more equal society without addressing the deep and persistent racial inequities embedded within the structure of American society and its schools.

Race continues to play a profound role in shaping the character of education in the United States. This is particularly the case in urban schools, but it is common in rural and suburban schools as well. Despite the position taken by the U.S. Supreme Court in *Students for Fair Admissions Inc. v. President and Fellows of Harvard College*, denying the persistence and presence of racial discrimination in education, and 70 years after the historic *Brown* decision, the legacy of educating students in racially separate and profoundly unequal schools endures. The persistence of deeply entrenched racial disparities in every aspect of life in America, particularly in educational and socioeconomic outcomes, provides the most poignant evidence that race cannot be ignored.

To make educational progress during a period of overt hostility to the rights of Black students, parents, and educators, we must ask ourselves: What are the possibilities for advancing racial equity and educational opportunity in schools at this time? The answer to this question will vary depending on the social context. The example of King-Drew Health Magnet School in Watts shows that under the right conditions, the constraints created by pervasive poverty and racial inequality can be mitigated. Yet we recognize that this does not mean that this can easily be done on a larger scale, especially given that King-Drew excludes students with the greatest needs. While we can learn from their model, school and district leaders must prioritize developing partnerships with outside organizations and service providers to ensure the needs of the most vulnerable are met. Schools cannot do this work alone, and much can be accomplished when we know our people and reorganize our systems accordingly. In states and communities where hostility to the education of Black children has come into the open with bans on books by Black authors, curricula identified as critical race theory, and diversity, equity, and inclusion efforts (Pollock et al., 2022), figuring out what can be done to advance racial equity will require ingenuity and struggle, as well as legal challenges.

Both authors have extensive experience working on school change efforts in communities throughout the country. Our experiences have led us to believe that greater progress will not be achieved unless Black parents, students, and community groups are involved in this work in a sustained way at the local level. It is too important to be left to consultants and academic researchers. Engagement can take the form of demanding more resources, such as A–G courses (these are the courses recognized by the University of California as meeting their requirements for eligibility), afterschool programs, laboratories, and computer labs, as the Community Coalition and Inner-City Struggle have done in Los Angeles (Noguera & Alicea, 2020). It can also involve policy efforts to push for the adoption of high-quality preschool, affordable housing, and community schools designed to provide more support to students. This will necessarily require greater cooperation between cities, county governments, and school districts across the country (Noguera & Wells, 2011).

To counter structural racism, it must be acknowledged that it is rooted in this nation's history of moral antipathy toward the plight of Black people, slavery, Jim Crow segregation, racial violence, redlining, and housing discrimination (Kendi & Reynolds, 2020; Rothstein, 2017), we must devise strategies that bring broad coalitions together to demand racial justice and equity in education. We must pursue policy changes at the state and local level to direct resources on behalf of our most vulnerable children and avoid the divide-and-rule tactic of pitting Black and Latinx communities against each other, or against other minoritized peoples. Historically oppressed racial and ethnic groups continue to be subjected to various forms of pernicious and unrelenting discrimination and mistreatment that go beyond *de facto* segregation in schools, including the denial of language and cultural rights, the withholding of basic human rights (i.e., denial of access to healthy food, clean water and air, gender-appropriate bathrooms, adequate housing and health care, etc.), and of course the failure to provide critical educational opportunities (e.g., highly skilled teachers, well-equipped schools, college prep courses, etc.). By building broad coalitions for racial equity in schools, we will be in a better position to defend and advance the rights of the marginalized and disenfranchised.

We must not take the position that until schools are no longer segregated, or until capitalism ends and poverty is alleviated, change is not possible. We readily acknowledge that schools often reproduce the inequities present in society (Bourdieu & Passeron, 1990; Bowles & Gintis, 1976); however; we also believe a great deal can be done to advance racial equity in schools even now. Over the course of U.S. history, individuals and groups have contested subjugation, resisted structural oppression, and fought to eliminate barriers to educational opportunity (Acuña, 2014; Warren, 2005). In fact, it was Oliver Brown's desire to challenge racial inequity that led to the class action lawsuit filed in federal court against the Topeka Board of Education. In his book *Faded Dreams* (1994), economist Martin Carnoy shows through a macrohistorical analysis of economic trends that the greatest strides in challenging and reducing racial inequality in education have been made during and immediately after periods when social movements were most active and successful in raising demands for change. School desegregation, affirmative action, need-based financial aid (Pell Grants), Head Start, free and reduced-price lunches (and breakfast), and a host of other reforms all came into existence as a byproduct of the Civil Rights Movements (Carnoy, 1994). While some of the advances brought about by these reforms have been reversed (e.g., school desegregation and affirmative action), others are now firmly entrenched and serve as the basis for continued expansion (e.g., from Head Start to universal preschool). We believe it is important for the next generation of activists to recognize that collective action made these changes in policy possible, and without it, reversals are not only possible but likely.

While it is important to recognize how social movements have countered racial inequality, it would be a mistake to conclude that until another large-scale movement emerges, change is impossible. In his book, *Spectacular Things Happen Along the Way* (2018), Brian Schultz, a former teacher in Chicago, describes how a harmless civic activity he undertook to get his students involved in their school and community ended up producing a major political conflict and embarrassment for public officials. When given the opportunity to name conditions in their schools and neighborhoods that they wanted to change, students generated a long list that included broken windows, rodents, lack of ventilation, and old books. They also pushed their teacher to allow them to present their concerns at a meeting of the Chicago School Board, and later at a press conference. Embarrassed by the public airing of the student's concerns, district and City officials promised to address them expeditiously. To their surprise and dismay, the officials soon found that the students would not be appeased by promises and continued to draw attention to the state of their school for a full year until corrective action was taken (Schultz, 2018).

Similarly, in recent years, teacher unions in urban school districts have expanded their demands beyond wage and benefit increases and become more outspoken about the woeful conditions that they and their students have long endured. They have begun raising these issues in labor negotiations, and in cities like Detroit, Chicago, Oakland, and Los Angeles, teachers have engaged in strikes and sickouts to call for lower class sizes, more counselors, social workers, and nurses—to address nonacademic issues that affect their students (Noguera, 2018). As teacher unions have drawn attention to structural and environmental conditions, their support from parents and students has grown.

To be clear, we are not suggesting that activists simply accept the nation's political and legal retreat from the promise of *Brown*. We have over 100 years of evidence that segregated schools are almost always blatantly unequal. However, we also know that the *Brown* decision and efforts to racially integrate our nation's schools will not be sufficient to overcome the resistance of those who oppose racial integration, racial equity, or the destruction of the social and economic barriers created by structural racism. Our contention is that the way forward is through organizing and struggle, and the pursuit of racial justice in education must continue on multiple fronts at the local, state, and national level.

As we commemorate the 70th anniversary of the historic *Brown* decision, we have an opportunity to take stock of where we are on the journey toward racial justice in education, and ask ourselves: Where do we go from here? Like Dr. Martin Luther King Jr., who posed the same question as he was organizing and planning the Poor People's March on Washington just months before his assassination in 1968, we believe that the only way to answer that question and to address the nation's lack of political will in supporting racial equality in education is through collective action. School and district leaders must not be afraid of such engagement. Our communities possess deep knowledge of the needs of those we serve, and by working in partnership to build capacity, we can organize our schools to be community-responsive learning institutions. To do this, new systems and practices must be developed and utilized. Wherever we go from here, we should move forward with a clear understanding that Black students deserve to gain deeper knowledge and appreciation of themselves and their people through schooling, to possess accurate knowledge of history and our current context, and to have both the space for reimagining new futures and real opportunities to pursue them.

REFERENCES

Acuña, R. (2014). *Occupied America: A history of Chicanos* (8th ed.). Pearson.

Ahram, R., Fergus, E., & Noguera, P. A. (2011). Addressing racial/ethnic disproportionality in special education: Case studies of suburban school districts. *Teachers College Record, 113*(19), 2233–2266.

Alliance for Children's Rights. (2020). *Who we serve and why*. https://alliancefor childrensrights.org/who-we-serve
Anderson, J. D. (1988). *The education of Blacks in the South, 1860–1935*. University of North Carolina Press.
Apple, M. W. (2001). Comparing neo-liberal projects and inequality in education. *Comparative Education, 37*(4), 409–423.
Bell, D. A., Jr. (1980). *Brown v. Board of Education* and the interest-convergence dilemma. *Harvard Law Review, 93*(3), 518–533.
Billingham, C. M., & Hunt, M. O. (2016). School racial composition and parental choice: New evidence on the preferences of white parents in the United States. *Sociology of Education, 89*(2), 99–117.
Bonilla-Silva, E. (2018). *Racism without racists: Colorblind racism and the persistence of racial inequality in America* (5th ed.). Rowman & Littlefield.
Boschma, J., & Brownstein, R. (2016, February 28). The concentration of poverty in American schools. *The Atlantic*.
Bourdieu, P., & Passeron, J. C. (1990). *Reproduction in education, society and culture* (Vol. 4). Sage.
Bowles, S., & Gintis, H. (1976). *Schooling in capitalist America: Educational reform and the contradictions of economic life*. Basic Books.
Bryk, A. S., Sebring, P. B., Allensworth, E., Luppescu, S., & Easton, J. Q. (2010). *Organizing schools for improvement: Lessons from Chicago*. University of Chicago Press.
Carnoy, M. (1994). *Faded dreams: The politics and economics of race in America*. Cambridge University Press.
Carver-Thomas, D., & Darling-Hammond, L. (2019). The trouble with teacher turnover: How teacher attrition affects students and schools. *Education Policy Analysis Archives, 27*(36).
Chetty, R., Grusky, D., Hell, M., Hendren, N., Manduca, R., & Narang, J. (2017). The fading American dream: Trends in absolute income mobility since 1940. *Science, 356*(6336), 398–406.
Children's Defense Fund. (2017). *The state of America's children*.
Crenshaw, K. W. (2006). Framing affirmative action. *Michigan Law Review First Impressions, 105*, 123–135.
Darling-Hammond, L. (2007). Race, inequality and educational accountability: The irony of 'No Child Left Behind.' *Race Ethnicity and Education, 10*(3), 245–260.
Denton, N. A. (1996). The persistence of segregation: Links between residential segregation and school segregation. *Minnesota Law Review, 80*, 795–824.
Du Bois, W. E. B. (1935). Does the Negro need separate schools? *Journal of Negro Education, 4*(3), 328–335.
Dudziak, M. L. (1988). Desegregation as a cold war imperative. *Stanford Law Review, 41*(1), 61–120.
Duncan, G. J., & Murnane, R. J. (Eds.). (2011). *Whither opportunity? Rising inequality, schools, and children's life chances*. Russell Sage Foundation.
EdBuild. (2019). *Fractured: The breakdown of America's school districts: 2019 update*. https://edbuild.org/content/fractured/fractured-full-report.pdf
Ed Data (n.d.) *County summary: Los Angeles County*. Education Data Partnership. http://www.ed-data.org/county/Los-Angeles

Edwards, E. J., & Noguera, P. A. (2022). Seeing our most vulnerable homeless students: The impact of systemic racism on the education of Black homeless youth in the United States. In H. Mahmoudi & R. Ray (Eds.), *Systemic racism in America: Sociological theory, education inequality, and social change* (pp. 112–138). Taylor & Francis.

Frey, W. (2020, July 1). *The nation is diversifying even faster than predicted, according to new census data*. Brookings Institution. https://www.brookings.edu/articles/new-census-data-shows-the-nation-is-diversifying-even-faster-than-predicted

Gamoran, A., & An, B. (2016). Effects of school segregation and school resources in a changing policy context. *Educational Evaluation and Policy Analysis, 38*(1), 43–64.

George, J., & Darling-Hammond, L. (2019). *The federal role and school integration*. Learning Policy Institute.

Givens, J. R. (2021). *Fugitive pedagogy: Carter G. Woodson and the art of Black teaching*. Harvard University Press.

Glaude, E. S., Jr. (2017). *Democracy in Black: How race still enslaves the American soul*. Crown.

Grant-Thomas, A., & Orfield, G. (Eds.). (2009). *Twenty-first century color lines*. Temple University Press.

Hacker, A. (2010). *Two nations: Black and White, separate, hostile, unequal*. Simon & Schuster.

Housing Matters. (2023, June 7). *School segregation is prevalent in the suburbs, not just between cities and suburbs*. https://housingmatters.urban.org/research-summary/school-segregation-prevalent-suburbs-not-just-between-cities-and-suburbs

Johnson, R. C. (2011). *Long-run impacts of school desegregation & school quality on adult attainments* (NBER Working Paper No. 16664). National Bureau of Economic Research. https://www.nber.org/papers/w16664

Johnson, R. C. (2019). *Children of the dream: Why school integration works*. Basic Books.

Jung, M., Costa Vargas, J. H., & Bonilla-Silva, E. (Eds.). (2011). *State of White supremacy: Racism, governance and the United States*. Stanford University Press.

Kendi, I., & Reynolds, J. (2020). *Stamped from the beginning: Racism, antiracism and you*. Little, Brown and Company.

King, J. E. (Ed.). (2006). *Black education: A transformative research and action agenda for the new century*. Routledge.

King, M. L. K., Jr. (1967). *Where do we go from here: Chaos or community?* Harper & Row.

Lipman, P. (2017). Economic crisis, accountability, and the state's coercive assault on public education in the USA. In B. Lingard, G. Rezai-Rashti, & W. Martino (Eds.), *Testing regimes, accountabilities and education policy* (pp. 29–45). Routledge.

Los Angeles Almanac. (2023). *Homelessness in Los Angeles County 2023*. http://www.laalmanac.com/social/so14.php

Love, B. L. (2019). *We want to do more than survive: Abolitionist teaching and the pursuit of educational freedom*. Beacon Press.

McRae, E. G. (2018). *Mothers of massive resistance: White women and the politics of White supremacy*. Oxford University Press.

Milner, H. R. (2021). *Start where you are, but don't stay there: Understanding diversity, opportunity gaps, and teaching in today's classrooms*. Harvard Education Press.

Mintrop, H. (2013). *Schools on probation: How accountability works (and doesn't)*. Teachers College Press.

Noguera, P. A. (2003). *City schools and the American dream: Reclaiming the promise of public education*. Teachers College Press.

Noguera, P. A. (2018). In pursuit of our common humanity: The role of education in overcoming the empathy gap and the crisis of connection. In Way N., Ali A., Gilligan C., & Noguera P. A. (Eds.), *The crisis of connection: Roots, consequences, and solutions*. New York University Press.

Noguera, P. A., & Alicea, J. (2020). Structural racism and the urban geography of education. *Phi Delta Kappan, 102*(3).

Noguera, P. A., & Syeed, E. (2020). *City schools and the American dream 2: Still pursuing the dream*. Teachers College Press.

Noguera, P. A., & Wells, L. (2011). The politics of school reform: A broader and bolder approach for Newark. *Berkeley Review of Education, 2*(1), 5–25.

Noguera, P. A., & Wing, J. Y. (Eds.). (2008). *Unfinished business: Closing the racial achievement gap in our schools*. John Wiley & Sons.

Noguera, P. A., Bishop, J., Howard, T., & Johnson, S. (2019). *Beyond the schoolhouse: Policy report*. Center for the Transformation of Schools, University of California–Los Angeles. https://transformschools.ucla.edu/wp-content/uploads/2019/10/beyond-the-schoolhouse.pdf

Orfield, G., & Ee, J. (2014). *Segregating California's future: Inequality and its alternative 60 years after* Brown v. Board of Education. Civil Rights Project / Proyecto Derechos Civiles. https://civilrightsproject.ucla.edu/research/k-12-education/integration-and-diversity/segregating-california2019s-future-inequality-and-its-alternative-60-years-after-brown-v.-board-of-education/orfield-ee-segregating-california-future-brown-at.pdf

Orfield, G., & Frankenburg, E. (2014). Brown *at 60: Great progress, a long retreat and an uncertain future*. The Civil Rights Project / Proyectos Derechos Civile. https://civilrightsproject.ucla.edu/research/k-12-education/integration-and-diversity/brown-at-60-great-progress-a-long-retreat-and-an-uncertain-future

Orfield, G., & Lee, C. (2004). Brown *at 50: King's Dream or* Plessy's *Nightmare?* Civil Rights Project.

Pollock, M., Rogers, J., Kwako, A., Matschiner, A., Kendall, R., Bingener, C., Reece, E., Kennedy, B., & Howard, J. (2022). *The conflict campaign: Exploring local experiences of the campaign to ban "Critical Race Theory" in public K–12 education in the U.S., 2020–2021*. UCLA Institute for Democracy, Education, and Access.

Porter, H. (2022). *School segregation in U.S. metro areas* [Report]. The Century Foundation. https://tcf.org/content/report/school-segregation-in-u-s-metro-areas/

Reardon, S. F. (2016). School segregation and racial academic achievement gaps. *RSF: The Russell Sage Foundation Journal of the Social Sciences, 2*(5), 34–57.

Robinson, C. J. (2000). *Black Marxism: The making of the Black radical tradition*. University of North Carolina Press. Original work published in 1983.

Rothstein, R. (2017). *The color of law: A forgotten history of how our government segregated America*. Liveright Publishing.

Schultz, B. D. (2018). *Spectacular things happen along the way: Lessons from an urban classroom*. Teachers College Press.

Siddle Walker, V. (2000). *Their highest potential: An African American school community in the segregated south*. University of North Carolina Press.

Simon, N., & Johnson, S. M. (2015). Teacher turnover in high-poverty schools: What we know and can do. *Teachers College Record, 117*(3), 1–36.

Stiglitz, J. E. (2012). *The price of inequality: How today's divided society endangers our future*. W. W. Norton & Company.

Students for Fair Admissions Inc. v. President and Fellows of Harvard College, 600 U.S. 181 (2023). https://www.supremecourt.gov/opinions/22pdf/20-1199_hgdj.pdf

Swanson, S. (2022). *Student Achievement Disparities in California*. California Policy Center.

U.S. Commission on Civil Rights. (2018, January). *Public education funding inequity in an era of increasing concentration of poverty and re-segregation* [Briefing report]. https://www.usccr.gov/pubs/2018/2018-01-10-Education-Inequity.pdf

Wang, Y. N. (2019). *How racial stereotypes in popular media affect people—and what Hollywood can do to become more inclusive*. In Race and Ethnicity, Media and Public Opinion, June 4th. Scholars Strategy Network.

Warren, M. (2005). Communities and schools: A new view of urban education reform. *Harvard Educational Review, 75*(2), 133–173.

Wilkerson, I. (2020). *Caste: The origins of our discontents*. Random House.

Williams, H. A. (2009). *Self-taught: African American education in slavery and freedom*. University of North Carolina Press.

Wise, T. (1998). Is sisterhood conditional? White women and the rollback of affirmative action. *NWSA Journal, 10*(23), 1–26.

CHAPTER 4

Reclaiming the Promise of *Brown*
The Integration of Desegregation and School Funding Reform

Rucker C. Johnson and Ary Amerikaner

Brown v. Board of Education propelled the Civil Rights Movement. The legacy of *Brown* is a symbol of America's commitment to racial integration, as the ruling struck down state-sponsored racial segregation and Jim Crow's state-enforced superstructure of racial hierarchy. Applying overtly to the nation's schoolchildren, symbolically *Brown* applied to all aspects of the entrenched system of racial hierarchy and was a catalyst that helped dismantle state-sanctioned racial apartheid in the United States more broadly. The vestiges of structural racism, branch by branch, would not go untouched—this was the promise and original meaning of *Brown*. Symbolically, yes, undeniably so—but substantively, the story is far more complicated, the journey a winding road with mountainous terrain, not a smooth straightforward path. And now we are at a crossroads—or destined for dead ends if new approaches are not embraced.

While the racial/ethnic and socioeconomic diversity of America's schoolchildren have never been greater, entrenched resegregation of American public schools has returned segregation to the levels that prevailed in the early 1970s, as support for integration efforts has waned substantially over the past 3 decades. This is no accident; it is, rather, the direct result of policy actions in education and policy inaction in housing. In many ways, the country has abandoned the ambition of integrated schools, and settled for a different and more politically comfortable vision. The prevailing view today amongst equity advocates is that education reform efforts should be directed solely at improving the quality of school resources that minority students receive, regardless of whether those students are in integrated or segregated schools. We have turned our back on the dream of *Brown*. In some places, violent opposition and hotly contested and antagonistic processes of implementation turned the dream into an avoidable nightmare in some communities. This at times led to disillusionment, and for many, the spirit of *Brown* seems to be lost. Where there was success, it was hidden from view, and there was less sharing of exemplars that might have informed best practices. How did we get here? Just as people have intergenerational lineages, so do policies. We must not have policy amnesia, but we must understand the policy lineage of equal education opportunity in this country. What lessons could we import from history that could inform contemporary policy debates about the best ways to address unequal opportunity in children's lives? Where there was success, what were schools doing right?

This chapter explores (1) the enduring relationship between racial segregation and unequal opportunity; (2) the divergent paths of "school integration" and "school resource equity" post *Brown*; (3) the urgent need for a recommitment to advancing integrated and well-resourced public schools; and (4) it begins to outline a path forward, if we are serious about achieving this vision. Ultimately, we argue that it is naïve to envision or assume that school funding reform can produce the same social benefits for children that racially and socioeconomically integrated schools can; nor, however, can greater educational opportunity be guaranteed just by engineering more diversity in schools through student–school assignment policy. The best available research evidence provides support of the pursuit of a holistic set of policy reforms that rethink how we assign students and resources to schools if we are ever to achieve equal educational opportunity that prepares all students to thrive in a multiracial democracy.

Segregation is not only about separation of people, but it is segregation—hoarding, in fact—of opportunity. Segregation is not uniquely Southern, nor a Black problem, but an American problem. Educational opportunity continues to be unequally distributed along race and class lines. *Brown* is rightly celebrated, but widely misunderstood—as though, instantaneously, a light switch was turned on. *Brown* struck down segregation, it did not say how its opposite—integration—should be enacted. *Brown* diagnosed the illness but did not prescribe the cure. It sketched the vision of a racially just society but left the details for someone else to fill in. There was nothing in the ruling about how specific districts were to be compelled into desegregation; nor was there an exact definition of what it would mean to have a desegregated school, or a deadline by which every district in the Jim Crow South would have to show itself in compliance with *Brown I & II* rulings.

Segregation has been protected and preserved in ways that go beyond laws and the trace of law, but embodies practices, resources, and values that live in individuals' hearts and minds. There is a false distinction between *de jure* and *de facto* segregation: Whether it occurs by law or by fact, the consequences are the same. Strategic city planning and residential segregation (via exclusionary housing zoning ordinances) pervasive throughout regions of the country outside the South effectively produce the same outcomes as Jim Crow laws in the South (Rothstein, 2017). This issue is penetrable, tractable—this is not a disease for which there is no known cure. It is a disease for which the deeply ingrained will to preserve racial segregation has not been matched by a sustained commitment to undo it. Integration is like a surgical procedure performed on a school system. It hurts, but it cures. Segregation is like a painkiller. It gives instant relief for families looking to avoid diversity, but has long-term side effects.

Integration is not only about assignments of children to schools by race and parental socioeconomic status (SES), but centrally about equitable school resources: funding, teacher quality and teacher diversity, curricular quality, facilities, guidance counselors, school nurse and health-related support staff. Indeed, advocating for more funding and resources in schools serving high concentrations of students living in poverty and students of color, without tackling the broken borders, boundaries, and policies that create the concentrations of poverty and racial isolation in the first place, will severely undermine forward progress. Achieving resource equity is most often not attainable without an explicit focus on desegregation because:

- segregation increases overall costs. The more socioeconomically segregated[1] schools are, the more money is needed overall to achieve equal educational opportunity, because student populations of concentrated poverty are expensive to serve well;
- segregation increases the need for redistribution. In a system funded largely by local property taxes, greater fragmentation and tiny isolated districts create a substantial need to shift money from one district to another to achieve equitable funding. Redistribution is politically unpopular and state policy made by elected officials doesn't—and won't—adequately address interdistrict tax inequities; and
- segregation ensures funding equity is not resource equity. Funding equity only matters to the extent it actually changes the student experience. Teacher churn, insufficient access to rigorous coursework, and overreliance on exclusionary discipline too often remain in segregated schools, even if funding is allocated more equitably.

It is thus paradoxical and ironic that, despite desegregation and school funding reforms sharing the goal of addressing educational opportunity gaps, school desegregation litigation and school finance litigation have taken two remarkably separate paths. The overlaps in aims, yet the divergence in methods to achieve them, should not be overlooked. Moreover, what is often underappreciated is that the pursuit of desegregation litigation and school finance litigation separately has contributed to the limited effectiveness of each. While the policy and legal process have historically viewed desegregation and school finance reform as policy substitutes (and continue to, but with perilous results), the reality is school resource equity in integrated schools and classrooms are complements and must be pursued in tandem, if either is to maximize effectiveness for student success.

DIVERGENT STRATEGIES POST-*BROWN*

Two U.S. Supreme Court cases in the mid-1970s helped create a gulf between those who worked toward resource equity and those who worked toward school integration. In 1973, the Supreme Court decided a seminal resource equity case: in *San Antonio Independent School District v. Rodriguez*, the Court decided there was no federal constitutional right to a public education. Resource equity advocates responded by shifting to state court litigation, pursuing cases demanding better and more equitable resources for schools serving high concentrations of students of color and from low-income families, based on state constitutional requirements to provide a public education. The following year, in an equally seminal integration case, the Court ruled, in *Milliken v. Bradley* (1974), that federal courts could not impose multidistrict, regional desegregation plans in the absence of any evidence that individual districts intentionally committed acts causing racial segregation. Integration advocates responded largely by pursuing federal court litigation and remedies focused on within-district integration. There have been a few meaningful state court efforts to pursue school integration, including *Sheff v. O'Neill* in Connecticut, *Latino Action Network et al. v. State of New Jersey*, *Cruz-Guzman v. State* in Minnesota, and *Paynter v. State* in New York. In the intervening 50 years, integration litigators and advocates have focused largely on federal courts and intradistrict desegregation strategies, while resource equity advocates have focused on state courts and interdistrict funding inequities.

The Court in *Milliken v. Bradley* ruled in 1974 that integration efforts could not cross district lines unless both districts were found to have discrimination policies on the books, planting early incentives for the secession movement, which reinforced and accelerated White and middle-class flight and the urban–suburban pattern of racial segregation and geography of unequal opportunity evident in most metropolitan areas today (Baum-Snow & Lutz, 2011). Consequences of the *Milliken* decision make it among the most important of desegregation court rulings outside of the original *Brown I and II*. Addressing the problem of racially and socioeconomically segregated districts does not have the same set of functional policy tools as the problem of segregated schools (within districts)—without housing policy reforms that support integrated, mixed-income housing developments.

These siloed strategies are created by more than Supreme Court jurisprudence and litigation. For example, data availability has reinforced the division between researchers focused on school funding and those focused on integration. Student race and family income information is widely available at the school level, meaning that researchers can study and model levels of integration/segregation between schools within districts fairly easily, and they do. But until recently, there was no widespread data on per-pupil spending at the school level; the only way to assess funding inequities at scale was to analyze interdistrict spending patterns, which reinforced the idea that school funding work is about district lines, while integration was about school assignment boundaries within districts. This kept the two fields working in often parallel paths without building relationships, connections, and knowledge about the ways that these two issues are intertwined and so deeply impact one another.

For those reasons and more, today's research, policy, legal, and advocacy landscape is strikingly siloed. There are a relatively small number of "school integration" organizations, researchers, and advocates that specifically dedicate time and attention to school funding formulas. A vast number of organizations, researchers, advocates, and networks of changemakers are dedicated to educational equity more broadly. While they talk about all types of resource equity—school funding, access to excellent educators, access to advanced coursework, school discipline inequities, social and emotional learning, STEM, arts, and more—they have been notably silent about the role school segregation and integration play in hindering or advancing the work.

Despite these siloed approaches, school finance and school desegregation litigation have a deeply interwoven history in some respects. The landmark *Green* decision in 1968 (*Green v. County School Board of New Kent County*, in Virginia) sketched a blueprint for desegregation plans. The Court created six "Green factors"—"students, faculty, staff, transportation, extracurricular activities and facilities"—and established the prototype that would define, across the country, district compliance with desegregation mandates, explicitly centering the importance of access to resources as a core reason to prioritize school integration. The judicial landmarks of the school desegregation cases provided part of the basis for the movement toward school finance reform and marked debates about the constitutionality of local finance systems that rely disproportionately on local property taxes to fund K–12 schools, creating inequality in school resources.

School desegregation aims to accomplish the goal of equal educational opportunity by redistributing schoolchildren; school finance reforms, by redistributing resources; and expansions of pre-K, by redistributing the timing of school investments back to the earliest years of cognitive development. They each have positive independent effects, but it is the synergies between them wherein the power to transform children's life chances lies. While desegregation focuses on race, pre-K–12 school funding reforms target poverty and resources. To undo the harms of segregation, one emphasizes the color of peers while the other the color of money; one centers on the power of diversity, the other(s) on the power of resources. Some advocates viewed the pursuit of integration as an end in and of itself, while others sought integration as a necessary means to the end: to realize the promise of equal opportunity.

While the overlap of the goals of these policies is clear, the overlap in the timing of implementation of them is less so, where the implementation timing differs considerably and depends on the specific district. But rarely have these three strategies been pursued in concert for extended periods of time. Rather, in most places and times, these policies have been advanced one at a time, unevenly and inconsistently, with each policy often framed initially as a panacea. The substantial variation in their timing and implementation across districts provides a rare testing ground for the first-generation suite of equal education opportunity policy initiatives. There is a difference between a collection of good, but separate, policies as we now have in some places, and a collaboration of interconnected policies, the ultimate goal. The separation of school finance litigation and school desegregation litigation mirrors the separation of poverty/SES and race in our diagnosis and formulation of the problem, and therefore the design of the policy prescription; it also mirrors the siloing of housing policy from education policy where residential segregation is now taken as immutable. Extant efforts at solving our educational woes detach health from education, early education from K–12 schooling, and so on. Current policy designs are as divided as our segregated classrooms—and must be combatted just as vigorously. This paper shifts the paradigm from a singular approach chasing after illusory silver bullets to an integrated solution that creates an aligned and coherent strategy for our children's long-term future.

The principle underlying the NAACP's desegregation strategy was that "green follows white": Money for well-resourced schools follows the White students. On the other hand, school finance litigation and reform are most often presented as if they have little to do with race and are all about poverty versus affluence in the struggle for school resources. Battles over school funding inequities have been waged in over 40 state supreme courts and over 40 state legislatures. These debates appear colorblind, focused solely on differing perspectives on the need for redistribution of resources, the efficacy of increased expenditures, and retaining local control over education, with race not explicitly mentioned, not centered, so far in the background it requires binoculars to view. But this is far from being the case. Race is always an undercurrent in these legislative and judicial cases, and while less visible to the naked eye, race often sets the tone for, and shapes the perceptions of, the nature of the problem and what policy action (if any) should be done. The way we view and define a problem ultimately determines how we try to solve it. Focusing on the right problem, fighting the right battle, requires both an awareness of the true costs of racial and economic isolation on the geography of opportunity, and needs the ammunition of new evidence on the costs of providing quality schools for children who live with the multidimensional disadvantages of concentrated poverty. Race is not a distraction, but a vitally important contextual factor. Colorblind analyses and "poverty-blind" analyses (i.e., analyses that do not carefully consider the intersectional relationship between poverty and race and their influence on the dynamics of race relations and policy adoption) can be both detrimental and, at times, dangerous, blurring a clear focus on the problem, and can undermine policy design and effectiveness.

Colorblindness in the natural world is a hereditary health condition that causes the inability to distinguish certain colors. My son, Rucker Jr., suffers from colorblindness, as did his grandfather; but we did not discover his ailment until his eyesight was formally checked by a physician. Research has the capacity to perform this diagnostic function for education policymakers and practitioners to illuminate root causes and consequences of policy reforms so that we do not become blinded by the (racial) politics of an issue. Without credible data and evidence, researchers would just be another set of people with an opinion. Seeing this, we assembled fresh, rigorous empirical evidence on what actually works that doesn't depend solely on hunches, good intentions, ideology, or the politics of reform. In this case, the inherited problem was state-sponsored (residential and educational) segregation; so it seems odd that race-conscious remedies would not be deemed requisite to addressing the enduring legacy of segregation—indeed, seeing race allows one to identify structural racism and perceive discrimination. Research, policy, and practitioner communities are all guilty of this tendency to obscure the intersectionality of race and class issues. The same can be said for the evolution of the academic research literature on the topic, in that studies of school funding reform rarely give explicit attention to issues of race, and especially not in framing the impacts analyzed; it is assumed to be mostly an issue of poverty/SES, where it is presumed that inclusion of simple controls for race/ethnicity are sufficient. In an analogous way, earlier literature on school desegregation was largely silent on the issue of socioeconomic integration. This separation gives rise to significant blind spots—in our policy designs, research designs, implementation designs—where research intersects with policy and practice.

After the Supreme Court held, in *San Antonio Independent School District v. Rodriguez* in 1973, that school funding inequities did not violate the U.S. Constitution, litigants directed their attention to state courts and raised claims under both equal protection and education provisions in state constitutions. State court interpretations of what this vague state constitutional language requires have differed substantially. Thus, school finance reform has traditionally been a state-by-state effort. Today about 75% of per-pupil spending disparities are between states (Evans et al., 2019). Inequality in school spending has risen since 2000 (after 3 decades of narrowing due to state school finance reforms), but rose especially sharply following the Great Recession, which resulted in large education funding cuts

(Evans et al., 2019). The recessionary drop in spending contributed to the end of decades-long national growth in test scores and college-going, and led to significant increases in the academic achievement gap and reduced college attendance rates (Jackson et al., 2021).

Both school finance reform and school desegregation are racially divisive issues—even when all groups stand to benefit from reforming the system. One can attempt to turn a blind eye to the dynamics of race relations when analyzing impacts of school finance litigation, but research from public opinion scholars has consistently shown that the level of support for school funding reform among Whites depends heavily upon racial attitudes (Reed, 1998; Tedin, 1994). Further, a meta-analysis of the history and success rate of predominantly minority districts in school finance litigation cases in the United States over the past 4 decades shows that the racial composition of the district(s) appears to play an influential role in determining its success or failure in school finance litigation and legislative reform. While there are a host of factors unrelated to race that affect the success of school finance litigation and the speed with which legislative remedies are implemented (e.g., antitax sentiment within the state, general urban/suburban/rural power struggles, and the state's economy all play a role), legislative responses to court decisions have differed markedly when predominantly minority or predominantly White districts have been lead plaintiff in a case. The record to date strongly suggests that, apart from desegregation funding imposed in federal court rulings (which has largely been eliminated with substantial releases from court supervision in recent decades), predominantly minority districts have fared less well in the political process in terms of securing more progressive state funding formulas and increases in state educational funds. While this evidence is suggestive, and not definitive causal evidence, it nonetheless must be considered, as public opinion about the value of (popular support for or opposition to) school finance reform is often colored through racialized lenses (Reed, 1998; Ryan, 1999a; Tedin, 1994). Anecdotally, to improve the chances of winning, plaintiffs' attorneys intentionally structured their cases to avoid racial issues (Ryan, 1999b).

INTENTIONALLY PURSUING AN INTEGRATED APPROACH

School desegregation, school funding reform, and pre-K, when implemented separately, lead to dead ends; but when integrated they make a path that, while a road unpaved and less traveled, is one that leads to the "promised land"—or at least a more promising land of opportunity—a land characterized by equal educational opportunities and racial tolerance and marked reductions of racial prejudice and bias. If this looks like a fairy tale, it is only because we have abandoned the commitment to address segregation. Neither school finance reform nor school desegregation can achieve equal educational opportunity when pursued separately and in isolation; the research has revealed the limits of school desegregation without school resource equity, and the limits of school funding reform in high-poverty and racially isolated schools. We are at a crossroads where the dead-end paths of school finance and school desegregation must come together in a new path so that the principles embodied in *Brown* can be realized today for contemporary cohorts. However, insufficient research attention has been paid to the relationship between school finance and desegregation and to the roles that race plays in school finance reform and that concentrated poverty plays in school integration efforts. Pursuing school integration and school finance reforms along separate, isolated paths has contributed to the joint policy failures reflected in the present-day realities that educational opportunity in most metropolitan areas remains deeply segregated and unequal. Our research findings regarding desegregation have revealed significant insights about school finance reform, and our analyses of the efficacy of school funding reform have revealed limits in achieving school resource equity amid persistently high rates of school segregation and concentrated poverty (Johnson, 2019).

This chapter focuses attention on the enduring relationship between racial segregation and unequal educational opportunity, and on the urgent need for policy prescriptions and revitalization of the ones that have worked in the past to create school resource equity in integrated classroom environments. It is vital that these efforts begin in the earliest years and are sustained throughout high school. This chapter lays out the evidence-based argument that the integration of race and class, housing and education policy, school resource equity in diverse schools and classrooms is the future (and was more of the focus in the early era following *Brown I* and *II*, before we lost our way). Restoring and reclaiming the promise and original meaning of *Brown* and extracting lessons from past policy successes and failures is critical for the future of school integration, and to change dead ends into hopeful new paths.

Litigation was a key agitator of change, but not necessarily the anchor of change. Anchors of change for education systems often occur at district and school levels, supported by state and federal equity policy. All systems' change begins with grassroots efforts mobilized on the ground, and this was true in each of the cases of school desegregation, school finance reform, and pre-K expansions. These battles were not only waged and vigorously fought in the courts, often embroiled in lengthy legal battles, but also swayed in the court of public opinion; demarcated along the color spectrum, class continuum, and regions of the country, and cut along generational lines, with younger generations having potential for development of more progressive racial attitudes, perhaps stemming from early formative experiences in integrated schools. Reformers embraced the perspective that "the belief can come after the mandate."

Our argument is not predicated on the false (and racist) notion that poor and minority children can't learn in schools without White and non-poor children. Such a belief itself has a racist underpinning, and it is woefully incomplete to characterize a school's quality solely by the racial composition of its students. Instead, we question what makes a segregated school system inherently unequal. It is in part the impacts of segregation on both school resources and school practices.

Beyond academic outcomes, it is important to consider potential impacts of integration on racial attitudes. The "Contact Hypothesis" posits that under appropriate conditions, interpersonal peer contact (particularly in formative years of development), can reduce prejudice, increase racial tolerance, and influence an individual's values (Boisjoly et al., 2006; Dobbie & Fryer, 2015; Pettigrew & Tropp, 2006). Ethnographic evidence highlights that awakenings occur from exposure to diverse school environments; prejudice and stereotypes are less likely to be enabled to live and grow. We test this contact hypothesis empirically. "Diversity is the art of thinking individually together," as Malcolm Forbes aptly described. It is difficult to become what you never see; therein lies the impact of role models and diversity of both teachers and students in schools.

As first documented in nationally representative survey data from the National Opinion Research Center, and summarized in *Learning for Justice* (Orfield, 2004), in 1940, 30% of Americans—40% of Northerners and 2% of Southerners—believed that Whites and Blacks should attend the same schools. By 1956, 49% of Americans—61% of Northerners and 15% of Southerners—believed that Whites and Blacks should attend the same schools. By 1963, on the eve of the federal passage of Civil Rights Act, 62% of Americans—73% of Northerners and 31% of Southerners—believed Blacks and Whites should attend the same schools (Schwartz, 1967). The pendulum was beginning to swing in a new direction; whether it pointed to a brighter future for children is the verdict that was still outstanding.

Almost no integration occurred during the first 10 years after *Brown*, which highlights where leaving it to "local control" got us despite the racially dual system being declared illegal—in fact, 99% of Black students still attended all-Black schools in the South in 1963. (See Figure 4.1.) Racial apartheid in access to educational opportunity and health care characterized much of the Jim Crow South. Developments in all three branches of government—judicial, executive, and legislative—were influential for both school and hospital integration.[2] This changed dramatically after 1964 due to federal intervention and required all three branches: from Congress, passage of the 1964 Civil Rights Act and 1965 Elementary and Secondary Education Act; enforcement by courts; actions by the Departments of Justice, and of Health, Education, and Welfare (HEW). Local communities would not have desegregated without the application of federal pressure and, in most cases, under court order. The Civil Rights Act of 1964 put teeth in enforcement

Figure 4.1. School Segregation

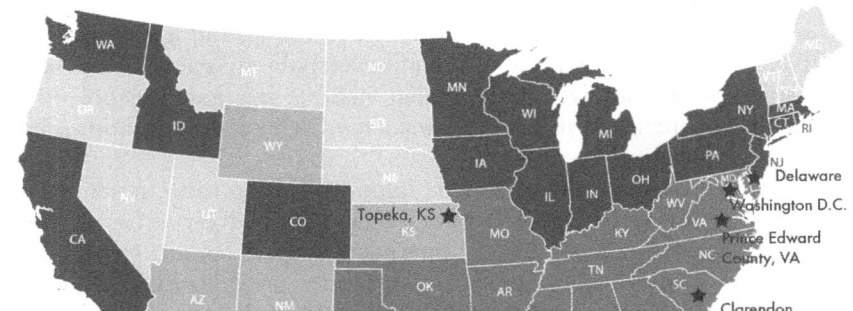

and prohibited discrimination in public schools and hospitals receiving federal financial assistance. This prohibition became potent with the passage of the Elementary and Secondary Education Act in 1965, which dramatically raised the amount of federal aid to education from a few million dollars to more than $1 billion a year. For the first time, the threat of withholding federal funds became a powerful inducement for school districts to comply with integration mandates. As the prominent lawyer Archibald Cox put it, the Civil Rights Act of 1964 made *Brown* "more firmly law" (Liu, 2006).

The fight against integration by no means ended. Instead, in many ways it adopted the same tactics as the Civil Rights Movement: mass protest, legal activism, and voter registration. A motivated and enlightened citizenry ultimately matters as much if not more than the decisions of the Supreme Court. As we witnessed with the Black Lives Matter grassroots movement, change can be catalyzed by the mobilization of a multiracial coalition of young people. The courts' decisions alone have not been sufficient, and at times have been oppositional to these goals. Congress exercised its power to enforce civil rights and advance racial justice and equality of opportunity, as the work of integration was achieved through legislative policy reforms and on-the-ground local policy implementation that (at its best) embraced the principles and spirit of the law, not just the cosmetic appearance. State and federal legislative bodies established guidelines and incentives for school districts to adopt integration plans that met educational quality standards and constitutional standards. These are some of the efforts that began in earnest but have since passed away.

One of the most enduring myths of school desegregation is that we tried it for a long time. But, in fact, significant efforts to integrate schools only occurred for about a 15-year window. We reached peak integration levels in 1988, and in every year since have regressed, ending up back at levels of segregation that prevailed before busing even began. With an attention to the integration efforts launched in that historical period, we next summarize research evidence on the long-run impacts of court-ordered school desegregation.[3]

Overview of Methodological and Empirical Approach. Because every child has unique abilities and faces a particular set of childhood conditions influenced by a complex set of parental, neighborhood, and school factors, it is impossible to say for certain how the quality of schools affected a child's subsequent life trajectory by simply looking at the correlation between school characteristics and student outcomes. Instead, much like the process of clinical trials designed to test new medications, it is necessary to examine a large number of children and school systems, followed over time, to gauge the impact of school quality.

Since the 1950s, when the first clinical trials of new drugs and other medical therapies were conducted, many researchers have emphasized randomized controlled trials (RCTs) as the preferred way to evaluate not only health interventions but also policy reforms in schools and elsewhere. In clinical drug trials (e.g., for hypertension or heart disease), doctors randomly assign participants to treatment and control groups, giving some the medication and others a placebo. Random assignment ensures that those receiving the medication and those receiving the placebo are statistically identical and, therefore, a comparison of their outcomes provides a clean test of the medicine's efficacy. These randomized experimental designs (and those that mimic them) are generally considered the gold standard in research designed to uncover the causal impacts of a policy reform or intervention.

As it turns out, the desegregation history and education policy innovation in the real world provides a similar kind of random assignment and natural experiments for the study of equal education opportunity policies in the United States. In particular, in the first study, we use the quasi-random timing of court-ordered school desegregation during the late 1950s through mid-1980s. We examine cohorts born between 1945 and 1970 who straddle the transformation from segregation to desegregation and were differentially exposed to integrated schools depending on place and year of birth. This includes a nationally representative sample of more than 10,000 Black and White children who have been followed from birth to adulthood over nearly 5 decades (1968–2015), all from districts that at some point underwent court-ordered school desegregation (not necessarily during their school-age years).

Because it is neither ethical nor practical to randomize children to variable school conditions (as they are not mice or guinea pigs), this subject cannot be studied purely within a formal RCT, but reseach can follow the same logic and be made equivalent to an RCT by using naturally occurring policy changes, for what is referred to as a *natural experiment*. The school policy reforms we examined, induced by (desegregation) court orders and implementation of new programs or funding, were enacted in ways that enabled some children to obtain better educational opportunities while leaving other, similar children in their previous substandard school contexts. This dramatic part of our policy history, which both shaped opportunity and influenced the dynamics of race relations, enabled us to capitalize on the timing of those policy changes to study the effect of school desegregation and resultant school spending changes on student outcomes.

Our central question examined whether integration works or fails (and by what yardstick)—that is, (1) whether it improves outcomes of children of all races, (2) whether it is a zero-sum game that improves the outcomes of some groups while worsening the outcomes of other groups, or (3) whether, indeed, it harms students generally. This is trickier to estimate than it may seem. Simply comparing the earnings and later-life success of people who were exposed to desegregated schools against those who weren't would not be evidence of a causal relationship, since the family backgrounds of children who attended integrated or well-funded schools may differ in important ways from those who didn't, and these differences may in turn affect their income potential. What is really needed is a source of randomization that takes a group of children of different races and assigns some of them into integrated and/or better-funded schools.

Just such a randomization tool was provided in the 1960s, 1970s, and 1980s by the staggered timing of desegregation implementation across districts resulting from the timing of judicial rulings of local federal court orders. This timing was influenced not by changes in family characteristics but instead by idiosyncratic chance that approximates randomness. Because of the high importance of legal precedent, the NAACP pursued the strategy of bringing suits first where and when they had the greatest chances of winning, not necessarily where Blacks would benefit most; thus, the timing was driven largely by factors other than systematic differences in family or neighborhood conditions that may have independently affected children's outcomes.

The Supreme Court ruled in the 1968 *Green* decision that all racial distinctions with regard to differences in access to school resources had to be totally eliminated in order to desegregate a school system—including differences in school spending, teacher quality (e.g., teacher experience and credentials, racial composition of teachers, principal experience and credentials), class size, curricular offerings, condition of school facilities, library resources and sufficiency of classroom textbooks, and other services. This was the new standard upon which the ruling would now define district compliance with desegregation mandates. The Court's insistence in *Green* on immediately destroying segregated schools "root and branch" hastened the pace of change. The percentage of Southern Black students attending integrated schools jumped from 32% in 1968–1969 to 79% in 1970–1971. In a private note to Justice Brennan, Justice Warren writes: "When this opinion is handed down, the traffic light will have changed from Brown to Green. Amen!"

The protracted timing of desegregation court orders therefore created a sharply defined period when integration efforts accelerated and were vigorously pursued, and plans were implemented and enforced, with most initial court orders occurring between 1965 and 1975. This process essentially placed otherwise similar children into a treatment group (those who were exposed to integrated schools) and a control group (those who weren't) by quasi-random timing of desegregation plans mandated by court rulings. By combining the legal data on all judicially mandated desegregation cases with the nationally representative longitudinal data of tens of thousands of children born between 1945 and 1970, and followed into adulthood, we were able to analyze the life trajectories of these two groups of children.

To evaluate the long-run impacts of desegregation, we followed representative birth cohorts over time and compared the adult outcomes of Black and White children from the same district before and after the implementation of court-ordered desegregation plans. Comparisons of children exposed to desegregation with those who were already older than 17–18 at the time of initial court order (and therefore were unexposed to desegregation and confined exclusively to segregated school environments throughout K–12 years) provide credible estimates of the effects of desegregation.

Due to the substantial changes school systems underwent following court orders, children born only a few years apart during this period may have experienced very different school environments. The timeline of school integration (and factors that influenced it) is not only important to accurately characterize the true nature of these efforts historically, but is also instrumental to our empirical approach for determining the causal impacts of desegregation.

Figure 4.2 shows the staggered rollout of desegregation court orders.

There was considerable geographic variation in both the timing and type of desegregation plan implemented across districts. This variation led to differences in the degree of racial school integration and resource equalization (improvement in access to school resources) achieved by initial court orders. At one end of the policy spectrum were desegregating districts in which school spending was raised for minority children to the level White children had always had access; this was achieved by the infusion of state funds to desegregating districts, as occurred in Louisiana (Reber, 2011). Other settings were typified by districts like Los Angeles Unified School District (LAUSD), where the sprawling urban form and segregation pattern

Figure 4.2. School Desegregation Court Order Dates

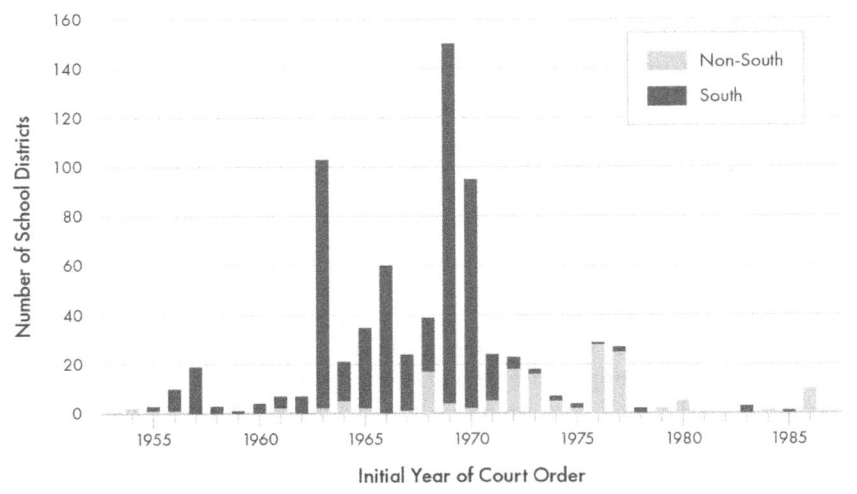

of Los Angeles made busing not a feasible long-term solution. Following a 1978 Los Angeles court-ordered desegregation plan (*Crawford v. Board of Education of Los Angeles*, 17 Cal.3d 280) that required compensatory spending to counteract the harms of school segregation, LAUSD schools in which more than 70% of students were minority were deemed eligible to receive: (1) additional funding to hire more teachers to reduce class sizes; (2) priority staffing program to help fill teacher vacancies; (3) access to pre-K "School Readiness Language Development Program"; (4) Medical-Counseling, Organizing and Recruiting (Med-COR program)—which provides extra support for high school students enrolled in the medical magnet schools; and (5) additional parent–teacher conferences and parent–education classes to better support parental involvement (Choy & Gifford, 1980).

Our research highlights the "*how*" of school reform matters as much as or more than the "*what.*" Beyond *what* policy (i.e., integration) works, we examine *how*, the type of implementation, to determine *why* it worked (or didn't).

LESSONS FROM THE PAST

To inform future integration efforts of what works, why and how, drawn from past experiences, we aspire to retain the positive aspects of integration experiences that we find in the best available research evidence, while also mitigating the negative features of implementation resistance that undermined integration success for students.

Reclaiming the Promise of *Brown*

Desegregation is a policy; *integration* is an outcome. Prior to desegregation, school district spending was disproportionately allocated to the majority-White schools within a district—this school practice was particularly acute in the South where Black teachers were systematically paid lower salaries, Black students confined to overcrowded classrooms, and school facilities in Black schools were older and systematically less well maintained. The strength and persistence of White resistance to integration efforts meant that little desegregation implementation occurred without a court order or before the 1964 Civil Rights Act put teeth in enforcement and the Elementary and Secondary Education Act of 1965 created financial incentives to be in compliance with *Brown* orders or risk losing substantial federal Title I funding (Cascio et al., 2010). Once desegregation was enforced, especially after *Green*, in many districts, resources for Black students were leveled up to match what White students were already receiving (Johnson, 2019; Reber, 2011).

After desegregation plans were enacted, there were not only substantial reductions in racial segregation among both students and teachers, but also sharp increases in per-pupil spending (by an average of 22.5%) and significant reductions in the average class sizes experienced by Black children (as shown in Figures 4.3 and 4.4).

The law alone was not enough to ensure compliance. Desegregation court orders did not necessarily ensure adherence to integration implementation in ways that fulfilled the *Green* criteria so that a school would no longer be racially identifiable, nor did they ensure the experience of being exposed to integrated schools with equitable resources (e.g., teachers,

Figure 4.3. Effect of Court-Ordered School Desegregation on Racial School Segregation

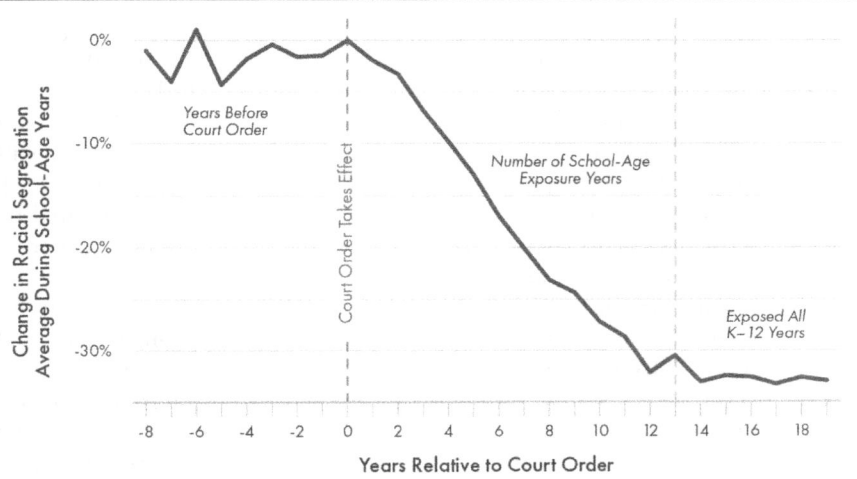

Figure 4.4. Effect of Court-Ordered School Desegregation on School Spreading for Blacks

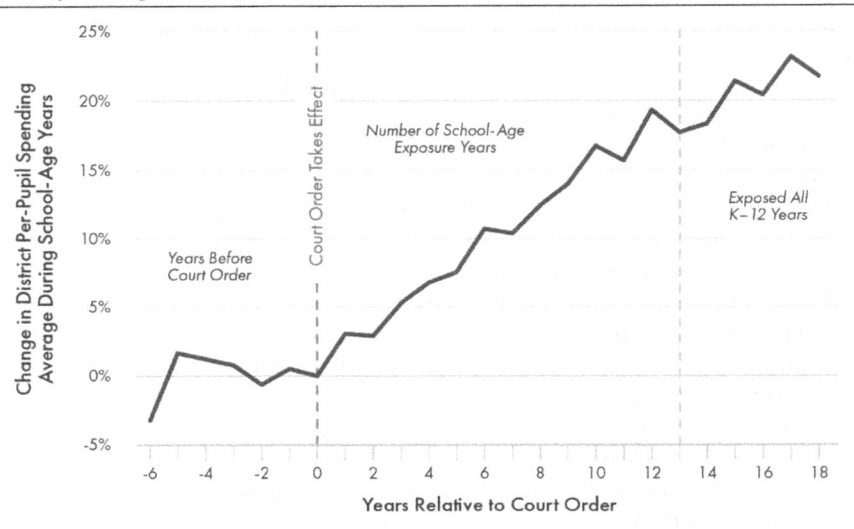

staffing, curricular quality, facilities). When desegregation policy impacts appear unsuccessful, one must be wary not to conflate desegregation implementation failures with ineffectiveness of school integration for student success; thus, impacts of desegregation court orders should be viewed as "intent-to-treat" estimates. Desegregation is the first step. Moving from desegregation to integration means moving from exposure to understanding; it means moving from access to inclusion.

Consider, for example, the unintended harmful effects of desegregation on racial teacher diversity when some racist administrators systematically laid off many Black teachers, as documented by Thompson (2022). The share of Black teachers employed in Deep South schools fell by 31.8% between 1964 and 1972, compared with the likely trajectory of teacher employment in the absence of desegregation. The unjust firing of Black teachers may have had significant deleterious effects on Black students, as highlighted by the long-term positive impacts of racial teacher diversity as demonstrated in the work of Gershenson et al. (2022).

Thus, it is important to bear in mind that the estimated total net effect[4] of desegregation court orders represents a combination of potential impacts of: (1) school resource equity; (2) peer effects; (3) racial resentment/violent resistance/hostility/school climate that was exclusionary (psychosocial impacts that were negative for Black children in many cases); (4) racial diversity of teachers/unjust firing of Black teachers. Likewise, potential heterogeneity in the estimated long-run effects reflects possible differences in reform-induced school conditions along several dimensions. The conditions of desegregation matter—the *how* as much as the *what*.

The Panel Study of Income Dynamics (PSID; psid.org), run by the Institute for Social Research at the University of Michigan, has come to be known as "America's family tree" due to its ability to follow generations of families, including siblings, over time. With more than a half century of data, it enables analyses of the multigenerational effects of education policy. It is the longest-running longitudinal panel data set in the world. The PSID combined with our research design enables the ability to compare the outcomes of otherwise similar children who differed in how many years of integration they experienced.

Using longitudinal data from the PSID, we find that for Black children, the experience of school integration has causal beneficial impacts on long-run socioeconomic attainment outcomes in adulthood, including significant increases in educational attainment (Figure 4.5) and earnings (Figure 4.6); reductions in the annual incidence of poverty (Figure 4.7) and decreased likelihood of ever being incarcerated; and improvements in overall health status and neighborhood quality in adulthood (likely resultant from an increase in SES).

Moreover, we find a dose-response in terms of both duration of school-age years of exposure and the intensity of treatment in which the longer students were treated for the symptoms of a segregated, poorly funded school, the larger the improvements were found to be (Figures 4.5–4.7); likewise, the more ambitious the scope of the integration efforts and

Figure 4.5. Effect of Court-Ordered School Desegregation on Educational Attainment by Race

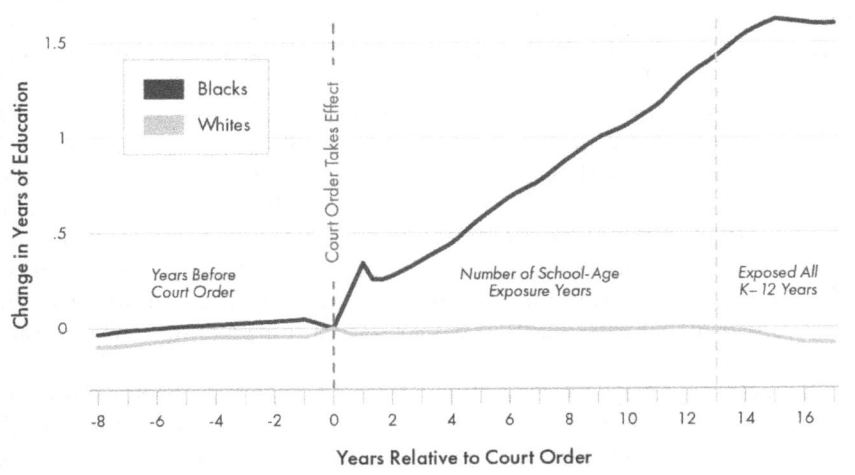

Figure 4.6. Effect of Court-Ordered School Desegregation on Adult Wages by Race, Ages 20–50

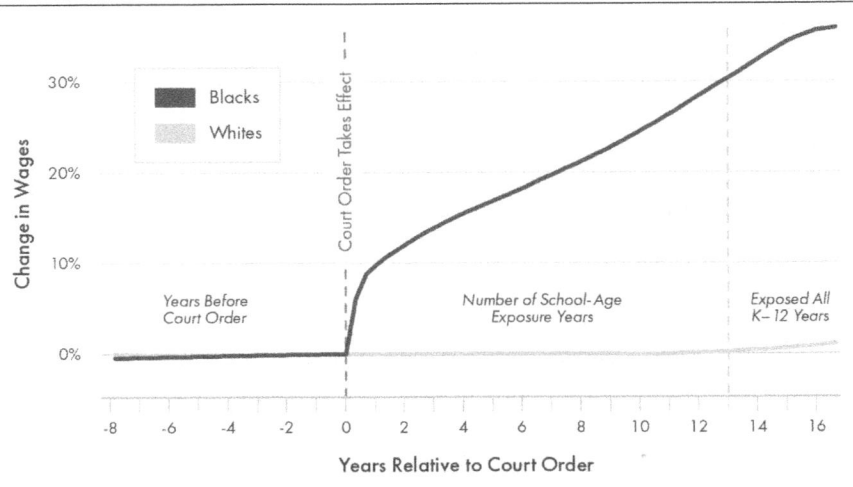

comprehensiveness of desegregation plans were, the larger the gains Blacks experienced. Conversely, we found small, insignificant effects of desegregation for Whites on each of these socioeconomic attainment outcomes. (See Johnson [2019] for fuller details, including multigenerational impacts.)

A more recent study by Garrett Anstreicher et al. (2023) also focuses on the most intensive period in which school desegregation efforts were pursued in the United States, to document long-term impacts of court orders on educational attainment and labor market outcomes of affected cohorts born between 1945 and 1985. The key innovation is their use of big data drawn from restricted-use administrative longitudinal data on labor market outcomes in adulthood, from the 2000 Long-form Census and 2001–2015 American Community Survey, for individuals ages 25–54. Using these data has many advantages, most notably, larger sample sizes that included 187 medium and large districts of more than 15,000 total students, which enables superior statistical power that was not possible in the prior work of Johnson (2011; 2019), Guryan (2004), Reber (2010), and others.[5] This data offers the opportunity to explore heterogeneity in effects of desegregation court orders and to examine their possible mechanisms. Importantly, the authors present estimated school desegregation impacts separately by race and region.

Largely following the research design and methods outlined in Johnson (2011), but analyzed on the larger samples that the Census Bureau's restricted-use data (RDC) enable, Anstreicher et al. (2023) find that for Blacks in the South, exposure to court-ordered desegregation throughout the school-age

Figure 4.7. Effect of Court-Ordered School Desegregation on Annual Incidence of Poverty in Adulthood by Race

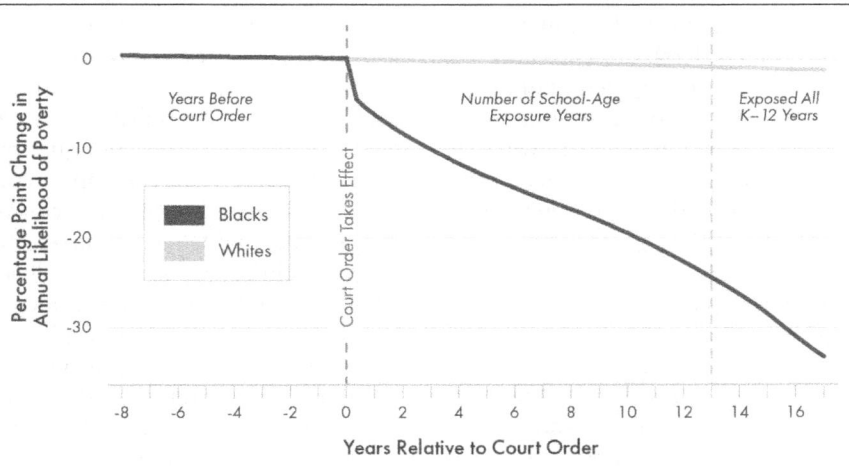

years was estimated to have increased educational attainment by a full year, high school graduation rates by approximately 15 percentage points, employment rates by approximately 10 percentage points, and annual wages by approximately 30%. Furthermore, they find small, insignificant effects among Southern Whites, suggesting that these gains among Black students did not come at the expense of Whites. These patterns and effect sizes are similar and on par with the estimates reported previously by Johnson (2019) (Figures 4.5–4.7).

Furthermore, the authors documented that the estimated desegregation effects were greater in counties with: (1) larger prior racial disparities, (2) larger Black enrollment shares (pre-reform), (3) less residential segregation, (4) fewer potentially competing school districts, and (5) stronger racial segregationist preferences (pre-reform).

In stark contrast, however, they find no significant beneficial effects for Blacks outside of the South. This data, with all its advantages, is not without its own limitations that have bearing on important interpretation issues, particularly estimated differential effects by region. The researchers cannot identify school districts, only the county of birth, and they have no information on schools attended. Countywide systems are far less common outside of the formerly Confederate states; this may explain why no effects were detected outside of the South (e.g., in the typical county, there was an average of 27 districts in the North and only 6 districts in the South).[6] This lack of geographic specificity could lead to mismeasurement of integration exposure in a way that likely dilutes estimated impacts in the North. Identifying the causal mechanism requires finer-grain geographic specificity data other than at the county level.[7] Greater district fragmentation (in response to desegregation court orders) could provide a counter-explanation for the null effects in the North (i.e., may act to mediate/moderate effects of desegregation court orders). For example, Cui (2024) shows in states that passed early legislation to desegregate public schools, Black in-migration had the largest effects on exclusionary zoning policy adoption, and housing policies were designed to exclude Blacks in ways that affected their access to school quality.

Taken together, this evidence further serves to underscore the importance of considering the interconnections between inclusionary housing and education policies and potential positive synergies when combined; and conversely, the consequences of each in isolation wherein exclusionary housing policies can undermine the effectiveness of school desegregation policies. The evidence that desegregation impacts appear stronger in counties with less residential segregation is suggestive of potential synergies between housing policies that promote integration and school assignment policies that aim to do the same. In line with this, results show that court-ordered desegregation had less impact in settings where there was a greater district fragmentation.

Other related corroborating evidence. Moving beyond the Black–White differences related to school desegregation, in a precursor to the *Brown* case, a federal appeals court in 1946 struck down segregated schooling for Mexican American and White students (*Mendez et al. v. Westminster School District of Orange County*, 64 F. Supp. 544 [1946]). The verdict prompted California Governor Earl Warren to repeal a state law calling for segregation of Mexican American, Native American, and Asian American students. Francisca Antman and Kalena Cortes, using the timing of *Mendez*, study the impacts of school desegregation on Mexican American students' adult attainments, and find remarkably similar patterns of large, beneficial effects of school desegregation exposure on success in adulthood for Mexican American cohorts that experienced these policy reforms relative to otherwise similar prior cohorts (Antman & Cortes, 2023).

TAKING STEPS BACKWARD

There has been a major school choice movement over the past 25 years emphasizing individual concerns over the public mission of education, with an apparent willingness to sacrifice the latter. The contemporary language used by some proponents of school choice (and its concomitant, privatization of public education) is eerily similar to the arguments of those who vehemently opposed integrated schools in the 1950s through the 1970s. We hear the same ideas reincarnated in the contemporary voices of the proponents of privatization (vouchers) without regard to the goals of equity, inclusion, and excellence, which, contrary to myth, can go hand in hand. "Local control" of public schools is the same language invoked by defenders of segregation before *Brown*.[8] This perspective is especially important given the current era of unprecedented racial and ethnic diversity among America's children, whose differences too often are not leveraged as assets in our schools, but viewed as deficits and barriers.

Beginning in the early 1990s, courts began ruling that school districts formerly under orders to integrate had reached "unitary" status, meaning their schools were sufficiently desegregated that they no longer needed to follow desegregation plans. In other words, so long as a school district had tried, it did not matter whether it had succeeded, nor did it matter what would be likely to happen if it ceased its efforts.[9]

The 2007 Supreme Court decision in *Parents Involved in Community Schools v. Seattle Dist. No. 1* (551 U.S. 701) ruled that it was unconstitutional for race to be the sole factor in student assignment plans to achieve school diversity. Chief Justice John Roberts wrote the decision's most famous line: "The way to stop discrimination on the basis of race is to stop discriminating on the basis of race." *Parents Involved* eliminated many of the most effective voluntary integration strategies for district leaders. The decision rendered all race-based admissions policies the same, equating racism (segregation) with attempts to end racism (integration). More recently, anti-integration advocates attempted to push even further, asking the Supreme Court to outlaw even the use of race-neutral efforts to promote diversity in schools. The Supreme Court declined to hear the case in 2024, leaving in place the 4th Circuit decision upholding the district's race neutral efforts to promote more diversity in the selective admissions school. (See *Coalition for TJ v. Fairfax County School Board*, U.S. Court of Appeals for the 4th Circuit. No. 22–1280 [2023]).

Chartering a Path to Segregation. North Carolina House Bill 514 was signed into law in June 2018. The bill allowed four wealthy, predominantly White suburbs in Mecklenburg County to create charter districts for their own residents, effectively permitting their secession from the Charlotte-Mecklenburg public school system. Because these charter schools receive government funding, taxpayers throughout the district—including those parents who might prefer integration—are being forced to subsidize these split-offs.

The resegregation of public schools in recent decades has been affected by other local policy decisions as well. Evidence has shown how changes in the political composition of a state's elected local school boards has affected school segregation through differences in the propensity to redraw school boundary zones in ways that promoted either integration or segregation (Macartney & Singelton, 2018). Republican-controlled school boards have been found to be more likely to gerrymander district boundaries to segregate. These patterns have been reinforced by Supreme Court decisions that sap opportunities for integration; state statutes that greenlight subsidized segregation via district lines; policies that allow communities to secede from their own school districts; and, in some cases, charter schools that act as White-flight schools (though it is worth noting that some charter schools are diverse by design; Monarrez, 2023; Monarrez et al., 2022; Monarrez & Schönholzer, 2023).

National evidence from Jang and Reardon (2019) shows that the socioeconomic gradient in academic achievement in reading and math is more than two grade levels on average, when comparing outcomes for students in low-income and affluent districts. However, it is important to not confuse symptoms with root causes. Wherever we see achievement gaps, we can trace them back to educational opportunity gaps that transpired earlier. To address inequities beyond resources, one must also consider school practices. Even in desegregated schools, there are often segregated classrooms, racialized tracking that begins in early elementary school grades and differential placement in college-preparatory curricular coursework (including advanced placement courses; Reardon et al., 2022). Evidence shows that even among high-achieving Black and White 3rd-graders with the same test scores, Black children are one-third less likely to be placed in gifted programs (Card & Giuliano, 2016; Grissom & Redding, 2016). Black and Hispanic students are disproportionately referred to special education and not referred to college-preparatory tracks, and experience differential disciplinary practices (Adukia et al., 2023). In this way, teacher segregation may accelerate student segregation at the classroom level and speed the flow of the school-to-prison pipeline (Bacher-Hichs et al., in press).

Currently, about two-thirds of segregation occurs between districts (not within them), and thus it has become imperative to use tools beyond busing to integrate schools. Housing policy is central, including reforms to counteract real estate steering practices (e.g., Choi et al.'s 2019 audit study "Long Island Divided"). That district lines are invisible does not make them less powerful tools of segregation. Among current school resource disparities, Johnson (2019) notes:

- Nationwide, schools in which the majority of enrollment is comprised of students of color have 15% less per-pupil spending (from state and local sources) than predominantly White, affluent ones, despite greater need due to higher proportions in poverty, with special needs, or who are English language learners;
- Only a third of public high schools with high Black/Latinx enrollment offer calculus, which is a gateway to majoring in STEM fields in college;
- Schools with high levels of Black/Latinx enrollment have almost twice as many first-year teachers as schools with low minority enrollment; in 33 states, minority students are more likely to be taught by inexperienced teachers than experienced ones;

- About 20% of teachers leave the profession within the first 5 years, and even higher rates of teacher turnover are found in concentrated poverty schools (up to 50%), disproportionately negatively affecting minority students.

The most significant school resource disparity, aside from money, is in teacher quality. That's among the most important resources that a school provides its children and a big part of what money buys, as roughly 80% of the school budget of a typical district is spent on teachers (determining both teacher salaries and class size). Concentrated poverty schools notoriously face greater challenges in consistent staffing of schools with high-quality teachers, particularly in math and science, and experience high teacher turnover and higher rates of burnout than better-resourced schools (Jackson, 2009). Minority and poor students thus more often have inexperienced and less effective teachers, and administrators as well. Research shows employees don't leave companies, they leave managers; this is also true of K–12 teachers (Bartanen et al., 2019; Boyd et al., 2011). Effective leadership at the principal and superintendent levels is central to recruitment, development, and retention of high-quality teachers, and evidence shows the diversity of the teaching workforce is an important aspect of that quality.

High-poverty schools are also often located in high crime areas and economically distressed communities. This makes attracting, developing, and retaining the best teachers and school leaders difficult because, all else being equal, teachers and administrators tend to choose schools with greater resources in supportive environments. Reardon et al. (2022) show that racial segregation leads to growing achievement gaps, and it does so in part through differences in school poverty (because racial segregation typically concentrates Black and Hispanic students in concentrated poverty schools that affects access to teacher quality).

School funding policies that make adjustments to per-pupil expenditure levels to capture the actual "buying power" of educational funds within different kinds of districts and account for the higher costs of providing equitable educational opportunities in concentrated poverty schools are important. Weighted student funding formulas incorporate cost and need adjustments to establish greater equity in school financing—e.g., differences in the relative costs of providing educational services that may include differences in costs of living and in the educational needs of students.

California bookends our analysis in that it's the home of the first successful state court–school finance litigation (*Serrano v. Priest*, 5 Cal.3d 584 [1971]), which was far less successful in improving student outcomes than if optimally designed because the funding formula's design features effectively leveled down spending, in connection with Proposition 13, the 1978 California constitutional amendment that strictly limited property taxes. But with the passage of Local Control Funding Formula (LCFF) in 2013,

California significantly increased funding overall and implemented what was among the most progressive school funding formulas in the country, with an $18 billion commitment over 8 years. We evaluated LCFF's impact on student outcomes using student-level data on the full universe of public school students in California from 2004 through 2019. Using quasi-experimental methods (2SLS-IV, difference-in-difference, and regression kink designs) to facilitate causal inference, we find positive and significant effects of LCFF-induced increases in per-pupil spending on academic achievement for every grade (3–8 and 11), every subject (math and reading), and for every school that experienced this new infusion of state funds, which targeted lower-income districts and students (Johnson, 2023). The impacts on student achievement increased with both school-age years of exposure to the greater funding and with the amount of increased funding that occurred due to LCFF. Furthermore, we find the increase in school spending subsequently increased the likelihood of graduating from high school and college readiness; and resulted in a significant narrowing of the average achievement gap by district socioeconomic status (SES) and race (Johnson, 2023).[10] This major progress notwithstanding, California public schools remain highly segregated and significant achievement gaps remain. Our future work aims to examine the extent to which the efficacy of school spending may be even more fruitful in more racially and socioeconomically integrated school environments beginning in the early years.

CHARTING A PATH FORWARD

It is not simply that resegregation portends a loss of opportunity, mobility, and unity (Chetty et al., 2020). It is that integration has the power to transform communities, and society, in ways we have only begun to realize. We must revive the dream, and bring together the people whom redlining, White flight, secession statutes, conservative Supreme Court precedent, gentrification, and other social forces would keep apart. But how? It is not that we are looking in the wrong places for policy solutions; rather we have made the faulty assumption that there is only one place to look. Whether it is desegregation, school finance reform, pre-K, or charter schools, all offer *an* answer, but none is a complete answer to address inequality. For that, we must turn to integrated solutions.

In this section we outline a holistic policy agenda that simultaneously advances early interventions, integration, resource equity, and access to high-quality teachers. This includes: adequately and equitably funding schools, changing district lines, making district lines more porous, moving dollars across district lines, ensuring within-district integration, creating positive student experiences in every school, and cultivating an education ecosystem that values and promotes integration and resource equity broadly. In the paragraphs below we flesh out each. Much of this policy agenda has been cocreated by a Community of Practice comprised of a wide variety of academic researchers, advocates, and litigators. The Community of Practice is convened by Brown's Promise, a new organization hosted by the Southern Education Foundation dedicated to advancing integrated, well-resourced public schools that prepare all students for success (learn more at www.brownspromise.org).

1. Adequately and Equitably Funding Schools

State funding policy should ensure that every district and school has the funding it needs to provide an adequate education, ensuring that all students can attend school in buildings that are safe, healthy, welcoming places, and that they have access to a rigorous, high-quality public education within those walls. The funding should also be equitable, targeting money to districts and schools based on the level of student need, and ensuring that all children have equal opportunity to achieve a common set of outcome goals. Districts with similar levels of need should receive similar levels of funding, and the same is true for schools. Turning away from a scarcity mentality in education will help pave the way for integrated schools and resource equity for schools; if we appropriately resource all schools, many of the policies described below to foster integration and equitable access to resources will be met with far less resistance.

2. Changing School District Lines

Tuttle (2019) provides compelling evidence from a case study of Jefferson County, Kentucky (including Louisville), and analyzes the long-run causal impacts of school desegregation on adult economic outcomes by race. Using conditional random assignment of students to schools, and confidential individual-level longitudinal data from the U.S. Census Bureau, he finds school desegregation had positive long-run effects on adult economic attainments for Black students by giving them access to better schools (e.g., schools with more capital investment, more credentialed teachers, lower drop-out rates, etc.), with negligible effects on the adult economic outcomes of White students from the same cohorts. This example from Louisville's countywide system is a particularly interesting one, in that Louisville was involved in the 1974 *Milliken* case; juxtaposed with Detroit, the system in which Louisville exists stands in stark contrast with Detroit's substantial district fragmentation, which has reinforced persistent segregation patterns for decades.

Changing district lines can allow students the opportunity to exchange ideas and perspectives by learning alongside people from different cultures and backgrounds and can ensure all students' schools have access to a reasonable and relatively even property wealth base from which to generate local revenue. In some places, this can be done by shifting to countywide districts or pursuing other integrative district consolidation. For example, Florida and West Virginia have true countywide districts (without the many exceptions to this general rule that are found in most Southern states).

In Starkville, Mississippi, the state consolidated two small districts to save money and provide a better education for students in an underresourced, racially isolated school district bordering a better resourced, more diverse district. Despite initial resistance, some families have even started to pull their children out of private schools to return to the newly integrated and better resourced public schools (Lewis, 2016). In Morristown, New Jersey, the state consolidated two districts explicitly to address racial segregation and created one of the most racially diverse districts in New Jersey, despite dire predictions of White flight at the time (Trachtenburg et al., 2016; Westhoven, 2022).

In other places, strategic redrawing of district lines to promote integration might not mean shifting to countywide districts or consolidation, and instead might simply mean minor shifts to existing lines. Strategic revision of district lines may enhance district diversity, minimize overall cost (by deconcentrating student poverty), and maintain reasonable student commute times, particularly in some states where existing district lines create hundreds of very tiny districts near one another. Researchers are beginning to use sophisticated tools to illustrate the possibilities. See, for example, Tyler Simko's work (2023) showing that New Jersey district lines essentially require school segregation today, and that the state could reduce segregation by nearly 40% in the median New Jersey county if students could be assigned to schools anywhere in the county, even within short commute distances.

One important part of this policy conversation is "playing defense" to prevent continued fracturing and White flight. This includes adopting or strengthening antisecession laws. Without careful attention to this, efforts to promote integration are likely to be met with backlash and backsliding, as happened in Tennessee after equity and integration leaders pursued an innovative effort to consolidate Memphis Schools into Shelby County School District (Zubrycki, 2013)—which was followed by quick secession of White, wealthy districts (Bauman, 2017). Examples of stronger policies that would have prevented such a response include (EdBuild, 2019): allowing secession only via a constitutional change (see Georgia and Florida) and statutory language requiring strong processes for secession (see California, where a state agency must review and approve after considering the impact on segregation, efficiency, and funding, and Connecticut, Arizona, Texas, and Vermont, which require voters in the "left behind" district to vote to approve any such change).

3. Making District Lines More Porous

Where district lines must remain fixed in the same places as they are today, we can minimize the damage by making it possible for students and dollars to move across them in intentional, equitable ways, by focusing on regional approaches to enrolling students.

This can be done by creating, strengthening, and expanding interdistrict transfer and magnet programs. It is important to note that, done badly or haphazardly, public school choice programs can, and do, exacerbate segregation and educational inequities. However, this approach can succeed with the right design elements built in to ensure equity (George et al., 2023). These must include:

- free transportation;
- lotteries that preference underserved communities—to eliminate selection policies that are biased and often discriminatory;
- siting policies that ensure
  » historically underserved students are not asked to bear disproportionate commute burden, and
  » communities of color and low-income communities/school districts receive resource infusions to create the new magnet programs, and do not disproportionally lose resources to wealthier neighboring districts;
- policies to recruit and retain educators of color;
- cohorting efforts to avoid students being "the only";
- automatic enrollment policies and other detracking supports within schools;
- inclusion in standard statewide accountability and oversight systems;
- promotion of restorative justice practices through teacher professional development on disparate discipline and building a culture of belonging; and
- additional supports for students enrolling in new schools across district lines.

For an example, we can look to Hartford, Connecticut. The greater Hartford area is marred by substantial segregation by race and income, but after a 1996 state court decision in *Sheff v. O'Neill*, the region has become a strong example of policies and practices that allow students to enroll across district lines, through a mix of magnet schools (some run by Hartford City School District and some run by the Capitol Region Education Council [CREC], a separate organization that serves 35 school districts in the region) and an interdistrict transfer program that allows students to enroll in traditional public schools across district lines (Quick, 2016). This is a two-way integration program in which students move both into and out of higher-wealth and lower-wealth districts, instead of only asking students of color to leave their neighborhoods. The magnet schools (with additional resources) located in the city serve primarily the students of color who live in the city (roughly 75%), increasing opportunities for access to well-resourced, integrated schools for students of color in districts where they live. It is the largest such program we are aware of, showing that this can be done at scale. It serves nearly 40,000 kids in interdistrict magnet schools each year (School and State Finance Project, 2023) and another 3,000 or so in an interdistrict open choice program (School and State Finance Project, 2022). Between one-third and one-half of all Hartford's students of color attend one of these schools each year; however, supply has not kept pace with demand (Megan, 2021; Putterman, 2023; Quick, 2016)

Evaluation of the programing in Hartford shows positive results. In addition to increasing integration along both race and income lines, participation provides more positive learning environments, (e.g. fewer teacher and student absences, more advanced math and world languages classes, lower grade retentions, higher peer support for academic achievement, support for college); a stronger sense of safety and belonging for students than reported in city nonmagnets (although weaker than in suburban nonmagnets), increases in student academic achievement outcomes (test proficiency), and an increased sense of cross-cultural/cross-racial friendships and connections for all students (Cobb et al., 2009).

That said, there are challenges. Hartford has created a complicated system that is difficult to understand for policymakers and families alike. Some believe the program is undercutting financial stability for the Hartford City Public School district, though others contest that allegation. It relies on parents and families navigating a complicated system of choices that undoubtedly leave some of the most vulnerable and marginalized students out of accessing the opportunity, and potentially in lower-resourced, and still racially isolated, schools as a result. We cannot ignore these challenges, but also cannot let the perfect be the enemy of the good.

Another example worth mentioning is the "50/50 Schools" in Dallas, Texas. This is a popular district-run program that draws students from outside the district and a wide variety of neighborhoods within the district to create an intentionally diverse student population. In each of these schools, 50% of students are considered economically disadvantaged and 50% are not (Rix, 2022). It relies on race-neutral measures of students' SES that are in line with today's limited Supreme Court guidance on how to promote diversity, and that are more nuanced than free and reduced lunch eligibility status, making it a helpful model that states should consider using in designing new programs.

4. Moving Dollars Across District Lines

By this point, it should not be surprising that in our integrated approach, it is not only students that can flow across current district lines, but also dollars and resources. Roughly 45% of all school funding in America comes from local sources (National Center for Education Statistics, 2023)—meaning it is closely tied to the wealth of the local community in which the district is located. State and federal dollars are often used to attempt to ameliorate the inequities in school funding this creates for students who live in low-wealth neighborhoods, but too often low-wealth communities continue to (1) have fewer dollars to support their school, especially relative to the often greater levels of student need in those communities; (2) have to tax themselves at disproportionately high levels to support their schools; or (3) both. Weakening the link between today's district lines and the ability to fund schools could be game changing for students of color and students in low-income neighborhoods, and might ultimately increase school integration by reducing the gap in perceptions of school quality created by inequities in school funding. State policy changes to advance this goal fall into two primary categories:

- **Redefining what "local" means** by creating revenue pooling across district lines (e.g., countywide pooling of funds or some other "regional," multidistrict version of pooling that does not rely on county lines). For example, in Wyoming, school districts are smaller than counties but have at least some countywide taxation for schools (EdBuild, 2024). In the Omaha Learning Community, a new regional governing body was to oversee a tax-sharing plan to redistribute revenue across 11 school districts located in two counties as well as an interdistrict student integration plan (Holme & Diem, 2015). The effort was created and implemented from 2005 to 2012, and despite the demise of much of the structure, including the revenue-sharing component, the unique legislative intent and process still has potential to inform new efforts (Blomstedt, 2013).
- **Reducing the share of funding from local sources and increasing share from statewide sources.** In Michigan, for example, Proposition A shifted schools from local to state funding, creating a state property tax designated for schools (Office of Revenue and Tax Analysis, 2002). While this is not a perfect system because of reliance on regressive sales and "sin" taxes and because the total amount raised is still probably too little and not equitably distributed, this shift to statewide funding is an important example (Cullen & Loeb, 2004). In Texas, the state shifts local funds raised in property wealthy districts into property poor districts (Swaby, 2019). This, too, is not a silver bullet; because of other issues in the

funding system, the state still has too little spending and inequitable spending, but this effort to shift local property tax funding from wealthier to less wealthy is also an important example. And in Vermont, the state sets tax rates and redistributes money, so it is really a state property tax to fund schools instead of a local one (Kolbe et al, 2020).

5. Ensuring Within-District Integration

States' responsibilities to ensure students have access to well-resourced, integrated public schools do not end where district lines begin. The state is ultimately responsible for the actual education received by each student, including the impact of decisions made by local district and school leaders. To that end, the state should also adopt policies that require, incentivize, and support local and school leaders in adopting and implementing policies that advance integration and resource equity. This might include adopting diversity requirements that, if not met, must be addressed by reworking student assignment policies, for example:

- No school in a district can have more than 10 percentage points more poverty than the districtwide average, but with exceptions for high-performing schools successfully serving historically underserved students well.
- If districts have high segregation and resource inequities, they must redraw boundaries.
- When districts choose to change school assignment policies for any reason (capacity, budget, new programming, etc.), they must conduct a diversity impact analysis and cannot move forward with the plan if it will exacerbate segregation or resource inequities.

Where charters are a substantial part of the public school ecosystem, states should regulate to support integration and equity by requiring (or incentivizing) the use of weighted lotteries to promote integration; requiring the provision of free and reduced-priced meals and transportation; requiring the use of a unified district/charter enrollment system to allow a single process to apply and help ameliorate inequities in access to and navigation of these systems; requiring charter schools to set enrollment targets based on the demographics of the communities served and take steps to reach those targets; allowing charter schools to enroll students from multiple school districts or across a region, without requiring a preference for in-district students; and tying approval of new charters to an analysis of predicted impact on overall school enrollment patterns in the region, including on concentration or deconcentration of poverty and racial segregation/integration (Potter & Nunberg, 2019).

6. Creating Positive Student Experiences in Every School

An integrated school is more than a diverse student body. States and districts must ensure that schools are led by diverse educators; students of color and students from low-income families are not disproportionately taught by novice, uncertified, or out-of-field educators; the curriculum reflects accurate history; the school climate is truly welcoming for all to be their authentic selves; academic tracking does not resegregate students within the walls of the building; and everyone has the opportunity to participate in extracurriculars that build a sense of belonging and community within the school.

There are robust state policy agendas from organizations that outline key steps states must take to support each of these critical policy elements. For example, see The Education Trust's key state policies to advance educator diversity and to ensure that Black and Latinx students are not disproportionately served by novice or uncertified educators (Mehrotra et al., 2021a; 2021b); policies to advance equity in social, emotional, and academic development (including a focus on climate, discipline, wrap around supports, and curriculum), created in collaboration with CASEL (Ed Trust & CASEL, 2021); and policies to advance equitable access to advanced coursework (Ed Trust, 2019).

These policies are critical statewide, but in designing and supporting cross-district integration programs, states must specifically attend to each of these elements within the impacted schools. For example

- **Educator quality and diversity:** If a state is investing in a new interdistrict transfer program, it should publish educator diversity and retention data for the program, set goals specifically for the schools that participate, target resources to support educator diversity in the program, and invest in opportunities to retain teachers of color in the program. If the state is creating new, magnet high schools in previously underserved school districts, it might consider making one or more of them part of a "Grow Your Own" program, or a Career and Technical Education program for Black students interested in teaching. The state should also require publication and tracking of data showing patterns in assignment to novice and uncertified educators for students by race, ethnicity, and socioeconomic status within the program and to set goals and hold adults responsible for addressing any inequities that emerge in that data.
- **Professional development:** States should explicitly require and fund evidence-based professional development for educators in schools participating in interdistrict integration efforts, including support for educators in understanding adult mindsets and asset-based

pedagogies; and provide antibias, diversity, equity, inclusion, and belonging training.
- **Student, family, and community engagement:** States should provide guidance, training, and funding focused on community engagement, specifically on the issues that are likely to arise for educators in integrating schools, including the need to ensure engagement from families who live further from a particular school or who speak different languages; provide guidance on leveraging community-based organizations (CBOs) to partner with the school to accelerate student learning and meet student needs, including CBOs in both the "sending" and "receiving" communities; creating parent and family advisory councils with actual power to participate in decision-making about the school's programming, practices, and policies that include families from underrepresented communities; require training and provide funding to provide ongoing support for community engagement work.
- **Access to advanced coursework:** States should require—and fund—schools participating in integration programs to do universal screening for participation in gifted-and-talented programs at the elementary level and implement automatic enrollment policies that automatically enroll all students who demonstrate readiness on any of a variety of metrics, including grades, end-of-course assessments, standardized tests, or teacher recommendations, in advanced courses. For example, see Dallas, Texas (Napolitano, 2023), Washington State (Blad, 2020), and a Maryland bill that did not advance to become law (Maryland House of Delegates, 2020).

7. Cultivating an Education Ecosystem That Values and Promotes Integration and Resource Equity

States should collect and report data to build understanding of segregation and resource inequities and, ultimately, build pressure for change. States can calculate and share on report cards information about measures of integration/segregation for each school as compared to the district as a whole; levels of segregation between schools for each district as a whole; and between-district segregation statewide and regionally. They can also calculate and share measures of resource (in)equities within each school and for each district as a whole (assessing how strategically and equitably the district has aligned resources—spending, non-novice educators, school counselors, psychologists, health supports, extracurriculars, etc.—to levels of need in different schools). For example, the National Coalition on School Diversity (2020, pp. 6–7) has model legislation that was the basis for a bill introduced in North Carolina in 2021 (Nordstrom, 2021).

States can also change accountability policy to support integration and resource equity within districts and schools. States can include measures of integration and resource equity as a "fifth indicator" under the Every Student Succeeds Act's accountability requirements, which set parameters around the grades schools are assigned by states (e.g., letter grades, star systems, colors, etc). States with distinct state accountability systems can also change those to add a focus on integration and resource equity. Note that accountability systems must hold leaders accountable for decisions in their locus of control: Individual schools should be rated on things that they can control (e.g., how they promote integration and allocate resources and opportunities within their school to different student groups; how well they recruit and retain diverse educators); similarly, districts should be held accountable for things that they can control (e.g., the level of segregation or integration between schools; the level of resource equity or inequities between schools within the district; how well they recruit and retain diverse educators). Both types of accountability are important, but the second half of this equation, district accountability, is often given too little attention. The inequities we are calling out at the 70th anniversary of *Brown* are systemic. Many cannot be resolved by the leaders and educators at a single school; states must change how students and resources are assigned to districts, and district leaders must then be held accountable for rethinking, in partnership with their communities, how they assign students and resources to schools to promote integration and resource equity. The National Coalition on School Diversity has model legislation (National Coalition for School Diversity, 2020, pp. 6–7) that was the basis for a bill introduced in North Carolina in 2021 (Nordstrom, 2021).

Finally, states can provide financial incentives and technical assistance to advance intradistrict and intraschool integration and resource equity, including, for example, additional formula funding per student in a district where all schools are within a certain percentage of each other in student poverty (but only for districts with at least some base amount of poverty to start with); grants to support addressing inequities in access to critical resources; integration strategies (such as grade-level schools—for example, see Pearl, Mississippi, and Clinton, Mississippi (Harris, 2020)—and school (re)assignment (Barshay, 2022); recruiting and retaining educators of color; detracking; restorative justice practices that end racialized exclusionary discipline practices; and cooperative learning opportunities within or in conjunction with integration efforts. States can also provide technical assistance and support by facilitating communities of practice and funding consultant support to assist districts in making these sorts of comprehensive policy changes.

Strategies and Tactics. Achieving the transformative redesign of our public school systems as described above—rethinking, essentially, how we assign both students and resources to schools to ensure they are integrated and adequately resourced to meet students' needs—will require building public will and the use of every "tool" in our collective toolkit: applied research to make the case and show what's possible; state court litigation to provide political cover and force state action; strategic communications and messaging to effectively build public and political will; and, undoubtedly most important, thoughtful and sustained community engagement, power building, and empowerment to center the expertise, experiences, and desires of those most directly impacted by today's patterns of segregated schools that underresource students of color and students from low-income families.

We are encouraged by two current state court lawsuits beginning to reinvigorate these conversations in states as different as New Jersey and Minnesota. *Latino Action Network v. State of New Jersey* is a case filed in 2018, led predominantly by the Latinx Action Network and NAACP of New Jersey, to hold the state accountable for the dramatic and unacceptable level of school segregation across the state. New Jersey's 600+ school district boundaries have trapped many kids in underresourced and underfunded schools for decades, and prevented Black, Latinx, and low-income kids from accessing a quality education. In its most recent decision (*Latino Action Network v. State*, No. L-1076-18 (N.J. Super. [2023]), the state superior court concluded that the state of New Jersey is responsible for addressing school segregation, and the "[plaintiffs] . . . have demonstrated marked and persistent racial imbalance in numerous school districts across the State that Defendants . . . have failed to remedy." This means that the seriousness and impact of school segregation is being acknowledged by state courts.

Halfway across the country, in December 2023, the Minnesota Supreme Court issued a decision on a crucial question in *Cruz-Guzman v. State of Minnesota*: whether the plaintiffs are required to show more than the existence of "racial imbalance" in schools in order to establish a violation of the education clause of the Minnesota Constitution. The court started by pointing out that plaintiffs need not show that the state intended to violate the constitution—or intended to segregate schools, in this case. That, in and of itself, is really important.

The court then went on to analyze whether plaintiffs were required, in order to prove a constitutional violation, to show: (1) that the state caused the racial imbalances in schools and (2) that the racial imbalances caused their children to receive an inadequate education. The court found that the plaintiffs are not required to prove that the state caused the racial imbalance. This is a big deal, because the state has argued that it cannot be held responsible for school segregation that has resulted from local, district policies.

The court did say that simply showing segregation in schools is not, itself, a violation of the constitution. The plaintiffs must establish that "the racial imbalances are a substantial factor in causing their children to receive an inadequate education." The court is essentially asking the plaintiffs to prove "separate is not equal" at trial. And while it feels a little funny to have to prove that in the year 2024, we know there is strong social science research and evidence available to make the case.

There is a long way to go but, overall, the decision is a positive step forward. The court found that the state, specifically the Minnesota legislature, can be found responsible for school segregation without the plaintiffs having to prove a particular state action that caused it. The Minnesota State Constitution's education clause is very similar to those in other states, making it a promising example for this work in other places. Advancing this kind of big-picture, transformative change will take all of us.

CONCLUSION

The surges of racial prejudice, racial intolerance, and polarization of political attitudes, and unprecedented economic inequality are not coincidental, but directly related to, and exacerbated by, the inequality of resources across our public schools and its lack of diversity. The world that existed during the era of integration and civil rights was not the same as the one we have inherited. The Black–White dichotomy is an old paradigm. We have shifted from Black and White communities to ones that are multiethnic in a globally competitive, international, 21st-century knowledge economy. Global community requires multicultural competencies. No matter where our children live and work in the future, their neighborhoods will be multicultural, part of the global community. Our failure will be in not adequately preparing them for that new reality.

REFERENCES

Adukia, A., Feigenberg, B., & Momeni, F. (2023). *From retributive to restorative: An alternative approach to justice* (Working paper #31675). National Bureau of Economic Research.

Anstreicher, G., Fletcher, J., & Thompson, O. (2023). *The long run impacts of court-ordered desegregation* (Working paper #29926). National Bureau of Economic Research.

Antman, F. M., & Cortes, K. E. (2023). The long-run impacts of Mexican American school desegregation. *Journal of Economic Literature, 61*(3), 888–905.

Ashenfelter, O., Collins, W., & Yoon, A. (2006). Evaluating the role of *Brown v. Board of Education* in school equalization, desegregation, and the income of African Americans. *American Law and Economics Review, 8*(2), 213–248.

Bacher-Hicks, A., Billings, S. B., & Deming, D J. (in press). The school to prison pipeline: Long-run impacts of school suspensions on adult crime. *American Economic Journal: Economic Policy.*

Barshay, J. (2022). *Proof points: Computer scientists create tool that can desegregate schools—and shorten bus routes.* Hechinger Report. https://hechingerreport

.org/proof-points-computer-scientists-create-tool-that-can-desegregate-schools-and-shorten-bus-routes

Bartanen, B., Grissom, J. A., & Rogers, L. K. (2019). The Impacts of Principal Turnover. *Educational Evaluation and Policy Analysis, 41*(3), 350–374.

Bauman, C. (2017). *Report: Demerger of schools in Shelby County cemented inequities in public education*. The Commercial Appeal. https://www.commercialappeal.com/story/news/local/2017/06/21/report-de-merger-schools-shelby-county-cements-inequities-public-education/416244001/

Baum-Snow, N., & Lutz, B. (2011). School desegregation, school choice and changes in residential location patterns by race. *American Economic Review, 101*(7), 3019–3046.

Bayer, P., & Charles, K. K. (2018). Divergent paths: A new perspective on earnings differences between Black and White men since 1940. *The Quarterly Journal of Economics, 133*(3), 1459–1501.

Bayer, P., Charles, K. K., & Park, J. (2021). *Separate and unequal: Race and the geography of the American housing market*. Federal Reserve Bank of Boston.

Blad, E. (2020). The simple policy change that's getting more students of color in advanced courses. *Education Week*. https://www.edweek.org/leadership/the-simple-policy-change-thats-getting-more-students-of-color-in-advanced-courses/2020/03

Blomstedt, M. (2013). *The legislative purposes and intent of the common levy in Nebraska's learning community* [Doctoral dissertation]. University of Nebraska–Lincoln. https://digitalcommons.unl.edu/cehsedaddiss/138

Boisjoly, J., Duncan, G. J., Kremer, M., Levy, D. M., & Eccles, J. (2006). "Empathy or antipathy? The impact of diversity." *American Economic Review, 96*(5): 1890–1905.

Boyd, D., Grossman, P., Ing, M., Lankford, H., Loeb, S., & Wyckoff, J. (2011). The influence of school administrators on teacher retention decisions. *American Educational Research Journal, 48*(2), 303–333.

Card, D., & Giuliano, L. (2016). Can tracking raise the test scores of high-ability minority students? *American Economic Review, 106*(10), 2783–2816.

Card, D., & Krueger, A. (1992a). Does school quality matter? Returns to education and the characteristics of public schools in the United States. *Journal of Political Economy, 100*(1), 1–40.

Card, D., & Krueger, A. (1992b). School quality and Black–White relative earnings: A direct assessment. *Quarterly Journal of Economics, 107*(1), 151–200.

Cascio, E., Gordon, N., Lewis, E., & Reber, S. (2010). Paying for progress: Conditional grants and the desegregation of Southern schools. *Quarterly Journal of Economics, 125*(1), 445–482.

Chetty, R., Hendren, N., Jones, M. R., & Porter, S. R. (2020). Race and economic opportunity in the United States: An intergenerational perspective. *The Quarterly Journal of Economics, 135*(2), 711–783.

Choi, A., Herbert, K., Winslow, O., & Browne, A. (2019, November 17). Long Island divided: Audit study. *Newsday*. https://projects.newsday.com/long-island/real-estate-agents-investigation/

Choy, R. K. H., & Gifford, B. R. (1980). Resource allocation in a segregated school system: The case of Los Angeles. *Journal of Education Finance, 6*(1), 34–50.

Clotfelter, C. T. (2004). *After Brown: The rise and retreat of school desegregation.* Princeton University.
Cobb, C., Bifulco, R., & Bell, C. (2009). *Evaluation of Connecticut's interdistrict magnet schools.* The Center for Education Policy Analysis, University of Connecticut. https://www.researchgate.net/publication/265581229_EVALUATION_OF_CONNECTICUT'S_INTERDISTRICT_MAGNET_SCHOOLS
Coleman, J., Campbell E., Hobson C., McPartland J., Mood, A., Weinfeld, F., & R. York. (1966). *Equality and educational opportunity.* National Center for Educational Statistics.
Cui, T. (2024). *Did race fence off the American city? The great migration and the evolution of exclusionary zoning* (Working paper). New York University Furman Center.
Cullen, J. B., & Loeb, S. (2004). School finance reform in Michigan: Evaluating Proposal A. In J. Yinger & W. Duncombe (Eds.), *Helping children left behind: State aid and the pursuit of educational equity* (pp. 215–250). MIT Press. https://econweb.ucsd.edu/~jbcullen/research/MIschfin.pdf
Dobbie, W., & Fryer, R. G., Jr. (2015). The impact of voluntary youth service on future outcomes: Evidence from Teach for America. *B.E. Journal of Economic Analysis and Policy, 15*(3), 1031–1065.
EdBuild. (2019). *Fractured: The accelerating breakdown of America's school districts.* https://edbuild.org/content/fractured/fractured-full-report.pdf
EdBuild. (2024). *FundEd: State policy analysis: Wyoming.* http://funded.edbuild.org/state/WY
Education Trust. (2019, December 9). *5 things to advance equity in access to and success in advanced coursework.* https://edtrust.org/resource/5-things-to-advance-equity-in-access-to-and-success-in-advanced-coursework
Education Trust & CASEL (2021). *Is your state prioritizing students' social, emotional, and academic development?* https://edtrust.org/is-your-state-prioritizing-sead
Evans, W. N., Schwab, R. M., & Wagner, K. L. (2019). The Great Recession and public education. *Education Finance and Policy, 14*(2), 298–326.
George, J., Darling-Hammond, L., and Plasencia, S. (2023). *Advancing integration and equity through magnet schools.* Learning Policy Institute. https://learningpolicyinstitute.org/product/advancing-integration-equity-magnet-schools-brief
Gershenson, S., Hart, C. M. D., Hyman, J., Lindsay, C. A., & Papageorge, N. W. (2022). The long-run impacts of same-race teachers. *American Economic Journal: Economic Policy, 14*(4), 300–342.
Greenberg, J. (2004). *Crusaders in the courts: How a dedicated band of lawyers fought for the civil rights revolution.* Basic Books.
Grissom, J. A., & Redding, C. (2016). Discretion and disproportionality: Explaining the underrepresentation of high-achieving students of color in gifted programs. *AERA Open, 2*(1), 1–25.
Guryan, J. (2004). Desegregation and Black dropout rates. *American Economic Review, 94*(4), 919–943.
Harris, B. (2020). '*We're stronger than we've ever been': A Mississippi district shows that integration pays off.* Hechinger Report. https://hechingerreport.org/were-stronger-than-weve-ever-been-a-mississippi-district-shows-that-integrated-schools-pay-off

Holme, J. J., & Diem, S. (2015). Regional governance in education: A case study of the Metro Area Learning Community in Omaha, Nebraska. *Peabody Journal of Education, 90*(1), 156–177. https://eric.ed.gov/?id=EJ1050829

Jackson, C. K. (2009). Student demographics, teacher sorting, and teacher quality: Evidence from the end of school desegregation. *Journal of Labor Economics, 27*(2), 213–256.

Jackson, C. K., Johnson, R. C., & Persico, C. (2016). The effects of school spending on educational & economic outcomes: Evidence from school finance reforms. *The Quarterly Journal of Economics, 131*(1), 157–218.

Jackson, C. K., Wigger, C., & Xiong, H. (2021). Do school spending cuts matter? Evidence from the Great Recession. *American Economic Journal: Economic Policy, 13*(2), 304–335.

Jang, H., & Reardon, S. F. (2019). States as sites of educational (in)equality: State contexts and the socioeconomic achievement gradient. *AERA Open, 5*(3).

Johnson, R. C. (2011). *Long-run impacts of school desegregation & school quality on adult attainments* (NBER working paper #16664). National Bureau of Economic Research. https://doi.org/10.3386/w16664 (Revised October 2016)

Johnson, R. C. (2019). *Children of the dream: Why school integration works*. Basic Books and Russell Sage Foundation Press.

Johnson, R. C. (2023). *School funding effectiveness: Evidence from California's local control funding formula*. Learning Policy Institute. https://learningpolicyinstitute.org/product/school-funding-effectiveness-ca-lcff-report

Kolbe, T., Atchison, D., Kearns, C., & Levin, J. (2020). *State finance reform vignettes: Vermont*. American Institutes of Research. https://carsey.unh.edu/sites/default/files/media/2020/06/20-11882_5._primer_statevignettes_vermont_air_formatted_v7_ed.pdf

Lafortune, J., Rothstein, J., & Schanzenbach, D. W. (2018). School finance reform and the distribution of student achievement. *American Economic Journal: Applied Economics, 10*(2), 1–26.

Lewis, N. (2016). *What happens when two separate and unequal school districts merge?* The Hechinger Report. https://hechingerreport.org/what-happens-when-two-separate-and-unequal-school-districts-merge/

Liu, G. (2006). The parted paths of school desegregation and school finance litigation. *Minnesota Journal of Law & Inequality, 24*(1), 81–106.

Logan, J. R. (2011). *"Separate and unequal: The neighborhood gap for Blacks, Hispanics, and Asians in metropolitan America."* Project US2010 Report, 1–22.

Lutz, B. (2011). The end of court-ordered desegregation. *American Economic Journal: Economic Policy, 3*(2), 130–68.

Macartney, H., & Singleton, J. D., 2018. School boards and student segregation. *Journal of Public Economics, 164*, 165–182.

Maryland House of Delegates. (2020). *House Bill 1421*. https://trackbill.com/bill/maryland-house-bill-1421-education-advanced-courses-automatic-enrollment/1889491

Megan, K. (2021). State says fewer Hartford students in integrated schools. *Connecticut Public Radio*. https://www.ctpublic.org/education/2021-01-19/state-says-fewer-hartford-students-in-integrated-schools

Mehrotra, S., Morgan, I., & Socol, A. R. (2021a). *Getting Black students better access to non-novice teachers*. The Education Trust. https://edtrust.org/resource/getting-latino-students-better-access-to-non-novice-teachers

Mehrotra, S., Morgan, I., & Socol, A. R. (2021b). *Getting Latino students better access to non-novice teachers*. The Education Trust. https://edtrust.org/resource/getting-latino-students-better-access-to-non-novice-teachers

Monarrez, T. E. (2023). School attendance boundaries and the segregation of public schools in the United States. *American Economic Journal: Applied Economics, 15*(3), 210–237.

Monarrez, T. E., Kisida, B., & Chingos, M. (2022). The effect of charter schools on school segregation. *American Economic Journal: Economic Policy, 14*(1), 301–340.

Monarrez, T. E., & Schönholzer, D. (2023). Dividing lines: Racial segregation across local government boundaries. *Journal of Economic Literature, 61*(3), 863–887.

Napolitano, J. (2023). *Dallas ISD's opt-out policy dramatically boosts diversity in honors classes*. The 74 Million. https://www.the74million.org/article/dallas-isds-opt-out-policy-dramatically-boosts-diversity-in-its-honors-classes

National Center for Education Statistics. (2023). *Public school revenue sources*. Condition of Education, U.S. Department of Education, Institute of Education Sciences. https://nces.ed.gov/programs/coe/indicator/cma/public-school-revenue

National Coalition on School Diversity. (2020). *Model state integration policies* (policy brief 11). Poverty and Race Research Action Council. https://school-diversity.org/wp-content/uploads/NCSDPB11_Final.pdf

Nordstrom, K. (2021, May 13). First-of-its-kind bill would incentivize integration of North Carolina Schools. *NC Newsline*. https://ncnewsline.com/briefs/first-of-its-kind-bill-would-incentivize-integration-of-north-carolina-schools/

Office of Revenue and Tax Analysis. (2002, December). *School finance reform in Michigan Proposal A: Retrospective*. Michigan Department of Treasury. https://www.michigan.gov/-/media/Project/Websites/treasury/MISC_8/propa.pdf

Orfield, G. (2004). *Brown v Board*: Timeline of school integration in the U.S. *Learning for Justice, Teaching Tolerance, 25*.

Pettigrew, T. F., & Tropp, L. R. (2006). A meta-analytic test of intergroup contact theory. *Journal of Personality and Social Psychology, 90*(5), 751–783.

Potter, H., & Nunberg, M. (2019). *Scoring states on charter school integration*. The Century Foundation. https://tcf.org/content/report/scoring-states-charter-school-integration

Putterman, A. (2023). Suburban CT schools accepted fewer Hartford students despite Sheff settlement, $300K in grants. *CT Insider*. https://www.ctinsider.com/news/article/Suburban-schools-Hartford-students-Open-Choice-17711120.php

Quick, K. (2016). *Hartford Public Schools: Striving for equity through interdistrict programs*. The Century Foundation. https://tcf.org/content/report/hartford-public-schools

Reardon, S. F., Fox, L., & Townsend, J. (2015). Neighborhood income composition by household race and income, 1990–2009. *The Annals of the American Academy of Political and Social Science, 660*(1), 78–97.

Reardon, S. F., Grewal, E., Kalogrides, D., & Greenberg, E. (2012). *Brown* fades: The end of court-ordered school desegregation and the resegregation of American public schools. *Journal of Policy Analysis and Management, 31*(4), 876–904.

Reardon, S. F., Weathers, E. S., Fahle, E. M., Jang, H., & Kalogrides, D. (2022). Is separate still unequal? New evidence on school segregation and racial academic achievement gaps (Working paper). Stanford University Center for Education Policy Analysis.

Reber, S. J. (2010). School desegregation and educational attainment for Blacks. *Journal of Human Resources, 45*(4), 893–914.

Reber, S. J. (2011). From separate and unequal to integrated and equal? School desegregation and school finance in Louisiana. *Review of Economics and Statistics, 93*(2), 404–415.

Reed, D. S. (1998). Twenty-five years after *Rodriguez*: School finance litigation and the impact of the new judicial federalism. *Law & Society Review, 32*(1), 175–220.

Rix, K. (2022). *Dallas parents flocking to schools that pull students from both rich and poor parts of town*. The Hechinger Report. https://hechingerreport.org/dallas-parents-flocking-to-schools-that-pull-students-from-both-rich-and-poor-parts-of-town/

Rothstein, R. (2017). *The color of law: A forgotten history of how our government segregated America*. Liveright.

Ryan, J. E. (1999a). Schools, race, and money. *The Yale Law Journal, 109*(2), 249–316.

Ryan, J. E. (1999b). The influence of race in school finance reform. *Michigan Law Review, 98*(2), 432–481.

School and State Finance Project. (2022). *Connecticut's open choice program*. https://schoolstatefinance.org/resource-assets/Connecticuts-Open-Choice-Program.pdf

School and State Finance Project. (2023). *Guide to Connecticut's magnet schools*. https://schoolstatefinance.org/resource-assets/Guide-to-CTs-Magnet-Schools.pdf

Schueler, B., Lyon, M. A., & Bleiberg, J. (2023, October 24). *Do state takeovers of school districts work?* Brookings Institution.

Schwartz, M. A. (1967). *Trends in White attitudes toward Negroes*. National Opinion Research Center. http://www.norc.org/PDFs/publications/NORCRpt_119.pdf

Simko, T. (2023). *School desegregation by redrawing district boundaries: Evidence from New Jersey*. https://drive.google.com/file/d/1pFJz2sVoU6KuwWpXhlho80MTtl2ZPhyq/view

Swaby, A. (2019, January 31). Many see 'Robin Hood' as a villain. But lawmakers rely on it to pay for schools. *The Texas Tribune*. https://www.texastribune.org/2019/01/31/texas-robin-hood-recapture-villain-texas-fix-school-finance/

Tedin, K. L. (1994). Self-interest, symbolic values, and the financial equalization of the public schools. *Journal of Politics, 56*(3), 628–649.

Thompson, O. (2022). School desegregation and Black teacher employment. *The Review of Economics and Statistics, 104*(5), 962–980.

Trachtenburg, P., Roda, A., & Coughlan, R. (2016). *Remedying school desegregation*. The Century Foundation. https://tcf.org/content/report/remedying-school-segregation/

Tuttle, C. (2019). *The long-run economic effects of school desegregation* (Paper). University of Maryland.

Westhoven, N. (2022). *Morris schools mark 50 years of integration that followed landmark civil rights ruling*. Daily Record. https://www.dailyrecord.com/story/news/2022/09/30/nj-school-integration-anniversary-jenkins-vs-township-of-morris-boe/69513428007/

Zubrzycki, J. (2013, July 9). Memphis-Shelby schools merge, amid uncertainty. *Education Week*. https://www.edweek.org/leadership/memphis-shelby-schools-merge-amid-uncertainty/2013/07

CHAPTER 5

But What About the Teachers?
The Forgotten Narratives of Black Teachers in the Midst of *Brown*

Gloria Ladson-Billings

INTRODUCTION

In 1960, Ruby Bridges was one of six Black students who passed a test to determine if they could attend an all-White school in New Orleans. Six-year-old Ruby entered the William Frantz Elementary School and was met by an angry mob of Whites who decried the school district's implementation of the landmark *Brown v. Board of Education* decision. So unsafe was the environment that Ruby was escorted to school each day by federal marshals. This daily parade was fixed in the American mind by Norman Rockwell's (1964) much-reproduced image, *The Problem We All Live With*, in which the young girl, dressed in white, is surrounded by marshals in suits, ensuring her right to go to 1st grade. Initially, no White parents permitted their students to attend the school. Gradually, a few parents enrolled their students, though none of the students would sit in a classroom with Ruby. No White teacher was willing to teach Ruby except Barbara Henry from Boston, MA. While we commend Ms. Henry for her courage and ethical commitment, how might things have been different for Ruby and the nine youth who desegregated Central High School in Little Rock (Bennett, 2020) if they had been accompanied to their new school settings by a group of caring, dedicated Black teachers?

In truth, we can expect that Black teachers attempting to desegregate a school would have faced harsher vitriol during this period in the United States even than children did. But it is important to consider the role of Black teachers during these early attempts at school desegregation. I am prompted to think about this because of a school desegregation conference I attended at the University of North Carolina–Chapel Hill in the 1990s. During that conference, members of the first group of Black students who desegregated Chapel Hill-Carrboro Schools discussed their experiences. The people appeared to be in their fifties to early sixties. They had completed their formal education, begun their work lives, married, raised children, and some were enjoying the benefits of grandparenting. However, during their retelling of their first year entering Chapel Hill-Carrboro High Schools, they struck a somber tone. Some began to weep as they recalled the loneliness of entering the high school where it was clear they were unwanted.

One man spoke with a quivering voice as he recounted, "We went over there by ourselves. All the trophies and medals our Black school had won over the years as football, basketball, baseball, and track champions stayed back at our old school. And our teachers did not go with us. We entered that building all by ourselves. We entered unprotected." The idea of sending students into a hostile environment without the care or protection of adults seems unusually cruel, indeed unfathomable, but it is exactly what Black students desegregating schools post-*Brown* experienced. The stories of what happened to the students have been told and retold (Waugh, 2012), but we rarely tell the stories of the teachers who were left behind during school desegregation.

BEFORE *BROWN*: SEPTIMA POINSETTE CLARK

While *Brown* was a landmark decision that marked the end of legal apartheid or state-sponsored segregation in the United States, it is not where the story of Black teachers begins. From their earliest days in the United States, Black people have been striving to equip themselves with education that would serve as a tool for liberation. Milla Granson (born Lilly Ann Granderson) was born in Petersburg, Virginia, ca. 1816 and is thought to have died in Natchez, Mississippi, about 1880 (Brooklyn Museum, n.d.). Soon after her birth Granson and her mother were sold to enslavers in Kentucky. As she grew, Granson developed a relationship with her captor's children, who began to teach her to read. Granson was once again sold to enslavers in Mississippi, where she went from a field hand to a house slave, and it was here she began her heroic mission of educating Black people.

Historian Gerda Lerner (1972) documented Granson's work in her book *Black Women in White America*. She describes what became known as Granson's "midnight" school. From 11 p.m. to about 2 a.m., Granson would take 12 enslaved Black people into an alleyway building and carry out the dangerous mission of teaching her charges to read and write. This was dangerous work because Mississippi, like many other states, made it illegal to teach Black people to read (Center for Black Educator Development [CBED], 2021). Granson's method was to teach a dozen students to read and write, "graduate" them, and take on another group of 12. Her "school" lasted for more than 7 years, and it is believed more than 200 enslaved people participated in her school. Some of her students used their newly acquired literacy skills to write their own "travel passes" that allowed them to escape slavery. Surprisingly, when news of Granson's school leaked, she was not sanctioned because the Mississippi law stated that no White person or free Black person could teach an enslaved person to read. The law said nothing about enslaved Blacks teaching each other. Granson could not be sanctioned because Mississippi's law said that a White person who taught a slave to read could be penalized, even imprisoned, but (unlike the laws of some other states) it did not specifically bar such teaching among enslaved people.

By the time Union troops reached Natchez, Mississippi, they found Granson well-equipped to teach the state's formerly enslaved people. She would go on to be a teacher in the Freedmen's Schools as a member of the American Missionary Association (CBED, 2021). Today schoolchildren can read of Granson's amazing efforts in Halfmann's 2018 children's book, *Midnight Teacher: Lilly Ann Granderson and Her Secret School*.

But one of the most fascinating teachers I encountered as I looked for examples of teaching excellence is Septima Poinsette Clark. Clark was known as the mother of the modern Civil Rights Movement, but her true calling was that of teacher. Born in 1896 (2 years after the *Plessy v. Ferguson* decision) to parents who were laborers, she was able to graduate from secondary school in Charleston in 1916 and spent more than 30 years teaching in South Carolina. McFadden (1996) described her as the "epitome of a community teacher, intuitive fighter for human rights and leader of her unlettered and disillusioned people" (p. 87). Septima Clark attended Benedict College, where she earned her bachelor's degree, and later Hampton Institute (now University), where she earned her master's degree. Both of these institutions were historically black colleges/universities (HBCUs); she later took summer courses at Columbia University in New York, since the Southern White colleges and universities did not allow Black students to enroll at the undergraduate or graduate level.

In her autobiography, edited by Cynthia Stokes Brown (Clark, 1990), Clark describes her work in poorly resourced, segregated schools in South Carolina. She worked tirelessly to help her students become literate because she recognized that South Carolina used literacy tests as a form of voter suppression. In addition to her work as a public school teacher with some of the nation's poorest students, Clark became active in the local chapter of the National Association for the Advancement of Colored People (NAACP). She was fired in 1956 by the Charleston Public Schools for her failure to disavow her membership in the NAACP.

Clark's dismissal led her to a new endeavor at Myles Horton's Highlander Folk School (now Highlander Research and Education Center) in Tennessee, founded in 1932 to build local leadership and by the 1950s focused on racial justice (Charron, 2009). In the mid-1950s she created a citizenship training program to empower African Americans to vote and pass the racist literacy tests established by many states to thwart the Black vote. For me, three things stand out from Clark's efforts. One, she educated a cadre of some of the most brilliant minds in the movement—Martin Luther King, Jr., Rosa Parks, Fannie Lou Hamer, and Hosea Williams, to name a few. Two, she did this work with an understanding of the power of people to liberate themselves when they possessed the right tools. And three, she developed a pedagogical model that was organic and not dependent on mainstream guides and texts.

Clark's work at Highlander laid the tactical strategy for civil rights leaders. The story of Rosa Parks as a tired seamstress acting impulsively fails in the clear light of her preparation by Clark at Highlander where she, along with Martin Luther King, Jr., learned more about nonviolent resistance strategies (Morris, 1984). Clark's years as a teacher likely informed her understanding of the limitless possibilities of people who are finally given a chance to acquire knowledge and skills that can empower them. Some years ago, I wrote a manuscript describing Clark as the forerunner to Paulo Freire and the journal editor dismissed my premise out of hand and rejected the manuscript. However, I contend the evidence is there. Clark was working with the poorest of the poor to move them to political, economic, social, and cultural power through an emancipatory literacy. Given that, Clark was a leader in adult literacy for liberation decades before Freire did similar work. And yet Freire is a keystone originating figure for discussions of teaching for social justice, while Clark is known, yes, but far less celebrated.

The third aspect of Clark's work that warrants inspection is her methodology. Where former adult literacy programs failed, Clark's thrived. She did not try to teach adults to read the way one might teach children. Instead of reading primers with their basic, childish vocabulary, Clark began by asking her students why they wanted to read and write. Their motivations for becoming literate ranged from being able to get a better job to being able to read to children or grandchildren or to read the Bible for themselves, and, of course, becoming able to vote in a time of literacy tests for voter registration. Clark then asked her students to develop vocabulary words from their area of interest. The students did not read things like, "A is for apple, B is for ball." Rather, they brought her words like "personnel office," "tabernacle," and "registration." As her citizenship schools grew, Clark recruited teachers from the community. She was adamant that she did not want "trained" (i.e., state-certified) teachers because they would likely talk down to the adults (Clark, 1990). Clark employed barbers and beauticians, bus drivers, cooks, and maids—people just like the students—to teach in churches, community centers, beauty salons, and barber shops. Clark understood that students needed to feel comfortable and welcome in the learning environment.

When teachers like Septima Clark disappeared from students' lives, what did we lose collectively? How were the annals of Black education irreparably destroyed? How could Black (and other) students have experienced a different and enriched schooling experience?

WHAT THE NUMBERS SAY

Edgar Epps (2002) asserts that about 38,000 teachers and principals in 17 Southern states lost their jobs between 1954 and 1965. Hudson and Holmes (1994) also suggest that it is possible to document the decline of Black teachers after 1954, claiming that before the landmark decision there were approximately 82,000 Black teachers responsible for educating the nation's 2 million African American public school students. Fultz (2004) describes both job loss and demotion among Black teachers. These losses and demotions are well documented. Thus, this chapter does not dwell on these obvious data. Instead, it offers narratives about Black teachers that demonstrate what those losses may have meant to generations of Black and other students. The chapter attempts to put flesh on the stark bones of the disturbing statistics. We know that there are approximately 228,000 Black teachers in the United States and the Black student population numbers about 7,400,000. That is just three Black teachers for every 100 Black students (National Center for Education Statistics, 2023a, 2023b). Because teachers are not assigned by race, it is very likely that many Black students never experience a Black teacher.

WHAT *BROWN* MEANT FOR THE BLACK TEACHER: PAULINE DUPREE

Pauline Dupree's classroom felt like the calm in the midst of a raging storm. Her school was riddled with disruptions, conflicts, and fights. The principal was relatively new, as were a number of the teachers, and the students sensed the inexperience. But in Pauline's room there was no such chaos. Pauline was impeccably dressed and soft-spoken. She began her day in high heels but shifted to comfortable flats shortly after the students arrived. "Miss Dupree, why you always come here so dressed up?" a student asked. "Because I am going to work and I work with very important people," she responded. A puzzled look came over the student's face and then she blurted out, "Who?" "You," came the reply. "Each and every one of you is important and I don't intend to show up in less than my best for you" (Ladson-Billings, 2022, p. 38). That simple act of affirmation made Mrs. Dupree's classroom decidedly different from those of her younger, inexperienced, mostly White colleagues.

Pauline Dupree (a pseudonym) is a teacher I had the pleasure of working with during my study of successful teachers of African American children. Listening to her describe her upbringing in rural Mississippi during the 1950s gave me some sense of what Black teachers experienced post-*Brown*.

Dupree was a graduate of Rust College, a historically Black college in Holly Springs, Mississippi. Holly Springs is a small town that today is home to fewer than 8,000 people, the majority (77%) of whom are Black (U.S. Census, 2023).

Rust College was founded shortly after the Civil War in 1866 by the Freedmen's Aid Society of the Methodist Episcopal Church. Northern missionaries opened a school in the Asbury Methodist Episcopal Church that accepted Blacks of all ages—children, youth, and adults—to teach them to read and to do elementary mathematics (see www.rustcollege.edu/about-rust-college/history). For many years Rust was the only place in the region where Black people could access formal education. The educational mission expanded into higher grades and even into a college-level program from which the first two students graduated in 1878. Rust's elementary school continued until 1930, and the institution maintained a high school until 1953 when public education became more widely available for Black students.

When the *Brown* decision was handed down it was met by massive resistance among Mississippi's White residents (Bolton, 2007). The state's powerful U.S. senator, James Eastland, vowed that Mississippi would never obey the U.S. Supreme Court's ruling, which applied not only to school desegregation, but also to public accommodations. To thwart the decision, Mississippi enacted a variety of laws aimed at suppressing the Black vote to reinforce the power of White citizens and elected officials. These measures included purging Blacks from the voter rolls through instituting a literacy test that required Blacks to be able to read and to provide a "reasonable" interpretation of portions of the state constitution" (Bolton, 2007). Additionally, the Sunflower Plantation owner, Robert B. Patterson, helped to institute the White Citizens' Council and the Ku Klux Klan terrorized and murdered Blacks who attempted to get Mississippi schools to desegregate. In 1955, Rev. George Lee, Gus Courts, and Lamar Smith, three Black leaders who championed school desegregation, were murdered by the Klan (Bolton, 2007). Later that year, 14-year-old Emmett Till from Chicago was murdered while visiting his relatives in Money, Mississippi, for allegedly speaking to (or whistling at) a White woman. His murderers were acquitted of what was one of the more brutal incidents of the post–Civil War South and his death became a catalyst of the modern Civil Rights Movement.

Pauline Dupree entered school almost a decade before the *Brown* decision was handed down. It had no impact on the life she led in Mississippi. She attended all-Black schools before *Brown* and she would continue to attend those schools after it, kindergarten through college. What she does recall is that Black teachers were among the most respected members of her community. They were among the few Black professionals she saw growing up. Unlike the domestics and laborers who made up the majority of the Black workers in her community, teachers dressed well; they wore tailored skirts or dresses, nylon hosiery, and high heels. For Pauline, Black teachers were not just the people who taught in her schools. Segregation, both of schools and of real estate, meant that despite having "middle class" jobs that would have allowed their White peers to move up and out of their home neighborhoods and perhaps into new suburbs, Black teachers remained in the neighborhoods they grew up in and worked in. She and classmates encountered their teachers in the local stores and at church. Her parents saw her teachers in beauty salons and barbershops, and when they needed help reading and understanding documents—contracts, legal notices, or employment rules— the Black community sought out those teachers for assistance. *Brown* did not diminish this vision of who Black teachers were. Pauline Dupree saw these teachers as people on the forefront of racial uplift (Moore, 2003). Her understanding of what it meant to be a teacher went beyond academics and extended into the responsibility to serve the community. Teachers, preachers, and nurses were the "chosen ones" in communities like Holly Springs, Mississippi (as well as in segregated communities across the United States).

Ms. Dupree took that same spirit of "community" or "racial uplift" (to use the terms introduced by Black leaders) with her when she moved to the west coast to become a teacher. The earlier description of "dressing up" clearly is a remnant of her perception of self-presentation that she learned in rural Mississippi. She emulated the Black teachers she experienced growing up in rural Mississippi and was determined to impress upon her young charges that they were valuable and worthy of the very best. Despite the fact that her younger, White colleagues came to work dressed in jeans and T-shirts, Ms. Dupree thought it was important that her students see themselves as worthy of respect through her style of dress. While this might seem a minor detail, it is reminiscent of the lawyers who volunteered to represent civil rights workers. These young, energetic White attorneys eagerly accepted civil rights cases (e.g., freedom riders, lunch counter protestors, and others who violated Jim Crow laws) but they resisted the protocols of dressing in a suit and tie. In an early case a Black defendant insisted that his lawyer wear a suit and tie. When the young lawyer objected, the Black client reportedly said, "Look, you're fighting for *my* life in that courtroom. The state's attorney will be wearing a suit and tie and under that robe the judge will have on suit pants, a shirt, and a tie. I will be the only one with a raggedy dressed lawyer. What do you think that tells the jury?"

Mrs. Dupree was about 50 years old when I began observing her classroom. She pulled heavily from her Black students' lives. For example, in one lesson she began, "Who knows what a proverb is?" One student said, "I think it's something in the Bible." "Yes," responded Ms. Dupree, "there is a book in the Bible called *Proverbs*, but what is a proverb?" The students sat silent and puzzled. "Have you ever heard someone say, 'A hard head makes a soft behind?' Ms. Dupree asked. Several students giggled as they nodded their heads. "My mama says that all the time," came a response. "Well,"

Ms. Dupree replied, "Your mother is using a proverb. We think of proverbs as wise sayings that use word pictures to convey a deeper meaning." She wrote the words, "word picture" and "deeper meaning" on the chalkboard. "Can you think of some other things your parents, grandparents, aunties, or neighbors say that remind you of the expression I shared?" After a few minutes students began offering what they thought were proverbs. "Every shut eye ain't sleep." "That's the pot calling the kettle black." "You move you lose—barbershop rules." "Spare the rod and spoil the child." As she wrote down the students' responses, she helped them to examine the deeper meaning associated with them. She told the students that they were going to gather as many proverbs as they could, starting with their family members. Ultimately, each student would select a favorite proverb, write a short description of what the proverb was trying to convey, and create an illustration to accompany their proverb.

When I talked to Mrs. Dupree about this lesson, she informed me that what she was teaching was not a part of the district's mandated curriculum. "When the state test comes, my students will have to understand things like metaphors and similes. The curriculum they require doesn't cover that. I know what skills the students will need to be able to perform well on the test but I'm not going to get up in my principal's face demanding my way. I just close my door and do what's right for my students." Dupree's response reminds me of Givens's (2021) notion of "fugitive pedagogy." Teachers like Dupree who had lived through segregated schooling and resistance to the *Brown* decision understood that Black teachers were expected to be subversive in their work to ensure their students received the education to which they were entitled.

While Septima Clark found a new career beyond traditional teaching, we know little about those Black teachers who remained in public education in the South after the *Brown* decision. To comply with the decision, many states and localities in the South began shuttering the doors of schools located in Black communities on the presumption that those schools were inferior. Siddle Walker (1996) argues that empirical evidence shows that there were Black community schools that offered a superior education for Black children despite their fiscal and material shortcomings. Fenwick (2022) describes that *en masse* displacement of Black teachers and principals in the South subsequent to the *Brown* decision. Although the Court declared school segregation of students illegal, it never suggested that the remedy was to close schools in Black communities and dismiss Black teachers and principals. One can only speculate that these dismissals were a form of retaliation designed to hurt Black teachers and by implication the Black community.

Black teachers were trained to do one thing—teach. Losing a teaching job did not open up other comparable professional opportunities. Thus, some Black teachers in the South ended up moving North or West to seek other teaching jobs. Those who remained in the South likely ended up in jobs that were beneath their previous status. They became domestic workers, clerks, factory workers, postal workers, and other lower-skilled employees. At the same time that Black teachers were being forced from classrooms in the South, White teachers were leaving public schools that were desegregating. But this exodus of White teachers from a changing public school landscape did not provide opportunities for Black teachers.

The *Brown* decision brought on what became known as "segregation academies."[1] These academies were founded in direct opposition to the Supreme Court's mandate to desegregate public schools. By 1971, about half a million White students attended segregated private schools. These schools or academies were low-cost, all-White schools that received passive or indirect financial and community support. For example, in Smallville, Louisiana, White parents organized an all-White private school that the local public school supported by "donating" all of the school's desks and library books. The fiscal burden was mitigated by a supplemental payment to the teachers from the state of Louisiana. Later when the State Supreme Court found those payments to be unconstitutional, the White teachers "retired" from their previous positions as public school teachers and received pensions that were, in effect, salary supplements (Champagne, 1973; Ladson-Billings, 2004). The very name of some of these academies evokes a glorification of the Confederacy—Andrew Jackson Academy, Jefferson Davis Academy, and Robert E. Lee Academy, to name a few.

NORTHERN BLACK TEACHERS AND THE NEED TO BE BETTER: ETHEL BENN[2]

Ethel Benn was exactly the teacher I did *not* want. She was an "older"[3] Black woman teaching 5th grade at Belmont Elementary School in West Philadelphia about 1957. I wanted to be assigned to the other 5th-grade teacher, Ms. Plunkett. Ms. Plunkett was an energetic young White teacher who seemed like she would be fun. Mrs. Benn was serious looking, never smiling, and she wore floral dresses, cotton stockings, and shoes we called "old lady comforters." They were the era's version of "sensible" orthopedic shoes. Everyone in the school knew she was a strict, no-nonsense teacher. Fun was not high on her agenda.

When I made a plea at the beginning of the school year to my mother to change me from Mrs. Benn's classroom, she remarked, "You haven't even given her a chance. I have no reason to consider changing you. After all, she's Reverend Benn's wife. I'm sure she's a nice Christian woman!" A few weeks into the school year my thoughts about Mrs. Benn's strictness were confirmed. She brooked no foolishness. She insisted on working us hard. Her standards were exacting. But she was also fair. She often told us how much she expected of us. She never talked down to us. She was also the school's chorus leader, and every member of her class was expected to sing in the chorus. It did not matter if you could sing, Mrs. Benn had you standing up in that chorus learning the songs. Our school chorus sang all over the city, at places many of us had never been. We sang what were then called "Negro spirituals," show tunes, and high church sacred music. I learned the song "Dona Nobis Pacem" in her chorus. She provided transportation by having her husband's congregants carpool us to the various concerts. It was during these trips that we began to see that our city was much larger than our little neighborhood. Somehow, she knew we needed to "be better." Mrs. Benn never treated her students as if they were unworthy. Instead, she was cognizant of the standard that many Black people heard growing up in Black communities—we have to work twice as hard to get half as far!

Mrs. Benn was also providing what Givens (2021) called "fugitive pedagogy." She is the person who initially introduced me to W. E. B. Du Bois. Mrs. Benn explained that Du Bois was the first Black person to earn a doctorate from Harvard. We found this information unbelievable, since we could not imagine Harvard as a place where Black people could attend school. But more than the information about Du Bois, Ethel Benn provided us with an extensive knowledge of Black history. She taught us about the kingdoms of Mali, Songhay, and Ghana. She taught us about the liberation struggles of Black people who included Denmark Vesey, Harriet Tubman, Robert Smalls, Frederick Douglass, Nat Turner, and others. She regularly urged us to take pride in being Black (I'm sure she said "Negro") and never to assume we could not achieve because of anything inherent in our racial makeup. Mrs. Benn is probably the first authority figure who made clear to me how important it was for us to be proud of being Black.

Although our school, filled to capacity with Baby Boomers, was 99.9% Black (there was one poor White family who attended the school), we were the recipients of a curriculum that rendered Black people invisible or as "slaves" (Woodson, 1933) incapable of intellectual, artistic, civic, or cultural excellence. Mrs. Benn regaled our class with stories of Black excellence and was adamant that we, too, could and should be great. It is only recently that I realized that Ethel Benn was following a model not unlike Givens's description of Tessie McGee in 1930s Louisiana. Mrs. Benn secretly taught all her Black students from books she brought from home on what was then known as "Negro History." While I had some degree of skepticism about what she was teaching, it did resonate with stories that were told as my parents and relatives sat around the kitchen table. My father insisted that Paul Robeson was a good and honorable man and I should not be swayed by the things being said about him as he sat before the House Sub-committee on Un-American Activities (i.e., the McCarthy Commission). I knew that the outstanding contralto Marian Anderson grew up in my neighborhood. I knew that Ralph Bunch had distinguished himself as a diplomat and, of course, Joe Louis was a boxing champ who carried the hopes of Black Americans with him each time he entered the ring.

But it was Ethel Benn who introduced me to Estavanico the Moor, who was the first Black person named as an explorer of the so-called New World. She taught us about the work of Black people who built Philadelphia and the antislavery movement. We learned of Richard Allen and Absalom Jones as the founders of the African Methodist Episcopal Church, and of the many Black abolitionists who made Philadelphia a "destination city" for formerly enslaved Blacks fleeing the South. More importantly, Ethel Benn convinced me of my own capabilities. I have a vivid recollection of her asking me, "What makes you think you can't be the best 5th-grader in this class?" "I don't know," I shrugged my shoulders. "What makes you think you can't be the best 5th-grader in this school?" Again, I had no answer. "What makes you think you can't be the best 5th-grader in this city?" While I was uncertain that was a possibility, I had no answer for her. Her questioning continued to expand to include the state, the nation, and the world. Mrs. Benn was planting a seed of excellence in me that I could not see. When I went on to an integrated[4] junior high and high school, it was Mrs. Benn's pointed questions that echoed in my head as I sat in classrooms with mostly White classmates. Indeed, I went on to win the Latin and the Chemistry awards. I worked hard and was successful at Morgan State University (an HBCU) and was equally successful at graduate studies at the University of Washington and Stanford University. I had my share of very good teachers and a few not so good ones, but it was Ethel Benn who made an important difference in spurring me on to excellence.

IT'S THE NORTH, ALSO

"How long can a city teach its black children that the road to success is to have a white face?"

—W. E. B. Du Bois

I highlighted the teaching of Ethel Benn and my experience in a Northern city post-*Brown* because much of the discourse about the *Brown* decision centers on the resistance of Southern cities and on Southern states' refusal to implement the Court's decree. The *Brown II*[5] decision, or consent decree, resulted in school closures, the proliferation of segregation academies (previously discussed) and outright resistance to admitting Black students into previously all-White schools. With the exception of Boston, the historical record tends to highlight Southern schools (e.g., New Orleans; Prince Edward County, Virginia; and Little Rock, Arkansas) but there is a story to be told about other Northern schools (Theoharis & Woodard, 2003).

Schools in cities like New York, Philadelphia, and Chicago flew under the school desegregation radar because they allowed their racially segregated housing policies to do their dirty work. For years I have argued that housing policy *is* education policy (Ladson-Billings, 2015). By maintaining redlining and unfair housing practices, Northern cities did not have to develop separate school systems. They declared that their schools were set up to ensure everyone could attend "neighborhood schools" without acknowledging that school district boundaries were effective tools for maintaining segregated schools. As long as Black families were denied access to housing in White communities, Black children would be cordoned off into all-Black schools. The major advantage of this segregation for Black families is that Black teachers were often assigned to teach in those communities because, like most workers, they wanted to minimize their commute and work closer to home.

Neighborhood segregation meant that Black communities included people from various social strata. Most of the residents were working class and held jobs like tradesmen (carpenters, plumbers, etc.), sanitation workers, nurses' aides, orderlies, and janitors. Those who traveled beyond neighborhood boundaries worked as domestics (in White households and hotels), chauffeurs, and factory workers. However, Black professionals also lived in Black communities. Often their homes were more spacious and luxurious, but nonetheless they were in Black communities. Black doctors, dentists, lawyers, and pastors lived in Black communities where they served Black clients almost exclusively. Among the Black professionals in these communities were Black teachers.

The advantage of having Black teachers in the community was that Black parents had ready access to them. They did not have to go to "Back to School nights" or progress report conferences to see their children's teachers. They saw them in the neighborhood grocery stores, in the local barbershops and beauty salons. They worshipped alongside them each Sunday in church. This proximity to teachers, these ordinary daily encounters, meant that Black parents could speak informally with their children's teachers and learn about their progress outside of formal in-school conferences.

Black teachers in segregated Northern cities were more than teachers. As a respected group within the community, Black teachers were called upon to help community members with a variety of tasks. Black teachers could help decode contracts and other legal documents such as leases, eviction notices, or tax information. Black teachers could help run interference for families with landlords, the utility company or an employer. The tacit understanding between Black families and Black teachers during the pre-*Brown* era was that the teachers were there to help the community and its children.

I was a 2nd grader when the *Brown* decision was handed down. I do not remember it because it appeared to have no impact on my schooling experience. Nothing really changed. I attended an almost all-Black school and had mostly Black teachers. None of my classmates was sent to a school across town to attend school with White students. No White students were bused to our school. This more dramatic action would not occur in Philadelphia for more than a decade (Franklin, 1979; Phillips, 2005). Similarly, cities like Chicago (Anderson & Pickering, 1986), Milwaukee (Dougherty, 2004), and New York (Taylor, 1997), experienced a similar lack of disruption in school assignment due to *Brown*. Rather than wait for a directive from the federal government to enforce the Brown decision, local activists lobbied the Pennsylvania Human Relations Commission (HRC) (Phillips, 2005). The upshot of this local activism was a statement by the School District of Philadelphia Board of Education that endorsed a nondiscrimination policy as its standing rule. However, this policy statement was not accompanied by enforcement at the local or state level. As community members pressed for school desegregation, they were met by an argument that the district had no resources to enforce the changes desegregation required.

Philadelphia, like most Northern cities in the post–World War II era, experienced a surge of migration from the South. Better-paying factory jobs and less overt racism were the draw that spurred the Great Migration (Wilkerson, 2010). Although Wilkerson documents a 6-decade movement of 6 million Black people from the U.S. South to the North, the postwar period was an especially active one. My own family, on both my mother's and father's sides, made their way from South Carolina to Philadelphia early in the 20th century. My mother experienced all of her schooling in the School District of Philadelphia, graduating in the midst of the Great Depression in 1934. My father arrived in Philadelphia with his older brother in 1927 to join relatives who had migrated to the city at least a decade earlier. He possessed a 3rd-grade education from the one-room, segregated rural school he attended along with his four older brothers and two older sisters. He never returned to school once he arrived in Philadelphia and he proceeded to work as a manual laborer and janitor for the next 64 years. My parents' stories were echoed across the North and reflected the changing demographics of Philadelphia and other large Northern cities.

As Northern cities' populations of Black citizens grew, Whites began moving to the outer reaches and suburban communities surrounding the cities. I have argued elsewhere (Ladson-Billings, 2015) that it is no coincidence that the Interstate Highway Act (1956) came one year after *Brown II*. The ability of Whites to move away from urban city centers via a well-financed highway system made suburban living an oft-chosen option for them. Those interstate highways not only took White residents out of cities, but they also took shopping (the suburban malls) and schools with them. In the late 1960s, the School District of Philadelphia had 280 schools serving approximately 280,000 students (Royal, 2022). The district was divided into eight geographic districts that mirrored the racial/ethnic housing patterns of the city. District 1 (West Philadelphia) and 4 (North Philadelphia) were predominately Black. District 2 and 3 served working-class White ethnic communities (i.e., Irish, Italian, Polish-descent families). District 5 served mostly Black and Latinx (mostly Puerto Rican) working-class families. District 6 was the "unicorn" that included a 50/50 split between poor/working-class neighborhoods and middle-class neighborhoods. District 7 represented another White ethnic working-class section with a growing number of Black and Latinx families. District 8, located in what was called "The Great Northeast," was almost exclusively White with middle- to upper-middle-class families.

The only feasible desegregation plan in 1968 had to include District 8; and District 8 parents were not interested in busing their children out of the Great Northeast. Slowly but surely Philadelphia began to resemble Detroit, where White families fled to the suburbs. White families made one of two choices: enrolling their children in private schools (mostly parochial schools) or moving outside the city limits. *Brown* would face a difficult future in Philadelphia. The 1974 *Milliken v. Bradley* case in Detroit ruled that urban school districts could not include suburban schools (schools across city or county lines) in their desegregation plan. Thus, the major metropolitan areas avoided compliance with *Brown* by creating incentives for Whites to move outside of the city limits to create Whites-only enclaves that could not be considered in urban desegregation plans.

BELIEVING THEY ALL CAN LEARN: KIMYA MOYO

I met Kimya Moyo a few years after I concluded my study on successful teachers of African American students. Moyo was one of the few African American teachers to pass the National Board for Professional Standards Test (NBPTS) in secondary mathematics. According to Leftwich (2005), Black teachers' success rate with the NBPTS is disproportionately lower than their White peers. Moyo reached out to me soon after she passed her certification exam with what I thought was a strange request. Moyo explained that she had participated in the almost yearlong process of assembling her information, answering written prompts, sharing lesson plans, student work, and student assessments, and videotaping her teaching performance. But the question that plagued her was: "Were my students actually learning?" Moyo was not convinced that showcasing her teaching as a "performance" was enough to make an argument that the students were actually learning. She asked me to review her NBPTS portfolio that contained a set of her videotaped lessons, and I was amazed. She was teaching mathematics in creative and imaginative ways. But first, it is important to share a bit of her background.

Kimya Moyo began teaching in 1969. She was a part of a small group of African American students who attended Northwestern University and ultimately forced the university to confront the level of dissatisfaction and alienation Black students experienced on campus (Ulalisa, 2023). Moyo stated that when she first arrived on campus, her dormitory roommate, a White woman, moved out "because she was not going to live with a Black person" (Ulalisa, 2023, p. 1). Moyo remained active in Black students' politics throughout her time at Northwestern, including a takeover of the university's bursar's office.

Kimya's teaching experiences took her to Chicago, Cincinnati, and West Africa. In 1993 she began directing a Saturday school experience for Black youth in grades 8–12 in her Cincinnati home. With the help of other Black teachers who volunteer, Moyo helps students in her Sankofa Enrichment Program improve their academic performance and learn about their culture. Second-year students participate in a trip to Detroit and Canadian Underground Railroad sites. Third-year students get to travel to the Sea Islands, a pivotal landing point of enslaved Black people after the harrowing Middle Passage. Students who continue with Sankofa into the fourth year earn the right to go to Ghana, West Africa.

My encounter with Moyo via her NBPTS portfolio was profound. I studied her tapes, and it seemed clear to me why she was board certified. She was teaching a group of students who were *not* recommended for algebra. They were initially assigned to "general math." Moyo decided that general math would limit their postsecondary possibilities and decided to offer an algebra class for the students. In her class, Moyo taught the students practical applications for algebra. For example, her students were required to plan, design, and create an article of clothing using large plastic trash bags. The students modeled their final products in a schoolwide fashion show.

In another lesson I saw Moyo write a simple equation on the board that read, "$4+3=x$" and ask, "What does this mean?" Initially, the students called out, "7!" "No," responded Moyo. I didn't ask you to solve the equation, I asked you to explain what it means." At that point you could see some puzzled looks on the students' faces. One student responded, "Well, 4 of something plus 3 of something equals an unknown something." "Pretty good," said Moyo, "but what information is missing? Again, after some hesitation a student finally chimed in, "Well, we don't know what the 'somethings' are!" "Exactly," boomed Moyo. "The 'somethings' will provide you with the context and without context mathematics doesn't make sense!" Rather than forcing students to do rote memorization of number facts or multiplication tables, Moyo wanted students who had previously not experienced success in mathematics to become more fluent in the language of mathematics.

A special touch that Ms. Moyo exhibited in her videotapes was her connection with her students' parents. Just before the end of the first progress report period, Moyo invited her students and their parents to her home. Crowded together into what looked like her living room and an adjoining three-seasons porch, the students sat beside their parents while Moyo extolled their effort and accomplishments. She then presented the group with a decorated cake and proclaimed, "Congratulations, you are a quarter of the way through!" Next, Moyo gave each student an envelope and said, "Your first-quarter grade is in the envelope. Open it up and then explain to your parent(s) why you received that grade." I watched as the students spoke with authority about what they achieved and what they still needed to improve on. Moyo stood to the side as the students took ownership of their academic progress. I was certain that her students were learning.

THE *BROWN* FALLOUT—WHAT HAS NOT CHANGED

As we reflect upon the 70 years since *Brown*, I know that my assignment for this chapter is to focus on the experiences of Black teachers before and up to the decision. However, I think it is important to consider the current conditions that make *Brown*'s goal of fair access to education difficult to achieve. Instead of focusing solely on access, Brown could have taken a stronger stance on equality of outcomes. Black teachers still comprise just 6.1% of the teaching population while White teachers make up 79.9%. Recruiting and retaining Black teachers are the main challenges facing many school districts. However, even if we increase the numbers of Black teachers, we must recognize the sociopolitical context of today's public schools.

In the mid-1950s, Nobel Prize–winning economist Milton Friedman insisted that public education should be subject to market forces. Friedman believed that parents should be given vouchers that would allow them to send their children to whatever schools they wanted—public or private (McGurn, 2023). Friedman believed the competition to get students and their parents to choose them would force schools to improve their educational offerings. However, his theory aided the cause of segregationists who saw vouchers as a way to avoid school desegregation. Friedman's argument seemed, in the 1950s, unlikely to be taken up. Today in 2024, there are 25 voucher programs in 16 states.[6] Most of these voucher programs exist in communities serving poor children of color (e.g., New Orleans, Milwaukee, Washington, DC) who are already attending schools that can be described as hyper-segregated.

As challenging as voucher programs may be for maintaining public education systems, another, more widespread option for what is being called "parental choice" is charter schools. Public school charters are not universally a bad option. Charter schools started and governed by local communities often provide important educational options for poor parents of color. Parents who identify a need can create a school that better meets that need. For example, after 1998, when California voters passed Proposition 227 (the Unz Amendment), which outlawed bilingual education

(Ryan, 2002), parents who wanted their children to maintain their language used the state's charter school laws to create bilingual schools. In Madison, Wisconsin, the persistent failure of Black children in the public schools prompted a community member to mobilize a group to create a preschool that has now expanded to a preK–8 school of about 400 children, mostly Black and Brown. In the fall of 2024, Appleton, Wisconsin, will open its first African-centered school, organized and chartered by a community-based nonprofit. However, the charter school laws have allowed large educational management organizations (EMOs) to move into urban communities and take over dozens of schools without posting any real academic improvement. One of the supposed positives of EMOs is that they hire Black teachers at a greater rate than traditional public schools (largely because they allow a greater degree of alternative certification). However, such schools are seen as primarily focusing on discipline and regimentation, and on rote learning. They have high rates of attrition when students fail to comply with school rules around wearing uniforms, sitting and standing at attention, or a vast array of regulations including things like failure to "track" the teacher[7] or not having parent engagement. In some communities, charter schools operate on an admissions system that excludes students with special needs. Although wholly funded by public monies, some charter schools function more like private schools and dismiss students who they perceive may lower the aggregate test scores.

In 2007 I asked a provocative question of a group of education researchers and law professors (Ladson-Billings, 2007). I asked, "Can we at least have *Plessy*?" I was suggesting that it was better to have a "real *Plessy*" than a "fake *Brown*." A real *Plessy* would mean that the separate schools Black and Brown children find themselves in would be required to have equitable funding, equally qualified teachers, and equal curricular materials as their White middle-income peers. I argued that it was clear that school districts were not going to ever truly desegregate and since Black and Brown children were going to remain in segregated enclaves, why can't we do right by them in their own communities?

Finally, it is important to note how White communities have successfully used *Brown* to their advantage. In 2007, the Supreme Court heard the case of *Parents Involved in Community Schools v. Seattle Public School District 1* (PICS). The Court ruled that it was unconstitutional for a school district to use race to assign students to a school to achieve demographic diversity. The Seattle School District had a policy of allowing students to apply to any high school in the district. Of course, some schools were oversubscribed because of their academic reputations. The district was forced to use a variety of factors as tiebreakers to determine who would be admitted. One factor was race. The Court found the use of race to be unconstitutional and ruled in favor of the parents. The PICS decision was coupled with another case, *McFarland v. Jefferson County, KY*; White parents in both Seattle and

Louisville won by claiming theirs was a victory for the *Brown* decision. This declaration reminded me of the late Derrick Bell, who insisted that there is never a civil rights decision that does not advantage White people. In his classic *Faces at the Bottom of the Well* (1992), Bell outlines the "Rules of Racial Standing." The first rule seems to apply when considering what has happened in the Supreme Court:

> The law grants litigants standing to come into court based on their having sufficient personal interest and involvement in the issue to justify judicial cognizance. Black people (while they may be able to get into court) are denied such standing legitimacy in the world generally when they discuss their negative experiences with racism or even when they attempt to give a positive evaluation of another black person or of his work. No matter what their experience or expertise, blacks' statements involving race are deemed "special pleading" and thus not entitled to serious consideration. (p. 111)

I contend that Black teachers understood that they were perceived to have no standing when it came to making decisions regarding the education of Black children. They knew their jobs were in jeopardy when *Brown* was decided, but if it meant that Black children would have better opportunities, they were willing to make the sacrifice. The role of Black teachers cannot be overstated in the history of the education of Black students. Black teachers often find themselves as advocates for Black students over issues such as special education assignment, representation in suspension and expulsion rates, and access to Advanced Placement and Honors programs and to quality cocurricular activities. But I also argue that Black teachers are important for *all* children. It is important for children of all races and ethnicities to experience expertise and skill that exists in people in every racial or ethnic group that reflects the diversity of the nation. Blazar (2024) documents the positive impact that Black teachers have on all students regardless of race or ethnicity. His study shows student improvements in reading and mathematics along with decreased absenteeism and increased student engagement and self-efficacy. The rapid disappearance of Black teachers is troubling and disheartening. When it comes to the education of Black students we must always ask, "But what about the Black teachers?"

REFERENCES

Anderson, A., & Pickering, G. W. (1986). *Confronting the color line: The broken promise of the Civil Rights Movement in Chicago*. University of Georgia Press.

Bell, D. (1992). *Faces at the bottom of the well: The permanence of racism*. Basic Books.

Bennett, B. (2020, September 5). *Little Rock Nine: Decades-long battle for school equity began with nine Black students facing an angry White mob.* Southern Poverty Law Center. https://www.splcenter.org/news/2020/09/25/little-rock-nine-decades-long-battle-school-equity-began-nine-black-students-facing-angry

Blazar, David. (2024). *Why Black teachers matter.* (EdWorkingPaper: 21-501). Annenberg Institute at Brown University: https://doi.org/10.26300/jym0-wz02

Bolton, C. C. (2007). *The hardest deal of all: The battle over school integration in Mississippi, 1870–1980.* University of Mississippi Press.

Brooklyn Museum. (n.d.). *The Dinner Party: Heritage Floor: Milla Granson.* https://www.brooklynmuseum.org/eascfa/dinner_party/heritage_floor/milla_granson

Brown v. Board of Education [II], 349 U.S. 294 (1955).

Brown v. Board of Education of Topeka, 347 U.S. 483 (1954).

Center for Black Educator Development. (2021, February 12). *Milla Granson (Lily Ann Granderson), Black Educator Hall of Fame.* Philly's 7th Ward. https://phillys7thward.org/2021/02/milla-granson-lily-ann-granderson-black-educator-hall-of-fame

Champagne, A. (1973). The segregation academy and the law. *Journal of Negro Education, 42*(1), 58–66.

Charron, K. M. (2009). *Freedom's teacher: The life of Septima Clark.* University of North Carolina Press.

Clark, S. P. (1990). *Ready from within: Septima Clark and the Civil Rights Movement, a first-person narrative* (C. S. Brown, Ed.). Africa World Press.

Dougherty, J. (2004). *More than one struggle: The evolution of school reform in Milwaukee.* University of North Carolina Press.

Epps, E. G. (2002). Race and school desegregation: Contemporary legal and educational issues. *Penn GSE Perspectives in Urban Education, 1*(1).

Fenwick, L. (2022). *Jim Crow's pink slip: The untold story of Black principal and teacher leadership.* Harvard University Press.

Franklin, V. P. (1979). *The education of Black Philadelphia: The social and educational history of a minority community.* University of Pennsylvania Press.

Fultz, M. (2004). The displacement of Black educators post-Brown: An overview and analysis. *History of Education Quarterly, 44*(1), 11–45.

Givens, J. (2021). *Fugitive pedagogy: Carter G. Woodson and the art of Black teaching.* Harvard University Press.

Halfmann, J. (2018). *Midnight teacher: Lilly Ann Granderson and her secret school.* Lee & Low Books.

Hudson, M. J., & Holmes, B. J. (1994). Missing teachers, impaired communities: The unintended consequences of *Brown v. Board of Education* on the African American teaching force at the pre-collegiate level. *The Journal of Negro Education, 63*(3), 388–393.

Ladson-Billings, G. (2004). Landing on the wrong note: The price we paid for *Brown. Education Researcher, 33*(7), 3–13.

Ladson-Billings, G. (2007). Can we at least have *Plessy*? The struggle for quality education. *North Carolina Law Review, 85*(5), 1279–1292.

Ladson-Billings, G. (2015). Getting to Sesame Street: Fifty years of compensatory education. *The Russell Sage Foundation Journal of the Social Sciences, 1*(3), 96–111.

Ladson-Billings, G. (2022). *The dreamkeepers: Successful teachers of African American children* (3rd ed.). Jossey-Bass.

Leftwich, P. J. (2005). *Discourse and disconnect: Black teachers and the quest for national board certification* [Unpublished dissertation]. University of South Florida.

Lerner, G. (Ed.) (1972). *Black women in White America: A documentary history*. Vintage Books.

McFadden, G. J. (1996). Septima P. Clark and the struggle for human rights. In C. Crawford, J. A. Rouse, & B. Woods (Eds.) *Women in the Civil Rights Movement: Trailblazers and torchbearers 1941–1965* (pp. 85–97). Indiana University Press.

McFarland v. Jefferson County Public Schools, 416 F.3d, 513 (2005).

McGurn, W. (2023, April 3). Milton Friedman's school choice revolution. *The Wall Street Journal*. https://www.wsj.com/articles/milton-friedmans-revolution-school-choice-education-vouchers-public-schools-unions-parents-virginia-c43e8ee9

Moore, J. M. (2003). *Booker T. Washington, W. E. B. Du Bois, and the struggle for racial uplift*. Scholarly Resources.

Morris, A. (1984). *The origins of the Civil Rights Movement: Black communities organizing for change*. Free Press.

National Center for Education Statistics. (2023a). *Condition of Education: Characteristics of public school teachers*. U.S. Department of Education, Institute of Education Sciences. https://nces.ed.gov/programs/coe/indicator/clr

National Center for Education Statistics. (2023b). *Condition of Education: Racial/ethnic enrollment in public schools*. U.S. Department of Education, Institute of Education Sciences. https://nces.ed.gov/programs/coe/indicator/cge

Parents Involved in Community Schools v. Seattle School Dist. No. 1, 551 U.S. 701 (2007).

Phillips, A. (2005). A history of the struggle for school desegregation in Philadelphia, 1955–1967. *Pennsylvania History: A Journal of Mid-Atlantic States*, 72(1), 49–76.

Plessy v. Ferguson, 163 U.S. 537 (1896).

Rockwell, N. (1964). *The problem we all live with* [Oil on canvas]. Norman Rockwell Museum, Stockbridge, MA. https://www.nrm.org/thinglink/text/ProblemLiveWith.html

Royal, C. (2022). *Not paved for us: Black educators and public school reform in Philadelphia*. Harvard University Press.

Ryan, W. (2002). The Unz Initiative and the abolition of bilingual education. *Boston College Law Review*, 43(2), 487–519.

Siddle Walker, V. (1996). *Their highest potential: An African American school community in the segregated South*. University of North Carolina Press.

Taylor, C. (1997). *Knocking at our own door: Milton A. Galamison and the struggle to integrate New York City schools*. Columbia University Press.

Theoharis, J., & Woodard, K. (2003). *Freedom north: Black freedom struggles outside the South, 1940–1980*. Palgrave Macmillan.

Ulalisa, T. (2023, April 20). Black NU alum reflect on campus hostility in '60s. *Evanston Roundtable*. https://evanstonroundtable.com/2023/04/20/northwestern-in-the-1960s-an-isolating-hostile-place-for-black-students/

U.S. Census Bureau. (2023). *Quick Facts: Holly Springs city, Mississippi.* https://www.census.gov/quickfacts/hollyspringscitymississippi

Waugh, D. L. (2012). From forgotten to remembered: The long process of school desegregation in Chapel Hill, North Carolina and Prince Edward County, Virginia [Doctoral dissertation, University of North Carolina–Chapel Hill].

Wilkerson, I. (2010). *The warmth of other suns: The epic story of America's great migration.* Random House.

Woodson, C. G. (1933). *The mis-education of the Negro.* Association Press.

CHAPTER 6

Facing the Rising Sun
Black Teachers' Positive Impact Post-*Brown*

Travis J. Bristol and Desiree Carver-Thomas

> *Sing a song full of the faith that the dark past has taught us,*
> *Sing a song full of the hope that the present has brought us;*
> *Facing the rising sun of our new day begun,*
> *Let us march on 'til victory is won.*
>
> —James Weldon Johnson (2019)

INTRODUCTION

The question "What is the importance of Black teachers in the 21st century?" is seemingly rhetorical, and yet particularly relevant given that scholars have termed this moment in U.S. history, 70 years after the *Brown v. Board* decision, the Second or New Nadir of race relations in the United States (Cha-Jua, 2010; Connolly et al., 2017). This naming is in response to Rayford Logan, who in 1954 characterized as "the Nadir" the period after Reconstruction through the early 1900s in which anti-Black racism was on public display, most notably through the rise of the Ku Klux Klan, the Supreme Court's 1896 *Plessy* ruling that sanctioned racial segregation, and Southern states' rescinding of voting rights (Logan, 1954).

The current sociopolitical climate is one in which pundits (Rufo, 2023) and policymakers (Florida Governor's Office, 2021) have publicly shared their playbook to push back against Black social and economic progress. Individuals and governmental institutions have presented affirmative action as reverse discrimination; enacted state and local legislation to ban books that centered the contributions of Black Americans (see Florida's House Bill 1467[1]); legislated against diversity, equity, and inclusion policies and practices in both the public and private sectors; coordinated the forced resignation of Harvard University's president Claudine Gay, a Black woman (Blow, 2024); increased voter suppression in predominantly Black communities

(Combs, 2016); and ruled in the Supreme Court to end affirmative action policies in higher education. These extensive examples are clear and present indications that we are in a Second Nadir.

As many of the chapters in this volume note, Black teachers were often the community members whose clarion calls about the assault on Black Americans' lives and liberties spurred a generation of Black students to demand that this country work on bringing to fruition the American Project: an inclusive multi-ethnoracial democracy in which the government works actively to remove structural barriers to ensure all persons have equal opportunity to move from the margins to the center. Black teachers served as an important source of knowledge and supported their students to understand the role of racism in shaping Black people's experiences. Schools staffed by Black teachers and administrators, in turn, were places to strategize and receive moral and practical support in the fight for equity. Black educators have taken part in the freedom struggles in this country, both as educators and individuals (Givens, 2021; Siddle Walker, 2001). However, the work of Black teachers has a cost.

In this current moment, a Second Nadir, Black teachers have one of the highest turnover rates among all groups of teachers. According to the most recent data from the U.S. Department of Education, Black teachers and Native American teachers were the subgroups of teachers whose percentage had the largest declines when compared to other groups of teachers (Taie & Lewis, 2023). Numerous circumstances account for this trend. Black teachers serve in the schools with the most administrator turnover and the least fiscal resources with which to do their work (Bristol, 2020). Black teachers are often asked by their colleagues to serve a multiplicity of roles to their students, such as educator, but also discipline enforcer and cultural translator (Bristol & Mentor, 2018). The working conditions of teachers, and Black teachers in particular, are related to these trends. These pressures create the stressful and poorly compensated working conditions in which Black teachers find themselves.

Over the past 60 years, one consistent finding from the research on Black teachers stands out: Black teachers have positive impacts on the academic, social, and emotional outcomes for all students. In this chapter, we draw attention to the extensive body of qualitative and quantitative research on Black teachers' impact for Black students as well as all students. We then present trends in Black teachers' representation in the workforce post-*Brown*. Next, we share more recent research on current issues related to recruiting and retaining Black teachers. We end by identifying federal, state, and local policy and practice efforts that can inform a comprehensive set of policies to recruit, develop, and retain Black teachers. Finally, it is important to note that as we draw attention to the importance of Black teachers for *all* children in U.S. public schools, simply being a Black teacher is not enough. As the research evidence presented in this chapter makes clear,

Black teachers are skilled professionals who think deeply about their practice and how to make their practice relevant and rigorous to their students (Alexander & Miller, 1989; King, 1993; Ladson-Billings & Henry, 1990).

QUALITATIVE IMPACT OF BLACK TEACHERS FOR BLACK STUDENT SUCCESS

Researchers have long documented the impact, or the transformational role, skilled and caring Black teachers have on Black students' lives (Hundley, 1965), a point underscored by Ladson-Billings in this volume. Historians have described how Black teachers and administrators in segregated schools before the *Brown* decision supported and prepared their Black students to navigate a society that was hostile to their very existence (Perlstein, 2019). Black students in *de jure* racially segregated schools in Washington, DC, Beaufort, North Carolina, Little Rock, Arkansas, and Louisville, Kentucky, recounted how their Black teachers provided them with a schooling characterized by educational excellence in underresourced publicly funded schools (Davis, 1996; Jones, 1981; Sowell, 1976; Tilford-Weathers, 1982).

Moreover, education historians Vanessa Siddle Walker and Jarvis Givens, through archival analysis, have drawn attention to the mechanisms used by Black teachers to support their Black students' academic and social and emotional learning in *de jure* segregated schools before *Brown*. Siddle Walker notes that Black teachers in the South taught rigorous curriculum, maintained high expectations, and consistently reminded their Black students that they had an innate capacity to succeed. As Daisy Durrah, a Black North Carolinian who attended segregated schools, recounted her Black teachers saying, "You can do anything you want to if you try hard enough. Not because you're Black necessarily, but because you're you" (Siddle Walker, 1996, p. 151).

While some of the research on the impact of Black teachers on their Black students examines the schooling experiences in the South during *de jure* segregation, before the *Brown* decision, a similar body of research has underscored the importance of Black teachers for the success of Black students in the North during what continues to be *de facto* segregation, post-*Brown* (Graybill, 1997; Irvine, 1990). This research, often centered in urban centers, describes how Black teachers, like their peers in the South, created learning environments that supported their Black students' academic success and social and emotional learning (Gottlieb, 1964; King, 1993). During the late 1960s in the Ocean Hill–Brownsville area of Brooklyn in New York City, a predominantly Black and Puerto Rican community, Black parents, community activists, and administrators described how Black teachers held higher expectations for their Black students when compared to their White teacher colleagues (D'Amico, 2016). Similarly, in northeastern urban centers such as Philadelphia (Royal, 2022) and Boston (Burkholder, 2010) as well as in Midwestern cities like Chicago (Todd-Breland, 2018; Wilson, 2023), researchers have documented how, in the 1970s and 1980s, Black teachers organized their classrooms to support Black and Latinx students' sociopolitical development and learning.

Michele Foster's 1997 book *Black Teachers on Teaching* builds on the burgeoning literature of the late 20th century. In this work, she draws attention to the practices that Black teachers employed to create the classroom conditions that supported student learning. Foster draws on the life histories of 20 veteran and novice Black teachers. One novice teacher, Leonard Collins, describes how he challenged the prescribed curriculum when teaching about Christopher Columbus "discovering" America: "[The textbook] does not discuss the disease and pestilence that they brought over from Europe. I have students examine that same historical event but from a different perspective. I present an alternate perspective and let the students come to their own conclusions" (Foster, 1997, p. 178). Black teachers like Collins have organized their classrooms to support rigor and relevance in service of student learning.

More contemporary scholarship on Black teachers continues to underscore their qualitative impact on their Black students (Farinde-Wu et al., 2017; Madkins, 2011). Researchers have documented how Black teachers' redesign of their content enables the enactment of culturally sustaining practices to increase engagement and learning (Acosta, 2019; Milner, 2016). Black teachers draw on their Black students' lived experiences to create classroom environments that center and celebrate Blackness (Cormier et al., 2022; Watson, 2018) and center and celebrate politicized care (McKinney de Royston et al., 2021). Black teachers, who continue to work in schools that have been underresourced by state and local governments, also support their students' sociopolitical consciousness (Jackson & Knight-Manuel, 2019; Lynn, 2002).

In response to the learning environments Black teachers create, Black students describe how their Black teachers create schooling environments that center care and attention to their social and emotional well-being (Jackson et al., 2014). McKinney de Royston et al. (2017) capture how one Black student's experience with a Black man teacher shows care for his social and emotional learning: "He taught us, like it's better to let out stuff than hold in stuff . . . like it's better to cry to let out your feelings" (p. 23). While Black students believed that all their teachers had the capacity to care for them, they also believed that Black teachers' demographic congruence meant that their Black teachers could also relate to their experiences navigating the world (McArthur & Lane, 2019; Nelson, 2016).

In addition to believing that their Black teachers cared for them, Black students also pointed to these teachers' expectations that students meet high academic standards (Lee et al., 2022). Goings and Bianco's (2016) interviews with Black students capture the specific practices their Black teachers used to maintain rigor. One Black student reflected on their experience with Ms. Bailey, a Black woman teacher:

> Like Ms. Bailey has pushed me but she's a teacher of color who I can say in my whole life has pushed me to the college level. I can turn something in and she can be like this isn't college work. This needs to be redone. She's one of the only teachers I know who will push me to do that. (p. 638)

For Black students, Black teachers' added value is not only evident in seeing these teachers as role models, but also in experiencing the rigor, relevance, and care extended toward them (Bristol & Martin-Fernandez, 2019).

QUALITATIVE IMPACT OF BLACK TEACHERS FOR *ALL* STUDENTS

While there is a large body of research on the qualitative impact Black teachers have in the lives of their Black students (Brown, 2012; Irvine, 1989), there is less research in this area that explores how students who are not Black experience their Black teachers. One possible reason for the dearth of research could be that the hyper-ethnoracial segregation of teachers and students in U.S. public schools (as Noguera and Noguera's chapter in this volume notes) makes it challenging for researchers to gather qualitative data in this area. Another explanation is that qualitative researchers continue to center Black students' experiences with Black teachers, with less attention, to date, to understanding how students who are not Black perceive their Black teachers. Nonetheless, scholars have underscored the importance of Black teachers for all students, particularly White students. Such sentiments were captured in the Carnegie Forum's 1986 analysis of what students who are not Black lose when they do not have opportunities to be taught by a Black teacher:

> The race and background of their teachers tells [sic] them something about authority and power in contemporary America. These messages influence children's attitudes towards school, their academic accomplishments and their views of their own and others' intrinsic worth. The views they form in school about justice and fairness also influence their future citizenship. (p. 79)

Approximately 32 years later, Gloria Ladson-Billings once again raises the urgency and underscores the importance of White children learning from Black teachers.

> It is important for White students to encounter Black people who are knowledgeable and hold some level of authority over them. Black students ALREADY

know that Black people have a wide range of capabilities. They see them in their homes, their neighborhoods, and their churches. They are the Sunday School teachers, their Scout leaders, their coaches, and family members. But what opportunities do White students have to see and experience Black competence? (Ferlazzo, 2018)

Given this sociopolitical moment, our Second Nadir, White children need skilled Black teachers who can interrupt their anti-Black beliefs (ross, 2021) as one effort, among many, to actualize the American Project. A limited number of studies investigate perceptions of Black teachers by students of other races and ethnicities. Carey explores Black and Latino young male high schoolers' perceptions of the pedagogies of their Black and Latino male teachers. In one instance, a Latino student reflects on the impact of his Black man teacher: Lucas, whose parents were born in El Salvador, describes Mr. Webber's class as "Engaging. You learn. It's not boring, man. You learn. You're supposed to have, you have group discussions with your table. Mr. Webber, he adds humor to it. He's funny, man. And it's fun, man" (Carey, 2020). Lucas, like his peers, describes how a Black teacher leverages humor to engage students. Given the limited number of empirical articles in this area, future qualitative studies should examine how students who are not Black perceive their Black teachers. As we highlight in the next section, a growing body of quantitative research measures Black teachers' impact on their students who are Black and of other ethnoracial groups.

QUANTITATIVE IMPACT OF BLACK TEACHERS FOR BLACK STUDENT SUCCESS

Over the last 50 years, there has been a clear body of quantitative research that finds that Black teachers have higher academic and social and emotional expectations of their Black students when compared to teachers of other ethnoracial groups (Love & Kruger, 2005; Redding, 2019). An analysis of surveys administered to Michigan teachers in the late 1970s found that when compared to White teachers, Black teachers were more likely to expect that their Black students would enter and complete college (Beady & Hansell, 1981). Subsequent studies in school districts in urban centers such as Baltimore, MD, and Rochester, NY, found that when compared to their White peers, Black teachers hold higher academic expectations of their Black students (Alexander et al., 1987; Pigott & Cowen, 2000). More recent studies have analyzed national data sets and corroborated these early findings (Fox, 2016). For example, one analysis of the Early Childhood Longitudinal Study-K: 1998, a nationally representative sample of U.S. kindergarteners through 5th-graders and their teachers, found that Black teachers, when compared to other teachers, had higher perceptions of Black students' math and reading abilities (Ouazad, 2014). Using this same data set, Grissom and Redding (2016) found that Black students were more likely to be assigned to gifted-and-talented programs when their teachers were Black compared to when their teachers were not Black. This pattern persists through high school: An analysis of the National Longitudinal Study, a nationally representative study of U.S. 10th-graders, found that Black teachers had higher expectations about Black students' potential educational attainment than teachers from other ethnoracial groups (Gershenson et al., 2016).

Beyond a greater belief in Black students' academic and social and emotional potential, Black teachers, when compared to their colleagues, rely less on exclusionary discipline practices toward Black students than teachers of other races (Liu et al., 2023). One of the initial quantitative studies of state-level (North Carolina) administrative data found that when Black elementary, middle, and high school students had a Black teacher, they experienced less exclusionary discipline than students taught by a White teacher (Lindsay & Hart, 2017). These findings on the reduced likelihood of Black students' suspension when matched to a Black teacher also extend to local school districts. An examination of a decade of data in the country's largest school district, New York City, found that assignment to a Black teacher decreased the likelihood of suspension for Black elementary students compared to Black students assigned to teachers who are not Black (Shirrell et al., 2023). Hayes et al.'s (2023) more recent study of Black middle and high school students in a large California urban school district and Hwang et al.'s (2024) study of K–5th-graders in Indiana both find that Black students have a lower probability of receiving a referral or suspension when their teachers are Black, as opposed to White.

Perhaps in response to Black teachers' high expectations, Black students, in turn, are more likely to report higher degrees of personal effort, happiness in class, feeling cared for, and motivated by their teacher when their teacher is Black compared to when their teacher is not Black (Egalite & Kisida, 2018). Black students are more likely to attend school in years when they have a Black teacher than in years when their teacher is not Black (Holt & Gershenson, 2015). The presence of Black teachers teaching an honors course is associated with an increased likelihood of Black students enrolling in that course compared to an honors course taught by a teacher who is not Black (Hart, 2020). Black high school students in a remote learning credit recovery course were more likely to remain logged into the digital platform and to attempt lessons when their online instructor was Black compared to when their teacher was not Black (Darling-Aduana, 2021). Finally, Black teachers' effect on their Black students extends beyond one academic year. Black elementary students in Tennessee who were randomly assigned to one Black teacher were more likely to graduate from high school and to matriculate into college when compared to their Black peers who were not assigned to a Black teacher (Gershenson et al., 2022).

In addition to the social and emotional benefits Black teachers provide to Black students (Liu et al., 2023; Ouazad, 2014), Black teachers are more likely to improve Black students' learning and achievement when compared to teachers from other demographic groups (Carver-Thomas, 2018; Gist & Bristol, 2022). Ehrenberg and colleagues' 1995 analysis of James Coleman's 1966 report to Congress entitled *Equality of Educational Opportunity* found a positive relationship between the concentration of Black teachers and standardized scores for Black students; similarly, the researchers found that Black students in schools with a higher percentage of White teachers had lower gain scores then their Black peers in schools with larger numbers of Black teachers (Ehrenberg et al., 1995). Hanushek, in 1992, found that Black teachers, when compared to White teachers, were more likely to improve Black students' reading achievement. To this end, Hanushek concludes, "[W]hite teachers do significantly worse than [B]lack teachers" (p. 111). A study during the mid- to late 1960s that focused on a standardized high school economic literacy exam found that Black teachers increased Black students' achievement when compared to White teachers (Evans, 1992).

In the 21st century, several studies have explored Black teachers' impact on Black students' achievement (Eddy & Easton-Brooks, 2011; Gershenson et al., 2022). One of the earlier studies was Dee's 2004 reanalysis of a Tennessee randomized control trial around class size in which he found that when Black elementary school students were assigned to Black teachers, their math and literacy scores increased, as compared to the scores of Black children with a White teacher. Subsequent studies that have used nationally representative data (Eddy & Easton-Brooks, 2011), state administrative data from Florida (Egalite et al., 2015) and North Carolina (Clotfelter et al., 2011), and local school districts' administrative records in Texas (Hanushek et al., 2005) and in California (Dee & Penner, 2021) continue to produce one consistent finding. Black teachers, when compared to outcomes for Black students with White teachers, are more likely to increase Black students' achievement. It is important to note that since these studies, for the most part, control for a host of variables, such as teacher preparation and school characteristics, they show that having a Black teacher alone is *not* necessarily sufficient to produce positive student outcomes, but rather provides an added benefit on top of the range of conditions that matter for student success.

BLACK TEACHERS' IMPACT ON *ALL* STUDENTS

Schools remain hypersegregated by race in 2024, as Orfield's chapter in this volume notes. Despite the large body of evidence on the positive impact

Black teachers have on their Black students' achievement and social and emotional learning, our primary premise is *not* to propagate the resegregation of schools or suggest that there be only Black teachers for Black students. In fact, Black teachers are associated with more positive outcomes for students of all races and ethnicities. One early study, using random assignment, examined the impact of the Houston Independent School District's 1960s and 1970s teacher desegregation policy on student learning. Researchers found that Latinx and White students' achievement, as measured by the Iowa Test of Basic Skills, increased when taught by Black teachers who were not required to transfer schools. The author concludes that Black teachers were "more effective with all students" (Sanders, 1984, p. 611).

In an analysis of survey responses from students across six large urban school districts, researchers found that Asian American, Black, Latine, and White students have more favorable perceptions of Black (and Latinx) teachers when compared to White teachers (Cherng & Halpin, 2016). Students, across all ethnoracial groups, also reported that Black teachers were more likely to hold them to higher academic standards and support their efforts to reach those standards. The largest and statistically significant effects were among Asian American students who reported that Black teachers, when compared to White teachers, challenged them academically, made content more engaging, and made connections across content that deepened learning. Black teachers' impact on Asian American students was also evident in Shirrell et al.'s 2023 analysis of a longitudinal data set of New York City Department of Education teachers and students; Asian American girls were less likely to be suspended in the years they were assigned a greater proportion of Black teachers. Finally, Blazar employs random assignment of teachers and students in a statewide data set and finds that assignment to Black teachers, when compared to White teachers, reduces the likelihood of chronic absenteeism, and increases math and ELA achievement for Asian American, Latinx, and White students (Blazar, 2022).

While there continues to be a growing body of research on Black teachers' positive impact on academic outcomes for *all* students, one recent study has measured Black teachers' impact on White novice teachers' student outcomes (Gershenson et al., 2023). Analyzing North Carolina administrative data, researchers find that when White beginning teachers (1–3 years) have a Black teacher on their grade level team, their Black students' math and reading achievement increases and the number of suspensions decrease.

As we have shown, a substantial body of research demonstrates that Black teachers are essential to the teacher workforce. Not only do Black teachers support the achievement and social–emotional development of Black students and students overall, but Black teachers also do the important work of helping American society live up to its ideals. In bringing a wealth of knowledge and personal experience to bear in the classroom and with colleagues, and in serving as role models of Black leadership to students of every background, Black teachers enrich public education. As we will show, however, the Black teacher population has been in decline, jeopardizing the important role Black teachers play in our nation's schools and communities.

TRENDS IN THE REPRESENTATION OF BLACK TEACHERS SINCE *BROWN*

Over the past 3 decades, one of the most profound changes to the teacher workforce has been the steady decline in the share of Black teachers. Based on an analysis of federal teacher survey data from the U.S. Department of Education National Center for Education Statistics's (NCES) National Teacher and Principal Survey (NTPS, 2015 to 2020) and its predecessor, the Schools and Staffing Survey (1987 to 2012) (NCES, n.d.), the proportion of Black teachers has dropped by nearly a third, from 8.6% of teachers in 1990 to 6.1% in 2020 (see Figure 6.1). In contrast, the proportion of teachers of color overall has increased dramatically since 1987 (from about 13% to 20%) and more new teachers are teachers of color today than were 30 years ago. This growth has been primarily driven by increasing numbers of Latinx and Asian American teachers, while the share of Black teachers has been in decline (Carver-Thomas et al., in press).

As a result of the shrinking share of Black teachers in the workforce, they are underrepresented with respect to the Black population in the United States, which was about 13% in 2020 (see Figure 6.2). The Black student-aged population was nearly 14% of children ages 5 to 17 in 2020. Black first-year teachers made up about 7% of first-year teachers, suggesting that if new Black teachers stay in the profession over time, the ranks of these teachers might be able to grow marginally.

THE ROLE OF TEACHER TURNOVER

High turnover rates threaten to undermine any gains made through increased Black teacher recruitment efforts. Based on nationally representative survey data, Black teachers indicated that they were more likely than White teachers to consider transferring schools or leaving the teaching profession. In the 2017–2018 NTPS, more than 35% of Black teachers agreed that they think about transferring schools, compared to 34% of teachers of color overall and 32% of White teachers (Carver-Thomas et al., in press). Further, about 41% of Black teachers reported they would leave teaching for a higher-paying job, compared to 38% of teachers of color overall and 34% of White teachers. These figures are significant, because a difference of even 1 percentage point in teacher turnover rates can amount to tens of thousands of teachers transferring school and leaving the teaching profession,

Figure 6.1. *The Share of Teachers of Color in the Teacher Workforce, 1987–2020*

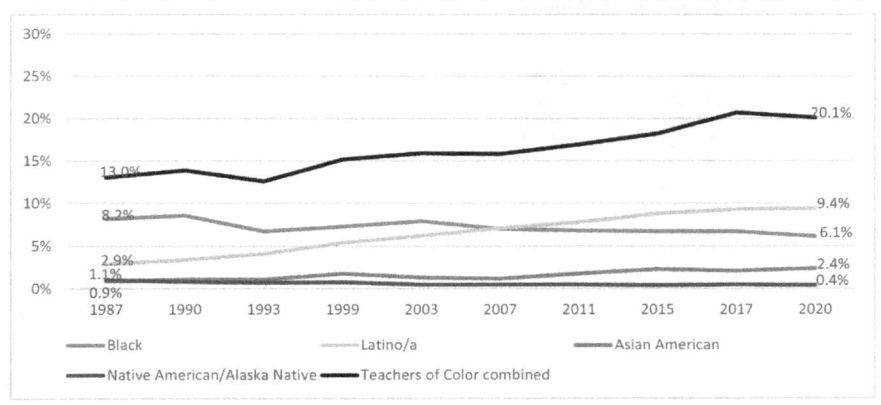

Note: Analysis by Learning Policy Institute. "Teachers of Color" combined includes all non-White teachers, including Native Hawaiian/Pacific Islander teachers and teachers reporting two or more races.
Sources: National Center for Education Statistics reports[2]

creating demand for new teacher hires and increasing the likelihood that schools suffer from teacher shortages (Sutcher et al., 2016). It is important to note, however, that these desires to either move schools or leave teaching may not necessarily reflect actual teacher turnover rates.

In addition to greater desires to transfer schools or leave teaching reported in the 2017–2018 teacher survey, 2021 survey data also show higher turnover rates among Black teachers. Between 2020–2021 and 2021–2022, approximately 8% of all teachers transferred schools and another 8% left the teaching profession (see Figure 6.3). These proportions were about the same for White teachers. Black teachers, however, had higher turnover rates, with about 9% of these teachers moving schools and nearly 11% of Black teachers leaving teaching.[3] Unless more Black teachers both enter the profession and persist in it, the downward trend in the share of Black teachers is likely to continue.

It is important to note that high turnover rates among Black teachers are not just a recent phenomenon. An analysis of 2012 data, for example, shows that between the 2011–2012 and 2012–2013 school year, nearly 22% of Black teachers either transferred schools or left the teaching profession entirely, a rate nearly 50% greater than the non-Black teacher turnover rate that year (Carver-Thomas & Darling-Hammond, 2017).

In 2012, in an era of school closings and layoffs in many cities, the rate of involuntary turnover was much higher for Black teachers than for all other teachers, constituting nearly a third of all turnover (Carver-Thomas & Darling-Hammond, 2017). Twelve percent of Black teachers who left

Figure 6.2. *Percentage distribution of the U.S. population (2020) and of teachers (2020–2021) by race/ethnicity*

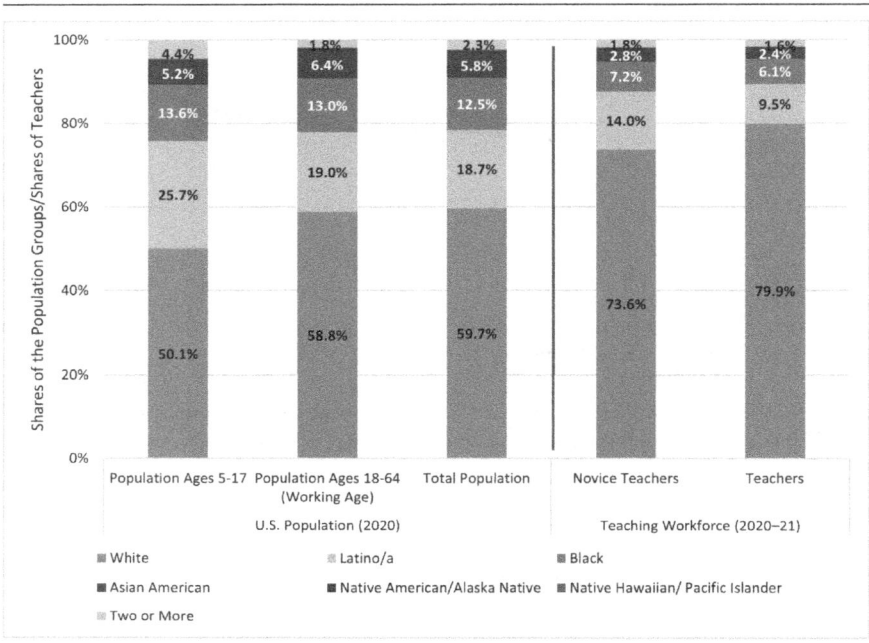

Notes: Hispanics are of any race (Hispanic origin is considered an ethnicity, not a race). Other races are non-Hispanic. Shares are built using U.S. Census Bureau, Population Division (2018). Shares for teachers are obtained from the NTPS 2020–2021 and include full-time, part-time, itinerant, and long-term substitute teachers. Novice teachers are teachers in their first year of teaching. Shares for Native American/Alaska Native populations are as follows: 0.8% ages 5–17, 0.8% ages 18–64, 0.7% total population, 0.4% novice teachers, 0.4% teachers. Shares for Native Hawaiian/Pacific Islander are as follows: 0.2% ages 5–17, 0.2% ages 18–64, 0.2% total population, 0.2% novice teachers, 0.2% teachers.

Sources: Own analyses of the National Teacher and Principal Survey, 2020–2021; U.S. Census Bureau, Population Division. (2018). *Main Projections Series for the United States, 2017–2060 Projected Population by Single Year of Age, Sex, Race, and Hispanic Origin for the United States: 2016 to 2060* (NP2017_D1). File: 2017 National Population Projections Tables. U.S. Census Bureau, Population Division. https://www.census.gov/data/tables/2017/demo/popproj/2017-summary-tables.html

the profession did so involuntarily, while 10% of teachers on average did (Sutcher et al., 2016). While about 30% of all movers left their schools involuntarily, over 50% of Black teachers moved involuntarily (Carver-Thomas & Darling-Hammond, 2017).

High involuntary turnover rates were substantially a function of teacher layoffs during the Great Recession, and of school closings in

Figure 6.3. *Percentage of Teachers Who Moved Schools or Left Teaching, 2020-2021 to 2021-2022*

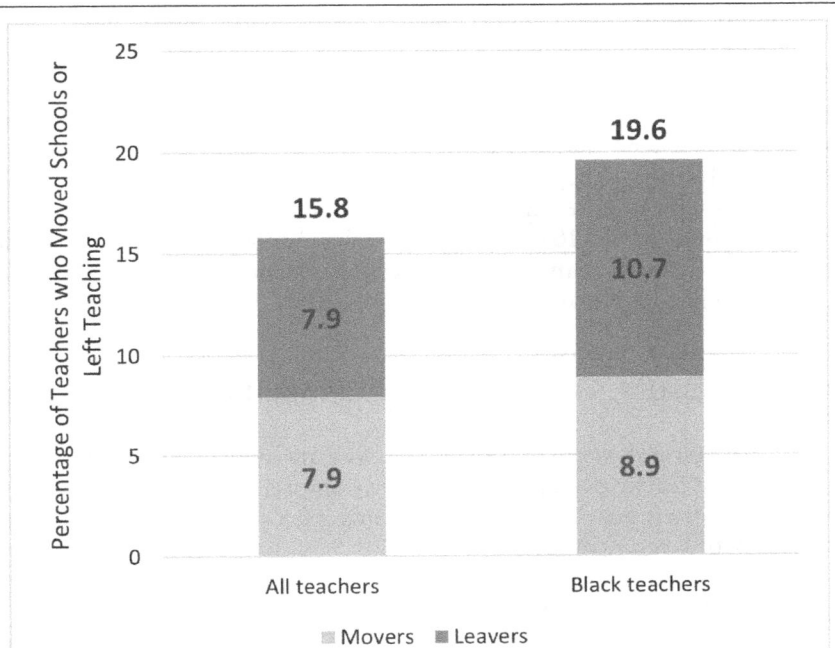

Notes: Data are weighted estimates of the population. "Movers" are teachers who were still teachers in the 2021–2022 Teacher Follow-up Survey (TFS) school year but had moved to a different school from their 2020–2021 NTPS school. "Leavers" are 2020–2021 NTPS teachers who were no longer teachers in the 2021–2022 TFS school year. Detail may not sum to totals because of rounding.

Source: Taie, S., & Lewis, L. (2023). *Teacher attrition and mobility. Results from the 2021–22 Teacher Follow-up Survey to the National Teacher and Principal Survey* (NCES 2024-039), Table A-2. U.S. Department of Education. National Center for Education Statistics. https://nces.ed.gov/pubsearch/pubsinfo.asp?pubid=2024039

urban districts due both to declining enrollments and sanctions targeted to schools with low test scores under No Child Left Behind (Garnett, 2014; U.S. Department of Education, 2011). Closures of traditional public schools reportedly increased from 717 in 2000–2001 to 1,069 in 2010–2011, an increase of about 50% (Layton, 2013). Further, closures disproportionately impact schools serving more Black students—where Black teachers are more likely to teach—especially when closures are related to accountability measures (Ewing, 2018). Indeed, evidence from school closures in Chicago Public Schools indicates that Black teachers were disproportionately impacted by school closures in the district, making up more than 51% of teachers terminated (Todd-Breland, 2018). Large-scale layoffs of Black teachers thus contribute to significant declines in the Black teacher workforce.

Decreases in the numbers of Black teachers have been proportionally much greater than decreases in the size of the overall teaching force in some of the nation's largest cities, listed in Table 6.1. In New Orleans, more than 7,000 teachers—most of whom were Black—were fired en masse after Hurricane Katrina. They were replaced by predominantly young, White teachers brought in to teach in the charter schools that replaced the district schools (Trujillo et al., 2017). As a result, the number of Black teachers declined there by more than 62%. In other major cities, the number of Black teachers declined by anywhere from 15% to 39%.

CURRENT ISSUES IN RECRUITING AND RETAINING BLACK TEACHERS

Decades of research show that several factors are associated with recruiting and retaining teachers, including access to comprehensive preservice preparation, supportive teaching conditions, ongoing professional development, and competitive compensation.

Access to Comprehensive Preservice Preparation

Prior research shows that access to comprehensive preservice preparation is associated with greater retention rates among teachers, in addition to supporting school stability and student achievement (Darling-Hammond, L., 2015). In what follows, we investigate the extent to which Black teachers

Table 6.1. Percentage Change in Teacher Population by Race and Ethnicity, 2002–2012

City	Overall	White	Black	Hispanic
Boston	−3.3	−0.8	−18.3	1.1
Chicago	−13.4	−3.2	−39.2	6.4
Cleveland	−17.4	−12.0	−33.9	−9.4
Los Angeles	−16.9	−28.0	−33.2	6.5
New Orleans	−44.4	3.3	−62.3	43.5
New York City	−2.0	−1.9	−15.1	2.4
San Francisco	−11.9	−21.9	−32.4	8.1

Source: Bond, B, Quintero, E., Casey, L., & Di Carlo, M. (2015). *The state of teacher diversity in American education*. Albert Shanker Institute. http://www.shankerinstitute.org/resource/teacherdiversity

have had access to preservice preparation, currently and over time. We also highlight the role that college debt may play in these trends.

Black teachers are less likely than White teachers to complete preservice preparation and to be fully certified. Black teachers are also more likely than White teachers to enter the profession through an alternative route, which typically offers little, if any, preservice coursework or student teaching. A staggering 45% of beginning Black teachers entered through such a route in 2017–2018, compared to 38% of teachers of color overall and just 24% of beginning White teachers (see Figure 6.4).[4]

Overrepresentation in alternative certification programs likely explains why beginning Black teachers were less likely than White teachers to have taken any preservice coursework (47% of beginning Black teachers did vs. 56% of beginning White teachers), and less likely to have done any student teaching (62% vs. 83%). Beginning Black teachers were also less likely to have access to the most comprehensive student teaching duration. About 38% of students taught for 12 weeks or more compared to 64% of beginning White teachers. Just 68% of beginning Black teachers are fully credentialed (holding either a regular or probationary certificate) in their state compared to about 84% of beginning White teachers. Having less access to preservice preparation is associated with higher turnover rates, undermining growth of the Black teacher workforce.

Figure 6.4. *Percentage of Beginning Teachers Who Entered Teaching Through an Alternative Route to Certification Program*

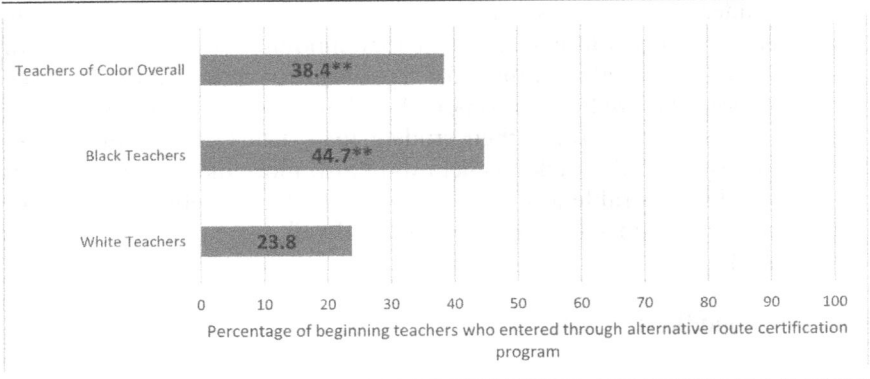

Notes: Sample includes teachers who are full time, part time, or itinerant in public schools. Beginning teachers are teachers with 3 or fewer years of experience. Statistical tests were conducted to compare Black teachers and teachers of color overall with White teachers. * $p < .05$, ** $p < .01$

Source: LPI analysis of the 2017–2018 National Teacher and Principal Survey (NTPS) microdata from the U.S. Department of Education, National Center for Education Statistics. https://nces.ed.gov/pubsearch/pubsinfo.asp?pubid=2020321

The Burden of Student Loan Debt

Access to financial supports likely plays a role in whether teachers of color are able to access teacher preparation (Fiddiman et al., 2019). According to a study of college loan debt, even expecting the same debt burden and postgraduation salary, Black undergraduate and graduate students were more likely than White students to report that loans limited their choice of educational institution (Baum & O'Malley, 2003). Black students were more likely to report that they wished they had borrowed less to fund their postsecondary education, that they changed their career plans because of their loans, or that their loan payments were burdensome. Given the persistent and growing racial wealth gap for Black families in particular, it is not hard to imagine that even with the same debt and salary expectations as White students, the cost of college and debt can present a greater relative burden (Perry et al., 2024). In 2016, the median White family had a net worth about 10 times as great ($171,000) as a median Black family (McIntosh et al., 2020). Having less of a safety net to rely on, on average, may explain why Black college students are more likely to report feeling burdened by loans.

Based on the 2020–2021 NTPS, Black teachers were more likely than other teachers to have taken out a student loan to pay for their undergraduate or graduate education (see Table 6.2). About 71% of Black teachers had taken out student loans compared to about 60% of teachers of color overall and 60% of White teachers (Carver-Thomas et al., in press). Black teachers were also more likely to still owe all the amount they had borrowed. Among student loan borrowers, nearly half (44%) of Black teachers who had taken out loans still owed all their loan amount compared to 32% of teachers of color overall and just 15.6% of White teachers. Further, Black teachers were far more likely to report that they experienced a high or very high level of stress regarding their student loan debt (72%) compared to White teachers (58%). Black teachers were also more likely to report that they took a less desirable job due to their student loan debt, although the survey instrument does not ask teachers to detail what makes these roles less desirable.

Teaching Conditions

Even when Black teachers enter the profession fully prepared, challenging teaching conditions can discourage persistence in the classroom (Carter Andrews et al., 2019). The conditions Black teachers experience on the job, including, for example, school characteristics and support from school leaders, can influence their decisions to stay in teaching (Young & Easton-Brooks, 2020).

Table 6.2. Student Loans and Debt by Race/Ethnicity, 2020-2021

	Black Teachers	Teachers of Color Overall	White Teachers
Did you take out any type of student loans for undergraduate or graduate education?	70.5**	60.1	59.8
(Of borrowers) Do you still owe all of the amount that you borrowed?	44.1**	32.2**	15.6
Level of stress regarding loan is high or very high	71.8**	66.8**	57.7
Did you have to work at more than one job at the same time because of student loan debt?	39	37.5	36.5
Did you take a less desirable job because of student loan debt?	28.6**	26.6**	20.5

Source: Analysis of the 2017–2018 National Teacher and Principal Survey (NTPS) microdata from the U.S. Department of Education, National Center for Education Statistics. https://nces.ed.gov/pubsearch/pubsinfo.asp?pubid=2020321

Notes: Teacher counts are rounded to the closest 10. Sample includes teachers who are full time, part time, or itinerant in public schools. Statistical tests were conducted to compare Black teachers and teachers of color overall with White teachers. * $p < .05$, ** $p < .01$.

School Characteristics

There is substantial evidence showing that school resources and characteristics play a role in teacher retention and attrition (Baker et al., 2024). Although prior research shows that Black teachers often report feeling drawn to teach in schools serving more students of color and students from working-class families (Manchanda et al., 2023), teacher attrition is often higher in these schools where resources are often strained (Baker et al., 2024; Carver-Thomas, 2018; Carver-Thomas & Darling-Hammond, 2017). Prior research shows that Black teachers in underresourced schools experience high levels of stress that can reduce job satisfaction and increase the likelihood of teacher turnover (Coleman-King et al., 2023).

Although the NTPS data do not provide details on school-funding levels, the data indicate that Black teachers, on average, are more likely to teach in settings that tend to receive inadequate resources. As noted, schools with more students of color and students from working-class families tend to receive inadequate funding relative to their need, and the magnitude of underfunding can be substantial (Borman & Dowling, 2008; Nguyen et al.,

2020). For Black teachers, about 80% of students in their schools are students of color, compared to about 43% for White teachers. Notably, this overall average masks just how concentrated Black teachers are in a fraction of schools. Nearly two-thirds of Black teachers teach in schools with more than 75% students of color (see Figure 6.5). By comparison, just 17% of White teachers teach in those settings. On the other end of the spectrum, just 3% of Black teachers teach in schools with 25% or fewer students

Figure 6.5. *Distribution of Teachers by Percentage of Students of Color, 2017-2018*

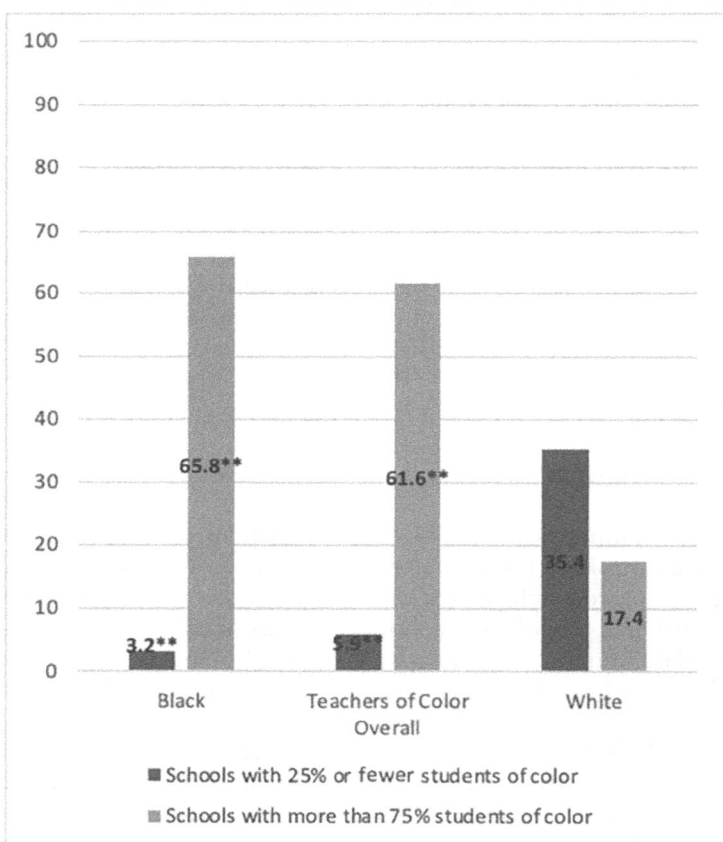

Source: Analysis of the 2017–2018 National Teacher and Principal Survey (NTPS) microdata from the U.S. Department of Education, National Center for Education Statistics. https://nces.ed.gov/pubsearch/pubsinfo.asp?pubid=2020321

Notes: Sample includes teachers who are full time, part time, or itinerant in public schools. Statistical tests were conducted to compare Black teachers and teachers of color overall with White teachers. * p < .05, ** p < .01

of color compared to more than 35% of White teachers. The disparity in school characteristics is similar, though less extreme, for teachers of color overall.

NTPS data show that Black teachers are also more likely to teach students from low-income families, as measured by eligibility for free and reduced-price lunch (FRPL) (Carver-Thomas et al., in press). Nearly 60% of Black teachers teach in schools where more than 75% of students are eligible for FRPL compared to just 23% of White teachers. Black teachers were the least likely to teach in low-poverty schools, which are likely to have disproportionately high resources (5% of Black teachers versus 21% of White teachers).

JOB SATISFACTION AND STRESS IN THE WORKPLACE

To examine Black teachers' experiences in schools requires, first, an understanding of the context in which they teach. As described above, the current conditions under which Black teachers teach, when compared to teachers of other ethnoracial groups, particularly White teachers, remains separate and unequal. There are at least two mechanisms that contribute to Black teachers being overrepresented in underresourced schools and underrepresented in well-resourced schools. Discriminatory practices in the hiring process often prevent Black teachers from teaching in more resourced schools (D'Amico et al., 2017), thereby tracking Black teachers into historically underresourced schools (Bristol, 2020). At the same time, Black teachers are also attracted to schools that serve large numbers of Black and Latinx students, further concentrating Black teachers into schools that tend to be underresourced (Stewart et al., 2023).

Despite having to make bricks without straw, Black teachers describe the joy they experience from teaching (Stanley, 2024). Like their predecessors who taught in *de jure* segregated schools, contemporary Black teachers in *de facto* segregated schools point to the transformative changes they are making in the lives of their predominantly Black and Latinx students as the North Star in their work (Vilson, 2014). Black teachers see the urgency of educating the next generation of Black students who, like them, can uplift the race (Dixson, 2003). These teachers see their presence as a counternarrative to the anti-Black beliefs to which their students are exposed from the media and other societal voices (Beauboeuf-Lafontant, 2002). Black teachers also see how their work contributes to the work of Black community-building (ross et al., 2016). Black parents, for example, describe the impact that Black teachers have on their students and share those appreciations with Black teachers.

While the school-based experiences that Black teachers have with their students are, on average, quite positive, this is less true in their interactions with colleagues who are not Black (White et al., 2020). Black teachers describe ongoing racial micro- and macroaggressions they experience with their White colleagues (Stovall & Mosely, 2023). These micro- and macroforms of aggression include being tasked to be the school's *de facto* disciplinarian or having colleagues use racial epithets to describe students (Brown & Thomas, 2020). These challenging school-based experiences may influence why a Black teacher who is the lone Black teacher on their faculty is less likely to ask colleagues for help around curricular concerns when compared to Black teachers working in schools with many more Black teachers (Bristol & Shirrell, 2019).

Compared to White teachers, Black teachers were less likely to strongly agree that they "like the way things are run at this school," an indicator of school leader support. Just 24% of Black teachers strongly agree that they like the way things are run at their school compared to 25% for teachers of color overall and about 28% for White teachers. Black teachers were also more likely to somewhat or strongly agree that stress and disappointments at their school were not worth it. More than 31% of Black teachers somewhat or strongly agree that stress and disappointments at their school aren't worth it, compared to 30% for teachers of color overall and 27% for White teachers. (See Table 6.3.)

Black teachers also point to their administrators as being another source of challenge to their school-based experiences (Campoli, 2017). The adage

Table 6.3. Teacher Satisfaction Indicators by Race/Ethnicity, 2017–2018

	Black Teachers	Teachers of Color Overall	White Teachers
I like the way things are run at this school			
Strongly Agree	24**	25.2**	27.8
Somewhat agree	46.0	45.2	44.2
Somewhat + strongly agree	70.0	70.4	72.0
The stress and disappointments involved in teaching at this school aren't really worth it			
Strongly Agree	8.4**	7.4**	5.6
Somewhat agree	23.1	22.8	21.8
Somewhat + strongly agree	31.5**	30.2**	27.3

Source: LPI analysis of the 2017–2018 National Teacher and Principal Survey (NTPS) microdata from the U.S. Department of Education, National Center for Education Statistics. https://nces.ed.gov/pubsearch/pubsinfo.asp?pubid=2020321

Notes: Statistical tests were conducted to compare Black teachers and teachers of color overall with white teachers. * $p < .05$, ** $p < .01$

"Teachers don't leave their students, but their principals," also applies to Black teachers. Black teachers who talk about teaching in schools with challenging working conditions describe principals, from all ethnoracial groups, as policing their practice to ensure fidelity to mandated scripted curriculum (Farinde et al., 2016). While it is the case that principals are, on average, enacting policies dictated by the district or charter management organization, Black teachers lay some of the blame on their principals for their in-school experiences. Finally, Black teachers also believe their principals are unable to create school environments that are responsive to their racialized experiences inside of the school.

In response to their challenging workplace environments, novice Black teachers have found refuge and guidance from more seasoned Black teachers in their schools. These school- and district-based efforts (Bristol, 2015) informed nonregulatory guidance tied to the 2015 Every Student Succeeds Act around providing time and space for differentiated support for all teachers, including affinity groups (U.S. Department of Education, 2016). States, supported by the Council of Chief State School Officers' (2018) Diverse & Learner-Ready Teachers Initiative and local school districts (New York City Department of Education's NYC Men Teach [n.d.] and Boston Public Schools' Women Educators of Color program [n.d.]) as well as nonprofits such as the Black Teacher Project (Mosely et al., n.d.) and the Center for Black Educator Development (n.d.) began to create professional learning communities for teachers, and in particular Black teachers. These professional learning communities provide social–emotional support to Black teachers and a space to reflect on practice—in service of student learning (Kohli, 2019).

DISCUSSION

The evidence, as we have provided above, makes clear Black teachers' present-day positive impact on the academic and social–emotional outcomes of Black students, students of color, and White students, and in aid of the continued work of this American Project. The characteristics of the schools in which many Black teachers teach is a sobering story. Seventy years after the *Brown* decision ruled that separate and equal schools were inherently unequal, Black teachers continue to teach in separate *and* unequal schools. In this Second Nadir of race relations in the United States, where Black teachers' workplace experiences are characterized by micro- and macroaggressions, we echo Justice Ketanji Brown Jackson's dissent in the Supreme Court case *Students for Fair Admissions v. Harvard* (2023): "Race still matters" (p. 25). We aimed in this chapter to underscore not only that Black teachers matter, but how they matter in the lives of our nation's children.

We know that our country continues to demonstrate its capacity to solve big problems when there is a will to do so. In the Space Race, after the Soviet Union sent a satellite into space, the United States responded 12 years later by sending a person to the moon. In 1 year, the United States developed the SARS-CoV-2 vaccine to end a once-in-a-lifetime pandemic. Black teachers' positive impact on American society and the higher rate at which they leave the profession when compared to their peers underscores the challenges our country faces related to retaining and, by extension, supporting and recruiting Black teachers. What we choose to do as a country to meaningfully and to comprehensively address these challenges is a matter of will. For current Black teachers, enacting policies and practices to support and retain them speaks both to the faith of the past and the hope of the present for improvements in the conditions under which they educate all children.

Policy and Practice Recommendations for Recruiting and Retaining Black Teachers

We end by offering policy and practice recommendations for recruiting and retaining Black teachers, given the urgency of having skilled Black teachers in our current sociopolitical moment, the body of research revealing Black teachers' positive impact for all students, and the constraints around entering and staying in the profession. Recent data indicate that Black teachers, on average, are significantly less likely to have access to comprehensive preservice preparation that offers a rigorous body of coursework and supervised student teaching. In addition, Black teachers are more likely to teach in underresourced schools that are associated with challenging teaching conditions. Despite this, evidence suggests that federal, state, and local agencies can improve the conditions to recruit and retain more Black teachers. Policies that increase access to comprehensive preparation by underwriting the cost of preparation have been shown to increase both the recruitment and retention of new Black teachers. In addition, on-the-job supports and opportunities for advancement through National Board certification can help to retain current Black teachers. Finally, given the disproportionate rate at which Black teachers leave their schools when compared to their peers and the central role school leaders play in shaping teachers' decisions to stay or leave their schools, building the capacity of principals to create positive working conditions will be critical.

Teacher Residencies and Apprenticeships

High-quality teacher residencies are partnerships between districts and universities that subsidize and improve teachers' training to teach in high-need schools and in high-demand subject areas (Guha et al., 2016). Participants spend a year working as residents with highly effective mentor teachers while completing related coursework at partnering universities (Rowland et al., 2024). Research on teacher residency programs shows that they are effective both in bringing more teachers of color into the profession and in preparing them to stay for the long term. Nationally, about 49% of residents are people of color, far more than the 20% of teachers who are people of color nationally (Guha et al., 2016). Principals find graduates of residency programs to be well-prepared and, in many cases, to be better prepared than typical new teachers. In addition, a review of residency program evaluations shows that residents tend to have higher retention rates over time than nonresident teachers (Guha et al., 2016; National Center for Teacher Residencies, 2016; Sloan & Blazevski , 2015; Solomon, 2009).

A registered apprenticeship is a new avenue for teacher preparation, approved by the federal government in 2021 (Will, 2022). States and districts can create apprenticeship programs and receive federal funding that goes toward wages, textbooks, and other supports. At Austin Peay State University in Tennessee—the first registered teaching apprenticeship in the country—apprentices can complete their teacher preparation free of charge, while they earn a salary and benefits working as educational assistants at partnering Clarksville-Montgomery County school district. States can also use the funds to support grow-your-own programs that support high school students to begin earning college credit before completing their teacher preparation at a partnering university. Much like residencies, the apprenticeship model addresses the student debt burden that disproportionately discourages potential teaching candidates of color from pursuing the profession, while providing the kind of comprehensive teacher preparation that builds the foundation for a successful career in teaching (Carver-Thomas, 2018).

Service Scholarships and Loan Forgiveness

Service scholarship and loan forgiveness programs have also been used to help teaching candidates of color to enter the profession with comprehensive preparation. These programs cover or reimburse a portion of tuition costs in exchange for a commitment to teach in high-need schools or subject areas, typically for 3–5 years. At the federal level, this includes the Teacher Education Assistance for College and Higher Education (TEACH) Grant Program, the Teacher Loan Forgiveness (TLF) Program, and the Public Service Loan Forgiveness (PSLF) Program, all of which have service commitments ranging from 4–10 years. Research indicates that loan forgiveness and service scholarship programs are effective at recruiting teachers, especially when they underwrite a significant portion of educational costs (Hansen et al., 2018; Podolsky et al., 2016).

The TEACH Grant Program provides scholarships of $4,000 per year to undergraduate and graduate students who are preparing for a career in teaching and who commit to teaching a high-need subject in a high-poverty school for 4 years.[5] It excludes early childhood educators and contains a harsh loan conversion penalty for those who do not complete their service commitment, which can be a disincentive for postsecondary students to use the program and ultimately go into teaching. Congress could make the TEACH Grant Program more effective by ending the automatic cuts to the award and increasing it to $8,000, reforming the loan conversion penalty, and ensuring early educators are eligible for benefits.

The TLF and PSLF programs require teachers to toil through years of monthly payments on low salaries before having part or all their federal student loan debt canceled. The PSLF Program, last significantly updated by Congress in 2007, requires 10 years of monthly payments while serving in a public service position before completely retiring the remaining federal loan balance. These programs could be reconstituted to have the federal government make teachers' monthly loan payments until they meet the service requirement to retire their debts completely. Doing so would save teachers hundreds of dollars each month and thousands of dollars over time while delivering a much-needed boost to both recruitment and retention.

NATIONAL BOARD CERTIFICATION

Increases in federal and state funding for teachers to pursue National Board Certification as well as increased compensation for teachers who attain and maintain certification can be one lever to recruit and retain more Black teachers. Established in 1987, National Board Certification serves as the "gold standard" of teacher certification. While just 3% of teachers pursue and receive Board certification, of these teachers more than 88% are White, which is higher than the 80% of White teachers who comprise the U.S. public schools workforce. The body of evidence shows that National Board Certification is associated with better student academic outcomes when compared to teachers who are not certified (Bristol & Esboldt, 2020).

Recent investments at the federal level and in several states seek to increase the number of teachers of color who pursue Board certification. For example, a 2022 $14 million grant from the U.S. Department of Education's (USDOE) Supporting Effective Educator Development (SEED) had an explicit focus on engaging and supporting educators of color (National Board for Professional Teaching Standards, n.d.). In 2023, California (California Department of Education, n.d.) increased its incentives, up to $25,000 over 5 years, for teachers who earn Board certification, and have provided resources to support teachers to pursue certification if they teach in a priority school (i.e., a school serving a majority of students who qualify for free or reduced-price lunch). These investments and policy efforts are leading to increases in educators of color pursuing Board certification. For example, the number of teachers in California pursuing National Board certification in high-priority schools increased from 415 in 2020–2021 to 1,727 in 2021–2022. During that same period, the number of Black, Indigenous, and People of Color (BIPOC) teachers pursuing National Board certification in California increased from 356 to 1,432. With the return on the public's investment in California that continues to increase the number of teachers of color pursuing Board certification, more states should consider expanding their fiscal incentives for teachers who work in high priority schools to become NBCTs.

Building the Capacity of School Leaders

Finally, given the evidence that Black teachers have higher turnover than their peers (Taie & Lewis, 2023) and cite school principals as a primary reason for leaving their schools (Bristol, 2020), national, state, and local policy efforts should focus on building the capacity of school leaders to create more positive teacher working conditions. There have been promising investments at the state and local levels that must be maintained and expanded. For example, the Department of Education's 2022 SEED Grant recipients reflected, quite possibly, the USDOE's priorities around building the capacity of school leaders. Of the 22 multi-million-dollar grants awarded, 11 went to organizations and programs focused on school leadership (Office of Elementary and Secondary Education, n.d.). Grantees included WestEd's Statewide Supports for Future Illinois Principals of Color and the University of Kansas's Supporting Effective School Leaders through Professional Learning and Resources for Equity Leadership & Educator Well-Being.

Several states, including Maryland, Massachusetts, Michigan, North Dakota, Ohio, Tennessee, Idaho, and Louisiana, have used their Every Student Succeeds Act (ESSA) funding to develop or to expand principal leadership programs (Espinoza & Cardichon, 2017). More states should use their ESSA Title II funds to invest in school leadership. These state investments in building the capacity of school building leaders are a critically important lever to improve school working conditions. Many of these states have targeted their investments to principals working in schools that have been historically underresourced. As states develop and expand their principal leadership programs, they should follow the USDOE's lead and prioritize funding to programs that center equity and seek to expand the number of teachers of color, in particular Black teachers who want to become principals.

REFERENCES

Acosta, M. M. (2019). The paradox of pedagogical excellence among exemplary Black women educators. *Journal of Teacher Education*, 70(1), 26–38.

Alexander, K. L., Entwisle, D. R., & Thompson, M. S. (1987). School performance, status relations, and the structure of sentiment: Bringing the teacher back in. *American Sociological Review, 52*(5), 665–682.

Alexander, L., & Miller, J. W. (1989). The recruitment, incentive and retention programs for minority preservice teachers. In A. M. Garibaldi, *Teacher recruitment and retention with a special focus on minority teachers* (pp. 45–51). National Education Association.

Baker, B. D., Di Carlo, M., & Weber, M. (2024). *The adequacy and fairness of state school finance systems* (6th ed.). Albert Shanker Institute, University of Miami School of Education and Human Development, and Rutgers Graduate School of Education. https://www.schoolfinancedata.org/the-adequacy-and-fairness-of-state-school-finance-systems-2024

Baum, S., & O'Malley, M. (2003). College on credit: How borrowers perceive their education debt. *Journal of Student Financial Aid, 33*(3), 7–19.

Beady, C. H. Jr., & Hansell, S. (1981). Teacher race and expectations for student achievement. *American Educational Research Journal, 18*(2), 191–206.

Beauboeuf-Lafontant, T. (2002). A womanist experience of caring: Understanding the pedagogy of exemplary Black women teachers. *The Urban Review, 34*, 71–86.

Blazar, D. (2022). *How and why do Black teachers benefit students? An experimental analysis of causal mediation* (EdWorking Paper 21–501). Annenberg Institute, Brown University. https://edworkingpapers.com/sites/default/files/Blazar_How%20and%20Why%20Do%20Black%20Teachers%20Benefit%20Students_Working%20Paper_0822.pdf

Blow, C. M. (2024, January 3). The persecution of Harvard's Claudine Gay. *The New York Times*, p. A19. https://www.nytimes.com/2024/01/03/opinion/harvard-claudine-gay-politics.html

Borman, G. D., & Dowling, N. M. (2008). Teacher attrition and retention: A meta-analytic and narrative review of the research. *Review of Educational Research, 78*(3), 367–409. https://doi.org/10.3102/0034654308321455

Boston Public Schools. (n.d.). Women educators of color (WEOC). https://www.teachboston.org/weoc

Bristol, T. J. (2015). Male teachers of color take a lesson from each other. *Phi Delta Kappan, 97*(2), 36–41.

Bristol, T. J. (2020). A tale of two types of schools: An exploration of how school working conditions influence Black male teacher turnover. *Teachers College Record, 122*(3), 1–41.

Bristol, T. J., & Esboldt, J. (2020). Curricular contradictions: Negotiating between pursuing national board certification and an urban district's direct instruction mandate. *Harvard Educational Review, 90*(3), 474–496.

Bristol, T. J., & Martin-Fernandez, J. (2019). The added value of Latinx and Black teachers for Latinx and Black students: Implications for policy. *Policy Insights from the Behavioral and Brain Sciences, 6*(2), 147–153.

Bristol, T. J., & Mentor, M. (2018). Policing and teaching: The positioning of Black male teachers as agents in the universal carceral apparatus. *The Urban Review, 50*, 218–234.

Bristol, T. J., & Shirrell, M. (2019). Who is here to help me?: The work-related social networks of staff of color in two mid-sized districts. *American Educational Research Journal, 56*(3), 868–898.

Brown, A. L. (2012). On human kinds and role models: A critical discussion about the African American male teacher. *Educational Studies*, *48*(3), 296–315.

Brown, A. L., & Thomas, D. J. III. (2020). A critical essay on Black male teacher recruitment discourse. *Peabody Journal of Education*, *95*(5), 456–471.

Burkholder, Z. (2010). From forced tolerance to forced busing: Wartime intercultural education and the rise of Black educational activism in Boston. *Harvard Educational Review*, *80*(3), 293–327.

California Department of Education. (n.d.). *NBCT certification incentive program information*. https://www.cde.ca.gov/pd/ps/npbtsprograminfo.asp

Campoli, A. K. (2017). Supportive principals and Black teacher turnover: ESSA as an opportunity to improve retention. *Journal of School Leadership*, *27*(5), 675–700.

Carey, R. L. (2020). Missing misters: Uncovering the pedagogies and positionalities of male teachers of color in the school lives of Black and Latino adolescent boys. *Race Ethnicity and Education*, *23*(3), 392–413.

Carnegie Forum on Education and the Economy. (1986). *A nation prepared: Teachers for the 21st century. (The report of the Task Force on Teaching as a Profession.)* Carnegie Forum on Education.

Carter Andrews, D. J., Castro, E., Cho, C. L., Petchauer, E., Richmond, G., & Floden, R. (2019). Changing the narrative on diversifying the teaching workforce: A look at historical and contemporary factors that inform recruitment and retention of teachers of color. *Journal of Teacher Education*, *70*(1), 6–12.

Carver-Thomas, D. (2018). *Diversifying the teaching profession: How to recruit and retain teachers of color*. Learning Policy Institute. https://doi.org/10.54300/559.310

Carver-Thomas, D., & Darling-Hammond, L. (2017). *Teacher turnover: Why it matters and what we can do about it*. Learning Policy Institute. https://doi.org/10.54300/454.278

Carver-Thomas, D., Leung-Gagné, M., García, E. (in press). *The state of teacher diversity*. Learning Policy Institute.

Center for Black Educator Development. (n.d.). *Liberating education*. https://thecenterblacked.org

Cha-Jua, S. K. (2010). The new nadir: The contemporary Black racial formation. *The Black Scholar*, *40*(1), 38–58.

Cherng, H.Y. S., & Halpin, P. F. (2016). The importance of minority teachers: Student perceptions of minority versus white teachers. *Educational Researcher*, *45*(7), 407–420. https://doi.org/10.3102/0013189x16671718

Clotfelter, C. T., Ladd, H. F., & Vigdor, J. L. (2011). Teacher mobility, school segregation, and pay-based policies to level the playing field. *Education Finance and Policy*, *6*(3), 399–438.

Coleman-King, C., Rosser, B. D., & Sanford, C. M. (2023). Beyond the institution: An informal partnership endeavored toward understanding and addressing Black teacher recruitment and retention. *The Urban Review*, *55*(4), 433–455.

Combs, B. H. (2016). Black (and Brown) bodies out of place: Towards a theoretical understanding of systematic voter suppression in the United States. *Critical Sociology*, *42*(4–5), 535–549.

Connolly, N. D., Johnson, W., & Kelley, R. D. (2017). This, our Second Nadir. *Boston Review*, 96–104.

Coopersmith, J. (2009). Characteristics of public, private, and Bureau of Indian Education elementary and secondary school teachers in the United States: Results from the 2007–08 Schools and Staffing Survey, Table 2. U.S. Department of Education. https://nces.ed.gov/pubs2009/2009324.pdf

Cormier, C. J., Scott, L. A., Powell, C., & Hall, K. (2022). Locked in glass classrooms: Black male special education teachers socialized as everything but educators. *Teacher Education and Special Education*, 45(1), 77–94.

Council of Chief State School Officers. (2018). *The diverse and learner-ready teachers initiative*. https://ccsso.org/topics/diverse-and-learner-ready-teachers-initiative

D'Amico, D. (2016). Teachers' rights versus students' rights: Race and professional authority in the New York City Public Schools, 1960–1986. *American Educational Research Journal*, 53(3), 541–572.

D'Amico, D., Pawlewicz, R. J., Earley, P. M., & McGeehan, A. P. (2017). Where are all the Black teachers? Discrimination in the teacher labor market. *Harvard Educational Review*, 87(1), 26–49.

Darling-Aduana, J. (2021). A remote instructor like me: Student–teacher congruence in online, high school courses. *AERA Open*, 7. https://doi.org/10.1177/2332858 4211018719.

Darling-Hammond, L. (2015). *The flat world and education: How America's commitment to equity will determine our future*. Teachers College Press.

Davis, B. H. (1996). Teacher of the future. *Journal of the American Society for Information Science*, 47(11), 849–853.

Dee, T. S. (2004). Teachers, race, and student achievement in a randomized experiment. *Review of Economics and Statistics*, 86(1), 195–210.

Dee, T. S., & Penner, E. K. (2021). My brother's keeper? The impact of targeted educational supports. *Journal of Policy Analysis and Management*, 40(4), 1171–1196.

Dixson, A. D. (2003). "Let's do this!" Black women teachers' politics and pedagogy. *Urban Education*, 38(2), 217–235.

Eddy, C., & Easton-Brooks, D. (2011). Ethnic matching, school placement, and mathematics achievement of African American students from kindergarten through fifth grade. *Urban Education*, 46(6), 1280–1299.

Egalite, A. J., & Kisida, B. (2018). The effects of teacher match on students' academic perceptions and attitudes. *Educational Evaluation and Policy Analysis*, 40(1), 59–81.

Egalite, A. J., Kisida, B., & Winters, M. A. (2015). Representation in the classroom: The effect of own-race teachers on student achievement. *Economics of Education Review*, 45, 44–52.

Ehrenberg, R. G., Goldhaber, D. D., & Brewer, D. J. (1995). Do teachers' race, gender, and ethnicity matter? Evidence from the National Educational Longitudinal Study of 1988. *ILR Review*, 48(3), 547–561.

Espinoza, D., & Cardichon, J. (2017, June). *Investing in effective school leadership: How states are taking advantage of opportunities under ESSA* [Policy brief]. Learning Policy Institute. https://learningpolicyinstitute.org/media/109/download?inline&file=Investing_Effective_School_Leadership_BRIEF.pdf

Evans, M. O. (1992). An estimate of race and gender role-model effects in teaching high school. *The Journal of Economic Education*, 23, 209–217.

Ewing, E. L. (2018). *Ghosts in the schoolyard: Racism and school closings on Chicago's South Side*. University of Chicago Press.

Farinde, A. A., Allen, A., & Lewis, C. W. (2016). Retaining Black teachers: An examination of Black female teachers' intentions to remain in K–12 classrooms. *Equity & Excellence in Education, 49*(1), 115–127.

Farinde-Wu, A., Glover, C. P., & Williams, N. N. (2017). It's not hard work; it's heart work: Strategies of effective, award-winning culturally responsive teachers. *The Urban Review, 49*(2), 279–299.

Ferlazzo, L. (2018, February 20). The importance of 'White students having Black teachers': Gloria Ladson-Billings on Education. *Education Week Opinion Blog*. https://www.edweek.org/education/opinion-the-importance-of-white-students-having-black-teachers-gloria-ladson-billings-on-education/2018/02

Fiddiman, B., Campbell, C., & Partelow, L. (2019). *Student debt: An overlooked barrier to increasing teacher diversity*. Center for American Progress.

Florida Governor's Office. (2021, December 15). *Governor DeSantis announces legislative proposal to stop WOKE activism and critical race theory in schools and corporations* [Press release]. https://www.flgov.com/2021/12/15/governor-desantis-announces-legislative-proposal-to-stop-w-o-k-e-activism-and-critical-race-theory-in-schools-and-corporations

Foster, M. (1997). *Black teachers on teaching*. The New Press.

Fox, L. (2016). Seeing potential: The effects of student–teacher demographic congruence on teacher expectations and recommendations. *AERA Open, 2*(1). https://doi.org/10.1177/2332858415623758

Garnett, N. S. (2014). Disparate impact, school closures, and parental choice. *University of Chicago Legal Forum 2014,* 5. https://chicagounbound.uchicago.edu/uclf/vol2014/iss1/5

Gershenson, S., Hart, C. M., Hyman, J., Lindsay, C. A., & Papageorge, N. W. (2022). The long-run impacts of same-race teachers. *American Economic Journal: Economic Policy, 14*(4), 300–342.

Gershenson, S., Holt, S. B., & Papageorge, N. W. (2016). Who believes in me? The effect of student–teacher demographic match on teacher expectations. *Economics of Education Review, 52*, 209–224.

Gershenson, S., Lindsay, C., Papageorge, N. W., Campbell, R., & Rendon, J. (2023). Spillover effects of Black teachers on White teachers' racial competency: Mixed methods evidence from North Carolina. *SSRN Electronic Journal*, https://doi.org/10.2139/ssrn.4490168

Gist, C. D., & Bristol, T. J. (Eds.). (2022). *Handbook of research on teachers of color and indigenous teachers*. American Educational Research Association.

Givens, J. R. (2021). *Fugitive pedagogy: Carter G. Woodson and the art of Black teaching*. Harvard University Press.

Goings, R. B., & Bianco, M. (2016). It's hard to be who you don't see: An exploration of Black male high school students' perspectives on becoming teachers. *The Urban Review, 48*, 628–646.

Gottlieb, D. (1964). Teaching and students: The views of Negro and White teachers. *Sociology of Education, 37*(4), 345. https://doi.org/10.2307/2112117

Graybill, S. W. (1997). Questions of race and culture: How they relate to the classroom for African American students. *The Clearing House: A Journal of Educational Strategies, Issues and Ideas, 70*(6), 311–318.

Grissom, J. A., & Redding, C. (2016). Discretion and disproportionality: Explaining the underrepresentation of high-achieving students of color in Gifted programs. *AERA Open, 2*(1), 1–25.

Guha, R., Hyler, M. E., & Darling-Hammond, L. (2016). *The teacher residency: An innovative model for preparing teachers.* Learning Policy Institute.

Hammer, C., & Gerald, E. (1990). *Selected characteristics of public and private school teachers: 1987–88* (NCES90–087), Table 1. U.S. Department of Education, National Center for Education Statistics. https://nces.ed.gov/pubs90/90087.pdf

Hansen, M., Quintero, D., & Feng, L. (2018). *Can money attract more minorities into the teaching profession?* Brookings Institution.

Hanushek, E. A. (1992). The trade-off between child quantity and quality. *Journal of Political Economy, 100*(1), 84–117.

Hanushek, E. A., Kain, J., O'Brien, D., & Rivkin, S. G. (2005). *The market for teacher quality* [Working paper 11154]. National Bureau of Economic Research. https://www.nber.org/papers/w11154

Hart, C. M. (2020). An honors teacher like me: Effects of access to same-race teachers on Black students' advanced-track enrollment and performance. *Educational Evaluation and Policy Analysis, 42*(2), 163–187.

Hayes, M. S., Liu, J., & Gershenson, S. (2023). Who refers whom? The effects of teacher characteristics on disciplinary office referrals. *Economics of Education Review, 93*, 102376.

Henke, R. R., Choy, S. P., Chen, X., Geis, S., Alt, M. N., & Broughman, S. P. (1997). *America's teachers: Profile of a profession, 1993–94* (NCES97–460), Table 2.3. U.S. Department of Education. National Center for Education Statistics. https://nces.ed.gov/pubs97/97460.pdf

Holt, S. B., & Gershenson, S. (2015). *The impact of teacher demographic representation on student attendance and suspensions* (Discussion paper 9554). Institute for the Study of Labor. https://docs.iza.org/dp9554.pdf

Hundley, M. G. (1965). *The Dunbar story (1870–1955).* Vantage Press.

Hwang, N., Graff, P., & Berends, M. (2024). Racialized early grade (mis) behavior: The links between same-race/ethnicity teachers and discipline in elementary school. *AERA Open, 10.* https://doi.org/10.1177/23328584231222185.

Irvine, J. J. (1989). Beyond role models: An examination of cultural influences on the pedagogical perspectives of Black teachers. *Peabody Journal of Education, 66*(4), 51–63.

Irvine, J. J. (1990). *Black students and school failure. Policies, practices, and prescriptions.* Greenwood Press.

Jackson, I., & Knight-Manuel, M. (2019). "Color does not equal consciousness": Educators of color learning to enact a sociopolitical consciousness. *Journal of Teacher Education, 70*(1), 65–78.

Jackson, I., Sealey-Ruiz, Y., & Watson, W. (2014). Reciprocal love: Mentoring Black and Latino males through an ethos of care. *Urban Education, 49*(4), 394–417.

Johnson, J. W. (2019). *Lift every voice and sing.* Bloomsbury Publishing USA.

Jones, J. (1981). Students' models of university teaching. *Higher Education, 10*(5), 529–549.

King, S. H. (1993). Why did we choose teaching careers and what will enable us to stay? Insights from one cohort of the African American teaching pool. *The Journal of Negro Education, 62*(4), 475–492.

Kohli, R. (2019). Lessons for teacher education: The role of critical professional development in teacher of color retention. *Journal of Teacher Education, 70*(1), 39–50.

Ladson-Billings, G., & Henry, A. (1990). Blurring the borders: Voices of African liberatory pedagogy in the United States and Canada. *Journal of Education, 172*(2), 72–88.

Layton, L. (2013, January 29). Activists to U.S. Education Department: Stop school closings now. *The Washington Post.* https://www.washingtonpost.com/local/education/activists-to-us-education-department-stop-school-closings-now/2013/01/29/7eb27f40-6a39-11e2-95b3-272d604a10a3_story.html

Lee, A., Henderson, D. X., Corneille, M., Morton, T., Prince, K., Burnett, S., & Roberson, T. (2022). Lifting Black student voices to identify teaching practices that discourage and encourage STEM engagement: Why Black teachers matter. *Urban Education, 59*(4), 979–1011. https://doi.org/10.1177/00420859211073898

Lindsay, C. A., & Hart, C. M. (2017). Exposure to same-race teachers and student disciplinary outcomes for Black students in North Carolina. *Educational Evaluation and Policy Analysis, 39*(3), 485–510. https://doi.org/10.3102/0162373717693109

Liu, J., Penner, E. K., & Gao, W. (2023). Troublemakers?: The role of frequent teacher referrers in expanding racial disciplinary disproportionalities. *Educational Researcher, 52*(8), 469–481. https://doi.org/10.3102/0013189X231179649

Logan, R. (1954). *The Negro in American life and thought: The nadir, 1877–1901.* Dial Press.

Love, A., & Kruger, A. C. (2005). Teacher beliefs and student achievement in urban schools serving African American students. *The Journal of Educational Research, 99*(2), 87–98.

Luekens, M. T., Lyter, D. M., & Fox, E. E. (2004). Teacher attrition and mobility: Results from the Teacher Follow-up Survey, 2000–01 (NCES2004–301), Table 3. U.S. Department of Education. National Center for Education Statistics. https://nces.ed.gov/pubs2004/2004301.pdf

Lynn, M. (2002). Critical race theory and the perspectives of Black men teachers in the Los Angeles public schools. *Equity & Excellence in Education, 35*(2), 119–130. https://doi.org/10.1080/713845287

Madkins, T. C. (2011). The Black teacher shortage: A literature review of historical and contemporary trends. *Journal of Negro Education, 80*(3), 417–427.

Manchanda, S., Bristol, T., & Moss, P. (2023). Getting Black men to the blackboard: Factors that promote Black men teachers' entry into the teaching profession. *Equity & Excellence in Education,* 1–14 https://doi.org/10.1080/10665684.2023.2265385

McArthur, S. A., & Lane, M. (2019). Schoolin' Black girls: Politicized caring and healing as pedagogical love. *The Urban Review, 51,* 65–80.

McIntosh, K., Moss, E., Nunn, R., & Shambaugh, J. (2020). *Examining the Black–white wealth gap.* The Brookings Institution. https://www.brookings.edu/blog/up-front/2020/02/27/examining-the-black-white-wealth-gap

McKinney de Royston, M., Madkins, T. C., Givens, J. R., & Nasir, N. I. S. (2021). "I'm a teacher, I'm gonna always protect you": Understanding Black educators' protection of Black children. *American Educational Research Journal, 58*(1), 68–106.

McKinney de Royston, M., Vakil, S., Nasir, N. I. S., Ross, K. M., Givens, J., & Holman, A. (2017). "He's more like a 'brother' than a teacher": Politicized caring in a program for African American males. *Teachers College Record, 119*(4), 1–40.

Milner, H. R., IV. (2016). A Black male teacher's culturally responsive practices. *The Journal of Negro Education, 85*(4), 417–432.

Mosely, M., Guillaume, C., & Yarbough, O. (n.d.). *Impact Report 2020–2023.* Black Teacher Project. https://static1.squarespace.com/static/5c01b0d6b98a78f723592deb/t/655d4dd6e3203141d193cf50/1700613598766/BTP+2020-23_Impact+Report.pdf

National Board for Professional Teaching Standards. (n.d.). *NBPCT awarded $14 million SEED grant.* http://www.nbpts.org/newsroom/national-board-for-professional-teaching-standards-awarded-14-million-seed-grant-from-the-us-department-of-education-to-grow-diverse-board-certified-teachers

National Center for Education Statistics. (n.d.). *National Teacher and Principal Survey.* U.S. Department of Education. https://nces.ed.gov/surveys/ntps

National Center for Education Statistics. (1994). *Schools and Staffing Survey: 1990–91 public use data file.* U.S. Department of Education. https://nces.ed.gov/surveys/sass/dataprod9092.asp

National Center for Education Statistics. (2012). *Schools and Staffing Survey.* U.S. Department of Education. https://nces.ed.gov/surveys/sass/

National Center for Education Statistics. (2013). *Schools and Staffing Survey, Table 1: Total number of public school teachers and percentage distribution of school teachers, by race/ethnicity and state: 2011–12.* U.S. Department of Education. https://nces.ed.gov/surveys/sass/tables/sass1112_2013314_t1s_001.asp

National Center for Teacher Residencies. (2016). *NCTR 2015 network impact overview* [Research brief]. https://nctresidencies.org/resource/nctr-2015-network-impact-overview

Nelson, J. D. (2016). Relational teaching with Black boys: Strategies for learning at a single-sex middle school for boys of color. *Teachers College Record, 118*(6), 1–30.

Nguyen, T. D., Pham, L. D., Crouch, M., & Springer, M. G. (2020). The correlates of teacher turnover: An updated and expanded meta-analysis of the literature. *Educational Research Review, 31*, 100355. https://doi.org/10.1016/j.edurev.2020.100355

NYC Men Teach. (n.d.). *Who we are.* https://www.nyc.gov/site/ymi/teach/nyc-men-teach.page

Office of Elementary and Secondary Education. (n.d.). *Supporting effective educator development grant program: Awards.* U.S. Department of Education. https://oese.ed.gov/offices/office-of-discretionary-grants-support-services/effective-educator-development-programs/supporting-effective-educator-development-grant-program/awards

Oliva, J. (2022, June 3). *House Bill 1467, K-12 Education, school district responsibilities* [Memorandum]. Florida Department of Education. https://info.fldoe.org/docushare/dsweb/Get/Document-9557/dps-2022-83.pdf

Ouazad, A. (2014). Assessed by a teacher like me: Race and teacher assessments. *Education Finance and Policy, 9*(3), 334–372.

Perlstein, D. (2019). Schooling the new Negro: Progressive education, black modernity, and the long Harlem Renaissance. In A. T. Erickson & E. Morrell (Eds.), *Educating Harlem: A century of schooling and resistance in a Black community* (pp. 31–54). Columbia University Press.

Perry, A. M., Stephens, H., Donoghoe, M. (2024). *Black wealth is increasing, but so is the racial wealth gap*. Brookings Institution. https://www.brookings.edu/articles/black-wealth-is-increasing-but-so-is-the-racial-wealth-gap

Pigott, R. L., & Cowen, E. L. (2000). Teacher race, child race, racial congruence, and teacher ratings of children's school adjustment. *Journal of School Psychology, 38*(2), 177–195.

Podolsky, A., Kini, T., Bishop, J., & Darling-Hammond, L. (2016). *Solving the teacher shortage: How to attract and retain excellent educators*. Learning Policy Institute.

Redding, C. (2019). A teacher like me: A review of the effect of student–teacher racial/ethnic matching on teacher perceptions of students and student academic and behavioral outcomes. *Review of Educational Research, 89*(4), 499–535.

ross, k. (2021). Anti-Blackness in education and the possibilities of redress: Toward educational reparations. *Amerikastudien/American Studies, 66* (1), 229–233.

ross, k. m., Nasir, N. I. S., Givens, J. R., McKinney de Royston, M., Vakil, S., Madkins, T. C., & Philoxene, D. (2016). "I do this for all of the reasons America doesn't want me to": The organic pedagogies of Black male instructors. *Equity & Excellence in Education, 49*(1), 85–99.

Rowland, C., Azar, T., Grossman, T., & Mottesi, G. (2024, January). *State policies to support teacher residencies: An overview*. National Center for Teacher Residencies. https://nctresidencies.org/wp-content/uploads/2024/01/State-Policies-to-Support-Teacher-Residencies-An-Overview-January-2024.pdf

Royal, C. (2022). *Not paved for us: Black educators and public school reform in Philadelphia*. Harvard Education Press.

Rufo, C. F. (2023). *America's cultural revolution: How the radical left conquered everything*. HarperCollins.

Sanders, J. M. (1984). Faculty desegregation and student achievement. *American Educational Research Journal, 21*(3), 605–616.

Shirrell, M., Bristol, T. J., & Britton, T. A. (2023). The Effects of Student–Teacher Ethnoracial Matching on Exclusionary Discipline for Asian American, Black, and Latinx Students: Evidence From New York City. *Educational Evaluation and Policy Analysis, 46*(3). https://doi.org/10.3102/01623737231175461

Siddle Walker, V. (1996). *Their highest potential: An African American school community in the segregated South*. University of North Carolina Press.

Siddle Walker, V. (2001). African American teaching in the South: 1940–1960. *American Educational Research Journal, 38*(4), 751–779.

Sloan, K., & Blazevski, J. (2015). *New Visions Hunter College Urban Teacher Residency: Measures of success*. Rockman.

Solomon, J. (2009). The Boston teacher residency: District-based teacher education. *Journal of Teacher Education, 60*(5), 478–488.

Sowell, T. (1976). Patterns of Black excellence. *Public Interest, 43*, 26–58

Stanley, D. A. (2024). *#Black Educators Matter: The experiences of Black teachers in an anti-Black world*. Harvard Education Press.

Stewart, N. D., Dunnigan, E. L., Purry, A. A., & Borom, C. C. (2023). Black liberatory educational policy: A systematic and unapologetic literature review on the advancement of Black teachers' pedagogies and practices. *Equity & Excellence in Education, 56*(4), 526–544.

Stovall, J. L., & Mosely, M. (2023). "We just do us": How Black teachers co-construct Black teacher fugitive space in the face of antiblackness. *Race Ethnicity and Education, 26*(3), 298–317.

Strizek, G. A., Pittsonberger, J. L., Riordan, K. E., Lyter, D. M., & Orlofsky, G. F. (2006). *Characteristics of schools, districts, teachers, principals, and school libraries in the United States: 2003–04: Schools and Staffing Survey* (NCES2006–313 Revised), Table 18. U.S. Department of Education, National Center for Education Statistics. https://nces.ed.gov/pubs2006/2006313.pdf

Students for Fair Admissions v. Harvard, 600 U.S. (2023). (Jackson, J, dissenting opinion). https://www.supremecourt.gov/opinions/22pdf/20-1199_hgdj.pdf

Sutcher, L., Darling-Hammond, L., & Carver-Thomas, D. (2016). *A coming crisis in teaching? Teacher supply, demand, and shortages in the U.S.* Learning Policy Institute. https://doi.org/10.54300/247.242

Taie, S., & Goldring, R. (2017). *Characteristics of public elementary and secondary school principals in the United States: Results from the 2015–16 National Teacher and Principal Survey* (NCES2017–070), Table 1. U.S. Department of Education. National Center for Education Statistics. https://files.eric.ed.gov/fulltext/ED575193.pdf

Taie, S., & Goldring, R. (2020). *Characteristics of public and private elementary and secondary school teachers in the United States: Results from the 2017–18 National Teacher and Principal Survey* (NCES2020–142), Table 1. U.S. Department of Education. National Center for Education Statistics. https://nces.ed.gov/pubs2020/2020142.pdf

Taie, S., & Lewis, L. (2022). *Characteristics of 2020–21 public and private K–12 school teachers in the United States: Results from the National Teacher and Principal Survey* (NCES2022–113), Table A-1. U.S. Department of Education. National Center for Education Statistics. https://nces.ed.gov/pubs2022/2022113.pdf

Taie, S., & Lewis, L. (2023). *Teacher attrition and mobility: Results from the 2021–22 Teacher Follow-up Survey to the National Teacher and Principal Survey* (NCES 2024–039). U.S. Department of Education, National Center for Education Statistics. https://nces.ed.gov/pubsearch/pubsinfo.asp?pubid=2024039

Tilford-Weathers, T. C. (1982). *A history of Louisville Central High School, 1882–1982.* General Printing Company.

Todd-Breland, E. (2018). *A political education: Black politics and education reform in Chicago since the 1960s.* University of North Carolina Press.

Trujillo, T., Scott, J., & Rivera, M. (2017). Follow the yellow brick road: Teach for America and the making of educational leaders. *American Journal of Education, 123*(3), 353–391.

U.S. Department of Education. (2011). *Guidance on Fiscal Year 2010 School Improvement Grants: Under Section 1003(g) of the Elementary and Secondary Education Act of 1965.* https://oese.ed.gov/files/2019/09/sigguidance11012010.pdf

U.S. Department of Education. (2016). *Non-regulatory guidance for Title II, Part A: Building systsems of support for excellent teaching and learning.* https://www2.ed.gov/policy/elsec/leg/essa/essatitleiipartaguidance.pdf

Vilson, J. (2014). *This is not a test: A new narrative on race, class, and education.* Haymarket Books.

Watson, V. M. (2018). *Transformative schooling: Towards racial equity in education*. Routledge.
White, T., Woodward, B., Graham, D., Milner, H. R., IV, & Howard, T. C. (2020). Education policy and Black teachers: Perspectives on race, policy, and teacher diversity. *Journal of Teacher Education*, 71(4), 449–463.
Will, M. (2022, October 31). Apprenticeships are the new frontier of teacher preparation. *Education Week*. https://www.edweek.org/teaching-learning/apprenticeships-are-the-new-frontier-of-teacher-preparation-heres-how-they-work/2022/10
Wilson, A. (2023). Returning to the source: Black teachers centering justice with Black students in Chicago public schools. *The Urban Review*, 1–21. https://doi.org/10.1007/s11256-023-00673-6
Young, J., & Easton-Brooks, D. (2020). Present but unaccounted for: Practical considerations for the recruitment and retention of Black women teachers. *Theory Into Practice*, 59(4), 389–399.

CHAPTER 7

The Complex Braid of *Brown*
How Conceptualizations and Initiatives Within the African American Community of Research, Practice, and Activism Have Influenced the Advance of Knowledge and Practice in Education

Carol D. Lee

On this, the 70th anniversary of the *Brown v. Board of Education* decision, we have the opportunity to reflect on its significance. At least two broad reflections have been well established over these decades: (1) legally, it was historic, and (2) the specific aim of desegregation of public schooling has not been achieved. Here, however, I want to situate the *Brown* decision as a metaphor, if you will, of what I think is a revolutionary understanding of American society; that is, that peoples of African descent have from the inception of the nation been essential as powerful levers of change, compelling the nation to wrestle in dynamic ways with the complex challenges presented by our democratic system of governance. I further argue that multiple communities in the country who currently and historically have struggled and faced systemic discrimination have been positively influenced by these efforts in the African American community. In the field of education specifically, many of the expansive goals we seek to address today have been informed by proactive work within African American education. These goals include the pursuit of the following:

- Rights of immigrant communities
- Language rights in education
- Rights of women
- Broader policies to address health and poverty
- Attention in schooling more recently regarding
    » Culturally relevant curriculum and pedagogy

> Attention to social and emotional well-being—the holistic development of children
> Community-based schooling

I seek to move in this chapter beyond crying, "Woe is me! We are discriminated against and disempowered!" to assert that we are a strong, active community on whom this nation depends and to whom this nation should feel deeply indebted.

The founders who developed the Declaration of Independence and eventually the U.S. Constitution contended with many complexities. While they made a theoretical universal appeal to the idea of fundamental human rights, in practice they lived in and participated in systems that discriminated against many groups of humans. When they wrote "We hold these truths to be self-evident, that all men are created equal, that they are endowed by their Creator with certain unalienable Rights, that among these are Life, Liberty and the pursuit of Happiness," their *all men* included only White men with property. It did not include White indentured servants, enslaved Africans, women, or the Indigenous populations whose lands they were in the process of taking. Unfortunately, historically and still today there have been very heated debates over whether these facts of our history should be taught in our schools, and over what these contradictions between the ideals articulated in our founding documents and the historical facts of discrimination and oppression say about how we see our national identity. However, these are literal facts.

The U.S. Constitution is a brilliant document. It creates structures and systems that allow for disputation across different levels of stakeholders. These disputes are reflected in relationships between the federal and state governments; among the executive, legislative, and judicial branches of government; and between majorities and minorities, as well as the rights of the individual. In the debates that fueled the writing of the document, the founders wrestled with the complexities of shared decision-making. They began as separate colonies under the rule of the British king but also including corporate capital entities such as the Virginia Company of London. They sought in what would become the Bill of Rights to identify a set of fundamental rights and built a system for making amendments. The amendment process was intentionally made difficult, with any amendment requiring approval by three-quarters of the states. Amendments to the Constitution have in many cases been deeply influenced by the political organizing of African Americans and those who support commitments to equity: for example, the 13th, 14th, and 15th Amendments after the Civil War, and the 19th Amendment in 1920 giving women the right to vote.

Civic decision-making requires a deep understanding of the dialogues among and relationships among multiple empowered stakeholders to influence political decision-making. None of the political battles we have fought has had a simple solution or achieved a straightforward outcome. Recognizing this, we understand, albeit in retrospect, that the *Brown* decision of 1954 in itself would not lead directly to desegregation of public schooling. Indeed, the political pushback from organized groups and states (not only Southern states) against *Brown I* led to *Brown II* obliging states to move toward desegregation but permitting compliance under their own timelines and processes, thus severely limiting the nationwide implementation of *Brown*. Starting 2 decades later, a series of additional court cases allowed states to engage in practices that would inhibit full implementation of *Brown*: *San Antonio School District v. Rodriguez* (1973), *Milliken v. Bradley* (1974), *Board of Education of Oklahoma v. Dowell* (1991), and *Freeman v. Pitts* (1992).

I begin by raising this complexity of political organizing, of which the *Brown* Supreme Court case stands as a revealing exemplar, to argue that it is very important that we place these efforts as they unfold in dynamic and ecological systems—that we not see them as standalone efforts that either achieve or do not achieve targeted goals. *Brown* is both a victory and an ongoing challenge, an enigma that captures what Du Bois (1903) calls the *double consciousness* of the African American, who seeks to integrate politically, economically, socially, and indeed culturally into the broader idea of America, while at the same time recognizing the importance of maintaining traditional values, beliefs, and practices that have sustained African and African-descent populations on the continent and across the diaspora. I will illustrate in this chapter efforts of self-determination around schooling that we have carried out in our communities while at the same time organizing for inclusive rights in the broader structures of the country.

The NAACP decided to focus on desegregation in schools because there was a long set of case histories on this issue (Bell, 2004). What they ultimately wanted to attack was broader public accommodations, but they did not believe the Supreme Court would be open to such a wide systemic illegalization of segregation.

It is both interesting and ironic to note the achievements made through the efforts of African American legislators in the South during Reconstruction around segregation in public schooling. Anderson (2015) notes:

> For example, in 1868, a new South Carolina Constitution was passed requiring that universities be free and open to all the children and youths of the State, without regard to race and color. The Louisiana Constitution held that "there shall be no separate schools or institution of learning established exclusively for any Race by the State of Louisiana." . . . Mississippi's Reconstruction constitutional convention barred school segregation from appearing in the state's new constitution. (p. 6)

Anderson also helps us understand the dynamic relations across the history of legislative cases with which *Brown* stands in conversation. For example, he argues, "There is a strong tendency in the historical scholarship to look to the *Plessy v. Ferguson* decision of 1896 as the precedent and even the catalyst for the kind of public school segregation and inequality that characterized the Jim Crow era . . . [however] the 'separate and unequal' school systems of the 20th-century South rested more on the disenfranchisement of the African American population than on the *Plessy v. Ferguson* decision" (Anderson, 2015, p. 11). Just as *Plessy* had less influence than the loss of voting rights in permitting segregation, *Brown* had less ultimate effect than the Voting Rights Act of 1964 in driving desegregation. Progress is influenced not by single foci but a broader understanding of the full ecologies in which these political, economic, and social inequalities live and are sustained. The complex relationships between federal legislation regarding voting rights and states' rights in determining how elections are carried out have continued from Reconstruction to Jim Crow to current contestations over gerrymandering in states. Desegregation of schools, desegregation in public accommodations, and voting rights are among the dynamic ecologies that must be navigated.

Among the most interesting conundrums in these school desegregation cases centers around the conception of race. The construct of race has been a moving target in the United States (Blackburn, 2000). At different points in our history and in different states (e.g., California, Texas) distinctions were made between Chinese and Japanese immigrants, where at one point Japanese were considered "Mongolian" and at other points White (Williamson et al., 2007). These distinctions were influenced by a combination of local politics and, at times, broader international politics; some have argued that one set of conditions that influenced a more receptive audience for the *Brown* case was the attention of other nations around continued systemic racism in the United States after World War II. The Nazi government sent representatives to the United States before World War II to study how eugenics operated within this country, identifying models for the uptake of eugenics in Germany that served as public warrants for the mass killing of Jews, Romas, and homosexuals (Kuhl, 2002).

Ladson-Billings (2006) discusses how U.S. officials recognized how the persistence of legal segregation and racism impacted the perceptions of this country around the world. After World War II, U.S. officials observed that the country's poor race relations affected its international standing. As early as 1946, Acting Attorney General Dean Acheson wrote a letter on this subject. In 1952, in preparing for some of the pre-*Brown* discrimination cases, a Justice Department lawyer asked Acheson for an authoritative statement and Acheson replied with a letter concluding that "the undeniable existence of racial discrimination gives unfriendly governments the most effective kind of ammunition for their propaganda warfare," a key concern during the Cold War. The letters are available with an essay by David Langbart (2015) from the National Archives.

The observation that segregation and racial disharmony are bad for the United States' reputation and can be used for adverse propaganda remains vivid today. Claims have been made that during the 2016 and 2020 election, the Russian government deployed political media ads on the internet that appealed to racial and other divisive tropes (Ribeiro et al., 2019).

BROWN AS EXEMPLAR OF CROSS-COMMUNITY COLLABORATIONS

The *Brown* case decided in 1954 grows out of a series of legal cases, some at the state level and others at the federal level, as would be expected. The *Brown* case also grows out of collaborations across multiple fields. These included the research community, specifically in psychology, with the work of Drs. Mamie and Kenneth Clark, whose well-known Doll Test was included in the NAACP brief and cited by the justices in the *Brown* opinion. Thirty years later, Dr. Kenneth Clark recalled in an interview:

> The Dolls Test was an attempt on the part of my wife and me to study the development of the sense of self-esteem in children. We worked with Negro children—I'll call black children—to see the extent to which their color, their sense of their own race and status, influenced their judgment about themselves, self-esteem. We've now—this research, by the way, was done long before we had any notion that the NAACP or that the public officials would be concerned with our results. In fact, we did the study fourteen years before *Brown*, and the lawyers of the NAACP learned about it and came and asked us if we thought it was relevant to what they were planning to do in terms of the *Brown* decision cases. And we told them it was up to them to make that decision and we did not do it for litigation. We did it to communicate to our colleagues in psychology the influence of race and color and status on the self-esteem of children. (Vecchione et al., 1995, 1987)

What is interesting is that Dr. Clark says that the original intent of the work was to "communicate with [their] colleagues in psychology." There has been much more research since the Dolls Test that has contested and complicated the findings of the Clarks, and that evolving research around racial identity has similarly informed legal cases as well as the focus on racial identity in educational practice. This evolving research in psychology and human development on racial identity has also influenced research around the construct of ethnic identity (Phinney et al., 1997). The connections between conceptualizations of race and ethnicity are essential to the challenges, discussed earlier, raised by Du Bois (1903) around double consciousness. *Race* is not a biological construct (Blackburn, 2000), but rather socially created specifically for the purposes of warranting deficit attributions to communities of humans based on melanin (Mills, 1997), and it is a shifting construct at that (Ignatiev, 1996). Think back to the earlier discussion of legal cases around school segregation among Asian and Latinx communities historically (Williamson et al., 2007). *Ethnicity*, on the other hand, is rooted in histories of experience, beliefs, and routine cultural practices that are real and documentable. At the same time, ethnicity is also complicated because it can include pan-ethnicity that brings together ethnic groups that are related by geographical region but separate within nation–states inside those regions. For example, we can think about *African* as a pan-ethnic group versus *Igbo* or *Akan* as specific ethnic groups; or we can think about *Chinese* as a nationality group versus *Han* or *Uyghur* as specific ethnic groups within China. Ethnicity and nationality can overlap.

There has been much criticism of the underlying claims from the Doll Test, namely that it was used to argue that somehow African American children's sense of self-worth is diminished when they are segregated. The great writer of the Harlem Renaissance, Zora Neale Hurston, wrote in an editorial in the *Orlando Sentinel* newspaper:

> If there are not adequate Negro schools in Florida, and there is some residual, some inherent and unchangeable quality in white schools, impossible to duplicate anywhere else, then I am the first to insist that Negro children of Florida be allowed to share this boon. But if there are adequate Negro schools and prepared instructors and instructions, then there is nothing different except the presence of white people.
>
> For this reason, I regard the ruling of the U.S. Supreme Court as insulting rather than honoring my race. Since the days of the never-to-be-sufficiently-deplored Reconstruction, there has been current the belief that there is no greater delight to Negroes than physical association with whites. . . .
>
> It is well known that I have no sympathy nor respect for the "tragedy of color" school of thought among us, whose fountain-head is the pressure group concerned in this court ruling. I can see no tragedy in being too dark to be invited to a white school social affair. The Supreme Court would have pleased me more if they had concerned themselves about enforcing the compulsory education provisions for Negroes in the South as is done for white children. The next 10 years would be better spent in appointing truant officers and looking after conditions in the homes from which the children come. Use to the limit what we already have.
>
> Thems my sentiments and I am sticking by them. Growth from within. Ethical and cultural desegregation. It is a contradiction in terms to scream race pride and equality while at the same time spurning Negro teachers and self-association. (Hurston, 1995)

Hurston's comments reflect this theme of double consciousness and the dilemma that underlies the complexity of the *Brown* case, its legal precedents and legal decisions and policies that have followed. Is school desegregation truly in the best interests of African Americans? Is it in the best interests of the nation?

The work building toward *Brown* also included activist work of Black educators on the ground. Ironically, one of the most significant downsides to the *Brown* decision was the loss of Black teachers and principals in schools, especially across the South. Vanessa Siddle Walker (2005) offers extensive documentation of work by African American educational organizations from the late 1800s through the Jim Crow era to advocate for school facilities, professional working conditions, transportation, and antiracist curriculum, among others. Black teacher organizations across the South actively pushed for educational equality and collaborated with organizations like the evolving NAACP. Not only were there statewide professional associations of Black teachers, but conferences, such as the 1901 Negro Common School Conference, which produced a comprehensive report (Du Bois, 1901; Du Bois & Dill, 1911).

The Howard University Law School was also an essential partner with the NAACP in helping to drive legal research and planning (Dark, 2004). Thurgood Marshall, who led the NAACP legal team arguing the *Brown* case, who would go on to be the first Black Supreme Court justice, was a faculty member in the Howard law school, among others. Many of the lawyers on the legal defense team of the NAACP-led *Brown* case were alumni of the Howard law school. Charles Hamilton Houston, who assumed the role of dean of the law school in 1929, is credited with laying the groundwork for the legal theory for *Brown*. In addition, a number of the specialists who were called on to testify in the *Brown* case were Howard University faculty in other departments.

Some have argued that collaboration between the legal community working toward dismantling the U.S. system of discrimination and the labor movement was also important to *Brown*. The Brotherhood of Sleeping Car Porters and Maids was founded in 1925, the first all-Black union recognized by the American Federation of Labor. The labor efforts of the Brotherhood helped to position workers as powerful enough to gain collective bargaining rights from corporations as big as the Pullman Company. A. Philip Randolph, one of the powerful leaders of the Brotherhood, was also intimately involved in leadership roles within the broader Civil Rights Movement. In addition to the Black labor movement, the United Auto Workers donated $75,000 to support the efforts of the NAACP. This kind of cross-community collaboration, reflected as well in the history of legal antisegregation cases led by different ethnic communities, is an important story in terms of *Brown*.

THE LEGACY OF PARALLEL PATHS

From the Holocaust of African Enslavement through the Civil War, from Reconstruction through Jim Crow and after, African American communities have followed parallel paths that reflect Du Bois's "double consciousness." African American communities have historically sustained cultural beliefs, practices, valued relationships, and creation of community-based organizations that in many respects maintain what we think of as African diasporic values (Boykin et al., 1997; Hilliard, 1995, 1998; Karenga & Carruthers, 1986). These include communalism, respect for elders, valuing of extended family, and the essentiality of communal relationships. While we have developed and sustained these relationships and communal systems, we have simultaneously organized resistance through efforts to change laws and social practices of the nation–state, organizing efforts that have benefited the African American community as well as other communities experiencing systemic inequities. This is the light in which, I am arguing, we should think about the meaning and impact of *Brown*.

During the Holocaust of Enslavement it was illegal for enslaved African Americans to learn to read or write. However, stories abound—mirroring the adage "each one teach one"—of enslaved Africans hiding books beneath the floors of slave quarters and literally risking their lives and harsh physical punishments for teaching one another (Cornelius, 1983; Gundaker, 2007; Span & Anderson, 2005). Directly after the Civil War, as Anderson (1988; 2023) documents, the newly freed African Americans in the South made independent decisions to establish their own schools, some 1,500 church-run and 500 community-run schools. He describes how, directly after the Civil War, representatives from the Freedman's Bureau came to the South to initiate efforts to establish education for the freed men and women, but found to their utter surprise that Black people had already established their own schools. What is important about the proposition of parallel paths—the idea that as African Americans work independently and internally to develop resources to support the uplift of our community, we simultaneously organize efforts that benefit the broader community and nation at large. In the former Confederate states, Black educators pushed local districts and states to fund public education, which at that time was not widely available even to poor Whites in the south. Du Bois (DuBois & Dill, 1911) credits these efforts of Black educators with the expansion of publicly funded education for all, although ironically as public funding became available, there were standardized inequalities in the distribution of resources to Black segregated schools. In many respects, we can think about these initial efforts after the Civil War as paving the path for the *Brown* case, even before *Plessy v. Ferguson*, which was about public accommodations more broadly.

Anderson (1988) goes on to document the independent spirit of African Americans around education during the Jim Crow era. He discusses how philanthropists like the Rosenwald Foundation went into small Southern school districts and offered money if they would abandon their curriculum in favor of curriculum focused on preparing Black children for low-income labor. Anderson (1988) documents how many of these districts refused the bribe and continued to primarily finance the education of their children on their own—building schools, providing community supports, and more. The Rosenwald Foundation is known for its contributions to the construction of segregated school buildings; less is known about the price exacted for such efforts.

Siddle Walker (1993; 1996, 2000) has conducted extensive research documenting the education of Blacks in the Jim Crow South. Siddle Walker (2018) explains how Lucy Laney, a Black educator from Georgia, pronounced at an NAACP meeting in 1919: "We are going to start anew in a way we know is going to be effective. We are going to start at the bottom with the children. We'll teach them history, vote, government" (p. 154). This was part of strategic efforts in Black segregated schools in the Jim Crow South to integrate African American history and culture as standards in Black schools, despite efforts—similar to what is happening today—to exclude any references to the history of racism in textbooks (codified by Mildred Lewis Rutherford in her 1920 pamphlet for the United Confederate Veterans, *A Measuring Rod to Test Text Books,* advocating textbooks that celebrated the Confederacy). In 1915, Carter G. Woodson established the Association for the Study of Negro Life and History, working closely with Black educators to integrate Black history and culture in the curriculum of schools. By 1926, they created National Negro History Week, which would go on to become Black History Month in 1976 (in the midst of the Black Power and Black Arts movements). Woodson's 1933 classic *The Mis-Education of the Negro* continues to serve as a blueprint for the centrality of inclusion of African American history and culture into the school curriculum. We have similar foundational arguments by Horace Mann Bond (1935, 1966, 1976) and Mary McLeod Bethune (1939, 1996) and more recently Barbara A. Sizemore (1973; 2007), to name only a few.

Siddle Walker (Siddle Walker et al., 2020) offers this rich description of how instruction on the ground in Black segregated schools in the Jim Crow South saw education as a resource for resilience and preparing leaders:

> In a third, equally significant strategy, Black educators built students who had the resilience to counter oppression. In English classes, teachers appropriated European poetry such as "If" or "Invictus" and insisted that Black children across the South memorize these and other poems with similar ideas. Lines such as "keeping [their] heads when all around them were losing [theirs] and blaming it on [them]" or being victimized by the "bludgeonings of chance" but having an "unconquerable soul" helped build students whose heads might later be "bloody, but unbowed" (Siddle

> Walker, 2018, pp. 155–156). As far as White school boards could discern, the teachers were teaching poetry. Yet the teachers themselves reportedly gave messages to students that told them to make sure they were listening to the words.
>
> The intentioned messaging also appeared in assemblies and widely-embraced Black teacher beliefs. Inside and outside classrooms, principals and teachers taught the students to aspire and to believe they could be anything they wanted to be, despite the truth that segregation confined their job opportunities (Siddle Walker, 2018). At assemblies, one principal reminded students that they needed to "love themselves" as Black people, notwithstanding the negative images they encountered in White America (Siddle Walker, 2018, p. 153). He told them they were more than the Little Black Sambo character that the Julius Rosenwald Foundation, through its library fund, first put into Black schools, and that indeed the pharaohs of Egypt looked like him, like them. In his words and the many replications in the other mandatory assemblies that comprised part of the curricula of Black schools, teachers and principals intentionally prepared the students to have the confidence to create and live in a world the educators fully expected would one day be created. As one president of the teachers' organization explained at a teachers' meeting in 1944, the job of the Black educator was to prepare the children "for the world of tomorrow" (Siddle Walker, 2018, p. 153).

There is a similar complex history in the evolution of historically Black colleges, navigating between the promise of financial rewards for focusing on labor preparation that would feed the labor needs of the Southern economy, versus preparing students to be competitive for professions beyond manual labor working for Whites. This was a period that had shifted from slave and sharecropping agricultural labor to an industrial base, but an industrial base for which White corporate interests sought a Black labor force. This shift in the South involved moving from manually picking cotton to use of the cotton gin and technical tools, but still required low-wage manual labor. These debates over the goals of education for Blacks are apparent in the history of the Tuskegee Institute, founded by Booker T. Washington, and in the historic debates between Washington and W. E. B. Du Bois. Du Bois (1903) argued the need for an intellectually rich education to prepare African Americans to compete in the larger economy and that education should prepare African Americans to resist racism and segregation. Washington, on the other hand, argued for practical technical education and not as preparation for active resistance to racism.

These debates over the goals of education for African Americans have been connected to how African Americans have considered their relationships with Africa and what such relationships mean for our senses of identity, reflected in DuBois's 1903 articulation of double consciousness.

This movement to recognize and build upon historical and cultural relations across communities of African descent, from the continent itself to the diaspora, historically goes back to the 1800s. One thread of the abolitionist movement involved the proposition that because of systemic racism in the United States, Black people should engage in efforts to return to Africa. The founding of Sierra Leone in 1787 and Liberia in 1847 are direct outgrowths of these efforts. Each, however, has its individual history, as they were initiated as sites for repatriated formerly enslaved Africans from the Caribbean, the United States, and, indeed, Great Britain. The Pan African Congresses were international meetings, held mostly in Europe, starting in 1900. Leaders from the continent and diaspora met to discuss and plan on how to resist the vestiges of racism and colonialism experienced as an outgrowth of the philosophy of white supremacy.

- 1900 in London
- 1919 in Paris
- 1921 in Brussels, London, and Paris
- 1923 in Lisbon and London
- 1927 in New York City
- 1945 in Manchester
- 1974 in Dar es Salaam
- 1994 in Kampala
- 2014 in Johannesburg

From 1919 forward, the NAACP was intimately involved in these conferences, with Du Bois as a major figure—the same NAACP that led the efforts to initiate the *Brown* case. It is noteworthy that at the 1945 conference, Du Bois met Kwame Nkrumah, then a student at Lincoln University in the United States. Nkrumah, of course, would go on to lead efforts to free Ghana, the first of the British colonial territories to gain its independence, and became the first president of an independent Ghana in 1957, 3 years after the initial *Brown* decision. More recently, the African Union (descended from the Organization of African Unity [1963–1999]) established the Diaspora Division with the following charge:

> The Diaspora Division serves as the focal point and hub for implementing the African Union decision to invite and encourage the African Diaspora to participate in the building and development of the African continent. Its main task, therefore, is to serve as a catalyst for rebuilding the global African family in the service of the development and integration agenda of the continent. (See Citizens and Diaspora Organizations Directorate, n.d.)

Of course, most people associate Pan-Africanism in the United States with the United Negro Improvement Association (UNIA) established by Marcus Garvey (1969) in 1914. But focusing on relationships between African Americans (and other persons of African descent across the diaspora) and Africa has been deeply embedded in African-diasporic communities since the Holocaust of Enslavement. As early as 1858, Richard R. Wright, principal of Augusta, GA's "Colored High School" (later renamed E. A. Ware High School), appears before the U.S. Senate Committee on Health, Education, Labor & Pensions. As Siddle Walker et al. (2020) note, at the senate committee hearing, when asked about "the race question" Wright said:

> It is generally admitted that religion has been a great means of human development and progress, and I think that all the great religions which have blest this world have come from the colored races—all. In other words, what is called the Aryan race has not originated a single great religion. I believe, too, that our methods of alphabetic writing all came from the colored race, and I think the majority of the sciences in their origin have come from the colored races ... Now I take the testimony of those people who know, and who, I feel are capable of instructing me on this point, and I find them saying that the Egyptians were actually wooly-haired negroes. In Humboldt's *Cosmos* ... you will find that testimony, and Humboldt, I presume, is a pretty good authority. The same is stated in Herodotus, and in a number of other authors with whom you gentlemen are doubtless familiar. Now if that is true, the idea that this negro race is inherently inferior seems to me to be at least a little limping. (Blair, 1885, p. 813, quoted in Siddle-Walker et al., 2020)

This commentary by Blair is evidence of not only how African Americans recognized their historical and cultural connections to the continent of Africa, but how such recognition entailed critical analyses of the deficit warrants that provided the rationale for racism, slavery, and, later, colonialism.

Many people do not know that the area known as Wall Street in New York City where the Civic Center presently stands there was an African burial ground where enslaved Africans buried their dead in the 17th and 18th centuries. Around 1990, the Schomburg Center for Black Culture organized community efforts to get the federal government to identify the African Burial Ground initially as a recognized landmark (designated 1993) and eventually as a national monument (designated 2007). There is a beautiful monument at the site in memory of those buried. The Schomburg Center also worked with archeologists from Howard University to dig up remains from the burial site. To no surprise, they found clear evidence of ill health. However, they were surprised to find that these enslaved Africans buried their dead with amulets, markings on the body, and in positions that essentially said, "I am Yoruba," "I am Igbo," "I am Akan." In other words, they buried their dead to tell whoever would discover their bodies that they did not see themselves as slaves, as property, but as human beings with ethnic identities that they never gave up, despite every effort by the slave system to destroy their identities, rituals, belief systems, and practices as Africans. The Schomburg Center itself has a rich history. It is part of the New York City public library system. It grew out of efforts in the 1920s and 1930s to establish public libraries in Black urban communities, including Harlem, when Black people did not have access to public libraries. Similar efforts took place across cities where Black people took the lead to make sure that books were readily available to Black communities. For example, founded in 1833 and incorporated in 1836, the Philadelphia Library Company of Colored People established a site for African Americans to have free access to books and other literacy artifacts. Porter (1936) documents the history of these early associations. In the case of the Schomburg Center, Arturo Schomburg, of Black and Puerto Rican ancestry, amassed a huge collection of artifacts of Black history and culture. The National Urban League helped to convince the Carnegie Foundation to purchase Schomburg's collection in 1926 and donate the collection to the Harlem branch library that would go on to be named after Schomburg. Schomburg served as the curator for the collection from 1932 until his death in 1938.

As we move into the late 1960s and early 1970s, we find the development of the African-centered education movement. This movement was influenced by the Black Power movement (Carmichael & Hamilton, 1967; Madhubuti, 1973) and the Black Arts movement (Bracey et al., 2015), both of which highlighted the need for Black empowerment through independent community building and international relationships with African-descent communities around the world.

The African-centered school movement sits inside this history of Pan-Africanism. The Council of Independent Black Institutions was established in 1972, representing independent Black schools across the country, in New York, Washington, DC, Chicago, Detroit, Los Angeles, Atlanta, New Orleans, Philadelphia, and others (King, 1990; Lee, 1994; Lee et al., 1990; Lomotey & Brookins, 1988; Shujaa, 1994; Shujaa & Afrik, 1996). Among the oldest of African-centered independent schools is New Concept School in Chicago, established in 1972 and still running under the aegis of the Institute of Positive Education (IPE, https://www.ipeclc.org). The Black Panther Party ran the Oakland Community School from 1971 to 1982. In the early 2000s, some independent African-centered schools transformed into charter schools to take advantage of public funding, no longer requiring that they charge tuition. The Betty Shabazz International Charter School network is probably the oldest of these independent schools transitioning to charter, an outgrowth of New Concept School and the Institute of Positive Education, established in 1998 and still in operation (https://www.bsics

.org). Parallel efforts in establishing community-based programs, outside of formal schooling, developed during the Civil Rights and Black Power movements: for example, the Student Nonviolent Coordinating Committee's Freedom Schools during the summer of 1964 in Mississippi (Payne, 2007). Siddle Walker et al. (2020) note:

> "The Freedom Schools blended the teaching of traditional academic subjects and what they called a "Citizenship Curriculum" with the explicit purpose of "train[ing] people to be active agents in bringing about social change" (Mississippi Freedom School Curriculum–1964, 1964/1991, p. 9). Charles Cobb, an architect of the schools, argued, 'If we are concerned with breaking the power structure, then we have to be concerned with building up our own institutions to replace the old, unjust, decadent ones which make up the existing power structure" (Cobb, 1963/1991, p. 36). Students were expected to use their newfound knowledge to force changes in their formal schools and work for racial equity inside and outside the classroom. (p. 202)

Warfield-Coppock (1992) has documented community-based rites of passage programs, with similar goals, across the country during this period. These programs recruited young people, largely adolescents, and taught African and African American history, included classes in the arts (African dance, drumming, and culturally inspired visual arts) and performances. The goals of these programs were to socialize positive identities among these young people as persons of African descent and to inspire a sense of purpose to support the African American community, reminiscent in some ways of Du Bois's (1903) vision of a talented tenth of educated African Americans who were active in community organizing.

Black schools run by African Americans have a rich history in this country. From the segregated schools in the Jim Crow South to the African-centered school movement from the late 1960s forward, they have filled an important role around the conception of *education for self-reliance*, articulated by Julius Nyerere, president of Tanzania, in 1968. In 1935, W. E. B. Du Bois said, about what Black run schools can do:

> Separate schools for Black youth are needed just so far as they are necessary for the proper education of the Negro race. The proper education of any people includes sympathetic touch between teacher and pupil; knowledge on the part of the teacher, not simply of the individual taught, but of his surroundings and background, and the history of his class and group; such contact between pupils, and between teacher and pupil, on the basis of perfect social equality, as will increase this sympathy and knowledge. If this is true, and if we recognize the present attitude of white America toward black America, then the Negro not only needs the vast majority of these schools, but it is a grave question if, in the near future, he will not need more such schools. (p. 328)

I raise this history because it is an interesting dynamic evolving in the same history as the efforts to desegregate schools and public accommodations highlighted by the *Brown* decision. I think this dual history embodies the dilemma raised by Du Bois's concept of double consciousness, and that the *Brown* case is a metaphor for a history of intertwined webs of activity. One thread captures independent activity within the African American community to sustain and uplift itself through sustenance of communal values and identities and collaborations across community institutions; the other thread captures efforts within the African American community to politically and economically organize and appeal to the political system to change laws and systemic practices that constrain life course opportunities for African Americans and other disenfranchised communities. It is this dynamic space that I argue should be highlighted and celebrated on this, the 70th anniversary of the *Brown* decision.

THE DILEMMA OF *BROWN*

The legal argument presented in the *Brown* case has a fundamental flaw, namely that African American students suffered a negative sense of identity because they attended segregated schools. On the one hand, the *Brown* case represents a monumental legal shift in declaring segregation in schools illegal. On the other hand, it represents an unfortunate warrant underlying its legal argument.

There is an underlying dilemma in the logic used to argue the *Brown* case. Ladson-Billings (2006) summarizes the dilemma as follows:

> The experts for the plaintiffs argued that black inferiority was exacerbated by segregation and that was the primary reason to overturn the separate but equal principle. By pathologizing the plaintiff instead of addressing the underlying pathology of the defendant—white supremacy—the ruling and its implementation were limited. Instead of seeing the ruling as something the nation was doing to live up to its own promise, it ultimately became something whites were doing for blacks. Thus, the failure of blacks to achieve in school is read as their inability to take advantage of the opportunity benevolent whites provided them. (p. 311)

Margaret Beale Spencer, an emeritus professor of human development at the University of Chicago, has replicated the Clarks' Dolls Test (Spencer, 2008). In the replication, her conclusion about the student population was informed by her theoretical framing in the Phenomenological Variant of Ecological Systems Theory (PVEST). PVEST (Spencer, 2006; Spencer et al., 1997) argues that resilience is not predictive simply from the experience of challenge. What matters is not simply the objective obstacles one faces, but rather the relationship between the sources of support available and those obstacles. The relationships between challenge and support then influence how people experience what she calls net stress, which then influences coping strategies that over time become internalized as part of one's emergent identity. In these processes, what she calls reactive coping strategies can be adaptative or maladaptive, leading to differential life course outcomes. These processes are developmental in that challenge and supports shift across the life course (Bowman, 1989).

In the replication, Spencer administered the Dolls Test to two age cohorts of Black children, young and middle childhood. Within the young cohort, she worked with one group of children in an African-centered educational program and the other in a program that did not emphasize the development of a positive sense of Black identity. As predicted from the Clark experiment, the young children not in the culturally focused program did identify the Black doll as the beautiful doll, but she documents how they did not internalize that observation as reflecting anything about them. Basically, Spencer argues, as is well established in child development literature, that these very young children are essentially egocentric. They understood that there is a social norm out in the world around whiteness as beauty, but because of their natural egocentrism, did not internalize that this social norm had anything to do with them. The Black children in the African-centered school, on the other hand, identified the Black doll as the beautiful doll. They were learning from their social environment that Black is indeed beautiful. Among the most interesting findings from Spencer's replication is her video footage showing that when she asked the older Black children about the dolls, their facial features clearly showed they were wrestling with the decision. Spencer argues that these older children are at a point in their development where, like the younger children, they recognize that there is a societal norm regarding whiteness as beauty, but in contrast to the younger children they realize that this deficit norming might now apply to them. Their ego protection makes the decision difficult.

This replication is vital to the dilemma of *Brown* and to Du Bois's discussion of double consciousness in the African American community. First, the legal argument made in the *Brown* case that Black children experience a sense of inferiority *because of racial segregation* is not true and overly simplistic. Second, it is clear that historically the African American community has intuitively understood the need for supports within the community, across multiple levels of our internal ecological system, to acknowledge, reinforce, and indeed embody our positive sense of ourselves as humans. These internal practices that I have briefly reviewed in this chapter serve as testimony. I think back to Zora Neale Hurston's 1928 admonition (Hurston, 2015), published in her essay "How It Feels to Be Colored Me":

But I am not tragically colored. There is no great sorrow dammed up in my soul, nor lurking behind my eyes. I do not mind at all. I do not belong to the sobbing school of Negrohood who hold that nature somehow has given them a lowdown dirty deal and whose feelings are all but about it. Even in the helter-skelter skirmish that is my life, I have seen that the world is to the strong regardless of a little pigmentation more or less. No, I do not weep at the world—I am too busy sharpening my oyster knife.

In the spirit of Zora, the fields of Black psychology and human development have contributed substantively to how we understand concepts like identity in relation to constructions of race and ethnicity. Racial identity is multidimensional (Sellers et al., 1998), deeply contextualized (Sellers et al., 2006), and heterogeneous. There are well-established measures of racial identity (Sellers et al., 1998). In learning environments, perceptions that learners have about themselves, the tasks, and the settings can influence how, for example, racial stereotypes are perceived and responded to (Steele, 2011). Very importantly, current research has documented relationships between positive senses of racial identity and academic outcomes (Chavous et al., 2003). In one of my own studies, we designed a literature curriculum to address the dual aims of developing strategic skills in literary reasoning and supporting a positive sense of racial identity through a literature curriculum rooted in African American literature. The 3-year longitudinal study took place in an urban high school located in a low-income neighborhood with African American students living in low-income neighborhoods. We found positive correlations among measures of their skills in literary reasoning, their epistemological orientations toward reading literature (as personally meaningful), their sense of self-efficacy and ability to cope, their perceptions of instructional experiences, and their sense of positive racial identity (Lee, 2016). A similar small-scale study was carried out in mathematics with similar results (Leatherwood, 2022).

So I think it is not the case that Black children need to sit beside White children in order to learn. Rather, the promise of school integration is its gift to the broader nation.

And as Du Bois argued back in his 1960 lecture "Whither Now and Why," given at the 25th Conference of the Association of Social Science Teachers at Johnson C. Smith University (https://credo.library.umass.edu/view/full/mums312-b250-i003), school integration should not mean that Black students must lose institutional supports for studying African American and African-diaspora culture and history in favor of studying curriculum that is Eurocentric and only addresses knowledge that has emerged from Europe and its diaspora. Keep in mind, these battles go back at least to the early 1900s and get revisited over and over again. Racial integration in public schooling is a gift to the nation in that it increases the likelihood that children and adolescents from very different backgrounds can learn to respect and empathize with one another. Mutual respect and the ability to empathize with others are essential to sustaining our democratic experiment. At the same time, to achieve such aims, the curriculum itself should be integrated, incorporating the contributions across cultural communities to knowledge across the academic disciplines.

The dilemma of *Brown* raises a question about what quality and focus of education does the nation require for all of its children, and for what purpose. Historically, Black educators in schools serving Black students and community-based supports for education have demonstrated our ability to provide quality education to our children, where quality means addressing the holistic needs of children and preparing children with the technical skills to navigate workforce challenges. I should add here that the criteria for excellence in schooling have shifted as public education has evolved in the 20th and 21st centuries. Keep in mind that prior to the late 1800s there was not a ubiquitous public education system across the nation, even for White children. Thus it is important to place the current data around discrepencies in educational outcomes in their historical context. The data on which we draw today to characterize Black children as failing has its own set of challenges. I am not arguing that our current challenges around achievement are not real, but they do not tell the full story. And we have much to learn today about the history of an internal, communal self-reliance that we do not have enough of today. This includes Wilson's (1987) warnings about class segregation in the Black community. While there have always been class distinctions and tensions within the Black community, during the period of Jim Crow they were not as stark. There is an interesting story of how Ida B. Wells decided to host a program to support poor Black people migrating up from the South to Chicago during the Great Migration at a site where her middle-class neighbors resisted her efforts. The resistance of her Black middle-class neighbors is an illustration of how class divisions have existed within the Black community. They did not want poor Blacks in their middle-class neighborhood.

THE STRUGGLE FOR *BROWN'S* CONTRIBUTIONS TO PRIORITIES IN EDUCATION TODAY

I started this chapter arguing that many of the priorities over which we wrestle today as goals in public education can be historically linked to the community organizing and political efforts that have been the foundation of the evolution of the *Brown* case. These include:

- Rights of immigrant communities
- Language rights in education
- Rights of women

- Broader policies to address health and poverty
- Attention in schooling more recently regarding
    » Culturally relevant curriculum and pedagogy
    » Attention to social and emotional well-being—the holistic development of children
    » Community-based schooling

Williamson et al. (2007) have documented the history of legal cases around segregation in public schooling initiated within Latinx and Asian American communities that the NAACP lawyers would have drawn on, all unfolding with parallel cases being brought by African Americans. These cases highlight how delicate and contextualized are constructions of race, who gets to be White when and under what circumstances.

Among the issues around inequity in education is that of language. The cases Williamson et al. (2007) reference include questions about the language rights of students. These include not only issues of bilingual education but also attention to African American English, as was taken up in federal district court for the Eastern District of Michigan as *Martin Luther King Junior Elementary School Children, et al. v. Ann Arbor School District Board*, 473 F. Supp. 1371 (E.D. Mich. 1979) which came to be known as the "Black English" case (Smitherman, 2004). In the *King* case, plaintiffs argued that African American children in the school who spoke Black English were being denied adequate supports for learning to speak and read Standard English. While there were and are controversies over recognizing Black English as a valid dialect of English, the question was and remains how it should be viewed and recruited to support learning in the academic content areas. The contribution of the *King* case was legal recognition that Black English had the status of a legitimate language variety that the school district was required to address, and in particular that it not be viewed as a deficit to be overcome. Prior to the *King* case, the College Composition and Communication Conference (CCCC), a division of the National Council of Teachers of English, issued the following proclamation—Students' Right to Their Own Language:

> We affirm the students' right to their own patterns and varieties of language—the dialects of their nurture or whatever dialects in which they find their own identity and style. Language scholars long ago denied that the myth of a standard American dialect has any validity. The claim that any one dialect is unacceptable amounts to an attempt of one social group to exert its dominance over another. Such a claim leads to false advice for speakers and writers and immoral advice for humans. A nation proud of its diverse heritage and its cultural and racial variety will preserve its heritage of dialects. We affirm strongly that teachers must have the experiences and training that will enable them to respect

diversity and uphold the right of students to their own language. (https://prod-ncte-cdn.azureedge.net/nctefiles/groups/cccc/newsrtol.pdf)

Nearly 20 years later, the Oakland School District in 1996 issued a "Resolution on Ebonics," deciding that African American English should be addressed in schools serving Black students in their district (Smitherman, 2004). Addressing Black English or African American English Vernacular (AAVE) has included supporting students in engaging in multiple features of the language in classroom discourse (e.g., rhyme, rhythm, overlapping talk), in explicit efforts to translate oral and written language from AAVE features to standard academic English. Lee (1995, 2005, 2007) has built a long-term program called Cultural Modeling in which an AAVE genre of talk called signifying—for example, ritual insult (Smitherman, 1977, 1994)—is scaffolded to support literary reasoning around figuration; and in which the rhetorical features of AAVE are recruited to support engagement in classroom discussions. Smitherman (2000) conducted a longitudinal study of student writing from the National Assessment of Educational Progress and found positive correlations between use of features of African American English and the quality of student writing.

The point of these examples of legal efforts influencing classroom pedagogical practices that positively engage AAVE is that they align with other efforts to recognize and support bilingualism in schools (see Williamson et al. [2007] for exemplary cases). The debates over whether the home languages of immigrant students should be maintained in schools and how those home languages can serve as positive resources for academic learning parallel similar debates around AAVE.

With regard to the rights of women, Black women have been intimately involved in that movement from its earliest instantiations. Sojourner Truth, known for her admonition "Ain't I a Woman?" was both an abolitionist and a fighter for women's rights. Her explicit efforts in the abolitionist movement to free African Americans from slavery was intimately connected to her understanding of the systemic discrimination against women in the United States. These collaborations of Black women deeply engaged in the politics of liberation within the African American community with political organizing for women's rights has a long history. Ida B. Wells participated in the first parade advocating women's rights in 1913, as the only Black member of the delegation from Illinois. She persisted in this support despite the fact that she was asked to move to the back of the parade. Wells would go on to serve as one of the founders of the NAACP along with W. E. B. Du Bois and others.

Drawing from the work of Siddle Walker (1993, 1996), Givens (2021), and others (Foster, 1997; Gay, 2000; Hollins, 1996; Ladson-Billings, 1994), it is clear that in the Black segregated schools of the Jim Crow South, collaboration among school, community, and family were essential, that teachers and schools were attuned to the holistic needs of children, and that curriculum that was explicit about teaching, in this case, African American history and culture, were the foundation of what schooling meant. It was commonplace for schools in the Jim Crow South that Black children would daily sing "Lift Every Voice and Sing," now known as the Black national anthem. The active push against restrictive teaching of history by Black educators has been going on since the early 1900s, and goes on as we revisit these questions today. Be clear, I am not naïvely arguing that these segregated schools did not have both internal and external problems. But it is equally clear that these strengths—school–community partnerships; attention to wholistic development; integration of African American history and culture—have not transferred to public schooling that most African American students experience today.

My point here is that *Brown* is not just a legal case that came before the Supreme Court in 1954, where the plaintiffs won and segregation in public schooling was officially made illegal. To conceive of this as the only significance of *Brown* leads to a sense of despair, as the goal of full integration has never been achieved, and because of the years of systematic decisions by the courts, Congress, and state legislators across the country to impede such desegregation. Rather, I see *Brown* as a metaphor, a symbolic act at a point in time that embodies all the community action, internal to the Black community and collaboratively across communities, that has been engaged to push the arc of justice slowly forward. As a metaphor, a symbolic act, we understand its power. We understand our own power. We understand the possibilities of this democratic experiment.

Wrestling with the possibilities and complexities of this democratic experiment at this, the 70th anniversary of the *Brown* decision, is as important as it has ever been. We face challenges today that in some ways we have experienced before, but unprecedented in other ways. We continue to wrestle disputations over race, class, and gender. However, not since the Civil War have we experienced such a direct attack on the processes of governance as occurred on January 6, 2021. One of the lessons of *Brown* and its history is that African Americans and other communities that have experienced persistent intergenerational discrimination have largely worked within the system of democratic decision-making to push for goals of equality.

This leads to my closing challenge, namely: What is the role of public education in preparing young people to engage in civic reasoning, problem solving, and discourse? The history I have recounted is replete with contestations over race, ethnicity, class, and gender. Considering these persistent challenges, the question we face is what do these challenges mean for curriculum, for teaching, for who teaches, and for the integration of students from across different backgrounds?

The National Academy of Education report *Educating for Civic Reasoning and Discourse* (Lee et al., 2021) offers some responses. The U.S. Constitution is a complex document. The founders debated vehemently about their differences. They wanted a nation, but were an evolving confederation of colonies that would become states. They had differences over slavery, with the irony that many of the original signers of the Declaration of Independence and authors of the Constitution thought they owned human beings. That contradiction has in so many ways been the foundational dilemma around which the nation has always been torn. And that underlying logic of a presumed white supremacy has bled out to infiltrate immigration policies, the eugenics movement in this country that the Nazi government officially studied as a model (Kuhl, 2002), discriminatory policies against virtually every group except White men with property. The current fights over how history is taught in our schools is fueled by a fear that if our children learn this history (Ward, 2007), they will not love America (see also PEN America's recent report at Meehan et al., [n.d.]). But those communities who have indeed been discriminated against persistently and historically show clear evidence that we do love America.

Our Constitution was designed to accommodate difference, to create a system that was sufficiently elastic, that had sufficient checks and balances that over time we could figure out ways to accommodate our differences, with democratic values and a sense of morality that would place the boundaries past which difference could not be accommodated (e.g., the adage that you can't falsely yell fire in a crowded theater—the limitations of free speech). You have the right as an individual to have racist, sexist, homophobic beliefs and negative beliefs against different religions. However, you don't have the right to act on them in ways that harm others. Still, even that becomes complicated if one thinks about the many legal cases that have tested that premise.

The NAEd report (Lee et al., 2021) argues that civic reasoning entails the following:

- Knowledge—conceptual and procedural, related to the topics that are addressed in the civic problem
- Epistemology—valuing complexity, resisting simplistic solutions to complex problems
- Ethics—values that are informed by not only perceptions of one's own needs, but also the needs of others; empathy for others; a belief in fairness; a desire for the health, happiness, and well-being of others
- Dispositions—to question, to weigh multiple points of view, to value evidence, to listen to others, to empathize with others

The report further argues that these dispositions can only be taught in public schooling, as the government cannot require families or private institutions to do so (Gutmann, 1999). The report further argues that these dispositions, because of their complexity and their developmental dimensions (young children versus adolescents, for example), must be taught across pre-K–12 grades, and within and across school subject matters. The report argues that the problems with which we wrestle in the public realm entail relevant conceptual knowledge across academic domains (e.g., knowledge of viral mutations related to COVID-19 in science; knowledge of mathematical displays used to understand distributions of public problems; knowledge of constitutional rights, of course; and of how literature offers opportunities to interrogate the human experience in ways that support empathy for others). The report offers illustrations of what such teaching can look like.

This civic challenge raises the further question: What are the civic demands of public education, and in this year of the 70th anniversary of *Brown*, what is the role of integration and what should integration entail?

I believe that children need to learn to interact with, learn from, play with children with whom they share much and who are different in many ways as well. I believe that all children deserve the benefit of interrogating the full breadth of knowledge accumulated across human civilizations and times, and should not be constrained by restrictive conceptions of the history and evolution of knowledge. We are an interconnected world in which human communities have always interacted, learned from, and contributed to one another; and no human community has the sole or primary claim to knowledge. I believe that all children should have access in their schools to infrastructures that create schools as robust learning communities.

We continue to have inequities in terms of funding of public schools, in the distribution of professional training among educators in different districts and different schools within districts, in the uptake of robust pedagogies. Residential and class segregation, particularly in urban school districts, contribute to these inequities.

As we move forward, we must continue to struggle to address these inequities. But in so doing, as African Americans we must always acknowledge our power (Du Bois, 1935). We must always continue along the dual path, the dynamic threads between internal development and external organizing. *Brown* epitomizes this dual path, the history I have tried, perhaps inadequately, to describe captures the internal development thread, and the legal cases leading to and following *Brown* capture the external organizing. We need both.

REFERENCES

Anderson, J. D. (1988). *The education of Blacks in the South, 1860–1935*. University of North Carolina Press.

Anderson, J. D. (2015). Eleventh annual *Brown* lecture in education research: A long shadow: The American pursuit of political justice and education equality. *Educational Researcher, 44*(6), 319–335.

Anderson, J. D. (2023). Ex-slaves and the rise of universal education in the South, 1860–1880. *Thinking about Black education: An interdisciplinary reader*. Perlego.

Bell, D. (2004). *Brown v. Board of Education*: Reliving and learning from our racial history. *University of Pittsburg Law Review, 66,* 21.

Bethune, M. M. (1939). The adaption of the history of the Negro to the capapcity of the child. *Journal of Negro History, 29,* 9–13.

Bethune, M. M. (1996). My last will and testament. In M. K. Asante & A. S. Abarry (Eds.), *African intellectual heritage: A book of source* (pp. 671–673). Temple University Press.

Blackburn, D. G. (2000). Why race is not a biological concept. *Race and Racism in Theory and Practice,* 3–26.

Blair, H. W. (1885). *Report of the committee of the Senate upon the relations between labor and capital, and testimony taken by the committee: In five volumes* (Vol. 2). U.S. Government Printing Office.

Bond, H. M. (1935). The curriculum of the Negro child. *Journal of Negro Education, 4*(2), 159–168.

Bond, H. M. (1966). *The education of the Negro in the American social order*. Octagon Books.

Bond, H. M. (1976). *Education for freedom*. Lincoln University Press.

Bowman, P. (1989). Research perspectives on Black men: Role strain and adaptation across the adult life cycle. In R. Jones (Ed.), *Black adult development and aging* (pp. 117–150). Cobbs & Henry.

Boykin, A. W., Jagers, R. J., Ellison, C. M., & Albury, A. (1997). Communalism: Conceptualization and measurement of an Afrocultural social orientation. *Journal of Black Studies, 409*–418.

Bracey, J. H., Sanchez, S., & Smethurst, J. (2015). *SOS—Calling all Black people: A Black arts movement reader*. University of Massachusetts Press.

Carmichael, S., & Hamilton, C. V. (1967). *Black power* (Vol. 48). Random House.

Chavous, T. M., Bernat, D. H., Schmeelk-Cone, K., Caldwell, C. H., Kohn-Wood, L., & Zimmerman, M. A. (2003). Racial identity and academic attainment among African American adolescents. *Child Development, 74*(4), 1076–1090.

Citizens and Diaspora Organizations Directorate. (n.d.). *The diaspora division*. African Union. https://au.int/en/diaspora-division

Cobb, C. (1991). Prospectus for a summer freedom school program. *Radical Teacher,* (40), 36.

Cornelius, J. (1983). "We slipped and learned to read": Slave accounts of the literacy process, 1830–1865. *Phylon (1960–), 44*(3), 171–186.

Dark, O. C. (2004). The role of Howard University School of Law in *Brown v. Board of Education. Washington History, 16*(2), 83–85.

Du Bois, W. E. B. (1901). *The Negro common school: Report of a social study . . . Together with the proceedings of the sixth conference for the study of the Negro problems,* held at Atlanta University, 1901. University Press.

Du Bois, W. E. B. (1903). *The souls of black folk*. Oxford University Press.

Du Bois, W. E. B. (1935). Does the Negro need separate schools? *Journal of Negro Education,* 328–335.

Du Bois, W. E. B., & Dill, A. G. (1911). *The common school and the Negro American*. Atlanta University Press.

Foster, M. (1997). *Black teachers on teaching*. The New Press.

Garvey, M. (1969). *Philosophy and opinion of Marcus Garvey*. (A. J. Garvey, Ed.). Atheneum.

Gay, G. (2000). *Culturally responsive teaching: theory, research, and practice*. Teachers College Press.

Givens, J. R. (2021). *Fugitive pedagogy: Carter G. Woodson and the art of Black teaching*: Harvard University Press.

Gundaker, G. (2007). Hidden education among African Americans during slavery. *Teachers College Record, 109*(7), 1591–1612.

Gutmann, A. (1999). *Democratic education*. Princeton University Press.

Hilliard, A. G. (1995). *The maroon within us: Selected essays on African American community socialization*. Black Classic Press.

Hilliard, A. G. (1998). *SBA: The reawakening of the African mind*. Makare Publishing Company.

Hollins, E. R. (1996). *Transforming curriculum for a culturally diverse society*. Erlbaum.

Hurston, Z. N. (1995). Court order can't make races mix. In C. A. Wall (Ed.), *Zora Neale Hurston: Folklore, memoirs, and other writings* (pp. 956–958). The Library of America.

Hurston, Z. N. (2015). *How it feels to be colored me*. Applewood Books.

Ignatiev, N. (1996). *How the Irish became white*. Routledge.

Karenga, M., & Carruthers, J. H. (Eds.). (1986). *Kemet and the African world view: Research, rescue and restoration*. University of Sankore Press.

King, J. E. (1990). In search of African liberation pedagogy: Multiple contexts of education and struggle. *Journal of Education, 172*(2).

Kuhl, S. (2002). *The Nazi connection: Eugenics, American racism, and German national socialism*: Oxford University Press.

Ladson-Billings, G. (1994). *The Dreamkeepers*. Jossey-Bass.

Ladson-Billings, G. (2006). The meaning of Brown . . . for now. *Teachers College Record, 108*(14), 298–315.

Langbart, D. (2015). *Foreign policy and domestic discrimination*. National Archives. https://text-message.blogs.archives.gov/2015/03/05/foreign-policy-and-domestic-discrimination

Leatherwood, C. (2022). *Ecological perspective on error orientations and interactions in African-centered middle school math classrooms*. Northwestern University,

Lee, C. D. (1994). The complexities of African centered pedagogy. In M. Shujaa (Ed.), *Too much schooling, too little education: A paradox in African-American life* (pp. 295–318). Africa World Press.

Lee, C. D. (1995). A culturally based cognitive apprenticeship: Teaching African American high school students skills in literary interpretation. *Reading Research Quarterly, 30*(4), 608–631.

Lee, C. D. (2005). Double voiced discourse: African American vernacular English as resource in cultural modeling classrooms. In A. F. Ball & S. W. Freedman (Eds.), *New literacies for new times: Bakhtinian perspectives on language, literacy, and learning for the 21st century*. Cambridge University Press.

Lee, C. D. (2007). *Culture, literacy and learning: Taking bloom in the midst of the whirlwind*. Teachers College Press.

Lee, C. D. (2016). *A longitudinal study of disciplinary literacy development in literature and history as a resource for identity development and psycho-social well being* (READi Technical Report #11). Project READi.

Lee, C. D., Lomotey, K., & Shujaa, M. (1990). How shall we sing our sacred song in a strange land? The dilemma of double consciousness and the complexities of an African–centered pedagogy. *Journal of Education, 172*(2), 45–61.

Lee, C. D., White, G., & Dong, D. (Eds.). (2021). *Educating for civic reasoning and discourse*. National Academy of Education

Lomotey, K., & Brookins, C. (1988). The independent Black institutions: A cultural perspective. In D. T. Slaughter & D. J. Johnson (Eds.), *Visible now: Black in private schools* (pp. 163–183). Greenwood Press.

Madhubuti, H. R. (1973). *From plan to planet: Life studies: The need for Afrikan minds and institutions*: Third World Press.

Meehan, K., Magnusson, T., Baeta, S., & Friedman, J. (n.d.). Banned in the USA: The mounting pressure to censor. PEN America. https://pen.org/report/book-bans-pressure-to-censor

Mills, C. W. (1997). *The racial contract*. Cornell University Press.

Nyerere, J. K. (1968). Education for self-reliance. *CrossCurrents, 18*(4), 415–434.

Payne, C. M. (2007). *I've got the light of freedom: The organizing tradition and the Mississippi freedom struggle*. University of California Press.

Phinney, J. S., Cantu, C. L., & Kurtz, D. A. (1997). Ethnic and American identity as predictors of self-esteem among African American, Latino, and White adolescents. *Journal of Youth and Adolescence, 26*(2), 165–185.

Porter, D. (1936). The organized educational activities of Negro literary societies, 1828–1846. *Journal of Negro Education, 5*(4), 555–576.

Ribeiro, F. N., Saha, K., Babaei, M., Henrique, L., Messias, J., Benevenuto, F., Goga, O., Gummadi, K. P., & Redmiles, E. M. (2019). *On microtargeting socially divisive ads: A case study of Russia-linked ad campaigns on Facebook* [Paper presentation]. Proceedings of the Conference on Fairness, Accountability, and Transparency. https://dl.acm.org/doi/10.1145/3287560.3287580

Rutherford, M. L. (1920). *A measuring rod to test text books and reference books in schools, colleges, and libraries*. At the request of the United Confederate Veterans.

Sellers, R. M., Copeland-Linder, N., Martin, P. P., & Lewis, R. H. (2006). Racial identity matters: The relationship between racial discrimination and psychological functioning in African American adolescents. *Journal of Research on Adolescence, 16*(2), 187–216.

Sellers, R., Shelton, N., Cooke, D., Chavous, T., Rowley, S. J., & Smith, M. (1998). A multidimensional model of racial identity: Assumptions, findings, and future directions. In R. Jones (Ed.), *African American identity development* (pp. 275–303). Cobb & Henry Publishers.

Shujaa, M. (1994). *Too much schooling, too little education: A paradox in Black life in White societies*. Africa World Press.

Shujaa, M. J., & Afrik, H. T. (1996). School desegregation, the politics of culture, and the Council of Independent Black Institutions. In M. J. Shujaa (Ed.),

Beyond desegregation: The politics of quality in African American schooling (pp. 253–268). Corwin.
Siddle Walker, E. V. (1993). Caswell county training school, 1933–1969: Relationships between community and school. *Harvard Educational Review, 63*(2), 161–182.
Siddle Walker, E. V. (1996). *Their highest potential: An African-American school community in the segregated south.* University of North Carolina Press.
Siddle Walker, E. V. (2000). Valued segregated schools for African American children in the South, 1935–1969: A review of common themes and characteristics. *Review of Educational Reseach, 70*(3), 253–285.
Siddle Walker, V. (2005). Organized resistance and Black educators' quest for school equality, 1878–1938. *Teachers College Record, 107*(3), 355–388.
Siddle Walker, V. (2018). *The lost education of Horace Tate: Uncovering the hidden heroes who fought for justice in schools.* The New Press.
Siddle Walker, E. V., Anderson, J., Williamson-Lott, J. A., & Lee, C. D. (2020). African American education as preparation for civic engagement, reasoning, and discourse. In C. D. Lee, G. White, & D. Dong (Eds.), *Educating for civic reasoning and discourse.* National Academy of Education.
Sizemore, B. A. (1973). Education for liberation. *The School Review, 81*(3), 389–404.
Sizemore, B. A. (2007). *Walking in circles: The Black struggle for school reform.* Third World Press.
Smitherman, G. (1977). *Talkin and testifyin: The language of Black America.* Houghton Mifflin.
Smitherman, G. (1994). The blacker the berry, the sweeter the juice: African American student writers. In A. Dyson & C. Genishi (Eds.), *The need for story: Cultural diversity in classroom and community* (pp. 80–101). National Council of Teachers of English.
Smitherman, G. (2000). African American student writers in the NAEP, 1969–1988/89 and "The blacker the berry, the sweeter the juice." In G. Smitherman (Ed.), *Talkin that talk: Language, culture and education in African America* (pp. 163–194). Routledge.
Smitherman, G. (2004). Language and African Americans: Movin on up a lil higher. *Journal of English Linguistics, 32*(3), 186–196.
Span, C. M., & Anderson, J. D. (2005). The quest for "book learning": African American education in slavery and freedom. In A. Hornsby Jr. (Ed.), *A companion to African American history* (pp. 295–311). John Wiley & Sons.
Spencer, M. B. (2006). Phenomenology and ecological systems theory: Development of diverse groups. In W. Damon & R. M. Lerner (Eds.), *Handbook of child psychology* (6th ed., Vol. 1, pp. 829–893). Wiley.
Spencer, M. B. (2008). Lessons learned and opportunities ignored since *Brown v. Board of Education*: Youth development and the myth of a color-blind society. *Educational Researcher, 37*(5), 253–266.
Spencer, M. B., Dupree, D., & Hartmann, T. (1997). A phenomenological variant of ecological systems theory (PVEST): A self-organization perspective in context. *Development and Psychopathology, 9*(4), 817–833.
Steele, C. M. (2011). *Whistling Vivaldi: And other clues to how stereotypes affect us* (Issues of Our Times series). WW Norton & Company.

Vecchione, J., Hampton, H., Bond, J., Fayer, S., Lacy, M. D., & DeVinney, J. A. (1995/1987). *Eyes on the prize: America's civil rights years*. [Documentary film]. PBS Home Video; Turner Home Entertainment (distributor).

Ward, K. (2007). *History in the making: An absorbing look at how American history has changed in the telling over the last 200 years*. The New Press.

Warfield-Coppock, N. (1992). The rites of passage movement: A resurgence of African-centered practices for socializing African American youth. *Journal of Negro Education, 61*(4), 471–482.

Williamson, J. A., Rhodes, L., & Dunson, M. (2007). A selected history of social justice in education. *Review of Research in Education, 31*, 195–224.

Wilson, W. J. (1987). *The truly disadvantaged: The inner city, the underclass, and public policy*. University of Chicago Press.

CHAPTER 8

Brown v. Board of Education and the Democratic Purposes of Public Education

Kent McGuire

INTRODUCTION

This chapter argues strongly that preparing young people for citizenship should be a central purpose of our education system. Specifically, our schools should provide students with ways of thinking about economic and social issues and equip them with the knowledge and skill to identify and advocate for addressing these issues. This purpose requires significant change in the design and operations of our schools. Schools should be designed and organized in ways that help students understand the obligations that members of a society owe one another. Such change carries implications for what we ask students to do while in school and how we account for what they learn.

Operationally, embracing the democratizing purpose of public education requires new ways of thinking about teaching and learning and includes a commitment to preparing an education workforce that sees this purpose as part of their charter. This new workforce must also see today's diverse learners for who they are: knowledgeable and interesting people who care about their peers and their communities. Our teachers will need time, flexibility, and support to embrace this charter. They will also need new tools—curriculum, instructional materials, and other resources that they can adapt to local context, customize to specific needs, and personalize to student learning styles.

Lest we think this refreshed or renewed purpose is out of reach, note that we have useful examples upon which to draw, especially at the policy level. With regard, for instance, to curriculum policy, much attention has been paid to civics course requirements. At least 42 states require students to take a course in civics and government, with eight of those states requiring a full year of civics (Viadero et al., 2018). Often the goal of these courses has been to ensure that students know the facts about the U.S. system of government: the branches of government and how they operate, the requirements of citizenship, and so on. Several states have also refined their graduation policies to include civic learning as a requirement (Kissinger, 2022).

While not out of reach, the very idea of education as a public good and as an institution whose purpose is to sustain a liberal democracy, is not promised. A divisive political climate, starting with a manufactured alarm about critical race theory, followed by assaults on gender identity and LGBTQ+ rights, is targeting our public schools. Over half the states have introduced bills or taken other actions to restrict whether and how teachers can discuss history, racism, and sexism (Stout & Wilburn, 2021). Stoking fear about schools bringing harm to White students is energizing efforts to privatize public education. Taken together, these efforts represent real threats to democracy. And this brings us to the fundamental significance of *Brown v. Board of Education*, for the core premise of this seminal court decision, I argue in this chapter, was to give rise, through education, to a vibrant multiracial democracy.

A RECOUNTING OF *BROWN'S* PROMISE

Seventy years ago, in *Brown v. Board of Education*, the U.S. Supreme Court declared that "separate educational facilities are inherently unequal." *Brown* signaled the end of legalized racial segregation in America's schools. There was an implied promise that if we leveled the playing field, a number of things would be true: That for children of color, high school graduation rates would rise; that these students would make successful transitions from school to work; that postsecondary participation would increase. Following this logic, these young people would take their place in our economy and democracy. *Brown* was about much more than just what happened in school. Kids who went to school together were much more likely to live in the same neighborhoods, more likely to become friends, and more likely to see each other as valued members of their communities.

The process of desegregating schools, imperfect though it was, did bring a significant increase in graduation and college-going rates. To the advocates for a fair and just public education system, this came as no surprise. A series of connected and reinforcing policy moves, building on *Brown*, contributed to the progress we observed between 1954 and the middle 1990s. These included a wave of school desegregation efforts, the school finance reforms of the 1970s and 1980s (Baker, 2021), and a corresponding effort to strengthen the quality of the education workforce. As these related policy moves took hold, we witnessed a steady reduction in race-related achievement gaps. The policy responses to *Brown* also contributed to raising adult income and economic power (Johnson, 2019).

Unfortunately, the connection between these post-*Brown* policy actions and their impact on academic achievement among Black and brown students was underappreciated, if recognized at all, by a generation of education reformers whose influence came into prominence several decades later. Rather than seeing an adequately resourced, equitable, and inclusive education as a prerequisite for civic participation and upward mobility, this new generation of reformers had been persuaded that wage stagnation and growing income inequality, well documented by then, were best explained by a broken education system (Kraus, 2023). Accordingly, fixing the schools would take priority over attention to business practices and tax policies. These education reformers would piggyback on a new chapter in federal education policy, the No Child Left Behind (2002) era advocating for and supporting a new suite of policies, from national standards to various accountability, human capital, and performance-oriented interventions. The reform strategies that ensued were based on a few key assumptions.

First, new education goals, expressed in terms of common standards, would pull the system toward excellence. States would gauge progress against those standards through summative tests of student knowledge. Performance management would become a key lever for improvement. A mix of punitive measures (closing schools, firing teachers) and incentives (merit pay) would coax the system along while pruning it of underperformers.

Second, following the logic of performance management, individuals and individual schools, rather than the structures that surrounded them, became the units of analysis. Students were deemed proficient or failing based on tests, and teachers and schools were judged by how much student test scores improved. Little if any attention was given to the unequal starting points *Brown* sought to address. The result was that students, teachers, and schools from neighborhoods with higher poverty and higher proportions of students of color were more likely to be labeled failing, and to face punitive rather than restorative measures.

Failing schools were given scant resources for improvement. In place of more resources or more attention to context or structure, *choice* would be the vehicle of school improvement. States were strongly encouraged to deregulate who could operate schools and create a market signal of quality among different schools that parents could easily understand (test scores). Parents, as customers, should rationally choose high-scoring schools, which would in turn create a virtuous cycle of competition where all schools in a geography would compete to improve, with the most successful expanding and the least effective closed.

Hence, the education reform movement that gained popularity roughly 50 years after *Brown* was firmly rooted in the broader neoliberal transformation of economic and social policy in the United States that first took hold in the 1980s. The central tenet of neoliberalism was and is that governments should not interfere with the functioning of markets, which are perfectly capable of shaping both economic and social outcomes. Today's dramatic income inequality and associated fissures in our democracy call into question whether markets, left unfettered, distribute economic returns widely. When they do not, history suggests that democracies often struggle (Wolf, 2023) and the current situation in the United States supports this assertion.

Herein lies today's challenge. During this (neoliberal) project, progress on school integration stalled. Students are now as racially segregated as they were in the late 1960s. And with this return to racial and economic segregation, we have, again, widespread inequality in educational opportunity. Among other things, the racial and socioeconomic makeup of schools has a significant impact on factors directly correlated with the quality of education, such as securing and retaining high-quality teachers (Jackson, 2009). Disparities in per-pupil expenditures, never fully addressed, widened once again. Instead of looking back to the years immediately following *Brown* for insights and ideas, education advocates and civil rights groups find themselves defending against a backlash to educational equity.

A NEW FRAME FOR ACHIEVING *BROWN'S* PROMISE

Serving as the ideological frame for reform, neoliberal thinking gave rise to a range of reform tactics. In addition to using test scores to identify and sanction ineffective schools, a lot of energy went into linking student-level data to teacher records to sort out effective from ineffective teachers (Sass et al., 2012). Governance reform was used to gain leverage on what were considered stubborn bureaucracies, giving rise to mayoral takeovers in several of the nation's big cities (Henig, 2013). State legislatures, and in some cases, state education agencies and local school districts, dramatically expanded the number of charter schools. These tactics did not, for the most part, live up to expectations. The tests were overly narrow and overly used, the methods for teacher performance management were flawed, the system wasn't resourced to improve, and structural factors like racism and poverty were largely ignored. Adding insult to injury, disparities in achievement between Whites, Blacks, and Hispanic students, which had been falling during the 1970s and 80s, tapered off in both reading and math to reinstate inequalities (Nation's Report Card, 2023).

Further, the school-age population has changed over the past 25 years. Between 2000, on the cusp of NCLB, and 2018, the public schools became much more racially diverse, as the percentage of White students fell from 62% to 47% (National Center for Education Statistics [NCES], 2022a). Just over 10% of all students were English language learners (NCES, 2022a). Of the roughly 50 million students now enrolled in the public schools, 50% attend school in middle to high poverty school districts (NCES, 2022a). The current system design was never intended to address the challenges associated with these new demographics. We should be open to new designs—structures and processes that leverage what we know today about how people learn and that respect the diverse majority of students in today's schools.

To drive home this last point, note that the most basic design behind our education system, the 185-day school year with the summer off, was created to fit an agrarian calendar. Within this structure, our education system has been retrofitted to align with an industrial age characterized by standardized modes of instruction and assessment where education content is controlled centrally and learning opportunities are delivered in fixed time blocks. To make this easier for teachers, the system groups students by age, ability, and often by race. A teacher's ability to manage their classrooms is a key factor in achieving tenure, as is their ability to keep pace with the scope and sequence of the centralized curriculum. Standardized tests provide cheap and reliable means of monitoring student performance. The irony, of course, is that this basic design, as noted above, has not altered race- and income-related achievement gaps, a point that should be of grave concern for the civil rights community.

Much more is known now than when we put this education system in place. We have advances in cognitive science that shed light on how people learn (National Research Council, 1999). There is now a science of learning which, owing to its interdisciplinary nature, gives us fuller pictures of our students and sheds light on how social context and culture influence how they learn, much less how to engage them in the process of learning (Learning Policy Institute and Turnaround for Children, 2021; Pellegrino & Hilton, 2012). This new knowledge has real implications for satisfying the conditions *Brown* sought to establish, which, I argue, were twofold. One, that like their White counterparts, students of color would be deeply educated, which meant that they would be supported to think critically and equipped with the tools to make sense of the times in which they lived; two, that students would emerge from their educational experiences with agency and purpose, interested in the economic and social issues of the day and ready to take them up, as citizens, consumers, parents, workers, and voters. The preconditions for these educational and developmental outcomes started with a well-resourced public education system and included the things that flow from this—rigorous curricula, quality teachers, and schools that were safe and welcoming (Robinson, 2021).

If these were the conditions *Brown* sought to create—that students would grow academically and participate fully in our democracy—we need to be explicit about what conditions must hold today, especially from a teaching and learning point of view. If neoliberal thinking falls short as a framework for academic success and social mobility, are new frames available through which to think about pursuing this aspiration? I offer below an idea or two for how we might reframe the debate about education reform and improvement. Thinking differently about the purpose of our public schools is a good place to start.

A Refreshed Purpose

The dominant axiom about education's purpose has been that it should get kids "college and career ready." This gave rise to an almost singular focus on reading and math in the development of new standards-aligned instructional resources and assessments. While this was justified, many aspects of a well-rounded education—civics, history, social studies, and the fine and performing arts—were deemphasized (Commission on No Child Left Behind, 2007; Hamilton et al., 2008). NCLB did not *require* that these subjects be deprioritized, but states felt the pressure to focus on the things that drove federal education aid (Polikoff et al., 2022). Even with this pressure, the country failed to make the achievement gains it had expected to make during this period (Lee, 2006; Loveless, 2015; NCES, 2005).

The strong hand of accountability, it can be argued, may well have discouraged much-needed policy innovation. It certainly kept low-performing schools from adopting practices that might have engaged and motivated their students. We should wonder what progress we might have made if the schools had been given resources to build their capacity to support their students, and students had been given opportunities to work on culturally relevant topics and projects that leverage their backgrounds and interests.

This is where purpose matters. Our preoccupation with skills, while necessary, may not be sufficient for today's students, who we know are longing for school experiences where it is obvious that educators are interested in who they are and in schoolwork that they see as worth their time and effort (YouthTruth, 2021). In my view, our schools should focus on competencies, skills, *and* civic reasoning. Programs around the country are demonstrating the engagement and learning dividends from a focus on civic learning.[1] Beyond this, I argue we desperately need our public schools to take *building our democracy* as a core purpose. Were we to do so, here are a few specific ideas for what might be emphasized.

1. *Our public schools should impart knowledge, skills, and dispositions for effective democratic and community engagement.* This sort of preparation is not at odds with being college and career ready. To the contrary, it is likely to be an essential component of being prepared for the jobs of the future.
2. *Our schools should do their part to convey common facts in a world where, increasingly, facts are contested.* A shared set of facts is perhaps the lowest common denominator for a good education and functioning democracy. But with the rise of misinformation, AI-altered media, and partisan echo chambers, our common fact

base is fragile. We should commit to strengthening schools as a public source of knowledge and an institution committed to helping children and their families use facts to advance the public good.
3. *Education should provide students with new frames for thinking about societal problems.* Today's neoliberal version of capitalism, just one of capitalism's many manifestations, is often assumed to be the only way to analyze and solve problems, when there are a range of ways we might balance the roles of governments and markets within a capitalist frame. If we want our future citizens to meet challenges such as inequality and climate change, which neoliberalism has been ill-suited to solve, it would behoove us to help young people expand their thinking around questions of power, wealth, choice, and freedom as early in their education as possible.

Design Ideas to Support a New Purpose

Charged though it may be to question the purpose of our public schools, challenging the core *design* is even more fraught. As noted above, the basic design has been with us since the turn of the century. While the leaders of today's education system struggle to reduce race- and income-related disparities, it is very difficult to engage in conversation about changing the current design. It is as if we are glued to our 100-year history, constrained by an outdated accountability construct, and trapped by today's contentious politics. And yet it is hard to imagine satisfying the conditions stated above, much less reproduce the academic success and social mobility we initially witnessed post *Brown,* if we cannot at least consider a few key changes in the system as we know it. In lieu of the broader treatment this question deserves, here are just three ideas that deserve more consideration than they receive today.

The first is implied by the discussion of purpose above. To provide a common and shared knowledge base, offer useful frames for understanding the world in which we live, and equip students with the skills and tools to understand and ultimately tackle the challenges of the day, we need new goals for teaching *and* learning. Today's continuing emphasis on memorizing prior knowledge must give way to helping students make sense of new information, including using what students are learning in one context to analyze and solve problems in another.

Second, new teaching and learning goals must be accompanied by expanded opportunities to learn. Within schools, this might mean doing more to personalize the student experience as a means of increasing engagement and motivation. Of course, schools are not the only setting in which learning occurs. If the pandemic taught us anything, it was how important community-based organizations, cultural institutions, businesses, and higher education institutions can be for engaging, motivating, and expanding learning opportunities. The structures for these opportunities take many forms—apprenticeships, dual enrollment, internships, service-learning opportunities, and some versions of what we popularly refer to as community schools. Although there are many examples across the country, they remain the exception, not the rule. Our current school design is not permeable enough to accommodate them.

Third, expanding learning opportunities also depends on how we think about and use time. Roughly a decade ago, the Ford Foundation and the James Irving Foundation supported a range of pilots to illustrate what is possible when time and space are considered variable. These included efforts to provide integrated supports and expanded learning opportunities for families and children as part of Promise Neighborhood initiatives in California and Minnesota; community school initiatives in Oakland, CA, and high school redesign efforts in Detroit that explicitly link academic, career, and workplace learning opportunities (Saunders et al., 2017). Each of these pilots sought to expand the settings and ways in which young people could learn and develop as students. One of the lessons coming out of the pandemic is that kids need more time, during the school year, to rebound from lost learning opportunities. Imagine the leverage we might gain on learning if we found ways to institutionalize recent efforts to include community organizations in the learning process, build high-dosage tutoring into the school day, or leverage the summer to provide more than remedial education.

One more point on design is warranted. Even when these expanded learning opportunities show promise, they face a common obstacle, the Carnegie Unit, which has been the central organizing feature of American education for more than a century. Valuable though it is as a common way of accounting for student effort, the Carnegie Unit has been criticized for limiting flexibility and innovation. Especially problematic is the fact that we have not found ways to acknowledge and extend credit for things that young people learn outside of school. While it would be unrealistic to simply abandon the Carnegie Unit—it is deeply embedded in our current education system—we could benefit from exploring alternatives and modifications to it. The modifications might include efforts to account for competency-based education experiences that are not linked to seat time, or project-based learning opportunities that occur over widely varying time frames.

Again, there are interesting new initiatives working now to expand how we think about time and space. Education Reimagined (https://education-reimagined.org) for instance, has presented a compelling case for dramatically more personalization that depends on settings outside as much as within schools. The organizing idea for their work is a community-based, learner-centered ecosystem in which young people can craft and navigate their own learning journeys. In some respects, Education Reimagined is picking up where the Ford–Irving pilots left off a decade earlier, arguing for an education system that is organized around the interests and needs of the students rather than the adults (Pittman & Irby, 2024).

These ideas are offered as suggestive of what is possible if we can just bring ourselves to appreciate the limitations of our current school and system design and imagine the possibilities for alternatives that reinforce a refreshed, if not entirely new, purpose for our schools.

Operational Possibilities: Preparing Our Diverse Majority as Engaged Citizens

Brown was about a lot more than schools. It was about securing a future for children of color every bit as promising as is understood to be possible for their White counterparts. All children stand to benefit from schools that are integrated, staffed by quality teachers, and providing learning opportunities that impart both basic skills and the advanced knowledge and skills needed to participate fully in our society. Over the past 2 decades, we have given plenty of attention to basic skills and relatively little to the knowledge and skills young people need to thrive in a dynamic and complex world.

To make all this happen, we will need to move beyond entrusting democratic preparation to a single high school U.S. government course that some students take as an elective. Yes, young people should still learn how a bill becomes a law, but they also need schools and communities that inculcate their agency and voice, offer curricula that promote inquiry into problems relevant to their lives, and staff the schools with educators who are trained to nurture civic skills and dispositions. This broader conception of civic learning, and the cross-curricular and real-world application it entails, will have a better chance at engaging kids in what we most want them to learn.

Here are a few examples of what is already happening in education that should give us a reason to believe we can move closer to a contemporary interpretation of *Brown*.

1. *Community schools.* Community schools (Blank et al., 2023) are receiving a welcome degree of new attention, with states like California supporting their expansion with multi-billion-dollar investments, and the federal government and many national organizations working as their champions. Racially integrated communities see schools as part of the social fabric. Flowing from the modern community schools movement, one would hope to see a renewed appreciation for the interdependence of education with other social determinants of learning, together with a rise in policy solutions and practices that knit these different sectors of community together.

2. *Civic learning.* There has been an increase in the number of states with civic learning graduation requirements or civic seals of engagement, and an increase in the number of nonprofit organizations helping students develop civic knowledge and skills (Darling-Hammond & McGuire, 2023). The rising civic learning movement, even if some of it does not extend beyond a few courses, is a likely opening for policy change, and well worth cultivating within the larger context of youth civic preparation.
3. *Affirming curricula.* Accompanied by the recent push for racial equity in education, a number of researchers, publishers, districts, and states have increased their attention to curricula and other educational resources that affirm the diverse identities of students. Of course, the backlash to educational equity has led to states removing references to race and gender in approved materials. Some adopters and providers have caved to pressure, but most are looking for guidance and support for the stand they are taking in support of culturally sustaining practices. In addition, educators will benefit greatly from advocacy for more affirmative standards and materials.
4. *Student voice.* Young people today tend to be more civically engaged than generations past, and adults slowly, finally, are starting to pay attention. Youth organizing develops a range of skills useful to democratic engagement, but it is not often connected to in-school experiences. There are also a number of education organizations that do an excellent job with student voice and engagement (e.g., Big Picture Learning, www.bigpicture.org), that are not often connected to civics conversations. Bridge building across these divides will be needed for a fuller understanding of the ways that young people nurture democratic skills and dispositions.
5. *AI.* AI is likely to change student learning; that is, learning that involves basic skills or the acquisition of facts will become mediated at least in part by algorithm, while learning that is collaborative, immersive, and applied will be more likely to be teacher-led. If done well, this could create more instructional time for the "good stuff" of an education. Mitigating the potential harmful effects of AI will be essential.

SECURING THE PROMISE OF *BROWN*

In 1954, the Supreme Court said that education had become the most important function of state and local government. Our public schools, the Court went on to argue, are the very foundation of good citizenship. The neoliberal project lost sight of this. Today's education narrative remains centered largely on market-based ideas for improvement (Lipman, 2011). These ideas emphasized weeding out ineffective teachers, closing failing schools, and creating escape valves for parents wanting to flee the public education systems. The culture wars and the advent of the parents' rights movement have added fuel to the fire. In the current political environment, giving visibility to the democratic purposes of our schools can be fraught (Rogers & Kahn, 2022).

But we must make the democratic purposes of our schools vivid and urgent. It is hard to imagine a society where people see clearly that their own happiness and welfare is wrapped up in supporting and embracing the welfare of others, if we do not leverage our schools to help young people see a common good. *Brown* created this possibility.

The norm in the civil rights community, rightly, has been to press for resources and fair treatment under the law. Historically, education advocacy among civil rights groups, possibly because they do not feel they have expertise, or perhaps because they have not viewed instructional issues as problematic, has not emphasized teaching and learning issues. But if we have learned anything over the past 2 years, with a well-organized national assault on what can be taught, what texts can be read, it is that focusing only on the money, while necessary, is insufficient. While we continue to argue for standardized tests, on the premise that more resources will flow to Black and brown children, 29 states now have legislation on the books diverting public resources to private schools (Public Funds Public Schools, n.d.).[2] Over half have passed bills placing restrictions on what can be taught in school.

Brown, most will argue, was the beginning of the Civil Rights Movement in this country. But much has changed in 70 years and the frames currently in place to identify and solve problems may not lend themselves to the solutions we need. A new civil rights agenda is needed, one that is less bound up in neoliberal thought. Given the scale of the current assault on public education *and* our democracy, we may need, as Robert Kim (2023) suggests, a new civil rights movement focused not only on defending our public schools, but on pursuing affirmative strategies to strengthen them. Here are a few things that might command the attention of such a movement.

Shifting the Focus of Advocacy Efforts From Proficiency to Critical Thinking

A new civil rights agenda would press for much greater access to experiences and coursework that prepare young people to be engaged citizens. It is widely understood that civics, history, and social studies courses are especially well-suited for increasing student engagement and academic performance. Civics is, by its nature, interdisciplinary, and as such provides opportunities for students to grow their skills in problem solving, collaboration, critical thinking, and a host of other competencies key to their future leadership and success. Providing these experiences across the curriculum is likely to be even more powerful (Lee et al., 2021).

Beyond civic learning, advocacy efforts need to focus even more on those aspects of the curriculum most associated with access to college, chiefly advanced placement, International Baccalaureate, and honors courses. Many of our high schools may have aligned their courses with college admission requirements, but that does not mean enough students are enrolled in these courses. National surveys suggest that school principals do not believe their students are college ready (NCES, 2024). Worse, it does not matter if you are ready if you do not enroll in these courses. Black student enrollment, at just over 10%, is disappointing. Among those who do enroll, only a third take the exam (Christian & McDermott, 2002). Education advocates and civil rights actors should press much harder to see Black and brown student participation rates increase. More than that, they should press for more engaging, relevant, and challenging coursework, for all students. The current preoccupation with basic literacy and remediation is counterproductive and plays into the hands of those who want to keep Black children undereducated.

Better Assessments

To complement high-quality curriculum and instruction, a new civil rights agenda must include arguments for aligned and varied assessments. This is a significant issue, since advocates and civil rights groups seem locked into backward-looking ideas about testing that provide little information about teaching and learning. Nor do these summative assessments succeed in distributing resources to students most in need of extra attention and support. To the contrary, the results often discourage greater education spending. What we need is greater emphasis on assessments *for* learning as much or more than *of*, so we can target resources in ways that improve teaching and learning.

Improving assessments will involve attention to their purpose, interpretation, and use. Today, accountability is the dominant purpose. In the context of neoliberal thinking, low performance means that a school is deemed failing and disqualified from receiving financial and other supports to improve student learning. This thinking simply makes no sense but remains in place. Interpretation of test scores is also largely outside the reach of advocates and stakeholders. Experts talk about standard scores, z-scores, T-scores, stanines, and grade equivalent scores; they use these scores to make decisions about remedial strategies, but rarely about advancement and enrichment. These tests can harm students in a number of ways: increasing pressure and anxiety in students, narrowing curricular focus, and limiting motivation and engagement. As these assessments became prevalent between 2001 and 2010, we learned a lot about the consequences of their use (Dee & Jacob, 2011). There were increases in math achievement, but very much at a cost in terms of mental health and well-being.

Advocates should push for tests that are aligned with learning goals. They should advocate for a broader range of assessments, to include project-based assessments, portfolios that contain evidence about student work, and other forms of assessment that provide a more holistic picture of a student's knowledge and skill. Given the emerging realities of today's workforce and AI, it is time for assessments that assess a student's understanding of content, not just their ability to remember facts. This involves the development and use of tests that measure critical thinking and problem-solving skills. Such tests exist, but they are not the focus of contemporary advocacy efforts. This needs to change.

A Prepared and More Diverse Teacher Workforce

Even if we succeed in making the thinking curriculum the norm and attend to better ways of assessing learning, we are unlikely to realize *Brown*'s promise if we do not advocate for a much more qualified and diverse teacher workforce. Effective teachers create the kinds of learning environments that foster thinking, problem-solving, and reasoning. Although we may be in agreement that teachers ought to help students acquire these competencies—including broader civic and social goals, such as preparing students for engaged civic participation in a diverse democracy—we are not set up today to produce these outcomes broadly in the education workforce.

As for the demographics of our workforce, remember that the diversity of the student population has increased markedly over the past 20 years; over the same period, however, the demographic makeup of the teacher workforce has seen little change. Advocates need to know that there is a growing body of evidence that teachers of color—in particular Black teachers—have important effects on student achievement, particularly for students of color (National Academies of Sciences, Engineering, and Medicine, 2019). They should push harder for efforts to bring the racial mix of teachers in line with that of students.

All this to say that in addition to a true thinking curriculum, and better ways to assess learning in relation to this curriculum, there remains the important task of creating a teacher workforce that can do its part to prepare students for work and civic life. If students are to evaluate new ideas and tie these ideas to the conclusions they reach, if they are to leverage prior knowledge to solve problems in their communities, we need a new vision of pedagogy, one that includes disciplinary modes of inquiry (such as literary analysis, historical analysis, and scientific investigation). These requirements need to find their way into a forward-looking civil rights agenda.

Better Equity Indicators

Keeping track of progress in this forward-looking agenda requires a more varied and evidence-based set of indicators. Advocates will want to know if students of color have access to high-quality curriculum and instruction. Such indicators would include both the availability of advanced placement and honors courses as well as measures of curricular breadth, such as access to the arts, social studies, science, and technology (National Academies, 2019).

We also need to be able to track disparities in access to effective teaching. Perhaps the most important indicators include data on teachers' credentials and areas of certification (NCES, 2000). All too often, low-income children and children of color do not have access to teachers certified in the subjects to which they have been assigned. Another troubling reality is that these students are, more often than not, exposed to novice teachers, so advocates need to monitor data on teachers' years of experience. Data on the racial and ethnic diversity of the education workforce are widely available and should be consulted to ensure that students of color see people who look like them in the classroom.

A new civil rights agenda in education needs to expand the availability of and access to data on supportive school and classroom environments (National Academies, 2019). The list of possible indicators is long and includes data from students on their perceptions of school safety, their relationships with teachers, and their access to academic support. Supports for emotional, behavioral, physical, and mental health form another important indicator, especially as national data confirm that student social and emotional well-being is a significant problem (NCES, 2022b).

CONCLUSION

There are many topics not addressed here. These include the challenges of resource inequality, and the absence of new strategies to address the resegregation of our communities and schools. Nor have I addressed issues like access to the internet, which many view as a civil right in an information society and modern democracy. But these issues are taken up in other contexts. A network of education funders has created the Resource Equity Funders Collaborative (REFC), to support research on resource equity, to increase awareness of inequality in school funding, and to support a number of state-level advocacy efforts across the country to press for school finance reform. Education Resource Strategies (ERS) is working to tackle similar issues at the district and school levels. The Southern Education Foundation (SEF) is host to a project called Brown's Promise, which is engaged in research, litigation, advocacy, and communications efforts, to identify new information needs, develop new legal theories and remedies, and foster a much-needed national discussion about the importance of ending school segregation. Their work needs to be incorporated into a refreshed civil rights agenda.

My core argument is that realizing the promise of *Brown* starts with reaffirming the purpose of public schools within our modern, diverse democracy. As suggested, this inclusive and forward-looking purpose opens our eyes to new roles for the schools to play, new designs for our education system, and many new operational possibilities, only a few of which have been noted herein. This is not a task for the civil rights community alone. It is a task for all of us. Rather than using education as a cynical political tool to deepen our divides, we need to remind ourselves of the real benefits that public schools can bring for young people. In the earliest days of our country's founding, a chief purpose of education was to prepare citizens to participate in our democratic republic. So, the idea of a civic purpose for public schools has ebbed and flowed through history, and, in a time of rising division, is in urgent need of renewal. Public schools that foster an appreciation for the lessons of history, alongside the skills and dispositions for citizenship, must be part of the long-term solution to the democratic and societal challenges we face today.

REFERENCES

Baker, B. D. (2021). *Educational inequality and school finance: Why money matters for America's students.* Harvard Education Press.

Blank, M., Harkavy, I., Quinn, J., Villarreal, L., & Goodman, D. (2023). *The community schools revolution: Building partnerships, transforming lives, advancing democracy.* Collaborative Communications Group.

Christian, P., & McDermott, L. (2022). *Disparities in advanced placement course enrollment and test taking: National and state-level perspectives.* Urban Institute.

Commission on No Child Left Behind (2007). *Beyond NCLB: Fulfilling the promise to our nation's children.* Aspen Institute.

Darling-Hammond, L., & McGuire, K. (2023). Policy for civic reasoning. In G. White, D. Dong, & D. E. Campbell, *Civic education in a time of crisis* (pp. 232–248). *The ANNALS of the American Academy of Political Science, 705*(1).

Dee, T., & Jacobs, B. (2011). The impact of No Child Left Behind on student achievement. *Journal of Policy Analysis and Management, 30*(3), 418–446.

Hamilton, L, Stecher, B., & Yuan, K. (2008). *Standards-based reform in the United States: History, research, and future directions.* RAND Corporation.

Henig, J. (2013). *The end of exceptionalism in American education: The changing politics of school reform.* Harvard Education Press.

Jackson, K. (2009) Student demographics, teacher sorting, and teacher quality: Evidence from the end of school desegregation. *Journal of Labor Economics, 27*(2), 213–256.

Johnson, R. C. (2019). *Children of the dream*. Basic Books.
Kim, R. (2023). The legal fight to preserve public education—and democracy. *Phi Delta Kapan, 104*(8), 60–62.
Kissinger, L., & the NCSS Seal of Civic Readiness Task Force. (2022). Civics diploma seals: Energizing civic education for students. *Social Education, 86*(3). https://www.socialstudies.org/system/files/2022-06/SE-860322209.pdf
Kraus, N. (2023). *The fantasy economy: Neoliberalism, inequality, and the education reform movement*. Temple University Press.
Learning Policy Institute & Turnaround for Children. (2021). *Design principles for schools: Putting the science of learning and development into action*. Learning Policy Institute. https://learningpolicyinstitute.org/sites/default/files/product-files/SoLD_Design_Principles_REPORT.pdf
Lee, C., White, G., & Dong, D. (Eds.). (2021). *Educating for civic reasoning and discourse*. National Academy of Education. https://naeducation.org/educating-for-civic-reasoning-and-discourse-report/
Lee, J. (2006) *Tracking achievement gaps and assessing the impact of NCLB on the gaps: An in-depth look into national and state reading and math outcome trends*. The Civil Rights Project, Harvard University.
Lipman, P. (2011). *The new political economy of urban education-neoliberalism, race, and the right to the city*. Routledge.
Loveless, T. (2015, March). *How well are American students learning?* (Vol. 3, No. 4). Brown Center on Education Policy at Brookings. https://www.brookings.edu/wp-content/uploads/2016/06/2015-Brown-Center-Report_FINAL.pdf
Nation's Report Card. (2023). *NAEP long-term trend assessment results: Reading and mathematics*. U.S. Department of Education, Institute of Education Sciences, National Center for Education Statistics. https://www.nationsreportcard.gov/ltt/?age=9
National Academies of Sciences, Engineering, and Medicine. (2019). *Monitoring educational equity*. The National Academies Press. https://doi.org/10.17226/25389
National Center for Education Statistics. (2000). *Monitoring school quality: An indicators report*. U.S. Department of Education. https://nces.ed.gov/pubs2001/2001030.pdf
National Center for Education Statistics. (2005). *National assessment of educational progress: The nation's report card*. U.S. Department of Education, Institute of Education Sciences.
National Center for Education Statistics. (2022a) *Digest of Education Statistics, Tables 203.50, 204.20 and 203.75*. U.S. Department of Education. https://nces.ed.gov/programs/digest/d22
National Center for Education Statistics (2022b). More than 80 percent of U.S. public schools report pandemic has negatively impacted student behavior and socio-emotional development. U.S. Department of Education. https://nces.ed.gov/whatsnew/press_releases/07_06_2022.asp
National Center for Education Statistics (2024). *School Pulse Panel: Responses to the pandemic and efforts toward recovery*. U.S. Department of Education, Institute of Education Sciences. https://nces.ed.gov/surveys/spp
National Research Council. (1999). *How people learn: Brain, mind, experience and school*. National Academies Press. https://nap.nationalacademies.org

/catalog/9853/how-people-learn-brain-mind-experience-and-school-expanded-edition

No Child Left Behind (NCLB) Act of 2001, Pub L, No 107-110, Stat. 1425 (2002).

Pellegrino, J., & Hilton, M. (2012). *Education for life and work: Developing transferable knowledge and skills in the 21st century.* National Academies Press.

Pittman, K., & Irby, M. (2024). *Too essential to fail: Why our big bet on public education needs a bold national response.* Education Reimagined.

Polikoff, M., Desimone, L., Porter, A., Garet, M., Stornaiuolo, A., Pak, K., Smith, T., Song, M., Flores, N., Fuchs, L., Fuchs, D., & Nichols, P. (2022). *The enduring struggle of standards-based reform: Lessons from a national research center on college and career-ready standards* (EdWorkingPaper 22-622). Annenberg Institute at Brown University. https://doi.org/10.26300/00ev-gk28

Public Funds Public Schools. (n.d.). *Bill tracker.* https://pfps.org/billtracker

Robinson, K. J. (2021). *Protecting education as a civil right: Remedying racial discrimination and ensuring a high-quality education.* Learning Policy Institute. https://doi.org/10.54300/407.455

Rogers, J., & Kahn, J. (2022). *Educating for a diverse democracy: The chilling role of political conflict in blue, purple and red communities.* UCLA Institute for Democracy, Education and Access.

Sass, T., Hannaway, J., Figlio, D., & Feng, L. (2012). *Value added of teachers in high-poverty schools and lower poverty schools.* UWRG Working Paper 45.

Saunders, M., Ruiz de Velasco, J., & Oakes, J. (Eds.). (2017). *Learning time: In pursuit of educational equity.* Harvard Education Press.

Stout, C., & Wilburn, T., (2021, June 9). CRT Map: Efforts to restrict teaching racism and bias have multiplied across the U.S. *Chalkbeat.*

Viadero, D., Jones, S., & Baker, L. (2018, October 23). Data: Most states require history, but not civics. *Education Week.* https://www.edweek.org/teaching-learning/data-most-states-require-history-but-not-civics/2018/10

Wolf, M. (2023). *The crisis of democratic capitalism.* Penguin Press.

YouthTruth. (2021). *Students weigh in.* YouthTruth Student Surveyhttps://youthtruthsurvey.org/resources/students-weigh-in-part-ii-learning-well-being-during-covid-19/

Notes

Chapter 1

    1. This paper draws in part on Darling-Hammond, L. (2018). Education and the path to one nation, indivisible. In F. Harris & A. Curtis (Eds.), *Healing our divided society: Investing in America fifty years after the Kerner report* (pp. 193–207). Temple University Press; and Darling-Hammond, K., & Darling-Hammond, L. (2022). *The civil rights road to deeper learning.* Teachers College Press.

    2. The Court found in a 5–4 decision that unequal funding of schools disadvantaging poor children in Texas was not a violation of the 14th Amendment because there is not a stated right to education in the Constitution.

Chapter 4

    1. Race is still meaningfully correlated with poverty overall in America, although the correlation has been reduced over the last 60 years. This pattern is also true specifically for children; Black, American Indian, and Latinx children are more than twice as likely to grow up in poverty as their non-Hispanic White and Asian and Pacific Islander peers. Even more distinctive than family poverty, though, is Black children's disproportionate exposure to high concentrated poverty neighborhoods. There are vast differences in the neighborhood quality in which Black and White families with children, *with identical incomes,* reside in metropolitan areas across the United States. Affluent Black households (those with income above $75,000) live in neighborhoods with a higher average poverty rate than poor White households (those with income below $40,000; Logan, 2011; Reardon et al. 2015). There is substantial neighborhood inequality by race throughout the entire household income distribution, and it is linked to racial parental wealth disparities. It takes more than $65,000 in household income for Black households to reside (on average) in the median American neighborhood (measured by income), while White households with just $21,000 in income reside in comparable neighborhoods (Bayer et al., 2021).

    2. We found that, by the end of 1966, 25% of the counties in the South—and 75% of the counties in the Mississippi Delta—were not yet in compliance with the order to desegregate hospitals.

    3. See Johnson's book *Children of the Dream* (2019) for fuller discussion.

    4. Often referred to as the "reduced-form" effect in empirical policy research.

    5. Earlier historical accounts and studies include Ashenfelter et al. (2006), Bayer & Charles (2018), Clotfelter (2004), Greenberg (2004), Orfield (1983), among others.

6. Most state constitutions in the South delegated the responsibility of providing public K–12 education to the county systems in those Southern states, as opposed to municipal districts or individual cities as was true for the North.

7. For example, in prior work when we've aggregated district per-pupil spending to the county level and used it as an outcome, we find desegregation no longer has detectable impacts on school resources (even though these impacts come through when per-pupil spending is properly measured at the school district level).

8. School choice without equity guidelines can exacerbate school segregation. In the spirit of elevating parent engagement, many charter schools put a heavy value on choice. But it is naive to assume that all parents equally understand and can manage the many options available to them. Most of our most vulnerable parents have limited skills to understand their school choice options; and without an aggressive community engagement effort on their behalf, it is likely that the better educated and more affluent families will be first in line to avail their children of opportunity. Further, charter schools have often not been required to submit to the same oversight as public schools (e.g., desegregation guidelines). Permissive district secession laws or unregulated charter school growth policies accelerate racial and socioeconomic school segregation patterns. The claim is "local control," but it's often designed to control the racial and socioeconomic composition of schools in segregative ways. We must remain vigilant to address modern-day forms of state-sanctioned discrimination affecting education opportunities by race and class.

9. Reardon et al. (2012) and Lutz (2011), using the timing of releases of desegregation court orders, show that they contributed significantly to the resegregation of public schools, and Lutz (2011) finds this led to significant increases in the probability of dropping out of high school for Black students.

10. The debate over whether money matters dates all the way back to Coleman et al. (1966), and this current work builds on a growing body of research on the causal impacts of school spending on student success. Other influential studies include Card and Krueger (1992a, 1992b), Jackson et al. (2016), Lafortune et al. (2018), among others.

Chapter 5

1. Portions of this section come from Ladson-Billings (2004).

2. I described Ethel Benn and my relationship with her in Ladson-Billings (2022).

3. I confess she was probably in her fifties, younger than this author at the time of this writing.

4. I use the term "integrated" as opposed to "desegregated" here because the junior high school and high school I attended were not under court orders. The schools' geographic boundaries included both Black and White communities. Each group was attending its neighborhood schools.

5. *Brown II* was handed down on May 31, 1955, a little more than a year after the *Brown* decision. *Brown II* left states and school districts with the ambiguous language of implementing school desegregation "with all deliberate speed," which meant there were years of resistance and foot-dragging before anything changed in many school districts.

6. Several states—Louisiana, Mississippi, Ohio, and Wisconsin—have multiple programs. Also, there is a voucher program in the District of Columbia.

7. Tracking requires students to follow teacher direction with their eyes at all times.

Chapter 6

1. For a description of the bill's requirements, see Oliva (2022).

2. 1987: Hammer & Gerald (1990); 1990: National Center for Education Statistics (1994); 1993: Henke et al., (1997); 1999: Luekens et al., (2004); 2003: Strizek et al., (2006); 2007: Coopersmith (2009); 2011: National Center for Education Statistics (2013); 2015: Taie & Goldring (2017); 2017: Taie & Goldring (2020); 2020: Taie & Lewis (2022).

3. Teacher Follow-Up Survey 2021–2022 data were not yet available at time of publication to conduct tests of significance to determine if the differences in mover and leaver rates were statistically significant.

4. Note that the statistical test compares outcomes for Black teachers and teachers of color to White teachers, as the overrepresented teacher group, and does not compare whether differences between Black teachers and teachers of color are statistically significant.

5. High-need fields under this program include bilingual education and English language acquisition, foreign language, mathematics, reading specialist, science, and special education, as well as any other field that has been identified as high need by the federal government, a state government, or a local education agency and that is included in the annual Teacher Shortage Areas Nationwide Listing.

Chapter 8

1. See for instance, Generation Citizen, https://www.generationcitizen.org, and Mikva Challenge, https://mikvachallenge.org

2. At least five states have such programs, often referred to as Education Savings Accounts (ESAs): Arizona, Florida, Mississippi, North Carolina, and Tennessee. Florida's program may now account for nearly 30% of all education funding in the state.

Index

Academic vs. vocational tracks, 32
Accountability: accountability systems, 41, 131; punitive, 85, 88, 229
"Accumulation of disadvantage," 85, 86–89
Acheson, Dean, 199
Achievement gaps: higher education, 19–21; high school attainment, 19; K-12, 16–19; quality teachers, access to, 28–33
Acosta, J., 38
Acosta, M. M., 164
Acuña, R., 92
Adams, L., 35
Adukia, A., 120
Adult literacy, 142–143
Affirmative action, 21, 57, 77, 82, 92, 161–162
African American cultural heritage, 202–210
African American English, 214–215
African American Vernacular English (AAVE), 215
African-centered education, 208
African Union, Diaspora Division, 206
Afrik, H. T., 208
Ahram, R., 88
Aladangady, A., 22
Alexander, K. L., 166
Alexander, L., 163
Alexander, M., 18, 40
Alicea, J., 91
Allen, Richard, 150
Allen, T., 37
Alliance for Children's Rights, 86
An American Dilemma (Myrdal), 58
American Missionary Association, 142
American Rescue Act, 19, 25, 40
Amerikaner, Ary, 3, 5, 7
An, B., 86
Anderson, A., 152

Anderson, J. D., 81, 87, 198–199, 203–204
Anderson, Marian, 149
Anstreicher, Garrett, 116
Antman, Francisca, 118
Apple, M. W., 82
Apprenticeships, 182–183
Armour, M., 39
Armstrong, S., 67
Artificial intelligence (AI), 233
Asante-Muhammad, D., 17
Assessments, 16–19, 31, 235–236. *See also* National Assessment of Educational Progress (NAEP)
Association for the Study of Negro Life and History, 204
Augustine, C. H., 38
Ayscue, J., 26

Bacher-Hicks, A., 34, 35, 120
Baker, B. D., 177, 225
Baker, M., 26, 38
Baldridge, B. J., 8
Barclay, C. M., 39
Barnett, S., 26
Barrett, N., 37
Barshay, J., 131
Bartanen, B., 121
Baum, S., 176
Bauman, C., 124
Baum-Snow, N., 101
Beady, C. H., Jr., 166
Beauboeuf-Lafontant, T., 179
Belasco, A. S., 37
Bell, Derrick, 7–8, 83, 157, 198
Benedict College, 142
Benjamin, Ruha, 10–11
Benn, Ethel, 148–150
Bennett, B., 140
Bethune, Mary McLeod, 204
Betty Shabazz International Charter School network, 208

Index

Beyond the Schoolhouse (Noguera et al.), 87
Bianco, M., 164–165
Biden administration, 19
Bilingual education, 155–156
Billingham, C. M., 84
Birmingham crisis, 61
Blackburn, D. G., 199, 200
Black English, 214–215
Black History Month, 204
Black Lives Matter movement, 108
Blackmun, Harry, 66, 67
Black Panther Party, 208
Black students: college admissions, 1, 88–89; in Los Angeles County, 86–88; per-pupil expenditures, 14; and school discipline, 33–34, 35–37, 167; student debt, 20–21; success of, 17–18, 29, 163–165, 166–168; tracking of, 88
Black teachers, 129; and activism, 202; and Africana American cultural heritage, 202–210; Black schools, history of, 209; and Black student success, 29, 163–165, 166–168; certification exams, 153, 184–185; and desegregation, 140–141; impact, analysis of, 181–184; impact on all students, 165–166, 168–170; job satisfaction, 179–181; National Board Certification, 184–185; in Northern cities, 151–153; recruitment and retention, 174–179, 182; and student achievement, 18; and students' sociopolitical development, 163–164; teacher turnover, 170–174; trends in representation post-*Brown v. Board*, 170
Black Teachers on Teaching (Foster), 164
Black Women in White America (Lerner), 141–142
Blad, E., 130
Blair, H. W., 207
Blank, M., 232
Blazar, David, 157, 169
Blazevski, J., 183
Blomstedt, M., 127
Blow, C. M., 161
Board of Education of Oklahoma City v. Dowell, 74–75, 198
Boisjoly, Johanne, 107
Bolton, C. C., 145
Bond, Horace Mann, 204
Bonilla-Silva, E., 87
Borman, G. D., 177
Boschma, J., 85, 86

Boston Public Schools' Women Educators of Color, 181
Bottiani, J. H., 35
Bourdieu, P., 92
Bowles, S., 92
Bowman, P., 211
Boyd, D., 121
Boyd, M., 29
Boykin, A. W., 203
Bracey, J. H., 208
Brangham, W., 19
Bransford, J, 30
Brennan, William J., Jr., 69, 71, 111
Brewer, D. J., 168
Bridges, Ruby, 140
Briggs v. Elliott, 59
Bristol, Travis J., 3–4, 29, 162, 165, 168, 179, 180, 181, 184, 185
Brittain, J., 41
Brookings Institution, 20
Brookins, C., 208
Brotherhood of Sleeping Car Porters, 202
Brown, A. L., 165, 180
Brown, Cynthia Stokes, 142
Brown, Linda, 67
Brown, Oliver, 92
Brown's Promise project (SEF), 123, 237–238, 239–240
Brownstein, R., 85, 86
Brown v. Board of Education of Topeka (1954), 83–86; African American cultural context, 202–210; background and context, 58–64; Black teachers, impact on, 144–148; *Brown II* decision (1955), 59, 198; civil rights lawsuits, 63; contemporary challenges, 10–11, 227–233; contemporary legacy, 213–218; context of, 13–15, 225–227; and cross-community collaborations, 200–202; future directions and hope, 233–237; harms of, 6–7; legacy and impact, 5–6, 8–10, 155–157, 196–200; legal arguments/theory, 202, 210–213; resistance among White residents, 145; used to White advantage, 156
Bryan, J., 37
Bryk, A. S., 89
Bueno, M., 26
Bunch, Ralph, 149–150
Burger, Warren E., 66, 67, 71
Burke, Fred, 30
Burkholder, Z., 164
Bush, George, 22

Bush, George W., 22
Butler, Octavia, 11

California: Local Control Funding Formula (LCFF), 121–122; Proposition 13, 121; Proposition 227, 155–156
Campoli, A. K., 180
Cannon, J. S., 25
Capitol Insurrection (2021), 216
Capitol Region Education Council (CREC), 125
Card, D., 120
Cardichon, J., 26, 28, 42, 185
Carey, R. L., 166
Carmichael, S., 208
Carnegie Forum, 165
Carnegie Units, 231
Carnoy, Martin, 92
Caro, R. A., 62
Carr, Peggy, 19
Carrell, S. E., 37
Carruthers, J. H., 203
Carter, K., 30
Carter, P. L., 21
Carter Andrews, D. J., 176
Carver-Thomas, Desiree, 3–4, 18, 29, 85, 168, 170, 171, 172, 176, 177, 179, 183
Cascio, E., 113
CASEL, 129
Center for Black Educator Development (CBED), 141, 142, 181
Centers for Disease Control and Prevention (CDC), 23
Cha-Jua, S. K., 161
Champagne, A., 148
Chapel Hill, North Carolina, 140–141
Charlotte-Mecklenburg, North Carolina, 119
Charron, K. M., 142
Charter schools, 18, 36, 119–120, 128, 155–156, 208
Chavous, T. M., 212
Cherng, H.Y.S., 169
Chetty, R., 83, 122
Chicago Consortium on School Improvement, 89
Children of the Dream (Johnson), 90
Children's Defense Fund, 85
Child tax credits, 23, 40
Choi, A., 120
Choy, R.K.H., 112
Christian, P., 235

City planning and segregation, 99–100
Civics/government coursework, 224–225, 232, 233, 234–235
Civil Rights Act (1964), 15, 61, 62; enforcement of, 107–108
Civil Rights Data Collection (CRDC), 28–29, 35–36, 42
Civil rights lawsuits, 63
Civil Rights Movement, 60–62, 234
The Civil Rights Road to Deeper Learning, 40
Clark, Kenneth, 200
Clark, Mamie, 200
Clark, Septima Poinsette, 142–144
Class stratification, 85, 152–153. *See also* Poverty
Clinton, Mississippi, 131
Clotfelter, C. T., 29, 168
Cobb, C., 126
Cohn, Avern, 72
Coleman, James, 168
Coleman-King, C., 177
Coles, J. A., 9
Collaborations, cross-community, 200–202
College Composition and Communication Conference (CCCC), 214
Collins, Leonard, 164
The Color of Law (Rothstein), 23
Combs, B. H., 162
Commission for Racial Justice, 24
Community-based organizations (CBOs), 130
Community-building practices, 38
Community Coalition and Inner-City Struggle, 91
Community schools, 232. *See also* Neighborhoods
Conflict resolution, 38, 39, 42
Connolly, N. D., 161
"Contact Hypothesis," 107
Cook, C. R., 38
Cooper v. Aaron, 60
Cormier, C. J., 164
Cornelius, J., 203
Cornell, D. G., 37
Cortes, Kalena, 118
Council of Chief State School Officers, 181
Council of Independent Black Institutions, 208
Counselors, school, 37–38
Courts, Gus, 145

Index

COVID-19 pandemic, 18–19
Cowen, E. L., 166
Cox, Archibald, 108
Crawford v. Board of Education of Los Angeles, 112
Crenshaw, K. W., 82
Critical thinking, 234–235
Cruz-Guzman v. State of Minnesota, 101, 132
Cubbage, J., 35
Cui, T., 118
Cullen, J. B., 127
Curran, F. C., 37
Curriculum: and achievement gaps, 29–30; need for challenging, 42

Dallas, Texas, 126
D'Amico, D., 163, 179
Dark, O. C., 202
Darling-Aduana, J., 167
Darling-Hammond, K., 40
Darling-Hammond, Linda, 1, 2, 5, 8, 15, 18, 28, 29, 30, 33, 38, 40, 41, 42, 85, 171, 172, 174, 177, 233
Darling-Hammond, Sean, 1, 2, 5, 8, 35, 36, 38, 39
Davis, B. H., 163
Davis, N. R., 8
Davis, S., 66
Dee, T. S., 168, 236
Denton, N. A., 9, 84
Desegregation: court orders, 111–112, *112*; enforcement of, 17; federal support for, 41; impacts of, *115*, 115–118, *116*, *117*; integration levels, peak, 109; randomized controlled trials (RCTs), 109–110; resistance to, 59; White allies, 90
DeSilver, D., 15
Detroit, Michigan; *Milliken v. Bradley* (1974), 71–74, 101, 123, 153, 198
Diem, S., 127
Dill, A. G., 202, 203
Discipline. *See* School discipline
Discrimination: housing, 151; individual cases, proving, 76; redlining, 14, 21, 24, 87–88, 91, 151
Diverse & Learner-Ready Teachers Initiative, 181
Diversity Act, 41
Dixson, A. D., 179
Dobbie, W., 107
Dolls Test, 200–201, 210–211
Double consciousness, 198, 203, 206, 210, 211

"Double segregation," 85
Dougherty, J., 152
Douglas, William O., 71, 72
Douglass, Frederick, 149
Dowd, Nancy, 6
Dowling, N. M., 177
Doyle, W., 30
Dred Scott decision, 58
Duarte, C. D., 34
Du Bois, W.E.B., 86, 149, 150, 198, 200, 202, 203, 205, 206, 209–210, 212, 218
Dudziak, M. L., 83
Dumas, M. J., 9
Duncan, G. J., 82
Duong, M. T., 38
Dupree, Pauline (pseudonym), 144–148
Durlak, J. A., 39
Durrah, Daisy, 163

Early Childhood Longitudinal Study, 166
Earthseed (Butler), 11
Eastland, James, 145
Easton-Brooks, D., 168, 176
Eaton, S., 72
Eberhardt, J. L., 37
Ebonics, 215
EdBuild, 84, 124, 127
Ed Data, 86
Eddy, C., 168
Ed Trust, 129
Educating for Civic Reasoning and Discourse (Lee), 217–218
Education: allocation of resources, 14; function of and hope for, 81–82; history of inequality, 14; market forces, 155; measurement and assessment, 16–19, 31, 235–236; right to, 41
Educational management organizations (EMOs), 156
Education Reimagined, 231–232
Education Resource Strategies (ERS), 237
Edwards, E. J., 87
Ee, J., 83
Egalite, A. J., 167, 168
Ehrenberg, R. G., 168
Eisenhower, Dwight, 59
Elementary and Secondary Education Act (ESEA), 15, 41, 63, 108; Title I funding, 90, 113
Emergency School Aid Act, 15
Engagement: and civic learning, 229, 233; student/family/community, 130, 242n8; and student voice, 233

Environmental hazards, 24
Epps, Edgar, 144
Equality of Educational Opportunity, 168
Equal Protection Clause, 21, 72
Equity: current status of, 15–21; equality as ideal, 13; indicators of, 237; resource equity, 100
Esboldt, J., 184
Espinoza, D., 185
Estavanico the Moor, 150
Ethical Ambition (Bell), 7–8
Ethnicity vs. race, 200–201
Eugenics, 31, 199
Evans, M. O., 168
Evans, W. N., 104–105
Every Student Succeeds Act (ESSA), 131, 181, 185
Ewing, E. L., 8, 173
Eyllon, M., 34

Fabelo, T., 34
Faces at the Bottom of the Well (Bell), 157
Faded Dreams (Carnoy), 92
Fair Housing Act (1968), 21, 62
Farinde, A. A., 181
Farinde-Wu, A., 164
Farrie, D., 18
Faubus, Orval, 59
Federal Interagency Forum on Child and Family Statistics, 23
Federalist Society, 73
Fenwick, L., 147
Fiddiman, B., 176
"50/50 Schools," 126
Fisher, B. W., 37
Flint, Michigan, 24
Florida Governor's Office, 161
Forbes, Malcolm, 107
Forde, A., 22
Ford Foundation, 231
Fortas, Abe, 65
Fortner, S., 24
Foster, M., 215
Foster, Michele, 164
Fothergill, K. E., 34
Fourteenth Amendment, 58
Fox, L., 166
Frady, M., 65
Frankenberg, E., 17, 85
Franklin, V. P., 152
Freedman's Bureau, 203
Freedmen's Aid Society, 145
"Freedom riders," 61

Freedom Schools, 209
Freeman v. Pitts, 75, 198
Freire, Paulo, 143
Frey, W., 83
Friedlaender, D., 31
Friedman, Milton, 155
Fryer, R. G., Jr., 107
"Fugitive pedagogy," 147, 149
Fultz, M., 144

Gage, N. A., 39
Gall, P., 65
Gamoran, A., 86
Garnett, N. S., 173
Garvey, Marcus, 207
Garza, F., 24
Gay, Claudine, 161
Gay, G., 215
George, J., 15, 85, 125
Gershenson, S., 114, 167–168, 169
Gifford, B. R., 112
Gifted and talented programs, 120, 130, 167
Gillespie, J., 34
Gilliam, W. S., 37
Gintis, H., 92
Gist, C. D., 168
Giuliano, L., 120
Givens, Jarvis, 5, 89, 147, 149, 162, 163, 215
Goe, L., 29
Goings, R. B., 164–165
Goldys, P., 38
González, T., 33, 38, 39
Gordon, M. F., 18
Gottlieb, D., 163
Gould, M. S., 34
Government Accountability Office (GAO), 33, 35
Granson, Milla, 141–142
Grant, A. A., 38
Grant-Thomas, A., 84
Grassroots movements, 9, 106, 108–109
Graybill, S. W., 163
Great Migration, 152, 2123
Great Recession (2008–2012), 18
Great Society programs, 16
"Green factors," 102, 113–114
Green v. New Kent County (1968), 64–66, 74, 102, 110–111
Gregory, A., 37, 38, 39
Griffin v. County School Board of Prince Edward County, 60
Grissom, J. A., 120, 167

Index 249

Grutter v. Bollinger, 21
Guha, R., 182, 183
Guidry, K., 37
Gundaker, G., 203
Guryan, J., 116
Gutmann, A., 218

Hacker, A., 84
Halfmann, Janet, 142
Halpin, P. F., 169
Hamer, Fannie Lou, 143
Hamilton, C. V., 208
Hamilton, L., 229
Hampton Institute, 142
Hansell, S., 166
Hansen, M., 183
Hanushek, Eric, 27, 71, 168
Harm-repair practices, 38, 39, 42
Harris, B., 131
Harris, T., 8
Hart, C. M., 167
Hartford, Connecticut, 125–126
Hashim, A., 38, 39
Hastings, D., 19
Hawken, L. S., 37
Hayes, Kelly, 9
Hayes, M. S., 167
Head Start program, 25, 92
Heckman, James, 26
Heglar, M. A., 6
Hemphill, S. A., 34
Henig, J., 227
Hennessy, E. A., 37
Henry, A., 163
Henry, Barbara, 140
Heritage Foundation, 73
Higher education: achievement gaps, 19–21; HBCUs, 142, 145, 150
Highlander Folk School, 142–143
High school attainment, 19
Hilliard, A. G., 203
Hilton, M., 228
Historically black colleges/universities (HBCUs), 142, 145, 150
Ho, E., 35, 36
Hoekstra, M., 37
Hollins, E. R., 215
Holly Springs, Mississippi, 145, 146
Holme, J. J., 127
Holmes, B. J., 144
Holt, S. B., 167
Horton, Myles, 142
Housing Matters, 84

Houston, Charles Hamilton, 202
Houston Independent School District, 169
Howard University Law School, 202
Huang, F. L., 37
Hudson, M. J., 144
Humphrey, Hubert, 65
Hundley, M. G., 163
Hunt, M. O., 84
Hurston, Zora Neale, 201, 211–212
Hwang, N., 167

Identity formation, racial, 212
Ignatiev, N., 200
Immigrant students, 31, 32
Inclusive school climates, 33–39
Inequity: future directions to improve, 39–43; K-12, 26–28; preschool, 25–26
Infrastructure Investment and Jobs Act (2021), 25, 40
Institute of Positive Education, 208–209
Integration: within districts, 128; integration vs. resource equity, 101–105; resistance to, 84; state court efforts, 101. *See also* Desegregation; Segregation
Intelligence tests, 31
Intelligence Tests and School Reorganization (Terman), 31
Interstate Highway Act (1956), 152
Iowa Test of Basic Skills, 169
Irby, M., 232
Irons, P., 14
Irvine, J. J., 163, 165

Jackson, C. K., 27, 28, 71, 105, 121
Jackson, K., 227
Jackson, Ketanji Brown, 181
Jackson, L., 164
Jacobs, B., 236
Jain, S., 38, 39
James-Galloway, A. D., 8
James Irving Foundation, 231
Jang, H., 120
Jefferson, Arthur, 72
Jefferson County, Kentucky, 123
Johnson, James Weldon, 161
Johnson, Lyndon B.: civil rights action, 61–62; civil rights policies, 63; as teacher, 90
Johnson, Rucker C., 3, 5, 7, 28, 83, 89–90, 106, 113, 116, 117, 120, 122, 225
Johnson, S. M., 85
Jones, Absalom, 150

Jones, J., 163
Jung, M., 84

Kaba, Mariame, 9
Kahn, J., 234
Karenga, M., 203
Karoly, L. A., 25
Keck, T. M., 73
Kendi, I., 91
Kennedy, John F., 61
Kerstetter, K., 39
Keyes v. School District No. 1 (1973), 68–69, 74
Kidane, S., 38
Kim, Robert, 234
King, J. E., 81, 208
King, Martin Luther, Jr., 57, 61, 81, 143
King, S. H., 163
King-Drew Health Science Magnet School, LA Count, 88–89, 90–91
Kisida, B., 167
Kissinger, L., 225
Kluger, R., 58
Knight-Manuel, M., 164
Kohli, R., 181
Kolbe, T., 128
Koruth, M. A., 28
Koutavas, A., 23
Kramer, U., 34
Kraus, N., 226
Kruger, A. C., 166
Kuhl, S., 199, 217
Ku Klux Klan, 73, 145, 161
Kyriakides, L., 29

Labor unions, 202
Lacoe, J., 35
Ladson-Billings, Gloria, 3, 6, 144, 148, 151, 152, 156, 163, 165–166, 199, 210, 215
Lane, M., 164
Laney, Lucy, 204
Langbart, David, 199
Lansing School District, 38
Lapan, R. T., 37
Latino Action Network et al. v. State of New Jersey, 101, 132
Latinx Action Network, 132
Latinx children, discrimination against, 68
Layton, L., 173
Lead poisoning, 24
Learning for Justice, 107
Learning Policy Institute, 228
Leatherwood, C., 212

Lee, A., 164
Lee, C., 84, 235
Lee, Carol D., 4, 10, 208, 212, 217–218
Lee, George, 145
Lee, J., 229
Leftwich, P. J., 153
Lepage, K., 37
Lerner, Gerda, 141–142
Let this Radicalize You (Hayes & Kaba), 9
Leung, M., 19, 29
Leung-Gagné, M., 33
Lewis, L., 162, 185
Lewis, N., 124
Lewis, S., 38
Li, J., 20
Liberia, 206
LiCalsi, C., 34
Life Academy of Health and Bioscience, 32–33
"Lift Every Voice and Sing," 216
Lindsay, C. A., 167
Linked Learning schools, 32
Lipman, P., 85, 234
Literacy tests, 142–143, 145
Litigation, as change agent, 106, 113–114, *114*
Liu, J., 167, 168
Local Control Funding Formula (LCFF), 121–122
Loeb, S., 127
Logan, Rayford, 161
Lomotey, K., 208
Los Angeles Almanac, 86
Los Angeles County Schools, 86–89
Los Angeles Unified School District (LAUSD), 3, 111–112
Losen, D. J., 34
Louis, Joe, 150
Louisville, Kentucky, 123
Love, A., 166
Love, B. L., 81
Loveless, T., 229
Lutz, B., 101
Lynn, M., 164

Macartney, H., 119
Mackevicius, C. L., 71
Madhubuti, H. R., 208
Madkins, T. C., 164
Mae W., N., 8
Magnet schools, 76
Magnet Schools Assistance Program, 41

Index

Maier, A., 25, 40
Manchanda, S., 177
Mansfield, K., 38
Marcus, J., 20
Marshall, Thurgood, 71, 72, 83, 202
Martin-Fernandez, J., 165
Maryland House of Delegates, 130
Massaro, V. A., 18, 40
Massey, D. S., 9
Masterov, D. V., 26
Maynard, R., 9
McArthur, S. A., 164
McCold, P., 38
McDermott, L., 235
McFadden, G. J., 142
McFarland v. Jefferson County, KY, 156–157
McGuire, Kent, 4, 5, 10, 233
McGurn, W., 155
McIntosh, K., 176
McKinney de Royston, M., 164
McLanahan, S. S., 37
McMorris, B. J., 38, 39
McRae, E. G., 83
A Measuring Rod to Test Text Books (Rutherford), 204
Meehan, K., 217
Megan, K., 126
Mehrotra, S., 129
Mehta, Jal, 30
Memphis Schools, 124
Mendez et al. v. Westminster School District, 118
Mental health, 34–35
Mentor, M., 162
Mexican American students, 118
Michigan: Proposition A, 127
Midnight Teacher (Halfmann), 142
Miller, J. W., 163
Millhiser, I., 17
Milliken v. Bradley (1974), 71–74, 101, 123, 153, 198
Mills, C. W., 200
Milner, H. R., IV, 82, 164
Mintrop, H., 85
The Mis-Education of the Negro (Woodson), 13, 204
Missouri v. Jenkins, 72, 75
Mitchell, John, 65
Monarrez, T. E., 120
Montgomery bus boycott (1956), 61
Moore, J. M., 146
Morgan State University, 150
Morris, A., 143
Morris, E. W., 34
Morristown, New Jersey, 124
Mosely, M., 180, 181
Moyo, Kimya, 153–155
Müller, B., 37
Murnane, R. J., 82
Myrdal, Gunnar, 58

NAACP (National Association for the Advancement of Colored People), 58, 142, 198; Legal Defense Fund, 78
Napolitano, J., 130
National Academies of Sciences, Engineering, and Medicine, 236, 237
National Academy of Education, 217–218
National Assessment of Educational Progress (NAEP), 17, 19, 215
National Board Certification, 184–185
National Board for Professional Teaching Standards (NBPTS), 42, 153–154, 184
National Center for Education Statistics (NCES), 16, 19, 20, 21, 22, 127, 144, 170, 227, 229, 235, 237
National Center for Teacher Residencies, 183
National Coalition on School Diversity, 130, 131
National Council of Teachers of English, 214
National Longitudinal Study, 167
National Negro History Week, 204
National Opinion Research Center, 107
National Research Council, 42, 228
National Student Clearinghouse Research Center, 20
National Teacher and Principal Survey (NTPS), 170, 176, 178–179
National Urban League, 208
Nation's Report Card, 227
Nazi Party, 199
Negro Common School Conference (1901), 202
Neighborhoods: community needs, 7–8; neighborhood school systems, 67–68, 127, 241n1; Promise Neighborhood initiatives, 231; segregated, 24, 75, 89, 151, 241n1
Nelson, J. D., 164
Nelson, L., 24
New Concept School, 208
New Jersey school district boundaries, 124, 132

New Orleans school integration, 140
Newport, F., 62
New York City Department of Education, 181
Nguyen, T. D., 177
Nickson, D., 8
Nixon, Richard: Civil Rights Act, enforcement of, 66; resegregation, 63; shift to right, 65
Nkrumah, Kwame, 206
No Child Left Behind (NCLB), 17, 173, 226, 227, 229
Noguera, Joaquin M. S., 1, 3, 5
Noguera, Pedro A., 1, 3, 5, 31, 37, 83, 84, 87, 88, 91, 93
Noltemeyer, A., 39
Nonviolent resistance strategy, 61, 143
Nordstrom, K., 130, 131
Norris, A., 39
North Carolina House Bill 514, 119
Nunberg, M., 128
Nyerere, Julius, 209

Oakes, J., 31
Oakland Community School, 208
Obama administration, 17, 33
Office of Elementary and Secondary Education, 185
Office of Revenue and Tax Analysis, 127
Ögülmüs, K., 39
Okonofua, J. A., 37
Omah Learning Community, 127
O'Malley, M., 176
Opportunity, hoarding of, 99
Opportunity gaps, 21
Orfield, Gary, 1, 2, 5, 62, 63, 72, 83, 84, 85, 107, 168
Organisation for Economic Co-operation and Development (OECD), 23
Ouazad, A., 167, 168
Out-of-school suspensions (OSS), 35–36. *See also* School discipline
Owens, J., 37

Pan-Africanism, 206–207
Panel Study of Income Dynamics (PSID), 115
Panetta, L. E., 65
Parents Involved in Community Schools v. Seattle District No. 1, 17, 75–78, 119, 156–157
Parks, Rosa, 143
Parmet, H. S., 61

Parolin, Z., 40
Passeron, J. C., 92
Pastor, Manuel, 24
Patterson, Robert B., 145
Payne, C. M., 209
Paynter v. State, 101
Pear, R., 17
Pearl, Mississippi, 131
Pearman, F. A., 18, 34
Pellegrino, J., 228
Peltason, J. W., 59
Penner, E. K., 168
Perlstein, D., 163
Perry, A. M., 176
Perry, B. L., 34
Pesta, R., 34
Pettigrew, T. F., 107
Phenomenological Variant of Ecological Systems Theory (PVEST), 210–211
Philadelphia, Pennsylvania, 152–153
Phillips, A., 152
Phinney, J. S., 200
Pickering, G. W., 152
Pigott, R. L., 166
Pittman, K., 232
Plessy v. Ferguson, 14, 58, 60, 70, 199
Podolsky, A., 29, 183
Police in schools, 37–38
Polikoff, M., 229
Pollock, M., 91
Porter, D., 208
Porter, H., 84, 85
Positive Behavioral Interventions and Support (PBIS), 39
Potter, H., 128
Poverty. *See also* Resource equity; childhood, 15; effects of, 21–25; high-poverty schools, 121
Powell, Adam Clayton, 61
Powell, Lewis, 65–66, 69
Powell, T., 9
Preschool education, 41; resources for, 25–26
Principals, 185
Privatization. *See* School vouchers
The Problem We All Live With (Rockwell), 140
Promise Neighborhood initiatives, 231
Psychologists, school, 37–38
Public Funds Public Schools, 234
Public Service Loan Forgiveness (PSLF) Program, 183–184
Putterman, A., 126

Index

Quick, K., 126

Racial issues: race vs. ethnicity, 200–201; racial identity, 212; racial uplift, 146; racism, structural, 87–88, 92; Second Nadir, 161–162, 166
Radical Brown (Spencer & Dowd), 5–6
Ramey, D. M., 34
Randolph, A. Philip, 202
Rauscher, E., 38
Reagan, Ronald, 17, 22, 33; resegregation, 63
Reardon, S. F., 83, 120, 121
Reber, S. J., 111, 113, 116
Reconstruction, 58, 161, 198
Redding, C., 120, 166, 167
Redlining, 14, 21, 24, 87–88, 91, 151
Reed, D. S., 105
Rehnquist, William, 66, 69, 74
Republican Party, 57
Resegregation, 17; contemporary state of, 98–99
Residencies, teacher, 182–183
Resource equity, 100; resource disparities, contemporary, 120–121; resource equity vs. school integration, 101–105
Resource Equity Funders Collaborative (REFC), 237
Restorative practices (RP), 38–39
Reynolds, A. J., 26
Reynolds, J., 91
Ribeiro, F. N., 200
Riestenberg, N., 38
Rix, K., 126
Roberts, John, 119
Robeson, Paul, 149
Robinson, K. J., 228
Rockwell, Norman, 140
Rogers, J., 234
Romney, George, 65
Romney, Mitt, 65
Ronfeldt, M., 29
Rosenthal, J., 65
Rosenwald Foundation, 203
ross, k. m., 166, 179
Rothstein, Richard, 21, 23, 91, 99
Rowland, C., 183
Royal, C., 152, 164
Rufo, C. F., 161
"Rules of Racial Standing" (Bell), 157
Rushton, J. L., 34
Rust College, 145
Rutherford, Mildred Lewis, 204

Ryan, J. E., 105
Ryan, W., 156

Sadler, J., 39
San Antonio Independent School District v. Rodriguez, 41, 70–71, 72, 101, 104, 198
Sanders, J. M., 169
Sass, T., 227
Saunders, M., 231
Schollenberger, T. L., 34, 35
Schomburg Center for Black Culture, 207–208
Schönholzer, D., 120
School and State Finance Project, 126
School counselors, 37–38
"School deserts," 18
School discipline, 33–34; discipline, exclusionary, 33–34, 35–37, 167; exclusionary, 34–35; persistence of racial disparities, 35–36; punishment, alternatives to, 38–39; punishment and racial disparities, 34–35; racial disparities, sources of, 36–37
School district boundaries, 119–120, 123–124, 125–126, 151
School finance reform, 26–28, 40–41; future directions, 122–133; history of, 112–118; integrated approaches to, 105–112; resegregation, 118–122; resource equity *vs.* school integration, 101–105
School lunch, free or reduced, 22
School police, 37–38
School psychologists, 37–38
Schools: high-performing, qualities of, 89; as sorting mechanism, 31; as vehicle for mobility, 57
School vouchers, 118, 155, 242n6
Schultz, Brian, 92
Schwartz, M. A., 107
Sciarra, D. G., 18
Scott-Clayton, J., 20
Seattle, Washington school district, 17
Second Nadir of race relations, 161–162, 166
Segregation: accumulated effects of, 21–25; costs of, 56–57; districts, between vs. within, 120; "double segregation," 85; as hoarding of opportunity, 99; increase in, 83–84; protection of, 99–100; in public schools, 198–199; residential, 21, 24, 99–100; by state, 108. *See also* Desegregation; Integration
"Segregation academies," 148
Sellers, R. M., 212

"Separate but equal," 14, 60, 66, 86. *See also Plessy v. Ferguson*
Serrano v. Priest, 121
Shapiro, T. M., 21
Sheff v. O'Neill, 101, 125
Shi, Y., 37
Shirrell, M., 167, 169, 180
Shivaram, D., 25
Shujaa, M. J., 208
Siddle Walker, Vanessa, 5, 11, 86, 147, 162, 163, 202, 204–205, 207, 215
Sierra Leone, 206
Simko, Tyler, 124
Simon, N., 85
Simpson, L. B., 9
Singleton, J. D., 119
Sizemore, Barbara A., 204
Slade, E. P., 34
Sloan, K., 183
Smalls, Robert, 149
Smallville, Louisiana, 148
Smith, Lamar, 145
Smitherman, G., 214, 215
Social and Emotional Learning (SEL) programs, 39
Solomon, J., 183
Southern Education Foundation (SEF), 123, 239–240
Southern strategy, 65
Sowell, T., 163
Span, C. M., 203
Spectacular Things Happen Along the Way (Schultz), 92
Spencer, Margaret Beale, 6, 210–211
Stanley, D. A., 179
Starkville, Mississippi, 124
Steele, C. M., 212
Steinberg, M. P., 35
Stevens, John Paul, 77
Stewart, N. D., 179
Stiglitz, J. E., 82
Stout, C., 225
Stovall, J. L., 180
Structural racism, 87–88, 92
Student experiences, 129–130
Student loan debt, 20, 175, 176, 177; loan forgiveness, 183–184
Student Nonviolent Coordinating Committee, 209
Students for Fair Admissions v. Harvard, 21, 57, 82, 90, 181
Students for Fair Admissions v. University of North Carolina, 21, 57

Student voice, 233
Sumner, D., 38
Supporting Effective Educator Development (SEED), 184
Supreme Court, composition of, 57
Sussman, J., 26
Sutcher, L., 171, 172
Swaby, A., 127
Swann v. Charlotte-Mecklenberg Board of Education, 15, 66–68
Swanson, S., 87
Syeed, E., 83, 88

Taeuber, A., 67
Taeuber, K., 67
Taie, S., 162, 185
Talluri, R., 34
Taylor, C., 152
Teacher Education Assistance for College and Higher Education (TEACH), 183–184
Teacher Loan Forgiveness (TLF) Program, 183–184
Teachers: alternative certification programs, 175; certification, 184–185; diversity, need for, 41–42; diversity in workforce, 236; loan forgiveness, 183–184; preservice preparation, 174–175; professional development, 129–130; quality teachers, access to, 28–33; recruitment and retention and school characteristics, 177–179; residencies and apprenticeships, 182–183; and school leadership, 185; service scholarships, 183–184; teacher turnover, 170–174. *See also* Black teachers
Teacher unions, concerns of, 93
Tedin, K. L., 105
Teles, S. M., 73
Terman, Lewis, 31
Terrill, S., 38
Theoharis, J., 150
Thierry, Augustin, 77
Thomas, D. J. III, 180
Thompson, O., 114
Thrumond, Strom, 73
Tilford-Weathers, T. C., 163
Till, Emmett, 145
Todd-Breland, E., 8, 164, 174
Toxic Wastes and Race (Commission for Racial Justice), 24
Trachtenburg, P., 124
Tracking systems, student, 30–31

Tropp, L. R., 107
Troubled Waters (Heglar), 6–7
Trujillo, T., 174
Trump, Donald, 17, 22, 42, 63–64, 73
Tubman, Harriet, 149
Turner, Nat, 149
Tuskegee Institute, 205
Tuttle, C., 123
Tyack, D., 14

Ulalisa, T., 154
United Confederate Veterans, 204
United Negro Improvement Association (UNIA), 207
U.S. Commission on Civil Rights, 85
U.S. Constitution, 197
U.S. Department of Education, 33, 173, 181
U.S. Department of Justice, 33

Vecchione, J., 200
Vesey, Denmark, 149
Viadero, D., 224
Vilson, J., 179
Viral Justice (Benjamin), 10–11
Virginia, private vouchers, 64
Vocational vs. academic tracks, 32
Vossoughi, S., 8
Voter suppression, 145
Voting Rights Acts (1964/1965), 62, 199
Voucher programs, 118, 155, 242n6
Vu, P., 37
Vuran, S., 39

Wallace, George, 65, 73
Wang, Y. N., 87
Ward, J. M., 73
Ward, K., 217
Warfield-Coppock, N., 209
Warren, Earl, 60, 111, 118
Warren, M., 92

Washington, Booker T., 205
Watson, V. M., 164
Waugh, D. L., 141
Way, S. M., 34
Wells, Ida B., 213, 215
Wells, L., 91
Welner, K. G., 21
Westhoven, N., 124
Whalen, B., 62
Whalen, C., 62
Whitaker, A., 38
White, Byron, 69, 71
White, T., 180
White Citizens' Council, 145
White flight, 84, 120
Whiteside, M., 33
White supremacy, 5–6, 206, 217
Wilburn, T., 225
Wilkerson, I., 84, 152
Will, M., 183
Williams, Hosea, 143
Williamson, J. A., 199, 201, 214, 215
Wilson, A., 164
Wilson, C. M., 8
Wilson, W. J., 213
Wing, J. Y., 84
Wise, T., 82
Wolf, M., 227
Woodard, K., 150
Woodson, Carter G., 13, 149, 204
Woodward, B., 67
Wright, Richard R., 207

Young, J., 176
YouthTruth, 229

Zeiser, K., 31
Zhu, B., 42
Zhu, M., 37
Zoning ordinances, 99–100
Zubrzycki, J., 124

About the Editors and Contributors

Linda Darling-Hammond is the president and CEO of the Learning Policy Institute. She is also the Charles E. Ducommun Professor of Education Emeritus at Stanford University where she founded the Stanford Center for Opportunity Policy in Education and served as the faculty sponsor of the Stanford Teacher Education Program, which she helped redesign.

Darling-Hammond is past president of the American Educational Research Association and recipient of its awards for Distinguished Contributions to Research, Lifetime Achievement, and Research-to-Policy. She is also a member of the American Association of Arts and Sciences and of the National Academy of Education. From 1994–2001, she was executive director of the National Commission on Teaching and America's Future, of which 1996 report *What Matters Most: Teaching for America's Future* was named one of the most influential reports affecting U.S. education in that decade. In 2006, Darling-Hammond was named one of the nation's 10 most influential people affecting educational policy. She led the Obama education policy transition team in 2008 and the Biden education transition team in 2020. In 2022, Darling-Hammond received the Yidan Prize for Education Research in recognition of her work that has shaped education policy and practice around the most equitable and effective ways to teach and learn.

Darling-Hammond began her career as a public school teacher and co-founded both a preschool and a public high school. She served as director of the RAND Corporation's education program and as an endowed professor at Columbia University, Teachers College. She has consulted widely with federal, state, and local officials and educators on strategies for improving education policies and practices. Among her more than 500 publications are a number of award-winning books, including *The Right to Learn*, *Teaching as the Learning Profession*, *Preparing Teachers for a Changing World*, and *The Flat World and Education*. She received an EdD from Temple University (with highest distinction) and a BA from Yale University (magna cum laude).

Na'ilah Suad Nasir is the sixth president of the Spencer Foundation, which funds education research nationally. Prior to joining Spencer, she held a faculty appointment in Education and African American Studies at the

University of California–Berkeley where she also served as the chair of African American Studies, then later as the Vice Chancellor for Equity and Inclusion. She also served on the faculty of the Stanford Graduate School of Education.

Nasir's research examines the racialized and cultural nature of learning and schooling, with a particular focus on the experiences of African American students in schools and communities. She coedited *The Handbook of the Cultural Foundations of Learning* (Routledge) and *We Dare Say Love: Supporting Achievement in the Educational Life of Black Boys*. She is also the author of *Racialized Identities: Race and Achievement for African American Youth*, published by Stanford University Press in 2012. Nasir is a member of the American Academy of Arts and Sciences and the National Academy of Education. She is a fellow of the American Educational Research Association and the International Society for the Learning Sciences. She was the president of the American Educational Research Association in 2021–2022. She serves on the board of Sage Publications, the National Equity Project, and the UC Berkeley Board of Visitors.

CONTRIBUTOR BIOS

Ary Amerikaner is the cofounder and executive director of Brown's Promise. She is an education policy leader with experience spanning federal and state government, advocacy, and the law. Ary served in President Obama's administration as a deputy assistant secretary at the Department of Education, where she led efforts to advance equity in school funding and access to excellent educators. Ary's federal experience also includes the Biden-Harris transition team and work on Capitol Hill. In Maryland, she served as the chief of staff at the state Department of Education and as an education advisor on Governor Wes Moore's transition team.

As Vice President for P12 Policy, Research, and Practice at The Education Trust, she and her team supported advocacy coalitions in 14 states while producing original data and policy analysis. Ary's legal experience includes serving as an expert in school funding litigation in Delaware, clerking for a federal judge, and being an editor at the *California Law Review*. Ary has a JD and MPP from the University of California–Berkeley, and a BA from Oberlin College. She grew up in West Virginia.

Travis J. Bristol is an associate professor of teacher education and education policy in Berkeley's School of Education and (by courtesy) the Department of African American Studies. Before joining Berkeley's faculty, he was a Peter Paul Assistant Professor at Boston University. Using qualitative methods, Dr. Bristol explores three related research strands: (1) the role of educational policies in shaping teacher workplace experiences and retention;

(2) district and school-based professional learning communities; and (3) the role of race and gender in educational settings. Dr. Bristol's research has appeared in over 60 peer-reviewed articles, book chapters, policy briefs, and opinion editorials including *Urban Education, American Educational Research Journal, Educational Evaluation and Policy Analysis, Journal of Teacher Education, Teachers College Record, Harvard Educational Review, Brookings*, and *The Washington Post*. He also coedited two volumes: *The Handbook of Research on Teachers of Color and Indigenous Teachers* (with Conra Gist), published by the American Educational Research Association (AERA) and *Men Educators of Color in U.S. Public Schools and Abroad* (with Ashley Woodson), published by Routledge.

The National Academy of Education/Spencer Foundation, Ford Foundation, and AERA awarded Dr. Bristol dissertation fellowships in 2013. In 2016, he received the inaugural teacher diversity research award from the American Association of Colleges for Teacher Education. In 2019, Dr. Bristol received a Ford Foundation Postdoctoral Fellowship and an emerging scholar award from the Comparative and International Education Society, African Diaspora SIG. In 2020, he received a National Academy of Education/Spencer Postdoctoral Fellowship. In 2021, Dr. Bristol received the Early Career Award from AERA (Division-K). More recently, in 2022, he received an AERA Outstanding Reviewer (Educational Researcher) Award.

Dr. Bristol has received more than $6 million in research funding from a diverse group of funders, including the New York City Department of Education, the National Education Association, the National Academy of Education, the State of California, the W.T. Grant Foundation, the California Department of Justice, the William and Flora Hewlett Foundation, the Chan Zuckerberg Initiative, the Walton Family Foundation, the Charles and Lynn Schusterman Family Philanthropies, and the United Nations International Children's Emergency Fund (UNICEF).

Dr. Bristol is on the editorial boards of *Urban Education, American Educational Research Journal*, and *Association for Education Finance and Policy Live Handbook*. He is also the chair of the National Board for Professional Teaching Standards Board of Directors and chairs the California Department of Education Teacher Diversity Advisory Group. Dr. Bristol is on the board of directors of Teach Plus; the National Center for Teacher Residencies; and the Albert Shanker Institute. He also serves on the advisory board for the National Academy of Education's Equity in Math Education Research Program. Dr. Bristol is a former student and teacher in New York City public schools and teacher educator with the Boston Teacher Residency program. Dr. Bristol received his AB from Amherst College; MA from Stanford University; and PhD from Teachers College, Columbia University.

Desiree Carver-Thomas is a senior researcher and policy analyst at the Learning Policy Institute and coleads LPI's Educator Quality team. Her work focuses on how educator quality, teacher diversity, and leadership development can promote equitable opportunities for teaching and learning. She also leads LPI's Racial Equity Leadership Network team. Before joining LPI, Carver-Thomas taught in New York City public elementary schools, where she had experience in bilingual education and special education, and as a mathematics lead. As a graduate student fellow with the Center for Cities and Schools at the University of California–Berkeley, she worked with the City of Richmond on implementing a full-service community schools initiative. She conducted similar work with the West Contra Costa Unified School District.

Carver-Thomas holds an MPP from the Goldman School of Public Policy at the University of California–Berkeley; an MS in Teaching from Fordham University; and a BA in Comparative Ethnic Studies with a concentration in anthropology from Columbia University.

Sean Darling-Hammond is an assistant professor of community health sciences and biostatistics at the University of California–Los Angeles Fielding School of Public Health. There, he seeks to expand belonging by combining his backgrounds in education, law, and public policy with methodological approaches stemming from psychology and econometrics. He holds a PhD in public policy from the University of California–Berkeley, earned his BA in sociology at Harvard College (2006), spent 5 years as the director of research at Hattaway Communications (a mission-driven firm in Washington, DC), earned his JD from UC Berkeley (2014), clerked for the district court for the District of Maryland, and worked in education law and policy for Hogan Lovells and Education Counsel. He also served as the director of Berkeley High School's restorative justice program and provided legal representation to special education students. He and his wife, Valentina, adore their baby boy, Kofi, who they welcomed into the world in April 2019. In his free time, he competes on NBC's *American Ninja Warrior* as "The Giving Ninja," devoted to donating to nonprofits that expand opportunity.

Rucker C. Johnson is the Chancellor's Professor of Public Policy in the Goldman School of Public Policy at the University of California–Berkeley, and faculty research associate at the National Bureau of Economic Research. As a labor economist who specializes in the economics of education, Johnson's work considers the role of poverty and inequality in affecting life chances. Johnson was inducted as the Sir Arthur Lewis Fellow of the American Academy of Political and Social Science, inducted as a member of the American Academy of Arts and Sciences, the National Academy of Education, and received the 2017 Andrew Carnegie Fellowship. His research has appeared in leading academic journals, and has been featured in mainstream media outlets. He has been invited to give policy briefings at the White House and on Capitol Hill. He is the author of the book *Children of the Dream: Why School Integration Works.*

Johnson is committed to advancing his scholarly agenda of fusing insights from multiple disciplinary perspectives to improve our understanding of the causes and consequences of—and remedies for—inequality in this country. Johnson earned his PhD in economics at the University of Michigan. At UC–Berkeley (2004–present), he teaches graduate and undergraduate courses in applied econometrics and topical courses in race, poverty, and inequality.

Gloria Ladson-Billings is the former Kellner Family Distinguished Professor of Urban Education in the Department of Curriculum and Instruction and faculty affiliate in the Department of Educational Policy Studies at the University of Wisconsin–Madison. She is a fellow of the British Academy, the American Academy of Arts and Sciences, and the Hagler Institute of Texas A&M University. She was the 2005–2006 president of the American Educational Research Association (AERA). Ladson-Billings's research examines the pedagogical practices of teachers who are successful with African American students. She also investigates critical race theory applications to education. She is the author of the critically acclaimed books *The Dreamkeepers: Successful Teachers of African American Children* and *Crossing Over to Canaan: The Journey of New Teachers in Diverse Classrooms*, and numerous journal articles and book chapters. She is the former editor of the *American Educational Research Journal* and a member of several editorial boards. Her work has won numerous scholarly awards including the H. I. Romnes Faculty Fellowship, the NAEd/Spencer Postdoctoral Fellowship, and the Palmer O. Johnson outstanding research award. During the 2003–2004 academic year, she was a fellow at the Center for Advanced Study in the Behavioral Sciences at Stanford University. In fall of 2004, she received the George and Louise Spindler Award from the Council on Anthropology and Education for significant and ongoing contributions to the field of educational anthropology. She holds honorary degrees from Umeå University (Umeå, Sweden), University of Massachusetts–Lowell, the University of Alicante (Alicante, Spain), the Erickson Institute (Chicago), and Morgan State University (Baltimore). She is a 2018 recipient of the AERA Distinguished Research Award, and she was elected to the American Academy of Arts and Sciences in 2018.

Carol D. Lee is professor emerita (the former Edwina S. Tarry Professor) of Education in the School of Education and Social Policy and in African American Studies at Northwestern University. Lee, the president of the National Academy of Education, is best known in academia for her 5 decades of work helping students from minority backgrounds excel in an environment of low expectations, poverty, negative stereotypes, and other barriers.

She was among the early scholars to scaffold children's everyday experiences as a resource for learning in school. Today her sophisticated ideas behind "cultural modeling" are a standard approach in the field. In 2021, Lee received the McGraw Prize in Education, the James Squire Award from the National Council of Teachers of English, and the Distinguished Contributions to Research in Education Award from the American Educational Research Association, the premier acknowledgment of outstanding achievement and success in education research. She is a member of the National Academy of Education in the United States, the American Academy of Arts and Sciences, a fellow of the American Educational Research Association, a fellow of the National Conference on Research in Language and Literacy, a member of the Reading Hall of Fame, and a former fellow at the Center for Advanced Studies in the Behavioral Sciences.

Lee received her doctorate from the University of Chicago. She is a past president of the American Educational Research Association (AERA), AERA's past representative to the World Educational Research Association, past vice-president of Division G (Social Contexts of Education) of the American Educational Research Association, past president of the National Conference on Research in Language and Literacy, and past cochair of the Research Assembly of the National Council of Teachers of English.

She received the Distinguished Service Award from the National Council of Teachers of English, Scholars of Color Distinguished Scholar Award from the American Educational Research Association, the Walder Award for Research Excellence at Northwestern University, the Distinguished Alumni Award from the College of Liberal Arts at the University of Illinois–Urbana, the President's Pacesetters Award from the American Association of Blacks in Higher Education, the Lifetime Achievement Award from the American Association of Colleges of Teacher Education, a Presidential Citation from the American Educational Research Association, and an honorary doctorate from the University of Pretoria (South Africa).

Kent McGuire is the program director of education at the William and Flora Hewlett Foundation. He leads the investments of teaching and learning and open educational resources strategies, with a focus on helping all students succeed in college, work, and civic life. Kent is a veteran of the national education movement for public education. Previously, Kent was the president and CEO of the Southern Education Foundation, an organization committed to advancing public education in the American South, with a focus on equity and excellence. Prior to that, he served as the dean of the College of Education at Temple University and was a tenured professor in the Department of Educational Leadership and Policy Studies.

From 2001 to 2003, Kent was a senior vice president at the Manpower Demonstration Research Corporation, where he split his time between research projects on school reform and directing its department on education, children, and youth. He has also been an education program officer at the Pew Charitable Trusts and directed the education program at the Lilly Endowment. Kent served as assistant secretary of the U.S. Department of Education from 1998 to 2001. Kent earned his PhD in public administration from the University of Colorado, an MA from Teachers College Columbia University, and a BA in economics from the University of Michigan. He serves on the boards of the Wallace Foundation, Teacher's College Columbia University, the Success for All Foundation, the National Public Education Support Fund, and the Institute for Citizens and Scholars.

Joaquín M. S. Noguera is an assistant professor in the School of Education at Loyola Marymount University. He has a PhD in social science and comparative education with a specialization in race, ethnic, and cultural studies from UCLA's Graduate School of Education. He also earned a master's degree in education from UCLA and a bachelor's degree in history from St. John's University. Prior to joining LMU, he was a postdoctoral fellow at the Center for Black Studies Research and a visiting professor in the Department of Black Studies at the University of California–Santa Barbara. He is a former social worker, K–12 teacher, school leader, and director of the International Youth Leadership Institute dedicated to serving Black and Latinx youth in New York City. He has also worked as a consultant and coach to school districts, educators, and other learning organizations throughout the country for more than a decade. His research is situated at the intersections of race, culture, power, education, and social justice, and engages three broad areas: the limits and possibilities for transformation and healing of education and schooling, particularly for Black, Latinx, and Indigenous communities and in low-income urban contexts; systems change that advances racial equity in organizational contexts; and critical analysis of society and culture and the impact of social and cultural patterns on the development and experiences of individuals and communities. Noguera's research and scholarship amplify anti/decolonizing, critical race, Indigenous, Black radical, and Ethnic Studies perspectives and draw from the knowledge produced by these traditions when responding to and remedying our individual and collective challenges. His work also centers well-being and holistic engagement while prioritizing relational awareness and accountability to forward sustainable transformation and healing.

Pedro A. Noguera is the Emery Stoops and Joyce King Stoops Dean of the University of Southern California Rossier School of Education. A sociologist, Noguera's research focuses on the ways in which schools are influenced by social and economic conditions, as well as by demographic trends in local, regional, and global contexts. He is the author, coauthor, and editor of 13 books. His most recent books are *The Crisis of Connection: Roots, Consequences and Solutions* with Niobe Way, Carol Gilligan, and Alisha

Ali (New York University Press, 2018) and *Race, Equity and Education: Sixty Years From Brown* with Jill Pierce and Roey Ahram (Springer, 2015).

He has published over 250 research articles in academic journals, book chapters in edited volumes, research reports, and editorials in major newspapers. He serves on the boards of numerous national and local organizations, including the Economic Policy Institute, the National Equity Project, and *The Nation*. Noguera appears as a regular commentator on educational issues on several national media outlets, and his editorials on educational issues have appeared in *The New York Times*, *The Washington Post*, *The Wall Street Journal*, *The Dallas Morning News*, and *Los Angeles Times*.

Prior to being appointed dean of the USC Rossier School of Education, Noguera served as a Distinguished Professor of Education at the Graduate School of Education and Information Studies at the University of California–Los Angeles. Before joining the faculty at UCLA, he served as a tenured professor and holder of endowed chairs at New York University (2004–2015), Harvard University (2000–2003), and the University of California–Berkeley (1990–2000).

Noguera was recently appointed to serve as a special advisor to the governor of New Mexico on education policy. He also advises the state departments of education in Washington, Oregon, and Nevada. From 2009–2012 he served as a trustee for the State University of New York as an appointee of the governor. In 2014 he was elected to the National Academy of Education and Phi Delta Kappa honor society, and in 2020 Noguera was elected to the American Academy of Arts and Sciences. Noguera has received seven honorary doctorates from American universities, and he recently received awards from the Center for the Advanced Study in the Behavioral Sciences at Stanford University, from the National Association of Secondary School Principals, and from the McSilver Institute for Poverty Policy and Research at NYU for his research and advocacy efforts aimed at fighting poverty.

Gary Orfield is Distinguished Research Professor of Education, Law, Political Science and Urban Planning at the University of California—Los Angeles. His research interests are in the study of civil rights, education policy, urban policy, and minority opportunity. He was cofounder and director of the Harvard Civil Rights Project, and now serves as codirector of the Civil Rights Project/Proyecto Derechos Civiles at UCLA. His central interest has been the development and implementation of social policy, particularly the impact of policy on equal opportunity for success in American society. Orfield is a member of the National Academy of Education and has received numerous awards, including the Teachers College Medal, Social Justice Award of the AERA, the American Political Science Association Charles Merriam Award for his "contribution to the art of government through the application of social science research," and honorary PhDs.

Orfield's research includes more than 12 coauthored or coedited books since 2004 and scores of articles and reports. In addition to scholarly work, he has served as expert witness or special master in more than three dozen class action civil rights cases, on school desegregation, housing discrimination, and other issues, and as consultant to many school districts, federal, state, and local governments, civil rights groups, and teacher organizations. He and various collaborators have organized amicus briefs to the U.S. Supreme Court on all the major school and affirmative action decisions over the last 2 decades.

Recent books include *The School Voucher Illusion: Exposing the Pretext of Equity* with K. Welner and L. Huerta, Teacher's College Press (2023); *The Walls Around College Opportunity: The Failure of Colorblind Policy,* Princeton University Press (2022); *Accountability and Opportunity in Higher Education: The Civil Rights Dimension* with N. Hillman, Harvard Education Press (2018), and *Discrimination in Elite Public Schools: Investigating Buffalo* with J. Ayscue, Teachers College Press (2018). Orfield also edited the 2017 Educational Testing Service report "Alternative Paths to Diversity: Exploring and Implementing Effective College Admissions Policies." "A Life in Civil Rights" appeared in the October 2010 issue of *PS: Political Science & Politics.*

Naomi Mae W. (Dr. Mae) is an assistant professor of educational policy studies in Fall 2024 and is currently an Anna Julia Cooper Fellow at the University of Wisconsin–Madison. Prior to Madison, Dr. Mae was an associate program officer and project manager at the Spencer Foundation. In this role, she reviewed proposals across the foundation's major grant programs and oversaw convenings that brought together scholars, practitioners, and policymakers across disciplines to address the most pressing issues in the field of education.

Dr. Mae is deeply informed by her upbringing and hometown of Southeast San Diego, CA, where she learned the beginnings of community and activism. She identifies as an activist scholar and community organizer, collaborating with Black student organizations, young people, and multiracial, multiethnic intergenerational community-based organizations for over 15 years. Dr. Mae is a qualitative researcher whose current work centers youth organizers of color as they build multiracial, multiethnic coalitions to fight for educational justice in underresourced urban districts. She uses community-based research methods, action research, and critical ethnography while leveraging youth resistance, critical race, and relational race theories to further the field's understanding of the praxis required to actualize greater justice and solidarity in partnership with young people and communities.